T0271201

Positive political economy investigates how observed differences in institutions affect political and economic outcomes in various social, economic, and political systems. It also examines how the institutions themselves change and develop in response to individual and collective beliefs, preferences, and strategies. This volume tackles both monetary and real topics in an integrated way, and represents the first coherent empirical investigation of positive models of political economy. The various constitutions discuss issues of great topicality, for European and other economies: Why do central banks matter? What determines their independence? How do central bank independence and exchange rate regimes affect monetary integration and activism? The volume also discusses the costs of a monetary union, unemployment benefits, and redistributive taxation.

Positive political economy: theory and evidence

Positive political economy: theory and evidence

Edited by
SYLVESTER EIJFFINGER
and
HARRY HUIZINGA
Center for Economic Research,
Tilburg University,
The Netherlands

CAMBRIDGE
UNIVERSITY PRESS

CAMBRIDGE UNIVERSITY PRESS
Cambridge, New York, Melbourne, Madrid, Cape Town, Singapore,
São Paulo, Delhi, Dubai, Tokyo

Cambridge University Press
The Edinburgh Building, Cambridge CB2 8RU, UK

Published in the United States of America by Cambridge University Press, New York

www.cambridge.org
Information on this title: www.cambridge.org/9780521572156

First published 1998

A catalogue record for this publication is available from the British Library

Library of Congress Cataloguing in Publication data

Positive political economy: theory and evidence / edited by Sylvester
    Eijffinger and Harry Huizinga.
        p.   cm.
    Includes index
    ISBN 0-521-57215-0
        1. Monetary policy–Congresses.   2. Banks and banking, Central–
Congresses.   3. Economic policy–Congresses.   I. Eijffinger,
Sylvester C. W.   II. Huizinga, Harry.
HG230.3.P68   1998
332.4′6–dc20   96–43850
                                                                    CIP

ISBN 978-0-521-57215-6 Hardback

Transferred to digital printing 2010

Contents

Figures

Tables

Contributors

LANS BOVENBERG	*CentER, Tilburg University*
ALEX CUKIERMAN	*Tel Aviv University and CentER, Tilburg University*
SEBASTIAN EDWARDS	*The World Bank*
SYLVESTER EIJFFINGER	*CentER, Tilburg University, College of Europe and Humboldt University of Berlin*
HÉLÈNE ERKEL-ROUSSE	*INSEE*
CASPER VAN EWIJK	*University of Amsterdam*
DANIEL GROS	*Centre for European Policy Studies*
JAKOB DE HAAN	*University of Groningen*
JÜRGEN VON HAGEN	*University of Mannheim*
DALE HENDERSON	*Board of Governors of the Federal Reserve System*
LEX HOOGDUIN	*De Nederlandsche Bank and University of Groningen*
HARRY HUIZINGA	*CentER, Tilburg University*
KEES KOEDIJK	*LIFE, University of Limburg*
SUSANNE LOHMANN	*University of California at Los Angeles*
JACQUES MÉLITZ	*INSEE*
GIAN-MARIA MILESI-FERRETTI	*International Monetary Fund*
PATRICK MINFORD	*University of Liverpool*
MANFRED NEUMANN	*University of Bonn*
PEDRO RODRIGUEZ	*The World Bank*
ERIC SCHALING	*Bank of England*
JACQUES SIJBEN	*CentER, Tilburg University*
HARALD UHLIG	*CentER, Tilburg University*
CASPER DE VRIES	*Tinbergen Institute, Erasmus University*
STEVEN B. WEBB	*The World Bank*
NING S. ZHU	*Board of Governors of the Federal Reserve System*

Foreword

On January 23–4, 1995, the CentER for Economic Research of Tilburg University organized an international conference with the theme "Positive political economy: theory and evidence." The conference was co-sponsored by the Royal Netherlands Academy of Sciences (KNAW). The aim was to discuss theoretical and empirical aspects of positive political economy among a group of experts from universities, research institutes, central banks, and international organizations. The authors, discussants, and other participants came from both Europe and the United States.

In this volume, an introduction by the editors, the conference papers and comments given by the discussants are published. The outline of this book closely follows the program of the conference. The organization of the conference and the publication of this book were possible only through the efforts of a number of people. In particular, I would like to thank the organizers, Professor Sylvester Eijffinger and Professor Harry Huizinga. Furthermore, I wish to express my gratitude to Mrs Jolanda Schellekens-Bakhuis and Mrs Marja Speekenbrink who constituted the conference secretariat. A special word of appreciation is due to Professor Theo van de Klundert and Professor Harrie Verbon for admirably chairing the sessions. Also, I want to thank Mrs Nicole Hultermans and Mrs Corina Maas for their assistance in compiling the conference volume, and to Marco Hoeberichts for making the index of this book. Of course, the conference benefited from the remarks of all participants. I hope the readers will benefit as much from the papers and comments as we at CentER enjoyed the conference.

Tilburg
February 1996

Professor Arie Kapteyn
Director of CentER

Introduction

SYLVESTER EIJFFINGER and HARRY HUIZINGA

Positive political economy investigates how observed differences in institutions affect political and economic outcomes in various social, economic and political systems. It also inquires how the institutions themselves change and develop in response to individual and collective beliefs, preferences and strategies. As stated by Persson and Tabellini (1990) in their book on macroeconomics and politics: "The future research agenda ought to give high priority to modeling the details of political institutions. Adding institutional content is necessary to sharpen the empirical predictions of the theory." The essays on political economy collected in this volume aim to be part of this research agenda.

The modern theory of macroeconomic policy, and of monetary policy in particular, focuses on the game-theoretic interactions between private agents and policy makers where the private sector rationally anticipates economic policy. The variety of interests at stake in the conduct of monetary and exchange rate policy renders it a fertile area for political economists. At the same time, monetary institutions are currently in a state of flux, especially in Europe. The prospect of a European Monetary Union by January 1999 has heightened the interest in the design of central banking institutions, while a renewed popularity of fixed exchange rate regimes worldwide has prompted a fresh academic interest in the choice between fixed and flexible exchange rates and in the determination of capital controls.

The CentER for Economic Research of Tilburg University organized an international conference with the title "Positive political economy: theory and evidence" on January 23–4, 1995. The conference papers which make up the chapters of this volume first address the role of central bank independence and the exchange rate system in the conduct of monetary policy. Also, the volume addresses the issue of monetary instrument selection, the cost of monetary union in Europe, the determination of capital controls, and, finally, unemployment benefits and redistributive taxation. The

1

vantage point of most if not all the contributions is one of political economy.

Reflecting the increasing importance of open-economy issues, two theoretical contributions (by Jürgen von Hagen, and by Dale Henderson and Ning Zhu) focus on game-theoretic facets of monetary policy in a multi-country setting. At its current stage of development, political economy as a discipline increasingly shifts its focus to empirical investigation. Correspondingly, half of the chapters in the volume have an empirical content. The empirical chapters address the determination of the degree of central bank independence, the role of central bank independence and the exchange rate system in the conduct of monetary policy, the political economy of the exchange rate system, the determination of capital controls, and, finally, the costs of monetary union in Europe. The five empirical chapters are all based on international data sets.

The main themes of this volume are, first, monetary institutions and policy and, second, exchange rate policy and other policies with redistributive implications. Reflecting these themes, the volume is organized into two separate parts. Part I features six contributions (by Susanne Lohmann; Jürgen von Hagen; Sylvester Eijffinger and Eric Schaling; Alex Cukierman, Pedro Rodriguez, and Steven Webb; Dale Henderson and Ning Zhu; and Hélène Erkel-Rousse and Jacques Mélitz) on the general topic of the conduct of monetary policy in various institutional settings and on the costs and benefits of alternative monetary arrangements. Part II consists of four contributions (by Sebastian Edwards; Gian Maria Milesi-Ferretti; Patrick Minford; and Harry Huizinga) on the political economy of exchange rate anchors, the determination of capital controls, exchange rate adjustments and manufacturing subsidies, and, finally, unemployment benefits and redistributive taxation. The chapter on unemployment benefits is the only one in the volume that does not deal with monetary phenomena.

The first chapter in part I, by *Susanne Lohmann* (University of California at Los Angeles), examines reputational versus institutional solutions to the time-consistency problem of monetary policy. She asks why the structure of monetary institutions, such as central banks, effects policy directly, and separately from policy makers' reputations for maintaining low inflation. Monetary institutions, created by policy makers, can in principle be altered or even abolished by the same policy makers. Why would institutions therefore be able to solve a credibility problem that cannot be dealt with by reputational means? This question implies that there is an "institutions don't matter" paradox. As a possible resolution to the paradox, Lohmann argues that institutional and reputational schemes differ in the implied policy responsiveness to economic shocks and in the relevant economy policy "audience" and, thus, in the costs of violating the expectations of this audience. The chapter by Lohmann is discussed by *Manfred J.M. Neumann* (University of Bonn).

Jürgen von Hagen (University of Mannheim and Indiana University) addresses the possibility of reciprocity-based political business cycles which are political business cycles that may occur as a result of decision making by a federation-wide central bank governing board. The central bank board is made up of representatives from the federation's constituent countries. The advantage of a many-state central bank council of national representatives over single-state central banks, namely that the decisive central banker is less likely to be subject to opportunistic political business cycle incentives, is generally not as strong in a repeated game setting as in single-shot voting games. If elections in participating countries are staggered, a main question is whether the federation-wide central bank will ever come to the aid of politicians in the election-country by way of creating a high federation-wide rate of inflation. Surprisingly, von Hagen shows that this may indeed be the case if the bargaining process among the country representatives follows a social norm that in essence entails that representatives from non-election countries will vote for relatively high inflation to "help" the election country, as they know they will be similarly helped in the future. The von Hagen chapter is discussed by *Kees Koedijk* (University of Limburg and LIFE).

The contribution by *Sylvester Eijffinger* (CentER, College of Europe, and Humboldt University of Berlin) and *Eric Schaling* (Bank of England) examines the theoretical and empirical determinants of the optimal degree of central bank independence or conservativeness. Building on Rogoff (1985), they are able to obtain a more precise characterization of the optimal degree of central bank independence with the aid of a graphical technique. The theory relates the optimal degree of central bank independence to underlying structural variables, such as the natural rate of unemployment, the benefits of unanticipated inflation, society's preferences for unemployment and inflation stabilization, and the variance of productivity shocks. Employing a latent variables method in order to distinguish between actual and optimal monetary regimes, Eijffinger and Schaling test these theoretical relationships using statutory measures of central bank independence and the relevant macroeconomic indicators for a set of nineteen industrial countries. The comment on the Eijffinger and Schaling chapter is by *Lex Hoogduin* (De Nederlandsche Bank and University of Groningen).

Alex Cukierman (Tel Aviv University and CentER), *Pedro Rodriguez* and *Steven Webb* (both World Bank) investigate how monetary policy is conducted in the face of a variety of macroeconomic shocks. From an open-economy macroeconomic model, they derive the optimal monetary reaction functions that indicate how monetary instruments (i.e., monetary aggregates or interest rates) are to be adjusted to economic disturbances under four different exchange rate system scenarios. Exchange rates can be either fixed or flexible, and countries' financial assets may or may not be perfect substitutes in private portfolios. The resulting monetary reaction functions are estimated for a pooled data set of seventeen industrial countries. The authors are specifically interested in how adjustment of monetary instruments to economic shocks depends on the degree of central bank independence and on the nature of the exchange rate system. They conclude, among other things, that wage inflation is less accommodated in countries with more independent central banks, and in countries with unilateral pegs. *Jakob de Haan* (University of Groningen) discusses their contribution.

The chapter by *Dale Henderson* (Board of Governors of the Federal Reserve System) and *Ning Zhu* (World Bank) addresses the role of economic uncertainty in the choice of monetary policy instruments in a two-country, game-theoretic setting. The monetary policy makers in each country can fix either the money supply or the nominal interest rate. This implies there is a total of four possible Nash equilibria in the game without (velocity) uncertainty. Building on work in the industrial economics area by Klemperer and Meyer (1986), the authors find that the introduction of uncertainty generally reduces the number of possible Nash equilibria to fewer than four. A conclusion is that introducing uncertainty can lead policy makers to select a unique equilibrium that corresponds to the equilibrium that yields the lowest payoff with no uncertainty. The paper by Henderson and Zhu is commented on by *Harald Uhlig* (CentER).

Hélène Erkel-Rousse and *Jacques Mélitz* (Centre de Recherche en Economie et Statistique) provide us with evidence on the costs of European monetary union resulting from the elimination of national monetary policies following monetary union. The magnitude of these costs depends on how important national monetary policies are at present in countering economic shocks, and on how well the remaining national fiscal policies can shoulder the burden of stabilizing national economies in their absence. Erkel-Rousse and Mélitz estimate a structural VAR model, based on the long-run identifying scheme pioneered by Blanchard and Quah (1989) and extended by others, for six members of the European Union (Germany, France, the United Kingdom, Italy, Spain, and The Netherlands) that allows the identification of five different types of shocks. By identifying separate shocks, they wish to see how much EU members stand to lose from surrendering their monetary policies given that fiscal policies are preserved. In summary, they find that national shocks are much less in tandem than is perhaps thought. If economic shocks are largely asymmetric, then fiscal policies are well-suited to respond to them. The macroeconomic costs of a European monetary union may, thus, be relatively small. Their chapter is discussed by *Daniel Gros* (Centre for European Policy Studies).

Part II contains four chapters on the topics of exchange rate systems and policy, capital controls, and unemployment benefits. *Sebastian Edwards* (World Bank and University of California at Los Angeles) investigates what determines a country's choice between fixed and flexible exchange rates, and whether exchange rate fixity imposes an effective constraint on monetary policy as evidenced by the rate of inflation. Starting from a theoretical model, Edwards proceeds to test what economic and political variables affect the choice for an exchange rate anchor in a sample of seventy advanced and developing countries. In addition, empirical results are presented on the extent to which fixed exchange rates in practice have contributed to a low rate of inflation. The evidence supports the view that fixed rates help reduce the inflationary bias, especially in countries with a history of already relatively stable prices. The comment on the Edwards chapter is by *Casper de Vries* (Erasmus University, Rotterdam).

The chapter by *Gian Maria Milesi-Ferretti* (International Monetary Fund) surveys the literature on the determination of foreign exchange restrictions and capital controls. The theory yields hypotheses relating various key structural and political variables to the existence of capital controls. These hypotheses are tested with a data set consisting of sixty-one industrialized and developing countries. The evidence suggests that the degree of central bank independence and several government finance indicators can explain in part the occurrence of restrictive exchange rate policy. Also, capital controls are more likely to be imposed in poorer countries, and in countries with a larger government. Finally, external sector variables are significantly correlated with capital controls. *Lans Bovenberg* (CentER) discusses the chapter of Milesi-Ferretti.

The contribution by *Patrick Minford* (University of Liverpool) turns to the political economy of the Exchange Rate Mechanism of the European Monetary System. Minford observes that there is a tendency on the part of participating countries, other than Germany, to experience a combination of real exchange rate appreciation and extensive subsidies for manufacturing. These policies are explained in a politico-economic model of an economy consisting of a traded goods and a non-traded goods sector. In bad times, there are pressures from manufacturers in the traded goods sector to devalue the exchange rate and to provide manufacturing subsidies. The model therefore gives rise to an asymmetric policy response to bad and good times: devaluation in bad times and no revaluation in good times. This policy outcome creates inflationary expectations so that the economy experiences a real exchange rate appreciation in good times. The Minford chapter is commented on by *Jacques Sijben* (CentER).

The chapter by *Harry Huizinga* (CentER) examines the role of unemployment benefits and redistributive taxation in a model where workers' labor productivities are influenced by the general level of labor quality. In the presence of such labor quality externalities, labor market quits by relatively low-quality workers may raise the productivity of remaining workers. In this setting, unemployment benefits have important efficiency as well as redistributive implications. The political economy of such unemployment benefits, financed by a proportional labor income tax or a lump sum tax, is examined in a median voter framework. Even an employed voter generally supports positive unemployment benefits financed by a proportional labor income tax. A coalition of the unemployed and the most qualified employed workers may favor a relatively high unemployment benefit, if it is financed by a lump sum tax on all. The Huizinga chapter is discussed by *Casper van Ewijk* (University of Amsterdam).

References

Blanchard, Olivier and Quah, Danny (1989), "The Dynamic Effects of Aggregate Demand and Supply Disturbances," *American Economic Review*, 79, 655–73.

Klemperer, Paul and Meyer, Margaret (1986), "Price Competition vs. Quantity Competition: the Role of Uncertainty," *Rand Journal of Economics*, 17, 618–38.

Persson, Torsten and Tabellini, Guido (1990), *Macroeconomic Policy, Credibility and Politics*, London: Harwood Academic Publishers.

Rogoff, Kenneth (1985), "The Optimal Degree of Commitment to an Intermediate Monetary Target," *Quarterly Journal of Economics*, 100, 1169–90.

I

Monetary institutions and policy

1 Reputational versus institutional solutions to the time-consistency problem in monetary policy

SUSANNE LOHMANN

1 Introduction

The classic time-consistency problem results in a counterproductive inflation bias to discretionary monetary policy (Kydland and Prescott, 1977; Barro and Gordon, 1983). The standard formulation of the problem is based on the following time sequence of events: wage setters negotiate nominal wage contracts, setting wage growth equal to expected inflation; the policy maker then sets the inflation rate. Output is stimulated if the inflation rate exceeds the nominal wage growth fixed in the wage setters' contracts. However, such output stimulation comes at the price of increased inflation. The equilibrium inflation rate trades off the policy maker's output stimulation and inflation stabilization goals. Wage setters are rational and thus understand the policy maker's decision rule. Consequently, their inflation expectations do not systematically deviate from actual inflation. It follows that, in equilibrium, the policy maker cannot stimulate output, but her futile attempt to do so leads to an inflation bias. The policy maker would be better off if she could credibly commit herself to refraining from attempting to stimulate output. Since she cannot fulfil her output goal, she could then at least achieve her inflation goal.

2 The reputational solution

In an infinite-horizon repeated game setting, there exists a *reputational solution* to the time-consistency problem in monetary policy (Barro and Gordon, 1983); that is, the inflation bias can be reduced via reputational trigger-punishment strategies (Friedman, 1971).[1]

Suppose the policy maker commits herself to eliminating the inflation bias in monetary policy. The wage setters consequently negotiate a lower rate of nominal wage growth. If she defects, the wage setters punish the policy maker by setting inflationary nominal wage growth in the future. The credibility of the policy maker's commitment is then a function of her discount factor. If the political discount factor is low, the temptation to defect dominates the future punishment of a reversion to the time-consistent equilibrium and commitment is infeasible. Conversely, if the policy maker's discount factor is high, the punishment exceeds the temptation to defect so that her monetary policy promises are credible.

3 Institutional solutions

3.1 Definition and examples

Taylor (1983) and Tabellini (1987) argue that societies alleviate the time-consistency problem by virtue of *institutional solutions*. An institution can be defined as a set of constraints that is initially the object of political choice at the "institutional design stage" but must subsequently be respected by the policy maker when setting policy at the "game stage" (Lohmann, 1992).

Scholars of monetary policy and theory have proposed a number of institutional arrangements, some of which have been implemented in practice: monetary targeting procedures, especially k-percent monetary growth rules (Friedman, 1968; McCallum, 1987; Canzoneri, 1985; Garfinkel and Oh, 1993; Flood and Isard, 1989); delegation to a conservative central banker (Rogoff, 1985; Lohmann, 1992; Waller, 1992; Eijffinger and Schaling, 1996); constitutionally guaranteed central bank independence (Neumann, 1991, 1992); fixed exchange rate regimes (Giavazzi and Giovannini, 1989; Giavazzi and Pagano, 1988; Mélitz, 1988; Cukierman, 1992; Cukierman, Kiguel, and Liviatan, 1994; Bordo and Kydland, 1995, 1996); and incentive contracts for central bankers (Persson and Tabellini, 1993; Walsh, 1995b).

3.2 Reputational versus institutional solutions

Institutional solutions to the time-consistency problem are based on the implicit assumption that the policy maker cannot credibly commit herself to a future path of monetary policy, whereas credible commitments to respect institutional constraints are feasible.[2]

One possible interpretation of this assumption is that institutional promises are *perfect commitments* that are impossible to "undo" without violating the laws of nature, whereas policy promises can be broken. However, the commitment to the central banking institutions listed above is imperfect in the sense that defections are *feasible*. (This does not exclude the possibility that policy makers may have *disincentives* to defect because of the costs imposed in the event of a defection.) In the context of central banking, credible commitments – whether policy or institutional promises

– can only arise if the shadow of the future is sufficiently strong. The feasibility of credible commitments is a function of the political discount factor, as noted above.

It follows that a policy maker can either make credible commitments, in which case there is no obvious role for institutional (rather than reputational) solutions, or she cannot make credible commitments, in which case institutions cannot solve the time-consistency problem. These two cases, which arise when the political discount factor is high or low, respectively, will now be examined in more detail.

If the policy maker cares strongly about the future, she can directly commit herself to the *ex ante* optimal monetary policy path. So why would she bother making institutional commitments, especially if these institutions have imperfections of their own?

For example, in 1978 several European countries formed the European Monetary System (EMS), thereby agreeing to limit bilateral exchange rate fluctuations within narrow margins around predetermined parities. This fixed exchange rate regime was originally set up as a cooperative system with symmetric intervention responsibilities. *De facto*, however, the Deutsche Bundesbank appears to have sterilized its exchange rate interventions to a large degree, with the acquiescence of other EMS member countries. The Deutschmark is now considered the anchor currency of the system. The inflation-averse and politically independent Bundesbank sets monetary policy at its discretion, and EMS member states are constrained to follow a low-inflation path to ensure that their currencies remain within EMS bands. The "disciplinary interpretation" of the EMS proposes that countries with traditionally high inflation rates such as France or Italy deliberately use EMS membership as a commitment device to achieve greater monetary discipline (Fratianni and von Hagen, 1992; see also Giavazzi and Giovannini, 1989; Giavazzi and Pagano, 1988; Mélitz, 1988; Cukierman, 1992).

The commitment of EMS member states to maintain EMS parities is fundamentally political in nature; that is, their promises can, as a matter of principle, be undone by political fiat. Nevertheless, devaluations and exits are costly. Not only do they raise inflation expectations, but governments that devalue or exit lose popularity and may consequently suffer electoral losses (Mélitz, 1988). A government that attempts to evade the monetary policy constraints implied by the EMS – by following an inflationary monetary policy while maintaining its EMS parities – may also trigger costly responses on the part of financial markets: destabilizing speculation, capital flight, and the like. In short, the commitment to the EMS is enforced by reputational trigger-punishment strategies, executed by wage setters, voters, and financial markets.

The institutional commitment via the EMS comes at a price. German monetary policy is responsive to a variety of domestic shocks. To the extent that German shocks are not perfectly correlated with the shocks impinging on the economies of other EMS member states, those countries not only forego the benefits arising from the stabilization role of monetary policy, but they also "import" monetary variability generated by the Bundesbank's domestic responsiveness. In the early 1990s, for example, the non-German EMS member states suffered recessionary consequences when German monetary policy was geared toward dealing with the potentially inflationary consequences of German unification.

The costly distortions generated by this institutional commitment mechanism raise a puzzle. Surely each non-German EMS member state would be better off if its government directly committed itself to follow a monetary policy path that is optimal from a domestic perspective rather than to bind itself to German monetary policy. Such a policy commitment could be enforced by reputational means: after all, the EMS success story (even taking into account the 1992/3 crises) suggests that the EMS member states are capable of entering at least partially credible commitments.

When conceiving of the EMS as an institutional commitment mechanism, it is not sufficient to identify the reputational means by which it is enforced, as some scholars have done (see, for example, Mélitz, 1988). Given that the institutional solution is associated with costly distortions, any explanation that fails to identify the benefits generated by the institutional solution over and above the reputational solution is incomplete.

If the political discount factor is low, then credible commitments are infeasible. In this case there is no obvious credibility differential between policy and institutional promises: the temptation to renege on the promise to adhere to a pre-specified future path of monetary policy is, after all, equal to the temptation of defecting, *ex post*, from a central banking institution that implements that same monetary policy rule. For this reason, proposals suggesting that a policy maker who faces a time-consistency problem with regard to policy promises can magically solve her problem by committing to an institution appear to be unfounded.

Indeed, governments have been known to renege on policy promises, but on occasion they have also failed to respect the constraints implied by institutional arrangements. For example, Italy not only repeatedly negotiated devaluations within the framework of the EMS, but in the course of the EMS crisis of 1992 it also exited.

Such instances of institutional breakdown can be interpreted as the exercise of costly escape options, rather than lack of commitment ability (Lohmann, 1992): after all, a government that cannot make credible commitments would not set up institutions in the first place. The EMS allows for negotiated devaluations but not for exits. At first blush, it might appear unreasonable to classify devaluations as an institutional defection, whereas exits are clearly a form of institutional defection. From an institutional design perspective, however, membership of the EMS might be interpreted as a commitment to maintain fixed parities within narrow bands, supplemented by two escape options that are characterized by differential costs.

Moreover, the observation of occasional institutional breakdown does not allow us to conclude that institutional commitment is ineffective – even if the defecting policy maker does not incur any reputational costs. For example, the Deutsche Bundesbank missed its pre-announced monetary targets eight out of thirteen times in the period 1975–87, while its inflation-fighting reputation has become, if anything, tougher rather than weaker. The puzzle raised by this observation can be resolved with reference to the "target audience" of the Bundesbank's money supply announcements. Most Germans are blissfully unaware of the fact that the Bundesbank is committed to follow a monetary target at all; they most certainly do not know the pre-announced value of the target, and for all practical purposes they face prohibitive costs of monitoring whether the Bundesbank fulfills its targets. Instead, the Bundesbank's monetary targeting procedure is directed at an elite community of Bundesbank watchers that monitors its performance – representatives of the banking sector, trade unions, and employer organizations. The cost of an unexcused defection from the target is given by the subsequent increase in inflation expectations formed by Bundesbank watchers, whose assessments shape a large number of nominal prices in the German economy. Interestingly, the Bundesbank tends to provide detailed explanations for its failures to fulfill its targets. Its well-informed audience is capable of judging whether the Bundesbank's excuses are acceptable, thereby allowing for "excused" (costless) defection when a variety of real and monetary shocks or unforeseen contingencies are realized (for a related interpretation of the gold standard, see Bordo and Kydland, 1995, 1996).

3.3 The credibility–flexibility tradeoff

Conventional analyses of optimal institutional design are incomplete and flawed if they fail to take into account the reputational underpinnings of institutional commitments. I demonstrate this with reference to the literature on the credibility–flexibility tradeoff in the design of central banking institutions (see, for example, Rogoff, 1985; Flood and Isard, 1989; Lohmann, 1992; Cukierman, 1992; Garfinkel and Oh, 1993; Eijffinger and Schaling, 1996).

Some scholars implicitly take into account reputational effects by assuming that the commitment to a central banking institution can be broken at a cost (Flood and Isard, 1989; Lohmann, 1992; Cukierman, 1992). For example, the policy maker might be committed to follow a simple zero-inflation rule, with the option of deviating from the rule at a cost. This "escape clause" is utilized when extreme monetary or real shocks are realized (Flood and Isard, 1989; see Lohmann, 1990, for a critique). The cost paid by the policy maker in such extreme circumstances can be interpreted as the reputational losses society incurs when the public observes a defection from the simple rule and revises its inflationary expectations upwards.

Other scholars fail to allow for the fact that institutional commitments must be enforced by reputational means (Rogoff, 1985; Garfinkel and Oh, 1993; Eijffinger and Schaling, 1996). Consider, for example, Rogoff's (1985) proposal that monetary policy be delegated to a "conservative" central banker who places a higher weight on the inflation objective than on the output objective, compared with his political principal. Such a central banker implements a lower time-consistent inflation rate on average, but from the policy maker's point of view the central banker underreacts to output shocks.

The policy maker can renege on her commitment to this delegation regime by dismissing the central banker or overriding his monetary policy decisions. The temptation to do so is larger for extreme output shocks than for moderate ones. Rogoff's assumption that the distribution of output shocks has infinite support (output shocks are normally distributed in his model) implies that the temptation to renege is unbounded. The principal is fully committed to Rogoff's institution if and only if the political cost of dismissing the central banker *ex post*, or overriding the central banker's decisions, is *infinite* (Lohmann, 1992). If the reputational mechanism by which the policy maker can commit to a conservative central banker were explicitly modeled, it would become apparent that the infinite-cost assumption is equivalent to the assumption that the policy maker has an infinite time horizon and a political discount factor equal to one.

If, instead, the discount factor lies strictly between zero and one, the reputational cost of dismissing or overriding the central banker is strictly positive and finite. In this situation, the conservative central banker is partially independent. He will set monetary policy independently in normal times, while accommodating the *ex post* demands of his political principal when extreme output shocks are realized. The central bank reaction function implemented by this institution thus differs from the one proposed by Rogoff and instead corresponds to the one derived by Lohmann (1992).

Implicitly underlying Rogoff's analysis is a dichotomous view of political commitments: commitments are credible, or they are not credible. This classification scheme is biased toward interpreting empirical instances of institutional breakdown as arising from a lack of credible commitment rather than the exercise of costly escape options. In contrast, Lohmann (1992) allows for partial commitments: in her model the degree of institutional commitment varies continuously with the cost incurred by the political principal in the event of a defection. As a consequence, the observation that the central bank occasionally accommodates inflationary political pressures does not necessarily imply that the political commitment to the central banking institution is an empty promise.

The literature on the credibility–flexibility tradeoff is subject to another weakness, which also arises because scholars fail to acknowledge explicitly the reputational underpinnings of institutional commitments. Institutional design proposals are typically based on a comparison of the levels of social welfare achieved under the proposed institutional solution and the discretionary solution (see, for example, Rogoff, 1985), or, more rarely, on a systematic assessment of the relative performance of various institutional solutions (see, for example, Lohmann, 1992). But overall the literature fails to compare the levels of social welfare achieved when credible commitments are sustained by institutional or (non-institutionalized) reputational means.

For example, in the Rogoff framework social welfare would be maximized if the monetary authority were fully committed to follow the *ex ante* optimal state-contingent rule. This rule implements the *ex ante* optimal inflation rate on average, while responding optimally to output shocks. The corresponding central bank reaction function can be implemented by reputational or institutional means if the political discount factor is sufficiently high.

The reputational solution involves a public commitment to the rule. The private sector then conditions its trigger-punishment strategies on the realization of the output shock. If the observed inflation rate differs from the one prescribed by the rule for the observed output shock, the private sector punishes the policy maker by revising its inflation expectations upwards. Since the state-contingent rule responds optimally to output shocks, the policy maker's temptation to renege is independent of the realization of the output shock. As a consequence, the policy maker is fully committed to follow the rule if the cost of reneging lies above a strictly positive but finite threshold. This condition is fulfilled if the political discount factor lies above a threshold that is strictly positive but smaller than one.

Alternatively, the *ex ante* optimal state-contingent rule is implemented by the following institutional solution: the policy maker delegates monetary policy to a central banker with the same objective function, except that the central banker's output "ideal point" is equal to the natural level (Persson and Tabellini, 1990, footnote 18; see also Neumann, 1992). Such a central banker does not face a time-consistency problem, and, from the policy maker's point of view, the central banker responds optimally to output shocks. As a consequence, the temptation to renege on this delegation regime is independent of the realization of the output shock. Thus, the policy maker is fully committed if the cost of reneging lies above a strictly positive but finite threshold. This cost can be interpreted as the reputational losses society incurs in the event of a defection: if the central banker is dismissed, or if his decisions are overriden, the public revises its inflation expectations upwards. It follows that the policy maker is fully committed to the delegation regime if the political discount factor lies above a threshold that is strictly positive but smaller than one.

Both the reputational and institutional solutions lead to the same level of social welfare (they implement the same central bank reaction function). Moreover, since both solutions implement the *ex ante* optimal state-contingent rule, they dominate the institutional solutions proposed by Rogoff (1985) and Lohmann (1992) both of which involve a costly distortionary response to output shocks. The Rogoff framework is implicitly based on the assumption that the policy maker is constrained to choose a central bank appointee from a pool of agents who differ in the weights they place on the output and inflation objectives. Given the lack of microfoundations for the central banker's objective function, this implicit constraint is completely *ad hoc*. Nevertheless, the Rogoff framework (that also underlies the Lohmann model) is thought to be valuable because it illustrates the credibility–flexibility tradeoff that might arise in the presence of empirical constraints on the choice of central banker "types." But the institutional solutions proposed by Rogoff and Lohmann, respectively, are subject to the critique that they are dominated by the (non-institutionalized) reputational solution that implements the *ex ante* optimal state-contingent rule.

This conclusion is, of course, based on a comparison of institutional solutions that are derived subject to constraints on the set of feasible central banking institutions, on the one hand, and the unconstrained reputational solution, on the other. It is plausible that the set of feasible trigger-punishment strategies is also subject to empirical constraints. For example, the reputational implementation of the *ex ante* optimal state-contingent rule requires the public to follow state-contingent punishment strategies. In the presence of transaction costs, informational asymmetries and bounded rationality, people may only be able to follow simple (that is, non-state-contingent) punishment strategies. In this case, the only rule that can be implemented without resort to an institution is a simple k-percent monetary growth or inflation rule. In the presence of unbounded output shocks, the commitment to such a rule is necessarily partial.

The simplicity constraint on the set of feasible trigger-punishment strategies does not affect the set of feasible central banking institutions considered by Lohmann. The political commitment to a conservative central banker can be sustained with a simple trigger-punishment strategy: if the central banker is dismissed, or if his decisions are overridden, society reverts to the high-inflation time-consistent equilibrium.

In conclusion, if the policy maker is constrained both with regard to the set of feasible central banking institutions and with regard to the set of feasible punishment strategies, as specified above, then she must in effect choose between the institutional solution of a partially independent conservative central banker and the reputational solution of partial commitment to a simple rule. In the Lohmann framework, the institutional solution leads to a better credibility–flexibility tradeoff (Lohmann, 1992).

3.4 Political versus legal commitments

So far, my discussion has been implicitly premised on the assumption that institutional promises are *political commitments*; that is, they are enforced by reputational trigger-punishment strategies rather than by the legal system.

Many central banking institutions do involve some degree of institutionalized enforcement via the legal system, among them constitutionally guaranteed central bank independence, legislated monetary targets, and incentive contracts for central bankers. The promise to respect the integrity of such institutions can be classified as a *legal commitment*.

Many scholars tend to think of legal commitments as close-to-perfectly credible. For example, Neumann (1991, 1992) proposes that monetary policy be delegated to a central banker who cares only about price stability or to a central banker whose output ideal point is equal to the natural level of output. Neither central bank has a time-consistency problem, but the policy maker obviously faces a commitment problem with regard to the credibility of the delegation regime if she constitutionally guarantees the independence of the central bank or at the very least requires that any change to the independent status of the central bank be subject to a two-thirds majority in parliament.

The implicit notion that legal commitments are close-to-perfect is problematic for a number of reasons (see Lohmann, 1995, for a more extensive discussion). First, such legal remedies are not generally effective. Measures of legal central bank independence are negatively correlated with the depreciation in the real value of money for *developed* countries; whereas the correlation is effectively zero for *developing* countries (Cukierman, 1992). Cukierman concludes that:

the divergence between the letter of the law and actual practice is substantially higher in developing than in developed countries. This may be due to a general norm of more adherence to the law in developed countries. (421)

Studies that focus on the *formal* independence of central banks are often based on the implicit assumption that the *behavioral* independence enjoyed by a central bank is invariant over time if the legal status of the central bank does not change (Lohmann, 1994). According to legal measures of central bank independence, the Deutsche Bundesbank is one of the most independent central banks in the world (Cukierman, 1992). Its legal status remained unchanged from 1957 to 1992. Yet, Lohmann (1994) finds that the degree to which German monetary policy was vulnerable to political pressures fluctuated considerably over this time period.

Second, the view that legal commitments are perfect is logically inconsistent with the widely held belief that different legal commitments are associated with different degrees of credibility. For example, most people would classify a k-percent money growth rule that is written into the constitution as "more credible" than a corresponding rule that has the legal status of a simple law. The underlying intuition is that these two institutional arrangements are associated with different probabilities that the legal commitment to the money growth rule will be politically undone. In a polity governed by heterogeneous legislative bodies, a law that can be changed by simple majority rule is more likely to be overturned some time in the future than a constitutional requirement that can only be changed with the votes of a supermajority.

Third, legal and political commitments are easily confounded. For example, in 1989 the New Zealand legislature revised the law governing the activities of the Reserve Bank of New Zealand. The new law requires that the governor of the central bank and the minister of finance establish public inflation targets for the Bank's operations. The governor is personally accountable if the Bank fails to fulfill its targets. The minister of finance has the prerogative to override the Bank's policy, but such a directive must be released to the public. The New Zealand targeting procedure thus appears to provide a legal constraint on the government's attempts to manipulate monetary policy for short-term gain. Numerous scholars have argued that this institutional arrangement provides monetary discipline via a legally enforceable incentive contract (see Walsh, 1995a, for a discussion). As a matter of principle, however, the New Zealand legislature can repeal the central bank law at any point in time. Of course, the legislature may choose not to do so because it would incur a political cost – for example, the government might be punished at the polls. But then we must conclude that the commitment to the New Zealand monetary regime is political in nature and not legal.

4 Conclusion

The conventional wisdom that "institutions matter" because they allow politicians to make credible commitments is deeply flawed. To the extent that a policy maker commits herself to respect the constraint implied by a central banking institution, the integrity of the institution must be protected by reputational means.

My argument is related to, but logically distinct from, the "institutions don't matter" view articulated by Posen (1993, 1994) who critiques the widespread notion that central bank independence "causes" low inflation. He argues that empirical findings of negative correlations between measures of central bank independence and inflation are consistent with a simple preference-based explanation: countries with preferences for low inflation (or governments pressured by powerful groups who have economic stakes in low-inflation outcomes) choose to set up independent central banks, whereas countries with preferences for high inflation (or governments who are subject to inflationary interest group pressures) tend to have dependent central banks. Thus, the empirical correlations that have been documented in the literature (see, for example, Cukierman, 1992) may be simply a consequence of preferences mapping directly into outcomes, with institutions being purely epiphenomenal.

To the extent that monetary policy is beset by time-consistency problems, Posen's preference-based argument obfuscates the distinction between *ex ante* and *ex post* preferences. In the absence of institutional commitment (or non-institutionalized reputational enforcement), the policy maker's *ex post* monetary policy preferences translate directly into monetary policy outcomes. But the purpose of institutions is to mute the impact of the policy maker's *ex post* preferences on monetary policy outcomes, consistent with the policy maker's *ex ante* preferences.

The institutional membrane that maps monetary policy preferences into outcomes is, of course, at some point in time the object of political choice. In this sense, central banking institutions are shaped by the preferences of the relevant political actors at the institutional design stage. Once a central banking institution is set up, however, any changes to the institution may be costly owing to reputational effects of the kind discussed in this chapter. The political costs of institutional change imply that the relevant political actors, their preferences or other factors determining their relative power may change while the institution remains constant (Lohmann, 1994).

At a common sense level of discourse, any conclusion that institutions don't matter is, of course, empirically contradicted by the considerable political efforts that go into the design and maintenance of central banking institutions. Rational policy makers would not expend such effort if they did not expect some payoff. It is hard to believe, for example, that the intense historical debates in the United States surrounding the commitment to the gold standard or the founding of the Federal Reserve System were "full of sound and fury, signifying nothing." In a companion article, I explore the possibility that institutions matter in the following sense: institutional solutions implement a socially preferred credibility–flexibility tradeoff, compared with their reputational counterparts (Lohmann, 1995).

Notes

Department of Political Science, University of California, Los Angeles. This chapter was presented at the Conference on "Positive political economy: theory and evidence" at the CentER for Economic Research, University of Tilburg, January 1995. It addresses some questions originally raised in joint work with Jonathan Bendor, whom I would like to thank for many insightful discussions. Manfred J.M. Neumann, Adam Posen, and Carl E. Walsh provided helpful comments on an earlier draft.

1 My terminology is consistent with that of the macro political economy literature, which speaks of reputational solutions in complete information settings (see, for example, Persson and Tabellini, 1990). Standard game theory has reputational effects arising in the presence of incomplete information (see, for example, Fudenberg and Tirole, 1991).

2 The following discussion builds on Bendor and Lohmann (1993); see also Lohmann (1995).

References

Barro, Robert and Gordon, David (1983), "Rules, Discretion and Reputation in a Model of Monetary Policy," *Journal of Monetary Economics*, 12, 101–21.

Bendor, Jonathan and Lohmann, Susanne (1993), "Institutions and Credible Commitment", mimeo, Stanford University.

Bordo, Michael and Kydland, Finn (1995), "The Gold Standard as a Rule: An Essay in Exploration," *Explorations in Economic History*. 32, 423–64.

(1996), "The Gold Standard as a Commitment Mechanism," In Tarnin Bayoumi, Barry Eichengreen and Mark Taylor, *Economic Perspectives on the Classical Gold Standard*, Cambridge: Cambridge University Press.

Canzoneri, Matthew (1985), "Monetary Policy Games and the Role of Private Information," *American Economic Review*, 75, 1056–70.

Cukierman, Alex (1992), *Central Bank Strategy, Credibility and Independence*, Cambridge, Mass.: MIT Press.

Cukierman, Alex, Kiguel, Miguel, and Liviatan, Nissan (1994), "How Much to Commit to an Exchange Rate Rule: Balancing Credibility and Flexibility," In Pierre Siklos (ed.), *Varieties of Monetary Reform: Lessons for European Monetary Union*, Dordrecht: Kluwer Academic Press.

Eijffinger, Sylvester and Schaling, Eric (1996), "The Ultimate Determinants of Central Bank Independence," this volume.

Flood, Robert and Isard, Peter (1989), "Monetary Policy Strategies," *International Monetary Fund Staff Papers*, 36, 612–32.

Fratianni, Michele and von Hagen, Jürgen (1992), *The European Monetary System and European Monetary Union*, Boulder: Westview Press.

Friedman, James (1971), "A Non-cooperative Equilibrium for Supergames," *Review of Economic Studies*, 38, 1–12.

Friedman, Milton (1968), "The Role of Monetary Policy," *American Economic Review*, 58, 1–17.

Fudenberg, Drew and Tirole, Jean (1991), *Game Theory*, Cambridge, Mass.: MIT Press.

Garfinkel, Michelle and Oh, Seonghwan (1993), "Strategic Discipline in Monetary Policy with Private Information: Optimal Targeting Horizons," *American Economic Review*, 83, 99–117.

Giavazzi, Francesco and Giovannini, Alberto, (1989), *Limiting Exchange Rate Flexibility: The European Monetary System*, Cambridge, Mass.: MIT Press.

Giavazzi, Francesco and Pagano, Marco (1988), "The Advantage of Tying One's Hands: EMS Discipline and Central Bank Credibility," *European Economic Review*, 32, 1055–82.

Kydland, Finn and Prescott, Edward (1977), "Rules Rather than Discretion: The Inconsistency of Optimal Plans," *Journal of Political Economy*, 85, 473–91.

Lohmann, Susanne (1990), "Monetary Policy Strategies – A Correction: Comment on Flood and Isard," *International Monetary Fund Staff Papers*, 37, 440–5.

(1992), "Optimal Commitment in Monetary Policy: Credibility versus Flexibility," *American Economic Review*, 82, 273–86.

(1994), "Federalism and Central Bank Autonomy: The Politics of German Monetary Policy, 1957–1992," mimeo, University of California, Los Angeles.

(1995), "Why Do Central Banking Institutions Matter?" mimeo, University of California, Los Angeles.

McCallum, Bennett (1987), "The Case for Rules in the Conduct of Monetary Policy: A Concrete Example," *Weltwirtschaftliches Archiv*, 123, 415–29.

Mélitz, Jacques (1988), "Monetary Discipline, Germany, and the European Monetary System: A Synthesis," in Francesco Giavazzi *et al.* (eds.), *The European Monetary System*, New York: Cambridge University Press.

Neumann, Manfred J.M. (1991), "Precommitment by Central Bank Independence," *Open Economies Review*, 2, 95–112.

(1992), "Binding durch Zentralbankunabhängigkeit," in Herman Albeck (ed.), *Wirtschaftsordnung and Geldverfassung*, Göttingen: Vandenhoeck & Ruprecht, 62–73.

Persson, Torsten and Tabellini, Guido (1990), *Macroeconomic Policy, Credibility and Politics*, Chur: Harwood Academic Publishers.

(1993), "Designing Institutions for Monetary Stability," *Carnegie-Rochester Conference Series on Public Policy*, 39, 53–84.

Posen, Adam (1993), "Why Central Bank Independence Does Not Cause Low Inflation: There Is No Institutional Fix for Politics," in Richard O'Brien (ed.), *Finance and the International Economy* vol. VII, Oxford: Oxford University Press.

(1994), "Is Central Bank Independence the Result of Effective Opposition to Inflation? Evidence of Endogenous Monetary Policy Institutions," mimeo, Federal Reserve Bank of New York.

Rogoff, Kenneth (1985), "The Optimal Degree of Commitment to an Intermediate Monetary Target," *Quarterly Journal of Economics,* 100, 1169–89.

Tabellini, Guido (1987), "Reputational Constraints on Monetary Policy: A Comment," *Carnegie-Rochester Conference Series on Public Policy*, 26, 183–90.

Taylor, John (1983), "Comments on 'Rules, Discretion and Reputation in a Model of Monetary Policy,'" *Journal of Monetary Economics*, 12, 123–5.

Waller, Christopher (1992), "The Choice of a Conservative Central Banker in a Multisector Economy," *American Economic Review*, 82, 1006–12.

Walsh, Carl (1995a), "Is New Zealand's Reserve Bank Act of 1989 an Optimal Central Bank Contract?" *Journal of Money, Credit and Banking*, 27, 1179–91.

(1995b), "Optimal Contracts for Central Bankers," *American Economic Review*, 85, 150–168.

Comment

MANFRED J.M. NEUMANN

Over recent years a consensus view has emerged in the macroeconomic literature on how governments may be able to overcome the deadlock of time-consistent inflation. The solution is handing the authority over monetary policy to an independent institution. In her chapter, Susanne Lohmann challenges this view. She even claims the conventional wisdom that institutions matter to be flawed.

In my comment, I will first provide a short overview of what we know about different institutional solutions to the time-consistency problem in monetary policy, next discuss why institutional solutions dominate reputational solutions, and, finally, take issue with a few related arguments.

Table 1.1 presents an overview of the different institutional approaches the government may choose for reducing the loss from time-consistent inflation. I believe it is useful to equate institutional solutions with precommitment rather than commitment. Commitment is just the promise of a specified policy path or conduct. Delivering on the promise yields credibility, the extent of which depends on how long good conduct is maintained. Thus, it takes time for the promise to be perceived as credible. Precommitment, in contrast, provides credibility on the spot, because it rests on legal constraints of government behavior.

Another point to note is that we need to spell out the nature of the constraints that make up an institutional solution. For example, delegating policy to a conservative central banker does not provide the lower expected or permanent rate of inflation computed by Rogoff (1985) if this banker can be dismissed at any time during his term. More generally, any institutional solution requires the provision that the central banker will not be dismissed during his term; without such a provision no institutional set-up will be perceived by the public as commitment. In table 1.1, I have listed three constraints on government that permit differentiating the main institutional solutions discussed by the literature.

Let the government's loss function be given by

$$L^G = (y - y^*)^2 = x\,\pi^2 \tag{1}$$

The government desires zero inflation, π, and the stabilization of output fluctuations relative to a desired level of output, y^*. Setting normal output at zero, the variable y^* represents a desired constant output gain. Let output be determined by

$$y = \pi - E_{-1}\pi + z \tag{2}$$

where z is a normally distributed supply shock.

In table 1.1, the completely government-dependent central bank, implied by the Barro and Gordon (1983) framework, serves as the benchmark case. This central bank subordinates to the government's loss function and, consequently, sets the rate of inflation at the discretionary level. As a result, the time-consistent average or regime rate of inflation is a positive function of the government's desired output gain

$$\overline{\pi}_{BG} = y^*/x \tag{3}$$

The subscript BG stands for Barro-Gordon.

Table 1.1 *Alternative solutions to the time-consistency problem of monetary policy*

	None	Non-perfect		
Government's commitment	None			
Constraints on government				
no dismissal		Yes	Yes	Yes
no overriding		No	Yes	Yes
CB free to disregard y^*		No	No	No
Status of central bank	Complete dependence	Partial dependence		Complete independence
	Barro–Gordon (1983)	Lohmann (1992)	Rogoff (1985)	Neumann (1991)
				0
				Neumann (1992)
Relative weight of output	$1/x$	$1/(x+\epsilon)$	$1/(x+\epsilon)$	$1/x$
Regime inflation	$\bar{\pi}_{BG} >$		$\bar{\pi}_L > \bar{\pi}_R$	$> \bar{\pi}_N = 0$
Cost of reneging	None	$\bar{\pi}_{BG} - \bar{\pi}_L < \bar{\pi}_{BG} - \bar{\pi}_R$	$\bar{\pi}_{BG} - \bar{\pi}_R$	$< \bar{\pi}_{BG}$

Note: $EL^G_{BG} > EL^G_L > EL^G_R > EL^G_N$.

Government can improve on the time-consistent solution by pre-committing to an institutional solution. A first institutional solution is the Lohmann (1992) bank. The government appoints a banker whose loss function is similar to the government's, except that he is more conservative than the government, $\epsilon > 0$.

$$L_L^{Cb} = (y - y^*)^2 + (x + \epsilon)\pi^2 \tag{4}$$

The subscript L stands for Lohmann.

The banker receives a contract that extends over the government's term. Since the government is *ex ante* constrained by the provision of no dismissal during the banker's term, the banker enjoys some independence against being forced to respond to output shocks differently from his conservative preference. However, the central bank statutes contain an escape clause for the government: in the case of large shocks the government holds the right of overriding the central bank if it does not respond more strongly to these large shocks. As a result, the Lohmann banker will provide a strictly positive regime rate of inflation that undercuts the time-consistent level of the Barro-Gordon banker

$$0 < \bar{\pi}_L < \bar{\pi}_{BG} \tag{5}$$

If the government eliminates from the central bank statutes the right of overriding, we arrive at the Rogoff (1985) bank. Now, the conservative banker will run policy according to his more conservative preference not just in normal times but always. Therefore, he will be able to reduce the government's inflation bias by more than the constrained Lohmann banker

$$0 < \bar{\pi}_R = y^*/(x + \epsilon) < \bar{\pi}_L \tag{6}$$

The subscript R stands for Rogoff.

Finally, we have the completely independent central bank. The special feature of independence is that the central banker is not forced by government to act on its preferences for an extra gain of output and employment. By eliminating the variable y^* from his loss function, the independent central banker frees the government from the self-created problem of unnecessary time-consistent inflation. In Neumann (1991) it was assumed that the independent banker completely eliminates the output objective. This implied that monetary policy is not used for stabilizing output fluctuations.[1] In Neumann (1992), in contrast, stabilization relative to normal output was admitted, but the government was advised to appoint a central banker of its own type, $\epsilon = 0$

$$L_N^{Cb} = y^2 + x\,\pi^2 \tag{7}$$

The subject N stands for Neumann.

Assuming that he is able to observe shocks to output without error, this non-conservative banker is the optimal independent central banker. He delivers a regime inflation rate of zero

$$\overline{\pi}_N = 0 \tag{8}$$

and, in addition, the optimal stabilization of output relative to its natural level. It follows that the expected loss of government, EL^G, will be lowest if monetary policy is handed to a non-conservative independent central banker.

Thus, we find that central bank independence dominates any other institutional solution. Of course, if the government is constrained to choose the central banker from a pool of agents who differ from itself in the weights they place on output and inflation objectives, as Lohmann assumes, then her and the Rogoff framework come into play. However, Lohmann admits that the assumed constraint is completely *ad hoc*. Why should government be unable to find a person of its own type? Therefore, I conclude: the government should love the independent central banker and we economists should stop playing with models of conservative bankers.

Finally note with Lohmann that governments may be tempted to renege on institutional solutions, say, by dismissing the central banker. This however comes at a cost in that the private sector will immediately revise inflation expectations upwards to the time-consistent level produced by the completely dependent Barro-Gordon banker. As the bottom line of table 1.1 indicates, the costs of reneging on the completely independent central bank are highest. It follows that this set-up provides the highest degree of precommitment for any type of government.

Reputational versus institutional solutions

The principal alternative to institutional solutions is reputation building. Lohmann claims that a government who cares strongly about the future has no need for institution-based commitment, because it can directly commit itself to the *ex ante* optimal path of monetary policy. To emphasize the claim, Lohmann invents an "institutions don't matter paradox." The paradox says: the government is either credible and it does not need an institutional solution, or the government is not credible, in which case credibility cannot be gained by an institutional solution. Though this is a nice paradox, it is misleading, as any paradox is.

Lohmann considers a virtuous government whose discount factor is sufficiently high. She argues that this government may either set up an independent central bank who will follow the *ex ante* optimal state-contingent rule or announce this rule publicly and run it by itself. To either regime the government will be fully committed if the cost of reneging lies above a strictly positive but finite threshold. It follows for this type of government that the institutional solution of central bank independence does not matter. So Lohmann seems to have a case.

However, the formal equivalence in equilibrium of the alternative solutions for some type of government is not sufficient to justify the strong assertion that institutions do not matter. Once we allow for less than perfect information, there are more aspects to consider. Since the private sector's inflation expectations depend on the perceived degree of commitment, central bank independence dominates the reputational solution. The reason is that the private sector knows that the costs of reneging differ between the two regimes. For any type of government the cost of reneging on central bank independence exceeds the cost of reneging on the reputational solution. While in both cases the inflation expectations are equally revised upwards, the net cost of reneging on the reputational solution is lower due to a one-time gain of output. The gain results from the fact that reneging on reputation is effected by unexpected high money growth. The sudden dismissal of the independent banker, in contrast, becomes immediately common knowledge, hence does not provide such gain.

Another aspect is that the political discount factor of any government may not be constant but decline over time with the time span left until the next election. If the government relies on the reputational solution, this will be perceived as a signal that it intends to renege on the solution just in time to secure a stimulation of the economy before the election. The alternative solution of central bank independence does not generate such a signal, because reneging on central bank independence does not provide an output gain. Consequently, inflation expectations will be higher under the reputational approach than under central bank independence.

It is worthwhile pointing out that Lohmann herself acknowledges that the set of feasible solutions changes, once we allow for the presence of informational asymmetries or transaction costs. She argues that in this case the government's options may be reduced to the choice between the reputational solution of partial commitment to a simple money rule and the institutional solution of the Lohmann (1992) banker. It comes as a small surprise when she concludes that the latter solution is to be preferred. Apparently, institutions may matter.

Legal versus political commitment

Lohmann presents different definitions of commitment whose cognitive value I find in doubt. For example, she defines "perfect commitment" as a promise that is "impossible to undo without violating the laws of nature."

Given that it is impossible to violate the laws of nature, the definition creates an empty set. So why have it? In fact, the notion of perfect commitment is in conflict with the assumption of rationality. It is not rational to abstain from reneging on a commitment under all circumstances.

Lohmann also speaks of legal and of political commitment. I believe we do not need such definitions. In contrast to reputational solutions, any institutional solution requires some legal form. However, whether a solution is to be kept or abolished is a purely political decision. In conclusion, any commitment by government, reputational as well as institutional, is political in nature.

Finally, Lohmann is right in pointing out that many scholars, including myself, have taken the law enforcement problem for granted when they proposed to write the constraints on government, i.e. the central bank statute, into the country's constitution. True, legal provisions are of no value if the government does not have to honor the law. But otherwise the degree of credibility will be the higher, the more difficult it is to change the chosen institutional solution by normal democratic procedures.[2]

Notes

1 Note that Neumann and Von Hagen (1993) cannot reject the hypothesis that the Bundesbank pays no attention to cyclical output movements.

2 Lohmann is right that legal provisons do not make a commitment "close-to-perfect," except I am not aware that anybody has made this claim.

References

Barro, Robert and Gordon, David (1983), "Rules, Discretion and Reputation in a Model of Monetary Policy," *Journal of Monetary Economics*, 12, 101–21.

Lohmann, Susanne (1992), "Optimal Commitment in Monetary Policy: Credibility versus Flexibility," *American Economic Review*, 82, 273–86.

Neumann, Manfred J.M. (1991), "Precommitment by Central Bank Independence," *Open Economies Review*, 2, 95–112.

—— (1992), "Bindung durch Zentralbankunabhängigkeit," in Herman Albeck (ed.), *Wirtschaftsordnung und Geldverfassung*, Göttingen: Vandenhoeck & Ruprecht, 62–73.

Neumann, Manfred J.M. and Von Hagen, Jürgen (1993), "Monetary Policy in Germany," in Michele Fratianni and Dominick Salvatore (eds.), *Monetary Policy in Developed Economies, Handbook of Comparative Economic Policies*, III, Westport: Greenwood, 299–334.

Rogoff, Kenneth (1985), "The Optimal Degree of Commitment to an Intermediate Monetary Target," *Quarterly Journal of Economics*, 100, 1169–89.

2 Reciprocity and political business cycles in federal monetary unions

JÜRGEN VON HAGEN

1 Introduction

A characteristic of monetary unions is that the governance of money has a federal structure. This is reflected in the fact that the central bank council consists of representatives of the member states of the union, possibly together with representatives of the federal government, if such a government exists, or with appointees of the central decision-making body of the union. For example, the Federal Open Market Committee (FOMC) has the presidents of five regional Federal Reserve Banks as voting members together with seven governors appointed by the US President and confirmed by Congress. The council of the Bundesbank consists of the presidents of all state central banks and the members of the Bundesbank Board. Where monetary unions do not coincide with political unions, such as in the Caribbean and in the African monetary unions, representatives of the independent member states sit on the council and decide on monetary policy collectively. This will also be true for the European Central Bank (ECB) according to the design of the Maastricht Treaty.

The federal structure of such unions raises the question of how to distribute the power over monetary policy between the center and the parts of the union. Von Hagen and Süppel (1994a, b) show that central appointees deliver more efficient monetary stabilization policies than state representatives. However, Von Hagen and Süppel also show that a central bank council of state representatives is less likely to produce political business cycles and, therefore, produce a lower long-run rate of inflation than central appointees. The reason is that, with uncoordinated election cycles in the member states, the median voter on the council is unlikely to represent a country holding an election. Due to the single-shot nature of the game Von Hagen and Süppel analyze, the median voter also has no reason to support the demands for easy monetary policy by other representatives for strategic reasons. Thus, the distribution of monetary policy authority involves a tradeoff between efficient stabilization and low inflation.

In this chapter, I show that the optimistic conclusion about central bank councils of state representatives is weakened when a repeated voting game is analyzed. With repeated voting, incentives for strategic behavior exist that may induce the median voter to support a fellow council member's demand for easy money even when this runs counter to her own, immediate interest. I will show that such strategic behavior entails positive inflation and real fluctuations even when election dates are completely staggered.

The existence and the potentially detrimental effects of strategic voting in federal decision-making bodies are long-standing themes of political economy. Of particular importance is the analysis of behavioral norms of reciprocity in federal parliaments such as the US Congress. Reciprocity prevails in a decision-making body, when some of its members vote against their sincere, short-run interests to render a favor to other members expecting that the latter will return such favors in the future.[1] Reciprocity can occur only in settings of repeated voting, since, as a behavioral norm, it is based on each player's expectation that all other players adhere to the same norm in the future.

A prominent example of such behavior is the existence of *pork-barrel* programs in US legislation, i.e., legislation that uses resources financed by tax revenue collected from all Congressional districts for purposes that benefit only a subset of all districts (Ferejohn, 1974). Examples for *pork* are local infrastructure projects funded with federal taxes. The notion of *pork* implies inefficient budgetary decisions: as each Congressman evaluates the full marginal benefit of the *pork* his district receives against the small part of the marginal tax burden to finance it falling on his district, Congress ends up voting for too much spending and, hence, excessive taxation.

The puzzle posed by the existence of pork-barrel legislation is, why does an individual Congressman vote in favor of legislation that provides *pork* for other districts? After all, such legislation only creates a cost (more taxes) but no immediate benefit for his district. The intuitive answer is that legislators will propose programs that give some *pork* to a parliamentary majority at the expense of the minority. However, standard social choice theory predicts that such programs cannot be supported by stable voting equilibria, since each Congressman wishes to attract as much *pork* to his district as possible and there are many possible permutations of a *majority* exploiting a *minority* in parliament.

In a recent set of papers, Baron (1991) and Baron and Ferejohn (1989) propose a model of bargaining in the legislature where making proposals and voting on them is time consuming, time is valuable, and Congressmen do not know which proposal will be made at the next stage of the bargaining process. In such a setting, a Congressman will accept a proposal promising him some but not the maximum possible *pork*, since he faces the risk that, if he votes the proposal down, he may find himself in the minority receiving no *pork* at all at a later stage of the game. The concept of reciprocity also lurks behind popular fears that the decision-making process on the European Central Bank Council will develop its own dynamics and voting patterns to the detriment of the European public. One version of this concern relates to the opportunistic version of the political business cycle. It suggests that the representatives of member states holding elections will demand easy monetary policy to improve their home governments' electoral chances, and that the other council members will support such demands, even when this does not fit their immediate interests, expecting that their own demands for easy money will be honored when their home governments face elections in a future period. If so, monetary union would not provide a way to escape political business cycles; much worse, it would be a way of importing political business cycles from other members.

The question I ask in this chapter is, can such reciprocity occur on the central bank council of a monetary union? The answer to this question requires two main steps: first, to establish an incentive to engage in strategic voting, and, second, to show how this incentive can prevail in equilibrium. The main point of this chapter is to construct an equilibrium in which reciprocity prevails and leads to an inefficient inflation bias. To keep the model tractable, I take the incentive for monetary ease in election periods as given and model it in the simplest possible way. This is admittedly a short-cut through a large literature showing that opportunistic political business cycles do not imply myopic nor irrational voters.[2] Nor do I tackle the question of how the equilibrium and the behavioral norms on which it rests came into being in the first place. As it turns out, the existence of an equilibrium with reciprocity depends on critical parameter restrictions and on the self-enforcing nature of an expectations-driven equilibrium. The main message of the chapter is, therefore, that reciprocity and political business cycles cannot be ruled out a priori for the central bank council of a federal monetary union. How important they will be in practice remains an empirical question.

The chapter proceeds as follows. Section 2 sets up a model of a monetary union and the central bank council. Section 3.1 shows that council members have an incentive to vote strategically to support their mutual interests. Section 3.2 constructs and characterizes the bargaining equilibrium. Section 4 concludes.

2 A model of monetary policy in a monetary union

2.1 The monetary union economy

The analysis uses a simplified version of the model presented in Von Hagen and Süppel (1994a). It is based on a standard model of monetary policy featuring a time-consistency problem (Barro and Gordon, 1983) extended for a monetary union composed of $n>1$ states, all indexed with $i=1, ..., n$, where n is odd. Below, a superscript "e" denotes a rational expectation based on information available at the end of the previous period. First, consider the aggregate economy of the monetary union. Output is given by the logarithmic supply function

$$Y_t = Y_0 + (\Pi_t - \Pi_t^e) \tag{1}$$

where Y denotes the level of union output, Y_0 is the normal level of output, and Π is the union inflation rate. Behind this supply function are nominal wages fixed in one-period standard contracts throughout the monetary union. I normalize $Y_0 = 0$. Trade with countries outside the monetary union is negligible, so that producer and consumer price inflation are identical. For the sake of simplicity, I take consumer price inflation as the central bank's policy instrument.

The member countries of the monetary union may differ in size, but they have similar economic structures. Output in country i is

$$y_{it} = b_i + (\pi_{it} - \pi_{it}^e) \tag{2}$$

where z_{it} is producer price inflation in country i, and b_i denotes the difference between normal output in country i and normal output in the monetary union.

With no differential shocks among the member states of the union, price changes are the same in all member states, so that consumer price inflation in each state is the same as union-wide inflation

$$\pi_{it} = \Pi_t \tag{3}$$

This gives solutions for country i's output

$$y_{it} = Y_t + b_i \tag{4}$$

Finally, let μ_i, $0 < \mu_i < 1$, be the relative size of country i's economy compared with the union economy. Consistency requires the following adding-up constraints

$$1 - \sum_{i=1}^{n} \mu_i = 0 = \sum_{i=1}^{n} \mu_i b_i \tag{5}$$

2.2   The central bank council

Monetary policy actions are the outcomes of decision making in the central bank council of the monetary union. The central bank council meets after wage contracts have been signed, so that there is scope for unanticipated monetary decisions to have real effects. The council members are appointed officials. All members are country representatives chosen by the individual member governments. There is one representative for each member country and all members have one vote. All council decisions are taken under simple majority rule. Council deliberations are not published, so that the public cannot base its expectations on the past voting behavior of the council members. Finally, we assume that the central bank council cannot enter into binding commitments with the public regarding its monetary policy.

The literature on purely opportunistic political business cycles argues that such cycles arise if monetary authorities use monetary policy to achieve the gains they perceive from surprise inflation in election periods.[3] Following that tradition, I assume that the typical council member dislikes inflation in her home state, but is willing to tolerate surprise inflation to reap a perceived gain $\delta_{i,t} > 0$ when her home state holds an election. I characterize these preferences by the utility functions

$$U_{it} = -\frac{\alpha}{2}\Pi_t^2 - \frac{1}{2}k_{it}(y_{it} - b_i - \delta_{it})^2 = -\frac{\alpha}{2}\Pi_t^2 - \frac{1}{2}k_{it}(\Pi_t - \Pi_t^e - \delta_{it})^2 \qquad (6)$$

where $\alpha > 0$, and the index variable k_{it} is one when state i runs an election and zero otherwise.[4] In non-election periods, council members are completely committed to the goal of price stability.

If central bank council members behave myopically, they cast their votes each period to maximize their current-period utility functions. The council decision is

$$\Pi_t = \underset{i=1,\dots,n}{\text{median}}[\underset{\Pi_t}{\arg\max}\ U_{i,t}]$$
$$\qquad (7)$$

which yields $\Pi_t = 0$ unless at least $(n+1)/2$ of the states hold elections simultaneously. This proves

Proposition 1: With myopic behavior, the monetary union will not be exposed to opportunistic political business cycles provided that election cycles in the member states are sufficiently asynchronized.

Strategic voting on the central bank council presupposes repeated voting and forward-looking behavior. Thus, I assume now that council members maximize the intertemporal utility functions

$$L_{it}^e = E[\sum_{j=0}^{\infty}\beta^j U_{it+j}] \qquad (8)$$

where $0 < \beta < 1$ and $E[.]$ denotes a rational expectation. Furthermore, I assume that election cycles in the member states are staggered such that there is an election in exactly one member state every period. Proposition 1 rules out political business cycles with myopic voting under these circumstances. The structure of the election cycles implies that subsequently it is sufficient to consider each member's subutility function extending over a span of n periods

$$\Lambda_{it}^e = E[\sum_{j=0}^{n-1} \beta^j U_{it-j}]$$ (9)

How can council members be enticed to support a fellow member's demands for higher inflation in a period when her home country does not hold an election? Reciprocity as a behavioral norm hints at an answer.[5] It suggests considering implicit agreements among the central bank council members to support each other's demands for easy money, even if doing so runs counter to a council member's own interest in price stability in periods when no elections are held in her home country. To obtain such agreements, two things are required. First, supporting the demands of an individual council member in a given period must attract a majority of votes on the council and, second, the agreement must be protected against reneging over time.

Political economy offers models for each element separately. Protecting implicit agreements against reneging is a theme familiar from the theory of repeated, non-cooperative games (Friedman, 1986). It is well-known from that theory that cooperative solutions can be enforced by an appropriate punishment of deviations from the agreement. In the context of monetary policy, this argument has been used in Barro and Gordon's (1983) analysis of reputation. Making individual demands consistent with majoritarian incentives is a theme explored in the political economy of parliamentarian decision making. The analysis in the next section brings these two arguments together.

3 Reciprocity, bargaining, and inflation

3.1 Reciprocity

Without loss of generality, let the countries be ordered such that country $i=1$ holds an election in period t, country $i=2$ holds an election in period $t+1$, etc.

Suppose that the following agreement is offered to a member i of the central bank council. If i supports a proposal to set $\pi_t > 0$ in period t, then with probability p a majority on the council will support a proposal to set $\pi_{t+j} > 0$ for $j=1, ..., n$, which includes the period when i's home country holds an election; with probability $(1-p)$ the deal will fall apart and the council will vote $\pi_{t+i} = 0$. Would such a deal find a majority?

The answer depends in part on the inflation rates proposed for t and $t+i$. Without loss of generality, let the proposal be $\epsilon(\Pi^e+\delta)$. For each member of the central bank council, we first find ϵ_i, the largest ϵ this member prefers over the proposal to set $\Pi_{t+j}=0$ for $j=1, ..., n$. ϵ_i is given by the restriction that

$$\Lambda_i = -\frac{\alpha}{2}[\epsilon_i^2(\Pi^e+\delta)^2 + p\sum_{j=1}^{n-1}\beta^j\epsilon_i^2(\Pi^e+\delta)^2] - \frac{p\beta^{i-1}}{2}(1-\epsilon_i)^2(\Pi^e+\delta)^2 \quad (10)$$

$$\geq -\frac{\beta^{i-1}}{2}(\Pi^e+\delta)^2$$

This yields

$$\epsilon_i = \frac{2p\beta^{i-1}}{\alpha + p(\alpha\sum_{j=1}^{n-1}\beta^j + \beta^{i-1})} \quad (11)$$

Note that ϵ_i increases as the survival of the deal becomes more likely and as the council member becomes more "conservative" (β increases). Furthermore, $\epsilon_i \geq \epsilon_{i+1}$. This implies that member $i=1$ supports higher inflation rates than any other member. The largest inflation rate proposed in this kind of deal is, therefore, the rate that maximizes the utility of member $i=1$

$$\Lambda_i = -\frac{\alpha}{2}[\Pi^2 + p\sum_{j=1}^{n-1}\beta^j\Pi^2] - \frac{p}{2}(\Pi-\Pi^e-\delta)^2] \quad (12)$$

which is[6]

$$\pi_1^* = \frac{p(\Pi^e+\delta)}{\alpha + p(\alpha\sum_{j=1}^{n-1}\beta^j + 1)} \quad (13)$$

If π_1^* was actually adopted in this way, rational expectations imply $\Pi^e = p\pi_1^*$, which yields

$$\pi_1^* = \frac{p\delta}{\alpha + p(\alpha\sum_{j=1}^{n-1}\beta^j + (1-p))} \quad (14)$$

In order for a deal to be feasible, it must be acceptable for at least $(n+1)/2$ members of the council. Thus, we now ask, what range of inflation rates would be acceptable for members $i=1, ..., (n+1)/2$. The answer is in

Proposition 2: Let $\beta > (1/2)^{2/(n-1)}$. The proposal to set $\pi_{t+j}=\pi^* \epsilon(0, \pi^*_1]$ for $j=0, ..., (n-1)/2$ is preferred to the proposal to set $\pi_{t+j}=0$ for $j=0, ..., (n-1)/2$, by a majority of council members.

Proof: We must show that $\Lambda_i(\pi_1^*) \geq \Lambda_i(0)$ for $i=(n+1)/2$. Inserting π_1^* from (11), this condition reduces to $p\beta^{i-1} \geq \alpha(1+p\Sigma_j\beta^j)(1-2\beta^{i-1})$. If β is large enough as required, the right-hand side is negative and, hence, the inequality holds for any value of p and α. It is straightforward to show that, if it holds for π_1^*, it holds for lower, strictly positive values, too. The restriction implies that member $(n+1)/2$ will find the proposal π_1^* attractive. Since the same must be true for members $i=1, ..., (n-1)/2$, $(n+1)/2$ is the median voter.

Proposition 2 establishes that the council members perceive gains from entering into implicit agreements among each other to support their demands for easy monetary policy in times of elections. However, these gains cannot be reaped easily. Suppose, that, in period t, a member $i \in [1, ..., (n-1)/2]$ proposes $\pi_{t+j}>0$ for $j=1, ..., n$. If member $(n+1)/2$ has reason to believe that a similar deal will be available in the future, she can improve her expected utility by rejecting the proposal and voting for zero inflation in period t and supporting the deal in period $t+1$, instead. Thus, a deal among the central bank council members needs enforcement to be sustainable.

The required enforcement mechanism can be provided by a behavioral norm prevailing among the council members. A plausible norm is the rule that council members that do not show concern for the electoral pressures felt by fellow members whose countries hold elections will be punished by the council's disregard of their own demands when their countries hold elections. Formally, define G_t as the group of countries holding elections in periods $t, t+1, ... t+(n-1)/2$. The behavioral norm is cast in

Assumption I: $\Pi_{t+k-1}=0$ if country k is in G_t and its representative votes "yes" on a proposal to set $\Pi_t=0$.

The restriction on β in proposition 2 ensures that, independently of the probability p, a member of group G_t will never vote in favor of zero inflation. Since G_t has a majority on the central bank council, an agreement among the council members will be supported. It follows that $p=1$.

3.2 The bargaining process

Although there is room for strategic cooperation, the members of group G_t prefer different rates of inflation in a given period. As we have seen above, the representative of the country $i=1$ wishes a higher inflation rate than any other council member. All other members of group G_t refrain from voting for zero inflation, but they like low inflation rates in the current period, nevertheless. Without further structure on the decision-making process, a voting equilibrium in the central bank council does not yet exist: since the council members not in group G_t vote against all proposals for positive inflation, each proposal will be rejected and the council will go through endless rounds of rejecting proposals for an inflation rate.

To introduce more structure, I follow Baron (1991) and Baron and Ferejohn (1989) in modeling the voting and bargaining process on the central bank council. At the start of a council meeting, a council member is selected randomly to make a proposal for the rate of inflation in the current period. The random selection mechanism reflects the assumption that council members are not recognized for proposal on the basis of their local interests. Once a proposal has been put forward, the council votes on it. If it is accepted, the central bank sets the inflation rate equal to the proposed rate. If it is rejected, a member of the council is chosen randomly to make the next proposal which is then put to vote, etc.

Following Baron and Baron and Ferejohn, I assume that time is valuable in the bargaining process. This is a particularly plausible assumption in our context, since central bank councils usually meet on fixed dates and decisions must be reached on those dates to avoid upsetting financial markets with the news of disagreement over monetary policy. I model the value of time by defining, first, the *intra-period* discount factor γ, $0<\gamma<1$, used to compare outcomes at different stages of the bargaining process. Second, I assume that there is a fixed cost v to entering a new round.[7]

I focus on stationary bargaining processes in the double sense that, (a) unless a member of group G_t deviates and votes for zero inflation, the expected bargaining outcome in period $t+j$, $j>0$, does not depend on the bargaining outcome in period t, and (b) a member's proposal does not depend on the stage of the bargaining process at which it is made. The first part of this assumption requires that the representative of the country whose election is k periods away in period $t+j$ makes the same proposal that the member from the country whose election is $k-1$ periods away made in period $t+j-1$.

Let π_{jt}^p be council member j's proposal. Council member i will accept this proposal, if the expected utility derived from it exceeds the expected utility from another round of bargaining

$$-\frac{\alpha}{2}(\pi_{jt}^p)^2 - \frac{k_{i,t}}{2}(\pi_{jt}^p - \Pi_t^e - \delta)^2 \geq \gamma V_i - v \tag{15}$$

Here, V_i is i's continuation value of the bargaining game, i.e., the expected value of reaching a decision at the next bargaining round. Note that the bargaining process concerns only the decision for period t, since the next period will begin with another council meeting. Therefore, the time subscript can now be dropped.

With our assumptions, $\pi_j^p > 0$ for $j \in G_t$, and $\pi_j^p = 0$ otherwise. A proposal to set inflation equal to zero will be rejected and only leads to a new round of bargaining. A proposal of zero occurs with probability $(n-1)/2n$, while a proposal for strictly positive inflation occurs with probability $(n+1)/2n$. Therefore, the continuation value of the bargaining game at each stage is

$$V_i = -\frac{1}{n} \sum_{j=1}^{(n+1)/2} [\frac{\alpha}{2}(\pi_j^p)^2 + \frac{k_i}{2}(\pi_j^p - \Pi^e - \delta)^2] + \frac{n-1}{2n}[\gamma V_i - v] \tag{16}$$

$$= -\phi \sum_{j=1}^{(n+1)/2} [\frac{\alpha}{2}(\pi_j^p)^2 + \frac{k_i}{2}(\pi_j^p - \Pi_t^e - \delta)^2] + \frac{n-1}{2n}v],$$

where $\phi = \dfrac{1}{n - \dfrac{n-1}{2}\gamma}$

Thus, a proposal will be accepted, if it satisfies the passing constraints of the central bank council

$$\sqrt{(\pi_j^p)^2 + \frac{1}{\alpha}(\pi_j^p - \pi^e - \delta)^2} \leq \sqrt{\frac{1}{\alpha(1-\gamma)}v} \qquad = N \tag{17}$$

for member $i=1$ and

$$\pi_j^p \leq N \tag{18}$$

for members $i=2, ..., (n+1)/2$.

Conditions (17) and (18) provide upper limits on the rates of inflation that find a council majority. We summarize them in

Proposition 3:
(a) A necessary condition for an equilibrium outcome with positive inflation is that the fixed cost of bargaining be strictly positive, $v>0$.
(b) Given the fixed cost of bargaining, the upper limit increases with the *intra-period* discount factor.
(c) The larger the utility weight on price stability, α, the smaller is the upper limit on inflation rates that pass the council.

Note also that member $i=1$ will support proposals for higher inflation than the other members of the council.

Taking propositions 2 and 3 together, we now have two intervals for the range of inflation rates a central bank council acting under a norm of reciprocity will adopt. We state this as

Proposition 4: Let $\beta > (0.5)^{2/(n-1)}$ and $N > 0$. Given assumption I, the council will adopt inflation rates in the interval $(0, \pi_1^*] \, \Lambda \, [0, N]$.

Proposition 4 gives the range of inflation rates that can be passed through the central bank council. All rational proposals for inflation rates made by members of group G_t must lie in this interval. Thus, proposition 4 allows us to determine the maximum inflation bias the monetary union may have as the upper limit of this interval.

However, this still leaves a range of possibilities for each council member. This implies that the public's expectations of inflation are still not determined. To pin down the actual proposals, we need to specify the council members' proposal strategies. This, in turn, requires another behavioral norm among the council members. One plausible norm can be derived from the notion that a member of group G_t is regarded as "cheating," if she proposes an inflation rate for period t that is lower than the rate she would propose if she could determine the rate of inflation in every one of the current and the next $(n-1)/2$ periods. The latter, π_i^p, can be derived in a similar way to π_1^* in equation (13), if the fixed cost of bargaining is large enough so that the majority constraints (17) and (18) are not binding. Otherwise, the council members must rationally propose smaller rates. For this case, I assume the proposal strategies $\pi_i^p = (\pi_i^* / -\pi_1^*)N$. This is plausible, since decreasing the cost of bargaining reduces the proposals, but preserves their order. Again, deviating behavior is punished by a future council decision. Thus, I pose

Assumption II: If member i, $i \in G_t$ proposes a rate $\pi' < \pi_i^p$, the council majority adopts $\Pi_{t+i-1} = \pi'$ in the period when i's home country holds an election.

With this assumption, we have immediately the following

Proposition 5: Each period, the central bank council adopts the first proposal for a strictly positive inflation rate.

Proof: Let $\pi' = \epsilon \pi_i^p$, $0 < \epsilon < 1$ for a council member $i \in G_t$. With assumption II, $\Lambda_i(\epsilon \pi_i^p) \geq \Lambda_i(\pi_i^p)$ if $(1-\epsilon^2) > -(\epsilon \beta^{i-1})^2/(1+\beta^{i-1})\beta^{i-1}$, which contradicts the assumption about ϵ. Thus, member i of group G_t proposes π_i^p. Since the latter obeys the majority constraint, it is accepted. If a council meeting begins with a proposal from a member $i \in G_t$, π_i^p is proposed and accepted immediately. If the council meeting begins with one or a series of proposals of zero inflation from members not included in group G_t, these proposals are rejected until a member of group G_t gets to propose.

Proposition 5 allows us to finally close the model by determining the public's inflation expectations

$$\Pi^e = \frac{2}{n+1} \sum_{j=1}^{(n+1)/2} \pi_j^p \tag{19}$$

Since the individual proposals generally differ from each other, the decision-making process on the central bank council creates uncertainty and actual and expected inflation will generally be different. This implies that the federal decision-making structure also creates real fluctuations through the ensuing inflation surprises.

A number of interesting characterizations remain to be drawn. First, increasing the number of member countries reduces the inflation bias of the union. By lengthening the electoral cycle for each member, it reduces the largest inflation rate accepted by the median voter on the council, since the period over which the reciprocity bargain extends becomes longer.

Second, contrary to conventional wisdom, "conservative" council members are more prone to inflation bias than those with small discount factors. The reason is that "conservative" members value future favors more than others, which is the basis for reciprocity. This indicates that, in the more general context of repeated voting and vote trading, the conventional wisdom that central bankers should be relatively conservative does not hold unambiguously.

Third, and again contrary to conventional wisdom, the union's inflation bias could be reduced by shortening the council members' appointments sufficiently, such that appointments are for less than an electoral cycle. This would reduce the scope for reciprocity on the council as each member would be off the council before she could realize the gain from strategic voting.[8]

Finally, adding a number of central appointees to the council, i.e., members with no allegiance to any government, reduces the inflation bias. The reason is that the existence of such members increases the number of state representatives required to obtain a majority each period. It follows from (11) that this reduces the range of inflation rates accepted by the necessary majority.

4 Conclusions

I have shown that, for a central bank council consisting only of the representatives of the member states of a monetary union, an equilibrium can be constructed that is characterized by positive expected inflation and stochastic fluctuations in prices and output due to opportunistic political business cycles motives. This equilibrium exists even though there is never more than one state holding an election in the union. The equilibrium is obviously undesirable from the point of view of the private sector that would be better off with zero inflation and output stability.

The equilibrium constructed in this chapter rests on social norms and expectations the members of the central bank council hold against each other. The fact that there is no explanation in the chapter of how these norms and expectations come into being in the first place is no argument to claim that such an equilibrium has no practical relevance. Intuitively, one might argue that the inefficient equilibrium studied in this chapter seems quite fragile, as it relies on the assumption that all central bank council members expect the same behavior of one another. Thus, if a sufficient number of council members break the convention, the equilibrium disappears. If one accepts this interpretation, the message of this chapter is quite optimistic: reciprocity-based political business cycle distortions are difficult to generate and vulnerable; hence, the fear of such behavior for the council of the European Central Bank would appear unfounded. Yet, examples of inefficient, expectations-driven equilibria exist in other areas and have been shown to be of practical relevance. The genesis of conventions and norms of behavior itself is still not well understood in the analysis of strategic games.[9]

Taking the case for such equilibria seriously, the main message of the chapter is that the advantage a central bank council of state representatives has over a council of central appointees – namely that the median council member is less likely to be directly exposed to opportunistic political business cycle incentives – is not as strong a safeguard against political business cycles as the analysis of single-shot voting games suggests. This strengthens the recommendation that the council should include a number, if not a majority, of central appointees.

Notes

This chapter was written in large part while I was a visitor at the Department of Economics, Tel Aviv University, whose hospitality is gratefully acknowledged.

1 See Calvert (1989) for a discussion.

2 For a review of that literature, see Davidson et al. (1990).

3 In a rational expectations framework, such benefits can be obtained even when voters are not myopic. The critical assumption then is an information asymmetry between the voting public and the monetary authority, see, e.g., Rogoff and Sibert (1988) or Cukierman and Meltzer (1986); for a literature review see Davidson et al. (1990). Here I neglect this issue for the sake of tractability.

4 The incentive for surprise inflation in election years stated in these utility functions can be interpreted as saying that the council members are not completely independent of their home governments in the sense that there is no congruence

of interest between the former and the latter. Obviously, the letter of the law saying that the ECB council members are independent is not enough to convince us that such non-congruence will always hold in practice. For a discussion of central bank independence in the context of the ECB see Fratianni *et al.* (1992).

5 An alternative approach would be to introduce a lag structure into the economic model, such that today's policy decisions create monetary surprises in the future, when the council member's home country holds an election. For example, in an economy with staggered nominal wage contracts such as Taylor's (1993) model, a rise in the rate of inflation that is unexpected on the basis of the information available at the start of period t creates real effects in periods $t+1$, $t+2$, ..., $t+m$, where m is the longest contract length in the economy. Suppose that such contracts prevail. Then a central bank council member whose country faces elections in period $t+m$ is willing to engage in surprise inflation in period t since she perceives that this will support her own government together with the governments facing elections between t and $t+m$. Thus, if $m \geq (n+1)/2$, the median council member will engage in opportunistic political business cycles. The drawback of this approach is that it obviously requires rather long contract durations if n is large.

6 Note that the public's expectations must be treated as a parameter at this stage.

7 For a general discussion of the importance of time for bargaining processes see Rubinstein (1982).

8 I owe this point to Ed Bomhoff's comment at the conference.

9 For some recent work in this area, see Young (1993).

References

Baron, David (1991), "Majoritarian Incentives, Pork Barrel Programs, and Procedural Control," *American Journal of Political Science*, 35, 57–90.

Baron, David and Ferejohn, John (1989), "Bargaining in Legislatures," *American Political Science Review*, 83, 1181–206.

Barro, Robert and Gordon, David (1983), "Rules, Discretion, and Reputation in a Model of Monetary Policy," *Journal of Monetary Economics*, 12, 101–22.

Calvert, Randall (1989), "Reciprocity Among Self-Interested Actors: Uncertainty, Asymmetry, and Distribution," in Peter Ordeshook (ed.), *Models of Strategic Choice in Politics*, Ann Arbor: Michigan University Press.

Cukierman, Alex and Meltzer, Allan (1986), "A Positive Theory of Discretionary Policy, the Cost of Democratic Government, and the Benefits of a Constitution", *Economic Inquiry*, 24, 367–88.

Davidson, Lawrence, Fratianni, Michele and Von Hagen, Jürgen (1990), "Testing for the Political Business Cycle," *Journal of Policy Modeling*, 12, 35–59.

Ferejohn, John (1974), *Pork Barrel Politics: Rivers and Harbors Legislation 1947–68*, Stanford: Stanford University Press.

Fratianni, Michele, Waller, Christopher and Von Hagen, Jürgen (1992), "The Maastricht Way to EMU", *Princeton Essays in International Finance*, Princeton: Princeton University Press.

(1993), "Central Banking as a Political Principal Agent Problem," CEPR Discussion Paper, No. 752.

Friedman, David (1986), *Game Theory with Applications to Economics*, Oxford: Oxford University Press.

Rogoff, Kenneth and Sibert, Anne (1988), "Elections and Macroeconomic Policy Cycles," *Review of Economic Studies*, 55, 11–16.

Rubinstein, Ariel (1982), "Perfect Equilibrium in a Bargaining Model," *Econometrica*, 50, 97–109.

Taylor, John (1993), *Macroeconomic Policy in a World Economy*, New York: W.W. Norton & Co.

Von Hagen, Jürgen and Süppel, Ralph (1994a), "Central Bank Constitutions for Federal Monetary Unions," *European Economic Review*, 36, 774–82.

(1994b), "Central Bank Constitutions for Monetary Unions," CEPR Discussion Paper.

Young, Peyton (1993), "The Evolution of Conventions," *Econometrica*, 61, 57–84.

Comment

KEES KOEDIJK

This chapter is one of a series of papers that Jürgen von Hagen has written on the institutional features of monetary union. A central theme in his work on monetary union is the recognition that the long-run inflation performance of such a union depends critically on its political structure and its institutional set-up. The work seems also relevant for the current discussion about the optimal road toward European Monetary Union and the design of a European Central Bank.

Monetary unions typically have a federal structure with a central bank council consisting of state representatives of the member states, in some cases together with central appointees. An important question related to the functioning of a monetary union is the division of power over monetary policy between the center and the parts of the union and, hence, between state representatives, who are supposed to defend, in their voting behavior, their country's interests, and central appointees on the central bank council, who are supposed to take a more neutral stand.

Contributions to the literature on the optimal design of a monetary union include work by Alesina (1988), Alesina and Grilli (1993), Casella (1992), and, more recently, Von Hagen and Süppel (1994). The Von Hagen and Süppel paper is of particular interest here because this chapter builds on that paper. In the Von Hagen and Süppel (1994) paper it is shown how a division of monetary policy authority between state representatives and central appointees may work out.

Von Hagen and Süppel (1994) show that in the context of a single-shot voting game a central bank of state representatives is less likely to produce a political business cycle with the associated inflation bias. The reason is the fact that with uncoordinated election cycles in the member states, the median voter on the council is unlikely to represent a country holding an election. Due to the single-shot nature of the game, the median voter also has no reason to support the demands for easy monetary policy by other representatives for strategic reasons.

In this chapter, the conclusion on the implications of a central bank council consisting of state representatives is reversed due to the introduction of strategic behavior in a repeated voting game. A central bank council consisting solely of state representatives is now a guarantee for creating political business cycles. Allowing for strategic behavior in the council of the central bank leads to positive inflation and real fluctuations. Strategic behavior is introduced through so-called behavioral norms of reciprocity. Reciprocity is defined as the situation where individual decision makers vote against there own sincere, short-run interests to render a favor to other decison makers expecting that they will receive favors in return in the future. Reciprocity stands for quid pro quo. Important is that reciprocity can only occur in settings of repeated voting, since it is based on each player's expectation that all other players adhere to the norm in the future. This concept may have direct practical relevance for discussion on the institutional set up of a future European Central Bank. Fear for too much reciprocity at a future European Central Bank council might also be behind the fear of some that establishing a European central bank and a monetary union would not be a guarantee against political business cycles, but instead a motive for enhancing and producing political business cycles. The idea would then be that representatives of member states of a monetary union that currently hold a general election will demand easy monetary policy to improve their government's electoral chances, and that other council members will support such demands even when it does not fit their own immediate interests, expecting that their own demands will be honored in a future period.

The model that Von Hagen uses to investigate strategic behavior in a European Central Bank council is a combination of the standard Barro-Gordon model of monetary policy extended for a monetary union composed of a number of states and the voting and bargaining models of Baron (1991) and Baron and Ferejohn (1989). Central to these latter models is the recognition that making proposals and voting is time consuming and moreover that time is valuable, and hence that some sort of bargaining is called for.

Important conditions for equilibrium in the model are that demands of an individual council member in a given period to stimulate their own economy must attract a majority of votes on the council, and that the agreement must be protected against reneging over time. Council members that do not show concern for the special needs created by electoral pressures of fellow members, who face elections in their home country, are punished by the council's disregard of their own demands when their countries hold elections.

Based on this framework, Von Hagen is able to derive several noteworthy results. First and foremost, he is able to construct an equilibrium in which reciprocity prevails and which leads to an inefficient inflation bias. In terms of the European Central Bank, this would mean that reciprocity and political business cycles cannot be ruled out. Second, increasing the number of member countries reduces the inflation bias of the union. Third, contrary to conventional wisdom so-called conservative council members are more prone to inflation bias than those with small discount factors. The reason is the fact that conservative council members value future favors more than others, which is the basis for reciprocity. Fourth, adding a number of central appointees to the council reduces the inflation bias.

The chapter presented by Von Hagen is well-written and in my view innovative. The combination of a Barro-Gordon model with political economy models of bargaining and reciprocity is well done. It should be noted, however, that the derived equilibrium with the inflation bias is very vulnerable and fragile, because it relies on the assumption that all central bank members expect the same behavior of each another. If sufficient members of the council break the convention, the equilibrium and hence the whole inflation basis and business cycle argument disappear.

Another drawback of the analysis may be that council deliberations are not published so that the public cannot base its expectations on the past voting behavior of the council. In the current set-up, there is no room for learning by the public about central bank policies. The model would certainly gain in relevance, if it would allow for such effects. A more likely scenario would be that the public learns that prior to every election, especially if the union consists of a large number of countries, there is a large probability that the central bank council will try to stimulate the economy. Eventually, the public will then adapt its inflationary expectations when an election is imminent and deprive the monetary stimulus package of its real effects.

With respect to the inflation bias argument, it would also be interesting to go back and see to what extent the kind of mechanism described in this chapter played a role in the founding of the Federal Reserve in the US and in the founding of the Bundesbank in Germany.

In the current chapter, there is no discussion of uncertainty with respect to the election dates. Thus we do not know whether the result with respect to the inflation bias would hold, if uncertainty about the election dates were introduced? Finally, it may be worthwile to include in the paper differences in bargaining power between the participating countries and hence the council members (e.g., as in Casella, 1992).

References

Alesina, A. (1988), "Macroeconomics and Politics," in Stanley Fisher (ed.), *NBER Macroeconomics Annual.*

Alesina, A. and Grilli, V. (1993), "On the Feasibility of European Monetary Union", *Economics and Politics*, 5, 145–66.

Baron, David P. (1991), "Majoritarian Incentives, Pork Barrel Programs, and Procedural Control," *American Journal of Political Sciences*, 35, 57–90.

Baron, David P. and Ferejohn, R. (1989), "Bargaining in Legislatures," *American Political Science Review*, 83, 1181–2096.

Cassella, A. (1992), "Participation in a Currency Union," *American Economic Review*, 82, 847–63.

Von Hagen, J. and Süppel, R. (1994), "Central Bank Constitutions for Federal Monetary Unions," *European Economic Review*, 36, 774–82.

3 The ultimate determinants of central bank independence

SYLVESTER EIJFFINGER and ERIC SCHALING

1 Introduction

Recently, in many countries both political and monetary authorities have shown an increasing interest in the objective of monetary stability and the position of the central bank. As pointed out by Persson and Tabellini (1993), recent policy reforms and historical experience suggest two different routes to price stability.

The first way is the *legislative* approach, namely to create by law a very independent central bank with an unequivocal mandate to focus on price stability. Interest in this approach is motivated by the success of the Deutsche Bundesbank in maintaining one of the lowest rates of inflation for several decades. Moreover, the accepted statute of the European Central Bank is strongly influenced by the law governing the Bundesbank. Moreover, France and Spain have reformed their central bank laws making the Banque de France and the Banco de España more independent of government. Furthermore, countries in Central and Eastern Europe, such as the Czech Republic, Hungary, and Poland, have increased the legal independence of their central banks. Finally, in Latin America there are also tendencies toward granting more independence to the central banks in Argentina, Chile, Mexico, and Venezuela. Academic contributions in this area are Rogoff (1985), Neumann (1991), and Lohmann (1992).

The second way is the *targeting* or *contracting* approach, namely to let the political principal of the central bank impose an explicit inflation target for monetary policy, and make the central bank governor explicitly accountable for his success in meeting this target. Recently, New Zealand, Canada, and the United Kingdom have made some progress along these lines. New Zealand enacted legislation that increased the independence of its Reserve Bank, whereas in the United Kingdom there is now a lively discussion of the desirability of making the Bank of England more independent.[1] Important theoretical work on this approach has been done by Walsh (1995) and Persson and Tabellini (1993).

Empirical work on the legislative approach (Alesina, 1988, 1989; Grilli, Masciandaro, and Tabellini, 1991; Cukierman, 1992; Eijffinger and Schaling, 1992, 1993a, 1993b; De Haan and Sturm, 1992; Alesina and Summers, 1993) has focused on quantifying independence using a number of legal attributes drawn from central bank laws. These studies focus on the *positive* issue of the relation between monetary regimes and economic performance. Broadly speaking, the conclusion is that the more independent the central bank, the lower inflation rate, whilst the rate of output growth is unaffected.

However, this literature does not explain the observed differences in central bank independence. For instance, no explanation is offered for the very high independence of the Bundesbank. It has often been pointed out that this independence may be explained by Germany's underlying aversion to inflation, associated with its experience of hyper-inflation in the 1920s.[2]

This brings us to a key issue in the political economy of central banking: the relation between institutional design and individual and collective preferences. Here the question to be dealt with is the *normative* issue of how independent a central bank should be, i.e., the optimal degree of central bank independence.

An important study in this field is Cukierman (1994). Building on the seminal paper of Lohmann (1992), he wants to identify the economic and political factors that induce politicians to delegate more or less authority to the central bank. His theory predicts that central bank independence will be higher, the larger the employment-motivated inflationary bias, the higher political instability and the larger the government debt.

These predictions were tested and, subsequently, rejected by De Haan and Van 't Hag (1995) using regression analysis (OLS method). In testing Cukierman's model, they employ measures of central bank independence that – in Rogoff's (1985) terminology – reflect the strength of the "conservative bias" of the central bank as embodied in the law. In Cukierman's model, following Lohmann (1992), central bank independence is defined as the *cost of overriding* the central bank, rather than as the degree of *conservativeness*. Cukierman's (1994) theory also generates propositions about *optimal* regimes, whilst the legal measures describe *actual* monetary regimes.

In this chapter we try to overcome these pitfalls. Building on the Rogoff (1985) model, we identify central bank independence as the degree of conservativeness rather than the political cost of overriding the central bank. Using a graphical method, we develop a new way of determining the optimal degree of conservativeness. As in Lohmann (1992), this degree depends on the balance between *credibility* and *flexibility*. However, unlike

Rogoff and Lohmann, we are able to express the upper and lower bounds of the interval containing the optimal degree of conservativeness in terms of the structural parameters of the model.

Furthermore, we derive several propositions concerning the relation between economic and political factors and the optimal degree of central bank independence. We show that optimal central bank independence is higher, the higher the natural rate of unemployment, the greater the benefits of unanticipated inflation (the slope of the Phillips curve), the less inflation-averse society, and the smaller the variance of productivity shocks. These propositions are tested for nineteen industrial countries (Australia, Austria, Belgium, Canada, Denmark, Finland, France, Germany, Ireland, Italy, Japan, The Netherlands, New Zealand, Norway, Spain, Sweden, Switzerland, the United Kingdom, and the United States) for the Bretton Woods period and after (1960–93). In testing the model, we employ a *latent variables* method (LISREL) in order to distinguish between actual and optimal monetary regimes.

The chapter is organized into four remaining sections, followed by three appendices. In section 2 we present the theoretical model. Section 3 contains the derivation of the optimal degree of central bank independence. In section 4 we test the model with the latent variables method. Our conclusions are given in section 5.

2 A simple macromodel

The main purpose of this section is to combine the Alogoskoufis (1994) model of wage and employment determination with the Rogoff (1985) model. We assume that there are two types of agents, *wage setters* (*the union*) and the *central bank*. Wage setters unilaterally choose the nominal wage every period, and the central bank controls monetary policy.

The sequence of events is as follows. In the first stage, wage-setters each period sign nominal wage contracts (Gray, 1976; Fischer, 1977). Wage setters know the domestic monetary regime. They take this information into account in forming their expectations. In the second stage, stochastic shocks to productivity are realized. These shocks are random and cannot be observed at the time the wage contracts are signed. In the third stage, the central bank observes the values of the shocks and – contingent on the chosen regime – reacts to the shocks accordingly. In the fourth and final stage, employment is determined by competitive firms. The timing of events is summarized in figure 3.1.

We now move to the supply side of the model.

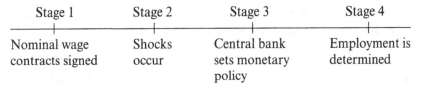

Stage 1	Stage 2	Stage 3	Stage 4
Nominal wage contracts signed	Shocks occur	Central bank sets monetary policy	Employment is determined

Figure 3.1 The sequence of events

2.1 Aggregate supply

Consider the following supply block. Capital will be assumed fixed, and output is given by a short-run Cobb–Douglas production function

$$y_t = \beta \ell_t + \mu_t \qquad\qquad 0 < \beta < 1 \qquad\qquad (1)$$

where lower-case letters refer to logarithmic deviations from steady-state values. Thus, y is the log of output, ℓ is the log of employment, and μ_t is a measure of productivity. The labor exponent, β, is less than unity.

Having described the level of output, it remains to be specified how productivity evolves over time. For simplicity, we assume that shocks to productivity are normally distributed with zero mean and finite variance

$$\mu_t = v_t^\mu \qquad\qquad v_t^\mu \sim N(0, \sigma_\mu^2) \qquad\qquad (2)$$

Firms determine employment by equalizing the marginal product of labor to the real wage $w_t - p_t$. This yields the following employment function

$$\ell_t = -\frac{1}{1-\beta}(w_t - p_t - \mu_t) \qquad\qquad (3)$$

where w is the log of the nominal wage and p the log of the price level.

The nominal wage is set at the beginning of each period and remains fixed for one period. The objective of the wage setters is to stabilize real wages and employment around their target levels. Thus wages in each period are set to minimize

$$W_t = E_{t-1}[\tfrac{1}{2}(\ell - \ell^*)^2] \qquad\qquad (4)$$

where E_{t-1} is the operator of rational expectations, conditional on information at the end of period $t-1$, and ℓ^* is the employment target of the union. We assume that $\ell^* \equiv \ell_i^s$, where ℓ_i^s is the number of insiders. Denoting the log of the labor force by ℓ^s, we assume that $\ell_i^s < \ell^s$. Thus we employ a variant of the insider–outsider approach to the labor market (Blanchard and Summers, 1986; Lindbeck and Snower, 1986). The minimization of (4) is subject to the labor demand function (3).

From the first-order conditions for a minimum of (4) subject to (3), the nominal wage is given by

$$w_t = E_{t-1}p_t - (1-\beta)\ell^* \tag{5}$$

Substituting (5) into the labor demand function (3), we get the following relationship between employment and unanticipated shocks

$$\ell_t = \ell^* + \frac{1}{1-\beta}(p_t - E_{t-1}p_t + \mu_t) \tag{6}$$

An unanticipated rise in prices $p_t - E_{t-1}p_t$ reduces the real wage, and causes firms to employ more labor. Thus, aggregate employment exhibits a transitory deviation from its equilibrium or "natural" rate ℓ^*.[3]

Subtracting (6) from the labor force ℓ^s, using the approximation that the rate of unemployment $u \approx \ell^s - \ell$, we get the following expression for the short-run determination of unemployment

$$u_t = \tilde{u} - \frac{1}{1-\beta}(p_t - E_{t-1}p_t + \mu_t) \tag{7}$$

where $\tilde{u} = \ell^s - \ell^*$. The variable $\tilde{u}$ can be thought of as the *equilibrium* or "*natural*" rate of unemployment in this model. Thus, (7) is the well-known expectations augmented Phillips curve. Unemployment deviates from its equilibrium rate only to the extent that there are unanticipated shocks to inflation or productivity. Anticipated shocks to inflation and productivity are reflected in wages (equation (5)) and do not affect unemployment. We can now incorporate the Phillips curve into a monetary policy game. This is the subject of the next section.

2.2 Time-consistent equilibrium under a "Conservative" central banker

As stated by Rogoff (1985, p. 1180), the adoption of central bank independence may be viewed as an institutional response to the time-consistency problem. Suppose, for example, that through a system of rewards and punishments the central bank's incentives are altered so that it places some direct weight on achieving a low rate of growth for a nominal variable such as the price level, nominal GNP, or the money supply. Rogoff demonstrates that society can make itself better off by selecting an agent to head the central bank who is known to place a greater weight on inflation stabilization (relative to unemployment stabilization) than is embodied in the social loss function, L_t. The social loss function, L, depends on deviations of unemployment and inflation from their *optimal* (socially desired) levels

$$L_t = \frac{1}{2}(\Delta p_t - \Delta p^*) + \frac{\chi}{2}(u_t - u^*)^2 \tag{8}$$

where $0 < \chi < \infty$ and Δp^* and u^* are society's inflation and unemployment targets. The parameter χ is the weight of unemployment stabilization relative to inflation stabilization in the preferences of society. Normalizing Δp^*, u^* and p_{t-1} at zero we get [4]

$$L_t = \frac{1}{2}p_t^2 + \frac{\chi}{2}u_t^2 \tag{9}$$

Rogoff shows that, in choosing among potential candidates, it is never optimal to choose an individual who is known to care "too little" about unemployment.

Suppose, for example, that in period $t-1$ society selects an agent to head the central bank in period t. The reputation of this individual is such that it is known that, if he is appointed to head the central bank, he will minimize the following loss function

$$I_t = \frac{(1+\epsilon)}{2}p_t^2 + \frac{\chi}{2}u_t^2 \quad 0 < \epsilon < \infty \tag{10}$$

If ϵ is strictly greater than zero, the agent places a greater relative weight on inflation stabilization than society does. Hence, following Eijffinger and Schaling (1993b, p. 5) we view the coefficient ϵ as a measure of the *political independence* of the central bank. The higher is ϵ, the more independent is the central bank. Note that if $\epsilon=0$, equation (10) reduces to the social loss function (9).

Thus, stochastic equilibrium is derived under the assumption that the monetary authorities attempt to minimize loss function I, given by equation (10) above.

Substituting the Phillips curve (7) in the loss function (10) yields

$$I_t = \frac{1+\epsilon}{2}p_t^2 + \frac{\chi}{2}[\tilde{u} - \frac{1}{1-\beta}p_t + \frac{1}{1-\beta}E_{t-1}P_t - \frac{1}{1-\beta}\mu_t]^2 \tag{11}$$

From the first-order conditions for a minimum of (11), i.e., $\delta I_t / \delta p_t = 0$, we obtain the central bank's reaction function to the union's inflationary expectations

$$p_t^I = \frac{\chi(1-\beta)}{(1-\beta)^2(1+\epsilon)+\chi}\tilde{u} + \frac{\chi}{(1-\beta)^2(1+\epsilon)+\chi}E_{t-1}P_t^I - \tag{12}$$

$$\frac{\chi}{(1-\beta)^2(1+\epsilon)+\chi}u_t$$

where superscript I stands for *independent* central bank regime.

Taking expectations conditional on information at $t-1$ of (12) gives

$$E_{t-1}p_t^I = \frac{\chi}{(1-\beta)(1+\epsilon)}\tilde{u}_t \tag{13}$$

Equation (13) is the reaction function of the union. The resulting price level and unemployment rate are

$$p_t^I = \frac{\chi}{(1-\beta)(1+\epsilon)}\tilde{u} - \frac{\chi}{(1-\beta)^2(1+\epsilon)+\chi}\mu_t \tag{14}$$

$$u_t^I = \tilde{u} - \frac{(1-\beta)(1+\epsilon)}{(1-\beta)^2(1+\epsilon)+\chi}\mu_t \tag{15}$$

3 Optimal commitment in monetary policy: credibility versus flexibility

3.1 Social welfare under central bank independence

We are now able to evaluate central bank independence from the perspective of society. To facilitate exposition in later sections, following Rogoff (1985, pp. 1175–6) we shall first develop a notation[5] for evaluating the expected value of society's loss function under any arbitrary monetary policy regime "A," $E_{t-1}L_t^A$

$$E_{t-1}L_t^A = \frac{1}{2}[\chi\,\tilde{u}^2] + \Pi^A + \Gamma^{A5} \tag{16}$$

where $\Pi^A \equiv 1/2\,(\tilde{p}_t^A)^2$, $\tilde{p}_t^A$ is the mean price level in period t, and

$$\Gamma^A \equiv \frac{1}{2}E_{t-1}\{\chi[\frac{\mu_t}{1-\beta} + (p_t^A - E_{t-1}p_t^A)/(1-\beta)]^2 + (p_t^A - E_{t-1}p_t^A)^2\}$$

Again, the first component of $E_{t-1}L_t^A$, $1/2[\chi\,\tilde{u}^2]$ is non-stochastic and invariant across monetary regimes. It represents the *deadweight loss* due to the labor market distortion ($\tilde{u}^2 > 0$). This loss cannot be reduced through monetary policy in a time-consistent rational expectations equilibrium. The second term, Π^A, depends on the mean inflation rate. This term is also non-stochastic, but does depend on the *choice* of monetary policy regime. The final term, Γ^A, represents the *stabilization component* of the loss function. It measures how succesfully the central bank offsets disturbances to stabilize unemployment and inflation around their mean values.

By substituting the results relevant for the central bank [(14) and (15)] into society's loss function (9) and taking expectations we obtain the I and regime counterpart of expression (16). Abstracting from the (common) deadweight loss, one gets

$$\Pi^I + \Gamma^I = \frac{\chi^2}{2[(1-\epsilon)(1+\beta)]^2}\tilde{u}^2 + \frac{\chi[(1+\epsilon)^2(1-\beta)^2+\chi]}{2(1-\epsilon)^2(1-\beta)^2+\chi]^2}\sigma_\mu^2 \qquad (17)$$

3.2 The Rogoff theorem

First, we reproduce Rogoff's (1985) proof that it is optimal for society (the principal) to select an agent to head the independent central bank that places a large, but finite weight on inflation. The *optimal degree* of central bank independence ϵ^* is defined as that value of ϵ that minimizes the expected value of the loss function of society $E_{t-1} L_t^I$.

To solve for the value of ϵ that minimizes $E_{t-1} L_t^I$, we can differentiate (17) with respect to ϵ to yield

$$\frac{\partial E_{t-1}L_t^I}{\partial \epsilon} = \frac{\partial \Pi^I}{\partial \epsilon} + \frac{\partial \Gamma^I}{\partial \epsilon} \qquad (18)$$

$$\frac{\partial \Gamma^I}{\partial \epsilon} = \frac{\chi^2(1-\beta)^2\epsilon\sigma_\mu^2}{[(1-\epsilon)(1-\beta)^2+\chi]^3} \qquad (19)$$

$$\frac{\partial \Pi^I}{\partial \chi} = \frac{-\chi^2 u^2}{(1-\epsilon)^3(1-\beta)^2} \qquad (20)$$

We are now ready to prove:

Proposition 1: With a *positive* natural rate of unemployment, the optimal degree of central bank independence lies between *zero* and *infinity* (for $\tilde{u}>0$, $0<e^*<\infty$).

Proof: Note that $\epsilon>-1$ by assumption. Thus, by inspection of (20), $\delta\Pi^I/\delta\epsilon$ is strictly negative. Note also, by inspection of (19), that $\delta\Gamma^I/\delta\epsilon$ is strictly negative for

$$\frac{-[\chi+(1-\beta)^2]}{(1-\beta)^2}<\epsilon<0, \text{ zero when } \epsilon=0 \text{ and positive for } \epsilon>0.$$

Therefore, $\delta E_{t-1} L_t^I/\delta\epsilon$ is strictly negative for $\epsilon\leq 0$. $\delta E_{t-1} L_t^I/\delta\epsilon$ must change from negative to positive at some sufficiently large value of ϵ, since as ϵ approaches positive infinity, $\delta\Gamma^I/\delta\epsilon$ converges to zero at rate ϵ^{-2}, whereas $\delta\Pi^I/\delta\epsilon$ converges to zero at rate ϵ^{-3}. Consequently, $\epsilon^*<\infty$.[6]

The intuition behind this result is the following. From (20), it can be seen that increasing the central bank's commitment to inflation stabilization decreases the credibility component of the social loss function. On the other hand, from (19) it follows that having a more independent central bank increases the stabilization component of the loss function.

Hence, optimal commitment in monetary policy involves trading off the *credibility* gains associated with lower average inflation versus loss of *flexibility* due to a distorted response to output shocks.

3.3 The ultimate determinants of central bank independence

Proposition 1 is Rogoff's theorem. Rogoff is unable to write down a closed-form solution for ϵ^*. Therefore, he is also unable to derive propositions concerning the comparative static properties of this equilibrium. This section can be seen as an *extension* of the Rogoff theorem.

Using a graphical method, we develop an alternative way of determining the optimal degree of central bank independence. Next, we show how this result is conditioned on the natural rate of unemployment ($\tilde{u}$), society's preferences for unemployment stabilization (χ), the variance of productivity shocks (σ_μ^2), and the slope of the Phillips curve ($(1-\beta)^{-1}$).

By setting (18) equal to zero, we obtain the first-order condition for a minimum of $E_{t-1} L^I_t$

$$0=\frac{\partial \Pi^I}{\partial \epsilon}+\frac{\partial \Gamma^I}{\partial \epsilon} \tag{21}$$

Substituting (19) and (20) into (21) yields

$$\frac{-\chi^2 \tilde{u}^2}{(1-\beta)^3 (1-\epsilon)^3}+\frac{\chi^2 (1-\beta)^2 \epsilon \sigma_\mu^2}{[(1-\epsilon)(1-\beta)^2+\chi]^3}=0 \tag{22}$$

Equation (22) determines ϵ^* as an implicit function of χ, $\tilde{u}$, σ_μ^2 and β. A solution for ϵ^* always exists and is unique.

To show this, we adapt a graphical method used by Cukierman (1992, pp. 170–2) in the context of a dynamic game.

Rewrite (22) as

$$\epsilon=\frac{[(1+\epsilon)(1-\beta)^2+\chi]^3 \tilde{u}^2}{\sigma_\mu^2 (1-\beta)^4 (1+\epsilon)^3} \equiv F(\epsilon) \tag{23}$$

The function $F(\epsilon)$ on the right-hand side of equation (23) is monotonically decreasing in ϵ as[7]

$$F(0)=\frac{[(1+\beta)^2+\chi]^3 \tilde{u}^2}{\sigma_\mu^2 (1-\beta)^4}, \quad \lim_{\epsilon \to \infty} F(\epsilon)=\frac{(1-\beta)^2 \tilde{u}^2}{\sigma_\mu^2} \quad \text{and}$$

$$\frac{(1-\beta)^2 \tilde{u}^2}{\sigma_\mu^2}<F(\epsilon)<\frac{[(1-\beta)^2+\chi]^3 \tilde{u}^2}{\sigma_\mu^2 (1-\beta)^4}$$

We are now ready to prove:

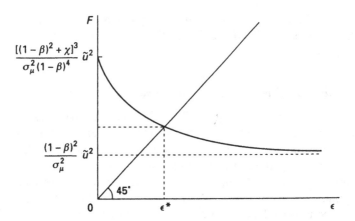

Figure 3.2 The optimal degree of central bank independence.

Proposition 2: $\dfrac{(1-\beta)^2\tilde{u}^2}{\sigma_\mu^2}<\epsilon^*<\dfrac{[(1-\beta)^2+\chi]^3\tilde{u}^2}{\sigma_\mu^2(1-\beta)^4}$

Proof: The left-hand side of (23) is a 45-degree straight line through the origin. Since

$$F(0)=\frac{[(1-\beta)^2+\chi]^3\tilde{u}^2}{\sigma_\mu^2(1-\beta)^4}\quad\text{and}\quad\frac{\partial F}{\partial \epsilon}<0,\text{ these two functions must}$$

intersect at one and only one point. Moreover, since

$$\frac{\tilde{u}^2(1-\beta)^2}{\sigma_\mu^2}<F(\epsilon)<\frac{[(1-\beta)^2+\chi]^3\tilde{u}^2}{\sigma_\mu^2(1-\beta)^4}$$

the intersection occurs at a value of ϵ that is bounded between $\dfrac{(1-\beta)^2\tilde{u}^2}{\sigma_\mu^2}$

and $\dfrac{[(1-\beta)^2+\chi]^3\tilde{u}^2}{\sigma_\mu^2(1-\beta)^4}$.

Figure 3.2 illustrates the argument graphically. Clearly, a solution for ϵ exists and is unique.

We are now ready to investigate the factors affecting the optimal degree of central bank independence. Hence, we identify *economic* and *political* factors that induce politicians to delegate more or less authority to this institution. We show that the delegation of authority to the central bank depends on the natural rate of unemployment, society's preferences for unemployment stabilization, the variance of productivity shocks, and the slope of the Phillips curve. The results are derived by performing comparative statics with respect to various parameters on figure 3.2. Derivations appear in appendix B. We summarize the main results in four propositions.

Proposition 3: The higher the natural rate of unemployment (the higher $\tilde{u}$), the higher the optimal degree of central bank independence.

Proof: Appendix B shows that $\dfrac{\partial F}{\partial \tilde{u}} > 0$, implying that when $\tilde{u}$ goes up, the curve $F(\epsilon)$ in figure 3.2 shifts upward. As a consequence, the equilibrium value of ϵ increases.

The intuition behind this result is the following. A higher natural rate of unemployment implies a higher time-consistent rate of inflation (see equation (14)) and, consequently, a higher credibility component of the social loss function. This means that society's credibility problem is increased. Hence, with an unaltered relative weight placed on inflation versus unemployment stabilization the monetary authorities' commitment to fight inflation is now too low.

Proposition 4: The higher *society's preferences for unemployment stabilization relative to inflation stabilization* (the higher χ), the higher the optimal degree of central bank independence.

Proof: Appendix B shows that $\dfrac{\partial F}{\partial \chi} > 0$, implying that when χ goes up, the curve $F(\epsilon)$ in figure 3.2 shifts upward. Thus, the equilibrium value of ϵ increases.

The underlying intuition is that, if society becomes more concerned with unemployment, the time-consistent inflation rate goes up (see equation (14)). Therefore, society's credibility problem becomes more pressing. With an unchanged relative weight placed on inflation stabilization, the balance between credibility and flexibility needs to be adjusted in favor of an increased commitment to fighting inflation.

Proposition 5: The higher the *variance of productivity shocks* (the higher σ_μ^2), the lower the optimal degree of central bank independence.

Proof: Appendix B shows that $\dfrac{\partial F}{\partial \sigma_\mu^2} < 0$, implying that when σ_μ^2 goes up, the curve $F(\epsilon)$ in figure 3.2 shifts downward. Therefore, the equilibrium value of ϵ decreases.

This result can be explained as follows. If the variance of productivity shocks increases, *ceteris paribus*, the economy becomes more unstable.

Thus, the need for active stabilization policy increases (the Γ^t component of the social loss function goes up).

With an unaltered relative weight placed on inflation stabilization, the balance between credibility and flexibility needs to be shifted toward more monetary accommodation.

Proposition 6: If society is relatively unconcerned with inflation $\left(\chi > \dfrac{(1+\epsilon)(1-\beta)^2}{2}\right)$, the greater the *benefits of unanticipated inflation* (the higher $(1-\beta)^{-1}$), the higher the optimal degree of central bank independence.

Proof: Appendix B shows that, if $\chi > \dfrac{(1+\epsilon)(1-\beta)^2}{2}$, $\dfrac{\partial F}{\partial (1-\beta)^{-1}} > 0$, implying that when $(1-\beta)^{-1}$ goes up, the curve $F(\epsilon)$ shifts upward. Consequently, the equilibrium value of ϵ increases.

The intuition behind this proposition is that, if the benefits of unanticipated inflation rise (see equation (7)), it becomes more tempting to inflate the economy. Therefore, society's credibility problem gains in importance. With the same emphasis on inflation stabilization, the balance between credibility and flexibility needs to be shifted toward increased commitment to price stability. Finally, we summarize the propositions from this section in table 3.1.

In order to confront these propositions with some cross-country evidence, we can now move on to the empirical evidence. This is the subject of the next section.

4 Empirical evidence

In this section, the ultimate determinants of central bank independence discussed before are empirically investigated. We will use, for that purpose, the latent variables method (LISREL) to make a distinction between the optimal and actual (legal) degree of central bank independence. The reasons for this distinction are two-fold. First, the propositions derived in the previous section are related to the optimal degree of central bank independence and not to the actual (legal) degree. These propositions formulate the relationship between the optimal degree and four economic and political factors in a country:

the natural rate of unemployment (positive relation);
society's preferences for unemployment stabilization relative to inflation stabilization (positive relation);

Table 3.1 *The ultimate determinants of central bank independence*

Economic and political factors			
$\tilde{u}$	χ	σ_μ^2	$(1-\beta)^{-1}$
Natural rate of unemployment	Society's preferences for unemployment stabilization	Variance of productivity shocks	Gains from unanticipated inflation (slope of Phillips curve)
$\dfrac{\partial \epsilon^*}{\partial \tilde{u}} > 0$	$\dfrac{\partial \epsilon^*}{\partial \chi} > 0$	$\dfrac{\partial \epsilon^*}{\partial \sigma_\mu^2} < 0$	$\dfrac{\partial \epsilon^*}{\partial (1-\beta)^{-1}} > 0$

the variance of productivity shocks (negative relation); and

the slope of the Phillips curve (conditional positive relation).

These determinants, reflecting the economic and political structure of a country, explain theoretically the optimal degree of central bank independence in that country.

Second, there is also an identification and measurement problem. Whereas the determinants of central bank independence change *frequently* during the sample period (i.e., the period 1960–93), the actual degree – approximated by the legal indices of central bank independence – hardly changes in the same period. The stickiness of actual (legal) central bank independence results from the fact that central bank laws are *very occasionally* adjusted in practice, especially in the industrial countries, during the post-war period.[8] Moreover, it could be questioned whether the legal indices of central bank independence are a good measure of actual central bank independence (see, for instance, Eijffinger and De Haan, 1996).

4.1 The data

As proxies for the ultimate determinants of central bank independence, we have chosen the following economic and political variables (see appendix C for a detailed account of these variables). For the natural rate of unemployment, the *non-accelerating inflation rate of unemployment* (*NAIRU*) is taken from Layard, Nickell, and Jackman (1991). They estimated the *NAIRU* for 19 industrial countries for the period 1960–88. The proxy for society's preferences for unemployment stabilization relative to inflation stabilization is the number of years that a *left-wing* (*socialist*) *party* has been in government as a share of the *total* number of years (*WLEFT*). For a left-wing government has a higher preference for unemployment stabilization and, therefore, the optimal degree of central bank independence increases under a left-wing government. The variance of productivity shocks is proxied by the *variance of output growth* (GDP) on an annual basis (*VPROD*). We compute the slope of the Phillips curve, using the labor income share in GDP.[9] Because data for the labor income share are not available for all countries in our sample, we have taken the ratio between the *compensation of employees* paid by resident producers to resident households and GDP (*SLOPE*).

Therefore, the *optimal* degree of central bank independence (*OPCBI*) is explained by the following variables, taken in deviation from their mean (*M*)

$$OPCBI = a_1 \cdot \overset{(+)}{[NAIRU\_M]} + a_2 \cdot \overset{(+)}{[WLEFT\_M]} + a_3 \cdot \overset{(-)}{[VPROD\_M]} +$$

$$\overset{(+)}{a_4 \cdot [SLOPE\_M]} \tag{24}$$

The expected signs are indicated above the explanatory variables. The optimal degree of central bank independence is assumed to be a *latent* variable in our empirical model. Next to the *observed* explanatory variables measured in deviation from their mean (*NAIRU_M, WLEFT_M, VPROD_M* and *SLOPE_M*), we need the actual (legal) degree of central bank independence as an *observed* variable. The actual degree of central bank independence is proxied by the legal degree, according to four main indices of central bank independence in the literature.

The index of Alesina (AL) is a narrow measure of independence and based on Alesina (1988, 1989). The total index of political and economic independence of Grilli, Masciandaro, and Tabellini (GMTT) is a broad measure based on Grilli, Masciandaro, and Tabellini (1991). The index of policy independence of Eijffinger and Schaling (ES) is, however, a narrow measure based on Eijffinger and Schaling (1992, 1993a) and extended by Eijffinger and Van Keulen (1995). The unweighted legal index of Cukierman (LVAU) is a very broad measure of independence and derived from Cukierman (1992).[10]

For our cross-country analysis, a set of 19 industrial (OECD) countries is taken that are ranked – with some exceptions – by the above-mentioned indices. The sample period that we have chosen covers more than 30 years, namely the period 1960–93 (for *NAIRU*: 1960–88). The reason to choose such a long period is that it contains many political and business cycles and, thus, comprises changes of the political and economic structure affecting the optimal degree of central bank independence.

4.2 The latent variables method

According to Bentler (1982), the essential characteristic of a *latent variable* is that a system of linear structural equations in which the latent variable appears cannot be manipulated so as to express this variable as a function of *measured* variables only.[11]

Aigner, Hsiao, Kapteyn, and Wansbeek (1984) state that, since 1970, there has been a resurgence of interest in econometrics in the topic of models involving latent variables. "That interest in such models had to be restimulated at all may seem surprising," in the opinion of Aigner *et al.*, "since there can be no doubt that economic quantities frequently are measured with error and, moreover, that many applications depend on the use of observable proxies for otherwise unobservable conceptual variables" (p. 1323).

Estimation of a simultaneous equations model with latent variables can be done by means of a computer program for the analysis of covariance structures, such a LISREL (Linear Structural Relations). The idea behind LISREL is to compare a sample covariance matrix with the parametric structure imposed on it by the hypothesized model. Under normality, LISREL delivers *Full Information Maximum Likelihood* (FIML) estimates of the model parameters. Because of its general availability, LISREL is the most widely used tool for handling latent variables.

The specification of the latent variables model to be analyzed by LISREL is as follows.[12] Let η be the latent *dependent* variable, i.e., the latent optimal degree of central bank independence, and let ξ be the latent *explanatory* variables, in our case the four ultimate determinants of central bank independence, satisfying a system of linear structural relations

$$\eta = B \cdot \xi + \zeta \tag{25}$$

where B is the coefficient matrix and ζ are the disturbances. It is assumed that η, ξ, and ζ have *zero* expectations, and that ξ and ζ are *uncorrelated*. Instead of the latent vectors η and ξ, the vectors y and x are *observed* so that

$$y = \Lambda_y \cdot \eta + \gamma \tag{26}$$

and

$$x = \Lambda_x \cdot \xi + \delta \tag{27}$$

where Λ_y and Λ_x are the coefficient matrices, and γ and δ are the vectors of measurement errors, *uncorrelated* with η, ξ, ζ, and each other, but possibly correlated among themselves. The observed vectors y and x are measured as deviations from their means, thus having *zero* expectations and a covariance equal to $E[x\ y]$. This implies, of course, that γ and δ also have zero expectations.

Therefore, y is a vector of *observed* legal indices of central bank independence (AL, $GMTT$, ES, and $LVAU$), measured in deviation from their respective means

$$y= \begin{bmatrix} AL\_M \\ GMTT\_M \\ LVAU\_M \\ ES\_M \\ LVAU\_M \end{bmatrix} \tag{28}$$

and x is a vector of the following observed explanatory variables: the non-accelerating inflation rate of unemployment ($NAIRU$), the percentage of years of a left-wing government ($WLEFT$), the variance of output growth ($VPROD$), and the compensation of employees as share of GDP ($SLOPE$), all measured in deviation from their means

$$x= \begin{bmatrix} NAIRU\_M \\ WLEFT\_M \\ VPROD\_M \\ SLOPE\_M \end{bmatrix} \tag{29}$$

So, equations (26) and (27) can be restated as

$$\begin{bmatrix} AL\_M \\ GMTT\_M \\ ES\_M \\ LVAU\_M \end{bmatrix} = \begin{bmatrix} \lambda_{y1} \\ \lambda_{y2} \\ \lambda_{y3} \\ \lambda_{y4} \end{bmatrix} \cdot \eta + \begin{bmatrix} \gamma_1 \\ \gamma_2 \\ \gamma_3 \\ \gamma_4 \end{bmatrix}$$

and

$$\begin{bmatrix} NAIRU\_M \\ WRLEFT\_M \\ VPROD\_M \\ SLOPE\_M \end{bmatrix} = \begin{bmatrix} \lambda_{x1} \\ \lambda_{x2} \\ \lambda_{x3} \\ \lambda_{x4} \end{bmatrix} \cdot \begin{bmatrix} \xi_1 \\ \xi_2 \\ \xi_3 \\ \xi_4 \end{bmatrix} + \begin{bmatrix} \delta_1 \\ \delta_2 \\ \delta_3 \\ \delta_4 \end{bmatrix} \tag{30}$$

Furthermore, Φ and Ψ are defined as the covariance matrix of ξ and the variance matrix of ζ, and Θ_γ and Θ_δ are the true variance–covariance matrices of γ and δ, respectively. Then it follows from the above assumptions that the variance–covariance matrix Σ of $[y', x']'$ can be written as

$$\Sigma = \begin{bmatrix} \Lambda_y\,[B\Phi B'+\Psi]\,\Lambda'_y+\theta\gamma & \Lambda_y B\Phi\Lambda'_x \\ \hline \Lambda_x\Phi B'\Lambda'_y & \Lambda_x\Phi\Lambda'_x+\Theta_\delta \end{bmatrix} \tag{31}$$

Assuming that the latent explanatory variables (ξ) equal the observed (x), thus $\xi = x$, we see that $\theta_\delta = 0$ and $\Lambda_x = I$, and that equation (31) simplifies to[13]

$$\Sigma = \begin{bmatrix} \Lambda_y [B\Phi B' + \Psi] \Lambda'_y \theta_\gamma & \Lambda_y B\Phi \\ \hdotsfor{2} \\ \Phi B' \Lambda'_y & \Phi \end{bmatrix} \qquad (32)$$

The parameters in Σ (Λ_y, B, Φ, Ψ, θ_γ) are estimated on the basis of the matrix S of second sample moments of x and y. In order to identify all parameters, *additional* restrictions on the parameters have to be imposed. Given these restrictions and the structure that equation (33) imposes on the data, LISREL computes FIML estimates of the parameters when $[y', x']$ is normally distributed, i.e., when the following criterion is minimized

$$\ln |\Sigma| + \text{tr} [S\Sigma^{-1}] \qquad (33)$$

To be able to identify all parameters of the model, we have made the following two additional restrictions:

(i) $\lambda_{y3} = 1$, which implies that the latent optimal degree of central bank independence (η) has the *same* unit of measurement as the observed legal index of Eijffinger and Schaling (*ES_M*);[14] and

(ii) θ_γ is diagonal, which implies that the correlation between the observed legal indices of central bank independence (y) is *only* caused by the latent optimal degree (η).[15]

4.3 The empirical results

On the basis of the restrictions given in the former subsection, LISREL computes *Full Information Maximum Likelihood* estimates of the parameters of the model. Computation with LISREL renders two different kind of estimations. First, the relationship between the *optimal* degree of central bank independence (η, here renamed *OPCBI*) and the explanatory variables (*NAIRU_M*, *WLEFT_M*, *VPROD_M*, and *SLOPE_M*), reflecting the ultimate *determinants* of central bank independence, is estimated.[16] Second, by estimating this relationship and calculating the optimal degree of central bank independence for each country (*OPCBI*), the comparison between the *optimal* degree and the *legal* indices of central bank independence (*AL*, *GMTT*, *ES*, and *LVAU*) can be made. Such a comparison is only possible if both the optimal degree and the legal indices are normalized on their theoretical scale (*OPCBI_N*, *AL_N*, *GMTT_N*, and *ES_N*, respectively).[17]

Next to the differences of individual legal indices with the optimal degree, the *average difference* (*AvDIFF*) may be calculated in the following way

$$AvDIFF=\frac{[AL\_N]+[GMTT\_N]+ES\_N]+LVAU}{4}-[OPCBI\_N] \qquad (34)$$

This average difference is *positive*, if the average of legal indices exceeds the optimal degree, and *negative*, if the optimal degree exceeds the average of legal indices. A positive average difference indicates that the legal degree of central bank independence should be *decreased*, whereas a negative average difference that the legal degree should be *increased* in order to bring it closer to the optimal degree based on the ultimate determinants of central bank independence.

Table 3.2 shows the estimation results, with all restrictions imposed in the former section, for the sample period 1960–93 (for *NAIRU*, the sample period 1960–88). From Table 3.2, it can be seen that all explanatory variables of the optimal degree, except *NAIRU*, have the expected sign.[18] Only one explanatory variable (*SLOPE*) is significant at a 90 per cent confidence level. The other explanatory variables have relatively low *t*-values. Nevertheless, we have calculated the optimal degree on the basis of the ultimate determinants for each country and, after normalization of the optimal degree and the legal indices, the average difference between these variables. Positive average differences – of 0.20 or higher – are found for Germany and Switzerland, implying that the legal degree of central bank independence exceeds the optimal degree and that the legal degree should be decreased.

Negative average differences – of 0.20 or lower – are observed for Australia, Norway, Sweden, and the United Kingdom, meaning that the optimal degree exceeds the legal degree and that the legal degree should be increased. For the other countries – Austria, Belgium, Canada, Denmark, Finland, France, Ireland, Italy, Japan, The Netherlands, New Zealand, Spain, and the United States – the average differences are relatively small, indicating that there is no reason to adjust the central bank law in these countries from the perspective of the ultimate determinants. In some countries – notably France and Spain – central banks have, recently, been made more independent of government which can be explained by another argument: a prerequisite for entering the third phase of Economic and Monetary Union in Europe is, among others, the independence of the *national* central banks of the participating countries. The relatively low *t*-values for the explanatory variables in table 3.2 can, probably, be attributed to the many severe restrictions imposed on the model by LISREL and the two additional restrictions made by us ($\lambda_{y3}=1$ and Θ_γ is diagonal) to identify all parameters of the model. Relaxing some of these restrictions might improve the *t*-values of the explanatory variables.[19]

Table 3.3 gives the empirical results, if we relax *only two* restrictions on the covariances, for the sample period 1960–93 (for *NAIRU*: 1960–88).

Table 3.2 *Table based on estimation with all restrictions*

Sample period 1960–93 for all variables (except for *NAIRU*: 1960–88)

$OPCBI = -0.098 * NAIRU\_M + 0.038 * WLEFT\_M - 0.039 * VPROD\_M + 2.025 * SLOPE\_M$
$\quad\quad\quad(-1.296)\quad\quad\quad(0.054)\quad\quad\quad(-0.638)\quad\quad\quad(2.008)$

Country	Indices				Transformed indices					Differences (INDEX − OPCBI)				
	AL	GMTT	ES	LVAU	AL_N	GMTT_N	ES_N	OPCBI	OPCBI_N	AL_N	GMTT_N	ES_N	LVAU	AvDIFF
Australia	1	9	1	0.31	0.00	0.56	0.00	−0.026	0.415	−0.42	0.15	−0.42	−0.11	−0.20
Austria	—	9	3	0.58	—	0.56	0.50	0.158	0.460	—	0.10	0.04	0.12	0.09
Belgium	2	7	3	0.19	0.33	0.44	0.50	−0.08	0.401	−0.07	0.04	0.10	−0.21	−0.04
Canada	2	11	1	0.46	0.33	0.69	0.00	−0.160	0.381	−0.05	0.31	−0.38	0.08	−0.01
Denmark	2	8	4	0.47	0.33	0.50	0.75	0.037	0.430	−0.10	0.07	0.32	0.04	0.08
Finland	2	—	3	0.27	0.33	—	0.50	−0.141	0.386	−0.06	—	0.11	−0.12	−0.02
France	2	7	2	0.28	0.33	0.44	0.25	−0.140	0.386	−0.06	0.05	−0.14	−0.11	−0.07
Germany	4	13	5	0.66	1.00	0.81	1.00	0.246	0.482	0.52	0.33	0.52	0.18	0.39
Ireland	—	7	—	0.39	—	0.44	—	−0.485	0.300	—	0.14	—	0.09	0.12
Italy	1.5	5	2	0.22	0.17	0.31	0.25	−0.659	0.256	−0.09	0.05	−0.01	−0.04	−0.02
Japan	3	6	3	0.16	0.67	0.38	0.50	−0.403	0.320	0.35	0.06	0.18	−0.16	0.11
The Netherlands	2	10	4	0.42	0.33	0.63	0.75	0.152	0.459	−0.13	0.17	0.29	−0.04	0.07
New Zealand	1	3	3	0.27	0.00	0.19	0.50	−0.393	0.323	−0.32	−0.13	0.18	−0.05	−0.08
Norway	2	—	2	0.14	0.33	—	0.25	0.281	0.491	−0.16	—	−0.24	−0.35	−0.25
Spain	1	5	1	0.21	0.00	0.31	0.00	−1.213	0.118	−0.12	0.19	−0.12	0.09	0.01
Sweden	2	—	2	0.27	0.33	—	0.25	1.072	0.689	−0.36	—	−0.44	−0.42	−0.41
Switzerland	4	12	5	0.68	1.00	0.75	1.00	0.852	0.634	0.37	0.12	0.37	0.05	0.23
UK	2	6	2	0.31	0.33	0.31	0.25	0.551	0.559	−0.23	−0.18	−0.31	−0.25	−0.24
US	3	12	3	0.51	0.67	0.75	0.50	0.632	0.579	0.09	0.17	−0.08	0.07	−0.03

Notes: _M means that variables are taken in deviation from their mean.
t-values in parentheses

Table 3.3 *Table based on estimation without restrictions on the covariances (γ_2, γ_3) and (γ_2, ζ)*

Sample period 1960–93 for all variables (except for NAIRU: 1960–88)

$$OPCBI = -0.008 * NAIRU\_M + 0.807 * WLEFT\_M - 0.436 * VPROD\_M + 0.923 * SLOPE\_M$$
$$\quad\quad (-0.237) \quad\quad\quad (1.529) \quad\quad\quad (-1.784) \quad\quad\quad (1.452)$$

Country	Indices				Transformed indices					Differences (INDEX − OPCBI)				
	AL	GMTT	ES	LVAU	AL_N	GMTT_N	ES_N	OPCBI	OPCBI_N	AL_N	GMTT_N	ES_N	LVAU	AvDIFF
Australia	1	9	1	0.31	0.00	0.56	0.00	0.461	0.536	−0.54	0.03	−0.54	−0.23	−0.32
Austria	—	9	3	0.58	—	0.56	0.50	1.223	0.727	—	−0.16	−0.23	−0.15	−0.18
Belgium	2	7	3	0.19	0.33	0.44	0.50	0.518	0.550	−0.22	−0.11	−0.05	−0.36	−0.19
Canada	2	11	1	0.46	0.33	0.69	0.00	0.438	0.530	−0.20	0.16	−0.53	−0.07	−0.16
Denmark	2	8	4	0.47	0.33	0.50	0.75	0.270	0.488	−0.16	−0.01	0.26	−0.02	0.02
Finland	2	—	3	0.27	0.33	—	0.50	0.625	0.577	−0.24	—	−0.08	−0.31	−0.21
France	2	7	2	0.28	0.33	0.44	0.25	0.959	0.661	−0.33	−0.22	−0.41	−0.38	−0.34
Germany	4	13	5	0.66	1.00	0.81	1.00	0.655	0.585	0.42	0.23	0.42	0.08	0.28
Ireland	—	7	—	0.39	—	0.44	—	0.238	0.480	—	−0.04	—	−0.09	−0.07
Italy	1.5	5	2	0.22	0.17	0.31	0.25	0.126	0.453	−0.29	−0.14	−0.20	−0.23	−0.22
Japan	3	6	3	0.16	0.67	0.38	0.50	−3.410	0.000	0.67	0.38	0.50	0.16	0.43
The Netherlands	2	10	4	0.42	0.33	0.63	0.75	0.260	0.486	−0.15	0.14	0.26	−0.07	0.05
New Zealand	1	3	3	0.27	0.00	0.19	0.50	−3.200	0.000	0.00	0.19	0.50	0.27	0.24
Norway	2	—	2	0.14	0.33	—	0.25	1.579	0.816	−0.48	—	−0.57	−0.68	−0.57
Spain	1	5	1	0.21	0.00	0.31	0.00	−1.925	0.000	0.00	0.31	0.00	0.21	0.13
Sweden	2	—	2	0.27	0.33	—	0.25	1.915	0.900	−0.57	—	−0.65	−0.63	−0.62
Switzerland	4	12	5	0.68	1.00	0.75	1.00	0.065	0.437	0.56	0.31	0.56	0.24	0.42
UK	2	6	2	0.31	0.33	0.38	0.25	1.077	0.690	−0.36	−0.32	−0.44	−0.38	−0.37
US	3	12	3	0.51	0.67	0.75	0.50	0.741	0.606	0.06	0.14	−0.11	−0.10	0.00

Notes: _M means that variables are taken in deviation from their mean.
t-values in parentheses

First, the restriction on the covariance of $[\gamma_2, \gamma_3]$ between the *GMTT*- and *ES*-indices is eliminated. This implies that the disturbances of these indices may be correlated. Second, the restriction on the covariance of $[\gamma_2, \zeta]$ between the *GMTT*-indices and the regression equation – equation (25) with $\xi = x$ – is lifted. This means that the disturbances between the *GMTT*-index and the regression equation can be correlated. All other restrictions on the model remain as before.

From table 3.3, it is clear that the t-values of all explanatory variables, except *SLOPE*, improve considerably. One of these explanatory variables (*VPROD*) becomes significant even at a 90 per cent confidence level. All explanatory variables, except *NAIRU*, have the expected sign. If we compare the coefficients of the explanatory variables in this table with those in table 3.2, the estimated coefficients do not seem very robust. Therefore, we have also calculated the optimal degree of central bank independence and the average difference with the legal indices for each country. The positive average differences for Germany and Switzerland appear to be still in place, while now Japan and New Zealand join this group. The negative average differences for Australia, Norway, Sweden, and the United Kingdom also remain, although these differences generally become bigger. Now this group is, however, joined by Finland, France, and Italy (negative average difference is –0.20 or lower). Almost no average differences are found for Denmark, Ireland, The Netherlands, and the United States. Apparently, these countries have central bank laws that correspond with their optimal degree based on the ultimate determinants, insofar as they are captured in the empirical model.

5 Conclusion

What may be concluded from the previous sections? First, it is possible to derive propositions on the basis of our theoretical model which formulates the relationship between the optimal degree of central bank independence and four ultimate determinants in a country: the natural rate of employment, the society's preferences for unemployment stabilization relative to inflation stabilization, the variance of productivity shocks, and the slope of the Phillips curve. These determinants, reflecting the economic and political structure of a country, refer only indirectly to the actual (legal) degree of central bank independence.

Second, to distinguish between the optimal and actual (legal) degree of central bank independence the latent variables method (LISREL) appears to be very useful as an empirical model. This method enables us to explain the optimal degree by proxies for the ultimate determinants (*NAIRU*, *WLEFT*, *VPROD*, and *SLOPE*), and it allows us to compare the optimal degree with the legal indices of central bank independence (*AL*, *GMTT*, *ES*, and *LVAU*). The latent variables analysis, based on 19 industrial countries, for the sample period 1960–93 (for *NAIRU*: 1960–1988) leads to estimation results that support our theoretical model reasonably well, if we relax two restrictions on covariances.

Third, the comparison between the optimal degree and the legal indices of central bank independence renders some interesting results. Germany and Switzerland specifically appear to have a sub-optimally high degree of central bank independence, whereas Australia, Norway, Sweden and the United Kingdom appear to have a suboptimally low degree. For Denmark, Ireland, The Netherlands, and the United States, we conclude that these countries have more or less an optimal degree of independence.

Finally, it should be mentioned that both our theoretical and empirical models can be extended to include other economic and political determinants of central bank independence. One could, for example, examine the role of the degree of openness of a country to allow for differences between small and large countries. These extensions are on our research agenda for the future.

Appendix A The derivation of the expected value of society's loss function under an arbitrary monetary policy regime

In this appendix following Rogoff (1985, pp. 1175–6), we develop the notation for evaluating the expected value of society's loss function under any arbitrary monetary policy regime "*A*," $E_{t-1} L_t^A$ (see equation (16) of the text). Unemployment under regime A is given by

$$u_t^A = \tilde{u} - \frac{1}{1-\beta} (p_t^A - E_{t-1}p_t^A + \mu_t) \tag{A1}$$

Squaring and taking expectations yields

$$E_{t-1}(u_t^A)^2 = \tilde{u}^2 + E_{t-1}\left[\frac{\mu_t}{1-\beta} + \frac{1}{1-\beta}(p_t^A - E_{t-1}p_t^A)\right]^2 \tag{A2}$$

The price level under regime A can be expanded as

$$p_t^A = \tilde{p}_t^A + (p_t^A - E_{t-1}p_t^A) \tag{A3}$$

where $\tilde{p}_t^A$ is the mean (expected) price level in period t. Squaring and taking expectations, in turn, yields

$$E_{t-1}(p_t^A)^2 = (\tilde{p}_t^A)^2 + E_{t-1}(p_t^A - E_{t-1}p_t^A)^2 \tag{A4}$$

The expected value of society's loss function under regime A is

$$E_{t-1}L_t^A = \frac{1}{2}E_{t-1}(p_t^A)^2 + \frac{\epsilon}{2}E_{t-1}(u_t^A)^2 \tag{A5}$$

Substituting (A2) and (A4) into (A5), yields equation (16) of the text.

Appendix B Derivation of the properties of the function $F(\epsilon)$ in the first-order condition.

(1) Demonstration that $\dfrac{\partial F}{\partial \epsilon} < 0$.

The first derivative of F with respect to ϵ is given by

$$\frac{\partial F}{\partial \epsilon} = \frac{3\tilde{u}^2\chi[1+\epsilon)(1-\beta)^2+\chi]^2}{\sigma_\mu^2(1-\beta)^4(1+\epsilon)^4} \tag{B1}$$

which is negative.

(2) Demonstration that $\dfrac{\partial^2 F}{\partial \epsilon^2} > 0$.

The second derivative of F with respect to ϵ is given by

$$\frac{\partial^2 F}{\partial \epsilon^2} = \frac{6\tilde{u}^2\chi\Gamma[\Gamma-\chi]}{(1-\beta)^4(1+\epsilon)^5\sigma_\mu^2} \tag{B2}$$

where $\Gamma \equiv (1+\epsilon)(1-\beta)^2 + 2\chi$, (B2) is positive.

(3) Demonstration that $F(0) = \dfrac{[(1-\beta)^2+\chi]^3\tilde{u}^2}{(1-\beta)^4}$.

This can be shown by a direct examination of the right-hand side of equation (23) at $\epsilon = 0$.

(4) Demonstration that $\dfrac{\tilde{u}^2(1-\beta)^2}{\sigma_\mu^2} < F(\epsilon) < \dfrac{[(1-\beta)^2+\chi]^3\tilde{u}^2}{(1-\beta)^4\sigma_\mu^2}$

Since $F(0) = \dfrac{[(1-\beta)^2+\chi]^3\tilde{u}^2}{\sigma_\mu^2(1-\beta)^4}$,

$\lim\limits_{\epsilon \to \infty} = \dfrac{\tilde{u}^2(1-\beta)^2}{\sigma_\mu^2}$ and $\dfrac{\partial F}{\partial \epsilon} < 0$, $F(\epsilon)$ must be bounded between

$\dfrac{\tilde{u}^2(1-\beta)^2}{\sigma_\mu^2}$ and $F(0)$.

(5)   Demonstration that $\dfrac{\partial F}{\partial \tilde{u}} > 0$.

The first derivative of F with respect to $\tilde{u}$ is given by

$$\frac{\partial F}{\partial \tilde{u}} = \frac{2[(1+\epsilon)(1-\beta)^2 + \chi]^3}{\sigma_\mu^2 (1-\beta)^4 (1+\epsilon)^3} \, \tilde{u} > 0 \tag{B3}$$

(6)   Demonstration that $\dfrac{\partial F}{\partial \chi} > 0$.

The first derivative of F with respect to χ is given by

$$\frac{3[(1+\epsilon)(1-\beta) + \chi]^2 \tilde{u}^2}{\sigma_\mu^2 (1-\beta)^4 (1+\epsilon)^3} > 0 \tag{B4}$$

(7)   Demonstration that $\dfrac{\partial F}{\partial \sigma_\mu^2} < 0$.

The first derivative of F with respect to σ_μ^2 is given by

$$\frac{\partial F}{\partial \sigma_\mu^2} = \frac{-[(1+\epsilon)(1-\beta)^2 + \chi]^3 \tilde{u}^2}{[\sigma_\mu^2 (1-\beta)^2]^2 (1+\epsilon)^3} < 0 \tag{B5}$$

(8)   Demonstration that $\dfrac{\partial F}{\partial (1-\beta)^{-1}} > 0$.

The first derivative of F with respect to $(1-\beta)^{-1}$ is given by

$$\frac{\partial F}{\partial (1-\beta)^{-1}} = \frac{2\tilde{u}^2 [2\chi - (1+\epsilon)(1-\beta)^2][(1+\epsilon)(1-\beta)^2 + \chi]^2}{\sigma_\mu^2 (1-\beta)^3 (1+\epsilon)^3} \tag{B6}$$

Note that (B6) is positive if $\chi > \dfrac{(1+\epsilon)(1-\beta)^2}{2}$.

Appendix C The data

VPROD: OECD, *Main Economic Indicators*, various issues.
Growth rate of GDP in US$ in 1985 prices and exchange rates, 1960–93.

NAIRU: R. Layard, S. Nickell, and R. Jackman, *Unemployment, Macroeconomic Performance and the Labour Market*, Oxford: Oxford University Press, 1991.
Estimates for NAIRU 1960–88, table 14, chapter 9.

WLEFT: *Winkler Prins Encyclopedie*, 1990; A.J. Day (ed.), *Political Parties of the World*, London: Longman, 1988.

(# years that a left-wing party has been in the government, either alone or in a coalition)/(total # years), 1960–93.

SLOPE: OECD, *National Accounts of OECD Countries*, 1960–77, 1977–89, 1978–92, Paris, 1979, 1991, 1994.
1/[1 – (Compensation of employees paid by resident producers/GDP)], in current prices.

Notes

The authors owe a debt of gratitude to Marco Hoeberichts for his empirical support. They are also grateful to Marno Verbeek for his valuable suggestions with respect to the latent variables method.

1 For a recent discussion about the independence of the Bank of England and the associated inflation targeting framework, see Centre for Economic Policy Research (1993).

2 See for instance Issing (1993).

3 Actual employment equals its natural rate when all expectations are fulfilled. Hence, the natural rate of employment equals ℓ^*.

4 Price-level targeting and inflation-rate targeting are equivalent here, since p_{t-1} is known at the time the central bank commits itself to achieving a target for $p_t - p_{t-1}$. Once monetary control errors are taken into account, it becomes important to make the distinction between a *zero inflation target and a target of price stability*. See Fischer (1994, pp. 33–4).

5 We derive equation (16) in appendix A.

6 As pointed out by Rogoff (1985, p. 1178), it is difficult to write down a closed-form solution for ϵ^*. Using an envelope theorem, Rogoff shows that this term must be positive and finite. Eijffinger, Hoeberichts, and Schaling (1995) give a closed-form solution based on Ferrari's method for solving a biquadratic equation.

7 These statements are demonstrated in appendix B to this chapter.

8 Recently, some countries within the European Union – e.g., France and Spain – have made their central banks more independent from government because this is required by the Maastricht Treaty on Economic and Monetary Union. These changes of central bank laws are, however, too infrequent to be applicable for our empirical analysis of the determinants in the industrial countries.

9 Since we use a Cobb–Douglas production function (equation (1)), the production elasticity of labor, β, equals labor's income share in GDP.

10 As a consequence of the latent variables method (LISREL), these observed indices of central bank independence are also measured in deviation from their means: *AL_M*, *GMTT_M*, *ES_M* and *LVAU_M*. If all variables have an expected value zero, then their covariance equals $E[x\,y]$.

11 For this definition of a latent variable, see: P.M. Bentler (1982). A clear overview of the latent variable method is given by: D.J. Aigner, C. Hsiao, A. Kapteyn and T. Wansbeek (1984).

12 In order to avoid overlapping symbols between sections 2 and 3 (theoretical

model) and section 4 (latent variables model), our notation differs from that of the LISREL manual. Having one latent dependent variable, we use B and γ, respectively, instead of the symbols Γ and ϵ for the LISREL manual. Compare also Aigner *et al.* (1984, pp. 1370–1) in this respect.

13 So, we make only a distinction between the *latent* optimal degree of central bank independence (η) and the *observed* actual degree (y) measured by the legal indices of central bank independence. Thus, the optimal degree of central bank independence is derived from the covariances of the four legal indices.

14 It is, however, also possible to choose as the unit of measurement for the latent optimal degree *one* of the other observed legal indices ($\lambda_{y1}=1$, $\lambda_{y2}=1$ or $\lambda_{y4}=1$). In principle, this choice will not make a difference regarding the identification of the parameters.

15 The measurement errors (γ) in equation (26) are, thereby, uncorrelated.

16 Because all variables are measured in deviation from their mean and have, thus, zero expectations, the constant is eliminated from the model.

17 Note that the legal index of Cukierman ($LVAU$) is already normalized on its theoretical scale, i.e., in theory its lowest value is 0 and its highest value 1.

18 The negatieve coefficient for the variable $NAIRU$ may, however, be explained by the existence of *reverse causation*: a high degree of central bank independence leads, apparently, to a low $NAIRU$ in the long run. Moreover, there is empirical evidence for an increase of $NAIRU$ in the OECD countries during the last decades.

19 See in this respect: Aigner, Hsiao, Kapteyn, and Wansbeek (1984, p. 1371). The relaxing of restrictions could imply that, although the latent variables method is still used, the assumptions of LISREL are not valid anymore.

References

Aigner, D., Hsiao, D., Kapteyn, A., and Wansbeek, T. (1984), "Latent Variable Models in Econometrics," in Z. Griliches and M. Intriligator (eds.), *Handbook of Econometrics*, Vol II, Amsterdam: Elsevier Science Publishers, 1321–93.

Alesina, A. (1988), "Macroeconomics and Politics," in: S. Fischer (ed.), *NBER Macroeconomics Annual*, Cambridge, Mass.: MIT Press, 13–61.

(1989), "Politics and Business Cycles in Industrial Democracies," *Economic Policy*, 8, 55–98.

Alesina, A. and Summers, L. (1993), "Central Bank Independence and Macroeconomic Performance: Some Comparative Evidence," *Journal of Money, Credit, and Banking*, 25, 151–62.

Alogoskoufis, S. (1994), "On Inflation, Unemployment and the Optimal Exchange Rate Regime," in F. van der Ploeg (ed.), *Handbook of International Macroeconomics*, Oxford: Basil Blackwell, 192–223.

Barro, R. and Gordon, D. (1983a), "Rules, Discretion and Reputation in a Model of Monetary Policy," *Journal of Monetary Economics*, 12, 101–22.

(1983b), "A Positive Theory of Monetary Policy in a Natural Rate Model," *Journal of Political Economy*, 91, 589–610.

Bentler, P.M. (1982), "Linear Systems with Multiple Levels and Types of Latent Variables," in K.G. Zöreskog and H. Wold (eds.), *Systems Under Indirect Observations: Causality Structure, Prediction*, Part I, Amsterdam: North-Holland Publishing Co., Chapter 5, pp. 101–30.

Blanchard, O. and Summers, L. (1986), "Hysteresis and the European Unemployment Problem," in S. Fischer (ed.), *NBER Macroeconomics Annual*, Cambridge, Mass.: MIT Press.

Centre for Economic Policy Research (1993), "Independent and Accountable: A New Mandate for the Bank of England," A Report of an Independent Panel Chaired by Eric Roll.

Cukierman, A. (1992), *Central Bank Strategy, Credibility and Independence: Theory and Evidence*, Cambridge, Mass.: MIT Press.

(1994), "Commitment through Delegation, Political Influence and Central Bank Independence," in J. de Beaufort Wijnholds, S. Eijffinger, and L. Hoogduin (eds.), *A Framework for Monetary Stability*, Dordrecht/Boston/London: Kluwer Academic Publishers, 55–74.

Eijffinger, S. (1994), "A Framework for Monetary Stability – General Report," in J. de Beaufort Wijnholds, S. Eijffinger, and L. Hoogduin (eds.), *A Framework for Monetary Stability*, Dordrecht/Boston/London: Kluwer Academic Publishers.

Eijffinger, S. and de Haan, J. (1997), "The Political Economy of Central-Bank Independence," *Princeton Special Papers in International Economics*, No. 19, May, International Finance Section, Princeton: Princeton University Press.

Eijffinger, S., Hoeberichts M., and Schaling, E. (1995), "Optimal Conservativeness in the Rogoff (1985) Model: A Graphical and Closed-Form Solution," CentER Discussion Paper, Tilburg University, No. 95121.

Eijffinger, S. and Schaling, E. (1992), "Central Bank Independence: Criteria and Indices," Research Memorandum, Tilburg University, No. 548. Also published in *Kredit und Kapital*, Special Issue 13, 1995, 185–218.

(1993a), "Central Bank Independence in Twelve Industrial Countries," *Banca Nazionale del Lavoro Quarterly Review*, 184, 1–41.

(1993b), "Central Bank Independence: Theory and Evidence," CentER Discussion Paper, Tilburg University, No. 9325.

Eijffinger, S. and Van Keulen, M. (1995), "Central Bank Independence in Another Eleven Countries," *Banca Nazionale del Lavoro Quarterly Review*, 192, 39–83.

Fischer, S. (1977a), "Wage Indexation and Macroeconomic Stability," *Carnegie-Rochester Conference Series on Public Policy*, 5, 107–147.

(1994), "Modern Central Banking," in F. Capie, C. Goodhart, S. Fischer, and N. Schnadt, *The Future of Central Banking*, Cambridge: Cambridge University Press, 262–308.

Gray, J. (1976), "Wage Indexation: A Macroeconomic Approach" *Journal of Monetary Economics*, 2, 221–35.

Grilli, V., Masciandaro, D., and Tabellini, G. (1991), "Political and Monetary Institutions and Public Financial Policies in the Industrial Countries," *Economic Policy*, 13, 341–92.

de Haan, J. and Van't Hag, G. (1995), "Variation in Central Bank Independence across Countries: Some Provisional Empirical Evidence," *Public Choice*, 85, 335–51.

de Haan, J. and Sturm, J. (1992), "The Case for Central Bank Independence," *Banca Nazionale del Lavoro Quarterly Review*, 182, 305–27.

Issing, O. (1993), "Central Bank Independence and Monetary Stability," Institute of Economic Affairs, Occasional Paper No. 89.

Layard, R., Nickell, S., and Jackman, R. (1991), *Unemployment, Macroeconomic Performance and the Labour Market*, Oxford: Oxford University Press.

Lindbeck, A. and Snower, D. (1986), "Wage Setting, Unemployment and Insider-Outsider Relations," *American Economic Review, Papers and Proceedings*, 76, 235–9.

Lohmann, S. (1992), "Optimal Commitment in Monetary Policy: Credibility versus Flexibility," *American Economic Review*, 82, 273–86.

Neumann, M. (1991), "Precommitment by Central Bank Independence," *Open Economies Review*, 2, 95–112.

Persson, T. and Tabellini, G. (1993), "Designing Institutions for Monetary Stability," *Carnegie-Rochester Conference Series on Public Policy*, 39, 53–84.

Rogoff, K. (1985), "The Optimal Degree of Commitment to an Intermediate Monetary Target," *Quarterly Journal of Economics*, 100, 1169–90.

Walsh, C. (1995), "Optimal Contracts for Central Bankers", *American Economic Review*, 85, 150–167.

Comment

LEX HOOGDUIN

Eijffinger and Schaling (for the sake of brevity, I shall refer to them as ES) have written an interesting and stimulating chapter. For some years now, the literature has paid considerable attention to the measurement of central bank independence and to its relationship with other economic variables. Time therefore has come to look more closely at the factors that explain the degree of central bank independence. In their chapter, ES make an original contribution in this area. On the basis of a formal model, they derive four factors governing the optimal degree of central bank independence. Using the latent-variables method, they then estimate the relationship between the optimal degree of central bank independence and these variables for 19 countries. Finally, they compare the actual with the optimal degree of central bank independence. The estimation period is 1960–93.

The variable ϵ plays a crucial role in the model of ES. This variable measures, or is at any rate a proxy for, the degree of central bank independence. I am not convinced of this. ϵ indicates to what extent price stability carries more weight in the central bank's loss function than in the social loss function. The greater the value of the variable ϵ, the greater the degree of central bank independence. In my view, however, independence has primarily to do with the extent to which the central bank is able make decisions without government interference. That is not exactly measured by the variable ϵ. It is very well possible, as for instance in Germany and The Netherlands, that society and the central bank are about equally averse to inflation (in the terms of the model, ϵ is small), while the central bank is able to make decisions with a high degree of independence of the government.

Following the definition of ϵ, the optimal degree of central bank independence is lower, the more averse society is to inflation. Within the logic of the model, this is true. The model, however, does not do adequate justice to the historical context that prompted the establishment of an independent central bank, at least in several countries. The model implicitly assumes that society is able to understand the time-inconsistency problem fairly well. Practice, however, has shown that in a number of countries the government has been permitted to create hyperinflation. Such hyperinflation has induced a high degree of aversion to inflation in society, while at the same time leading to central bank independence. This suggests a positive – rather than a negative – relationship between the social degree of aversion to inflation and central bank independence. Stated in more general terms, past experiences with inflation and unemployment, to my mind, are a factor of major significance in explaining the institutional design of economic policy.

This leads me to suggest that it might be useful to supplement the formal approach adopted by ES with an historical approach. Besides serving as a source of inspiration for the formal approach, an historical approach may also make an independent contribution to our knowledge. The formal approach necessarily seems to involve a measure of rigidity. Can it, for instance, do adequate justice to differences between countries? In their analysis, ES lump all countries together and force them within the confines of one and the same model. Also, how sensitive are the model results to changes in the underlying assumptions (rational expectations, information structure, the introduction of lags, the elimination of the insider/outsider assumption in the labor market, etc.)? In part, one could counter the latter point by saying that this should be shown by further research. I am prepared to admit this, but I do wonder whether this will help us much. The number of formal models to be studied is very large, if at least one wishes to keep them manageable.

A difficulty which would appear to be inherent in the chosen approach is that it is not easy to see what variations in ϵ precisely mean for the concrete institutional design of the central bank. Or, more specifically, under what circumstances is the German model optimal and under what circumstances the British one? The estimates show, for instance, that the central banks of Germany and Switzerland are actually too independent. Which concrete measures might prompt a move towards the optimum? Are ES able to explain their empirical results in more concrete terms? They do not have to do so now, but do they see clues for fruitful further research in this area? Does the fact that the Bundesbank is too independent imply that the average German inflation rate over the period 1960–93 has been too low according to ES? But the average inflation rate was already higher than 2 per cent, the highest level considered to be compatible with price stability by the Bundesbank and other European central banks. Do the results of ES imply that price stability is generally not the correct objective of monetary policy, or does it merely imply that this objective though correct is unattainable? If the former is the case, I would be interested in a formal analysis of the optimal rate of inflation within the model of ES. If the latter is the case, the question of what this means for the credibility of the central bank and the monetary strategy arises.

Let me add an institutional question in this context. ES and others implicitly assume that the degree of central bank independence is a variable which allows for an exact dosage or, in other words, is more or less continuous. I wonder whether things are as simple as that in reality. Let me try to explain my problem by means of an example. It is sometimes argued that the central bank should, in principle, be independent, but that corrections on the part of the government must be possible in the event of supply shocks, since an independent central bank would then tend to pursue an unduly restrictive policy. In itself, this is logically correct. The problem though, is that often the nature of a shock will not be immediately apparent. The proposed institutional structure could thus lead to a situation where the government might abuse its powers. The time-inconsistency problem for which central bank independence seeks to provide a solution then resurfaces to make itself felt with full force. Doesn't the limited knowledge of economic reality which is available to both the government and the central bank call for the clearest possible institutional structure? The number of workable degrees of central bank independence might then turn out to be smaller than that assumed in models such as that of ES. In practice, the pursuit of an optimum might prove overly ambitious. What seems feasible and is highly important is to prevent major mishaps and to ensure a satisfactory economic development on average. If that is possible within an institutional structure with a highly independent central bank, I am prepared to accept that the central bank will not invariably be able to warrant the best outcome. Here, as in other fields, we must prevent the best from becoming the enemy of the good.

Finally, I would briefly say a few words about the empirical results of the model. I already touched upon this subject earlier and shall keep things brief here, as I am not enough of an expert in the estimation methods used to provide any well-founded assessment. I would suggest, however, that others who are more familiar with the techniques used should undertake this task, as the estimation results do not make a very robust impression. In all fairness, I must add that this is not claimed by ES. Is it not true, nonetheless, that their empirical results prompt them to draw conclusions which may go beyond what is justified?

4 Central bank autonomy and exchange rate regimes – their effects on monetary accommodation and activism

ALEX CUKIERMAN, PEDRO RODRIGUEZ, and STEVEN B. WEBB

1 Introduction

Policy makers usually adjust the money supply in response to various developments in order to achieve several objectives such as a high level of economic activity, maintenance of the real exchange rate within a desired range, and price stability. The relative importance assigned to alternative objectives is one of the factors affecting the magnitude and the direction of the response of the money supply to various economic developments. For example, if policy makers are mostly concerned with economic activity and employment, they are likely to, at least partially, accommodate recent wage increases. By contrast, if they are concerned mostly with price stability they are likely to "lean against the wind" by reducing money supply growth in response to accelerations in wage inflation. If they are concerned mostly with international competitiveness and the level of the real exchange rate they are likely to loosen the money supply in response to increases in foreign prices. However, if they are concerned mostly with price stability they may actually reduce money growth in response to increases in foreign inflation.

Countries with central banks that have a clear mandate to focus on price stability, and which are relatively independent from political authorities, are therefore more likely to lean against both domestic and foreign inflationary impulses by making money growth independent of those impulses – or even by reducing money growth in response to increases in domestic wage inflation or foreign price inflation. Following recent literature, we refer to central banks with more authority and a clearer mandate to focus on price stability as more independent.[1] Such considerations lead us to expect that there might be systematic links between the coefficients of the monetary policy reaction function and the degree of central bank autonomy. *Actual* monetary policy, in many cases, is the result of a compromise between the objectives of the political authorities and those of the central bank (CB). The less independent is the CB, the more likely it is that the objective of price stability has lower priority and that actual policy is more accommodative, as well as more activist.

The degree of accommodation, and the monetary policy reaction function generally, is also likely to be influenced by the exchange rate regime in effect. For example, a serious commitment to a fixed exchange rate, as under the Bretton Wood system, is likely to reduce the degree of accommodation in comparison to a flexible rate. Evidence presented in Alogoskoufis and Smith (1991) and in Alogoskoufis (1992) suggests that inflation persists more under flexible exchange rate regimes than under fixed rates. Since more accommodative policies lead to more inflation persistence, this finding is consistent with the view that monetary policy is more accommodative under flexible than under fixed rates of exchange.

The main objective of this chapter is to determine empirically whether accommodation and the degree of policy activism differ systematically across countries with different degrees of central bank independence (CBI) and different types of exchange rate regimes. This is done in two stages. First reaction functions and response coefficients are estimated in each country by running time series regressions. The resulting monetary policy response coefficients are then related to CBI and the type of exchange rate regime. One novelty of the chapter is that it allows for the possibility that the effects of institutions on the accommodation of domestic wage inflation and of foreign inflation are different.

The short-run impact of high-powered monetary expansion on economic activity, inflation, and the real exchange rate depends on the type of exchange rate regime and also on whether there is perfect or imperfect substitutability between domestic and foreign currency denominated assets. With perfect substitutability (and fixed rates), sterilized intervention is ineffective. Hence, policy makers cannot pick the rate of monetary expansion and the nominal exchange rate independently and they have essentially only one monetary policy instrument. With imperfect substitutability, however, authorities can, at least for a while, choose the two variables independently, by using sterilized interventions in the foreign exchange market to offset the effects of monetary expansion on the nominal rate. Since our sample includes countries which are likely to be in the first group (such as the US, the UK and Japan), as well as countries which are likely to be in the second group (like Italy and Spain) it is necessary to distinguish between perfect and imperfect asset substitutability.[2]

Although the main focus of the paper is empirical, it is instructive to interpret the policy response coefficients in a conceptual framework in which policy makers try to achieve their objectives. Given these objectives, policy reaction functions depend on the type of exchange rate regime as well as on whether sterilized interventions are effective or ineffective. The paper, accordingly, presents a conceptual framework in which policy reaction functions depend on the type of exchange rate regime and on the effectiveness of sterilized interventions.

The conceptual framework is presented in section 2. The data and the estimation of country specific reaction functions for 17 industrialized countries are presented in section 3. Evidence on the relations between accommodation and policy activism on one hand, and CBI and type of exchange rate regime on the other is presented in section 4. This is followed by concluding remarks.

2 An organizational framework for the interpretation of monetary reaction functions

This section presents an organizing framework for interpreting monetary policy reaction functions in four cases:

Flexible rate (or dirty float) under perfect substitutability;

Fixed peg under perfect substitutability;

Flexible rate (or dirty float) under imperfect substitutability;

Fixed peg under imperfect substitutability.

We postulate that, given the relevant institutional constraints, monetary and exchange rate policies are chosen so as to minimize the following cost function

$$\frac{A}{2}[N^* - N]^2 + \frac{B}{2}[r^* - r]^2 + \frac{1}{2}(\pi^p)^2 \tag{1}$$

Here, N and N^* are the (current) actual and desired levels of employment, r and r^* are the (current) actual and desired levels of the real exchange rate and π^p is the rate of inflation in the basket of goods purchased by domestic residents. The real exchange rate is measured as the ratio of the price of domestically produced goods to that of foreign goods where both are denominated in terms of a common currency. Hence, an increase in r corresponds to an appreciation of the real exchange rate as in the IMF definition.[3]

The parameter A reflects the relative emphasis of policy on achievement of the economic activity objective versus price stability. The higher is A the stronger is the relative emphasis of policy on the first objective. The parameter B reflects the emphasis of policy on achieving real exchange rate objectives in comparison to price stability. The higher is B the larger the relative emphasis of policy on the real exchange rate objective. The objective function in equation (1) should be viewed as the outcome of policy inputs by *both* the CB and political authorities. The level of CBI is expected therefore to affect the size of the parameters A and B. In particular, we hypothesize that the larger is CBI the lower is A.[4]

We now turn to the structure of the economy which is characterized by a short-run Phillips curve due to wage contracts of the Fischer–Taylor type; the relation of π^p to inflation of domestically and foreign-produced goods; the relation of prices of domestically produced goods to wage inflation (high-powered) money growth; changes in foreign prices and the exchange rate; and a relation between the rate of change in the (nominal) exchange rate; on the one hand, and sterilized and unsterilized interventions, on the other. The short-run Phillips curve is given by

$$N-N_{-1}=\alpha_d(\pi-w_{-1})+\alpha_f(\pi^*+e-w_{-1})+\epsilon \tag{2}$$

where π and π^* are the rates of inflation in domestically produced, and in foreign goods respectively, w is the rate of increase in wages, e is the rate of change in the domestic currency price of foreign exchange, and α_d and α_f are non-negative parameters. A minus one subscript designates a one-period lag. Unsubscripted variables refer to current values. Equation (2) states that the over time change in the level of employment is positively related to the difference between the rate of inflation in the prices of domestic goods and last period wage inflation and to the difference between the rate of inflation in the (domestic currency) price of foreign goods and last period wage inflation.

The lag on wage inflation captures the effect of Fischer (1977) – Taylor (1980) type contractual elements of wage formation on employment. Given last period's wage settlements, increases in either domestic or foreign prices raise current employment by raising profit margins on production for domestic uses as well as for exports.[5] ϵ captures changes in employment which are unrelated to changes in profit margins due to changes in real wages. We assume that ϵ is a white noise process.

The rate of inflation in the cost of goods used by domestic residents is a weighted average of the rate of inflation in domestically produced goods and of the rate of inflation in the (home currency) cost of imported foreign goods. This relationship is given by

$$\pi^p=\gamma(\pi^*+e)+(1-\gamma)\pi, \quad 0\le\gamma\le1 \tag{3}$$

The rate of inflation in prices of domestically produced goods is affected both by cost-push and by demand-pull elements. This is formalized by the following equation

$$\pi=\delta_2\mu+\delta_1 w_{-1}+\delta_3(\pi^*+e),\quad 0\leq\delta_i\leq1 \tag{4}$$

where μ is the rate of growth of high-powered money. The effect of μ reflects the influence of demand-pull on the prices of home goods. The second and third terms reflect the effects of increases in costs on the rate of inflation. The first term reflects the effect of wages and the last term reflects the effect of increases in the cost of imported intermediate inputs. (This effect has been stressed by Dornbusch (1982) in the context of exchange rate rules.) The lag on wages reflects the presumption that prices adjust to changes in domestic costs with a lag – which in the empirical work is a semester. This specification is at least partly adopted to avoid reverse causality – from money growth to wage inflation.

We turn next to the specification of the relationship between the rate of change in the nominal exchange rate and the rate of change in relevant financial stocks. The general relationship is

$$e=\theta f+\psi\mu-\psi^*\mu^*+e_p, \psi,\psi^*>0, \theta\geq0 \tag{5}$$

where μ^* is a vector of rates of expansion of high powered money in "relevant" other countries,[6] f is the rate at which the CB engages in sterilized purchases of foreign exchange, and e_p is the rate of change in the exchange rate that would have materialized in the absence of either sterilized or unsterilized interventions of any kind. We assume that e_p is a white noise process. Under perfect substitutability of financial assets $\theta=0$ and only unsterilized (domestic or foreign) interventions affect the (nominal) exchange rate. In the presence of some substitutability between domestic and foreign financial assets $\theta>0$ and policy makers have the ability to affect the nominal exchange rate even by relying only on sterilized interventions.

Other things being equal, the real exchange r depreciates (r goes down) when foreign prices and the nominal exchange rate increase. It appreciates (r goes up) when domestic prices go up. We approximate this relation by[7]

$$r-r_{-1}=\beta(\pi-\pi^*-e) \tag{6}$$

3 Policy choices with a flexible rate or a dirty float under perfect substitutability

Perfect substitutability of domestic and foreign currency denominated assets ($\theta=0$) implies, via equation (5) that the choice of money base growth fully determines the nominal exchange rate given e_p and μ^*. Hence the choice of π by home policy makers affects their objective function both directly as well as through the effect that base money expansion has on nominal depreciation or appreciation. We assume that in choosing π they take all channels into account. Formally, the choice of base money expansion is obtained by minimizing equation (1) subject to the constraints in equations (2) through (6) and the perfect substitutability condition, $\theta=0$. Substituting the constraints into the objective function we obtain the following problem

$$\min_{\mu} \frac{A}{2}[s_{-1}-\alpha_d(\pi-w_{-1})-\alpha_f(\pi^*+e_p+\psi\mu-\psi^*\mu^*)-w_{-1}-\epsilon]^2$$

$$+\frac{B}{2}[r_{-1}-r^*+\beta(\pi-\pi^*-[e_p+\psi\mu-\psi\mu^*])]^2+\frac{1}{2}[(\gamma+(1-\gamma)\delta_3)$$

$$(\pi^*+e_p+\psi\mu-\psi^*\mu)+(1-\delta)\delta_1w_{-1}+(1-\gamma)\delta_2u]^2 \tag{7}$$

where

$$s_{-1}\equiv N^*-N_{-1} \tag{8}$$

Differentiating with respect to π, equating to zero and rearranging we obtain the reaction function of policy makers for the case of a flexible rate under perfect substitutability

$$\mu=\frac{1}{D}\left\{ \begin{array}{c} [AK_1(\alpha_f+(1-\delta_1)\alpha_d)-B\beta^2\delta_1K_2-K_3(1-\gamma)\delta_1]w_{-1} \\[2mm] +[-AK_1K_4+B\beta^2K_2-K_3K_5]\pi^*+AK_1(s_{-1}-\epsilon)+B\beta K_2(r^*-r_{-1}) \\[2mm] +[AK_1K_4+B\beta^2K_2(1-\delta_3)+K_3K_5]\psi^*\mu^*+K_6e_p \end{array} \right\} \tag{9}$$

where

$D \equiv AK_1^2+B\beta^2K_2^2+K_3^2.$
$K_1\equiv\alpha_d\delta_2+[\alpha_d\delta_3+\alpha_f]\psi.$
$K_2\equiv\delta_2-(1-\delta_3)\psi.$
$K_3\equiv[\gamma+(1-\gamma)\delta_3]\psi+(1-\gamma)\delta_2.$
$K_4\equiv\alpha_d\delta_3+\alpha_f.$
$K_5\equiv\gamma+(1-\gamma)\delta_3.$

Note that except for K_2 all the combinations of parameters are positive. K_2 is probably positive, since the direct effects of money growth on prices (δ_2) and on the exchange rate (ψ) would be of about the same magnitude, leaving the indirect effect of money on domestic prices through the exchange rate ($\delta_3\psi$) to make the whole expression positive. The explicit forms of K_6 is not displayed since it has no importance for the rest of the discussion. The coefficients of the variables on the right-hand side of equation (9) are response coefficients. Each of them characterizes the response of high-powered money expansion to the appropriate right-hand variable.

The coefficient of w_{-1}, when it is positive, measures the tendency of monetary authorities to accommodate wages. However, a glance at this coefficient reveals it is not necessarily positive. It is positive if policy makers have a high concern for achieving their employment objective (A is high), and it is negative if they are mostly concerned with price stability (A and B are small). In the first case they accommodate wage inflation, and in the second they lean against it.

The effect on the response coefficient of wages of the relative emphasis of policy on real exchange rate objectives (B) is generally ambiguous. The reason for this is that an increase in μ has two opposing effects on the real exchange rate, r. On the one hand, by raising the domestic rate of inflation π, an increase in μ raises the real exchange rate. On the other hand, by accelerating the rate of depreciation of the nominal exchange rate e, it lowers the real exchange rate. To the extent that in the short run the effect of μ through financial markets dominates its direct effect on domestic inflation, an increase in μ causes a real depreciation (r goes down), and K_2 is negative. In this case, a relatively strong emphasis on real exchange rate objectives reinforces the tendency to accommodate wages. However, when the direct effect of μ on domestic inflation dominates the indirect effect through the exchange rate, a relatively strong emphasis on real exchange rate objectives weakens the tendency to accommodate wages ($K_2>0$ in this case).

The coefficient of foreign inflation, π^*, is likely to be negative. Note that both the price stability motive and the employment motive contribute to this negative sign. The intuition underlying the first effect is obvious; concern for price stability induces policy makers to lean against foreign inflation. The contribution of employment is negative because, other things being equal, an increase in foreign prices raises domestic employment by raising profit margins of exporters. As a consequence, the urge to stimulate employment by means of monetary expansion diminishes.

The coefficient of lagged unemployment, s_{-1}, is positive and larger the larger is the relative emphasis of policy on employment considerations. It reflects the well-known Barro-Gordon inflationary bias.[8] The (absolute value of the) coefficient of the discrepancy in the previous period, between the desired and the actual real exchange rate is larger, the larger is B. Its sign depends on K_2. When K_2 is negative, a larger discrepancy is associated with a lower rate of monetary expansion, since an increase in μ reduces the real exchange rate. Monetary expansion in other countries is likely to cause home monetary expansion. Domestic policy makers tend to accommodate foreign monetary expansion in this case, even if they lean against foreign inflation.

3.1 Policy choices under a peg and perfect substitutability

Perfect substitutability ($\theta=0$) implies via equation (5) that the choice of money base expansion fully determines the nominal exchange rate, given e_p and μ^*. With the exchange rate pegged ($e=0$)μ has to be chosen so as to maintain it fixed. It follows from equation (5) that

$$\mu=\frac{1}{\psi}[\psi^*\mu^*-e_p] \tag{10}$$

Hence, under a peg with perfect substitutability there is no accommodation of, nor leaning against, wage and foreign price inflation. However, *there is* accommodation of foreign money growth.

3.2 Policy choices under a peg and imperfect substitutability

With imperfect substitutability ($\theta>0$) the fixed peg ($e=0$) can be maintained for any given rate of monetary expansion, by appropriate choice of sterilized interventions (f) in the foreign exchange market.[9] It follows from (5) that

$$f=\frac{1}{\theta}[\psi^*\mu^*-\psi\mu-e_p] \tag{11}$$

This leaves the rate of growth of high-powered money free for the minimization of the objective function in equation (1). Using the constraints in equations (2) through (6) and the constraint $e=0$ in equation (1) we obtain

$$\min_{\mu}\frac{A}{2}s_{-1}-\alpha_d[\delta_1 w_{-1}+\delta_2\mu+\delta_3\pi^*-w_{-1}-\alpha_f(\pi^*-w_{-1})-\epsilon]^2$$

$$+\frac{B}{2}[r_{-1}-r^*+\beta(\delta_1 w_{-1}+\delta_2\mu+\delta_3\pi^*-\pi^*)]^2+\frac{1}{2}[\gamma\pi^*+$$

$$(1-\gamma)(d_1 w_{-1}+\delta_2\mu+\delta_3\pi^*)] \tag{12}$$

After rearrangement the first-order condition for this problem yields the following reaction function:[10]

$$\mu=\frac{1}{D'}\left\{\begin{matrix}[A\alpha_d(\alpha_f+(1-\delta_1)\alpha_d)-B\beta^2\delta_1-(1-\gamma)[\gamma+(1-\gamma)\delta_3]]w_{-1}\\ -[-A\alpha_d(\alpha_d\delta_3+\alpha_f)+B\beta^2-(1-\gamma)[\gamma+\\ (1-\gamma)\delta_3]]\pi^*+A\alpha_d(s_{-1}-\epsilon)+B\beta(r^*-r_{-1})\end{matrix}\right\} \tag{13}$$

where

$$D' \equiv \delta_2(A\alpha^2_d + B\beta^2 + (1-\gamma)^2) > 0 \tag{14}$$

The main difference between this reaction function and the one in equation (9), for perfect substitutability, is that the parameters ψ and ψ^* and the variable e_p do not appear in it. The reason is that under a peg and imperfect substitutability their values are of no consequence since (as is clear from equation (11)) their effects on μ are neutralized by appropriate choice of f.

Examination of the reaction function in equation (13) reveals that, as was the case under a flexible rate with perfect substitutability, policy makers are more likely to accommodate wages the larger is A. However, unlike in that case, a larger B makes it more likely that policy makers will lean against wage inflation since now an increase in μ raises the real exchange rate – as does wage inflation. Hence a higher concern for the real exchange rate is associated with a stronger effort to offset the effect of wages on the real exchange rate by means of a lower rate of monetary expansion. Thus, *ceteris paribus*, the coefficient of lagged wage inflation is more likely to be negative under a peg with imperfect substitutability than under a flexible rate with perfect substitutability.

If B is sufficiently large in comparison to A, the coefficient of foreign inflation is positive. Foreign inflation reduces the real exchange rate and, under a peg with imperfect substitutability, base growth increases it. This induces an accommodative pattern between μ and π^*. This accommodative tendency rises with the relative concern of policy for achieving its real exchange rate objective. As was the case under a flexible rate with perfect substitutability, the coefficient of unemployment is positive reflecting a Barro-Gordon inflationary bias. However, the coefficient of $r^* - r_{-1}$ is now unambiguously positive since an increase in μ induces a real appreciation by raising domestic prices.

An important feature of the reaction function for a peg under imperfect substitutability is that base expansion *does not* depend on the rates of base expansion in other countries. The reason obviously is that this link is neutralized by means of sterilized interventions that maintain the nominal exchange rate at a fixed parity.

3.3 Policy choices under a flexible rate and imperfect substitutability

With a flexible exchange rate and imperfect substitutability of assets ($\theta > 0$) base growth, μ, and the rate of nominal depreciation, e, can be chosen independently by appropriate choice of sterilized interventions, f (see (5)). It follows that policy makers have two instruments for achieving their objectives, μ and e.[11] Using the constraints in equations (2) through (6) in equation (1) we obtain the following problem for this case

$$\min_{\mu,e} \frac{A}{2}[s_{-1}-\alpha_d(\pi-w_{-1})-\alpha_f(\pi^*+e-w_{-1})-\epsilon]^2+\frac{B}{2}$$

$$[r_{-1}-r^*+\beta(\pi-\pi^*)-e]^2+\frac{1}{2}[\gamma(\pi^*+e)+(1-\gamma)\pi]^2 \tag{15}$$

Differentiating with respect to μ and e, equating each of those first-order conditions to 0 and solving for μ we obtain (after substantial algebra) the following reaction function

$$\mu=\frac{1}{\delta_2 D''}\left\{\begin{array}{c}[AB\beta^2(\alpha_d+\alpha_f)(1-\delta_1-\delta_3)+\\ A[\gamma\alpha_d-(1-\gamma)\alpha_f][\delta_1\alpha_f+\{[1-\delta_1-\delta_3]\gamma+\delta_3\}\{\alpha_d+\alpha_f\}]\\ +B\beta^2\delta_1((1-2\gamma)[\gamma+(1-\gamma)\delta_3]]w_{-1}\\ +A[(\gamma+(1-\gamma)\delta_3)(\gamma\alpha_d-(1-\gamma)\alpha_f)+B\beta^2(1-\delta_3)(\alpha_d+\alpha_f)]\\ (s_{-1}-\epsilon)+B\beta^2[A(\alpha_d\delta_3+\alpha_f)(\alpha_d+\alpha_f)+\gamma+(1-\gamma)\delta_3](r^*-r_{-1})\end{array}\right\} \tag{16}$$

where

$$D''\equiv A[\gamma\alpha_d-(1-\gamma)\alpha_f]^2+B\beta^2[1+A(\alpha_d+\alpha_f)^2] \tag{17}$$

As was the case under a fixed exchange rate with imperfect substitutability, foreign rates of monetary base expansion do not appear in the reaction function. The reason is the same. Any undesired effect of foreign monetary expansion on the nominal exchange rate is offset by appropriate sterilized interventions in the foreign exchange market. Contrary to the case of a fixed peg, however, foreign inflation also does not enter into the reaction function. The intuitive reason is that now nominal exchange rate changes offset any effect of foreign inflation on the sum π^*+e.

Examination of equation (16) reveals that the coefficient of lagged wages is likely to be (but is not necessarily) positive. A sufficient (but not necessary) condition for accommodation of wages by policy makers is

$$\frac{\gamma}{1-\gamma}>\frac{\alpha_f}{\alpha_d} \tag{18}$$

This condition states that the weight of foreign inflation, relative to that of domestic inflation in the cost of goods used by domestic residents, is larger than the ratio of the effects on unemployment (equation (2)) of foreign inflation and of domestic inflation.

Contrary to all other cases, the coefficient of $s_{-1}-\epsilon$ is not necessarily positive, although that seems to be likely. Equation (18) is a sufficient (but not necessary) condition for this to be the case. Finally the coefficient of r^*-r_{-1} is positive. Positive discrepancies between the desired and the lagged actual real exchange rate are accommodated. The reason is that any effects of μ on objectives via e are neutralized by means of sterilized interventions in the foreign exchange market, leaving only the direct effect of μ on the real exchange rate. This raises the rate of inflation in the price of domestically produced goods, thereby pushing the real exchange rate upward.

3.4 The effect of central bank independence on the accommodation of wages

A commonly held view is that the central bank is relatively more concerned with price stability than the central government or the treasury. This view implies that the paramter A in equation (1) is lower the higher the degree of CBI. A fuller exposition of this hypothesis and its bases appears in chapter 18 of Cukierman (1992). The main message of this sub-section is that, under plausible conditions, the tendency to accommodate wages is stronger the higher is A.[12] In conjunction with the hypothesis above, this implies that the degree of accommodation of wages and CBI are inversely related.

3.5 Summary of qualitative implications

Table 4.1 summarizes the main qualitative implications for policy reaction functions under alternative exchange rate regimes and alternative assumptions about the effectiveness of (sterilized) interventions.

The simplest case is pegged with perfect substitutability of foreign and domestic assets; in this case domestic money accommodates only foreign money growth and leans against random shocks to the exchange rate. With a floating rate and perfect substitutability, the latter two relations hold, and, in addition, the domestic monetary authorities can accommodate or lean against the effects of lagged wages, the lagged real exchange rate, unemployment, and foreign inflation. With imperfect substitutability, the need to accommodate foreign money growth and exchange market shocks is less or even zero with either pegged or floating rates. Finally with a float there is also no need to react to foreign inflation.

Importantly, table 4.1 suggests that money growth does not react to foreign rates of monetary expansion when sterilized interventions are effective. The reason is that, in this case, the effects of foreign rates of monetary expansion on objectives is offset by means of sterilized interventions alone.

4 Estimation of country specific reaction functions

This section presents estimates of monetary reaction functions for seventeen industrial economies. Since (at least initially) we do not know whether

Table 4.1 *Summary of qualitative implications*

Degree of substitutability Exchange rate regime	No effective sterilized interventions (perfect substitutability)	Effective sterilized interventions (imperfect substitutability)
Flexible or dirty float	1 C of $w_{-1}>0$ for sufficiently large $A-s$ and $B-s$ provided $K_2<0$.	1 C of $w_{-1}>0$ under condition (18) and $\gamma<1/2$ or a sufficiently small B.
	2 C of $\pi^*<0$ if $K_2<0$.	2 C of $\pi^*=0$.
	3 C of $s_{-1}-\epsilon>0$.	3 C of $s_{-1}-\epsilon>0$ under condition (18) or for a sufficiently large B.
	4 C of $r_{-1}>0$ if $K_2<0$.	4 C of $r_{-1}<0$.
	5 C of $\psi^*\mu^*>0$ if $K_2<0$.	5 C of $\psi^*\mu^*=0$.
	6 C of $e_p<0$ if $K_2<0$.	6 C of $e_p=0$.
Peg	1 C of $w_{-1}=0$.	1 C of $w_{-1}<0$ for sufficiently small $A-s$ and large $B-s$.
	2 C of $\pi^*=0$.	2 C of $\pi^*<0$ for sufficiently large $A-s$ and small $B-s$.
	3 C of $s_{-1}-\epsilon=0$.	3 C of $s_{-1}-\epsilon>0$.
	4 C of $r_{-1}=0$.	4 C of $r_{-1}<0$.
	5 C of $\psi^*\mu^*>0$.	5 C of $\psi^*\mu^*=0$.
	6 C of $e_p<0$.	6 C of $e_p=0$.

Note: C=coefficient.

sterilized interventions are, or are not, effective we estimate two alternative sets of reaction functions.[13] One – which corresponds to the first case – includes foreign rates of monetary expansion along with the other variables as regressors. The other – which corresponds to the second case – constrains the coefficients of foreign rates of monetary expansion to zero.

4.1 Sample and data

Monetary reaction functions were estimated for seventeen industrial economies from the mid seventies to the end of the eighties using semi-annual data. For most countries the sample period is from the second semester of 1975 to the second semester of 1990.[14] The sample period is largely dictated by the availability of data.

The semi-annual rate of base money growth is calculated as the rate of expansion of average quarterly levels, between quarter t and quarter $t - 2$, of reserve money from the International Monetary Fund, *International Financial Statistics* (IFS).[15] The real exchange rate is also from the IFS. The IMF defines it as the ratio between an index of domestic prices and a weighted average of foreign prices, where both are expressed in terms of a common currency. This definition implies that an increase in the index corresponds to a real appreciation and a decrease to a real depreciation. The IFS provide a number of such indices based on alternative measures of domestic and foreign prices. We experimented with measures that are based on unit labor costs, normalized unit labor costs, and export unit values. Since the results are broadly insensitive to the choice of index, all the empirical results are for real exchange rates in terms of a single measure – the real exchange rate in terms of export unit values. A rise (fall) in the index corresponds to a loss (gain) in competitiveness. The weights of foreign prices are derived from the share of each country in total manufacturing exports.[16] The original data are quarterly. Semi-annual observations are simple averages of the quarterly observations. In line with the discussion of the previous section the lagged value of this variable is entered as a regressor.

Foreign price inflation is proxied by the rate of inflation in the weighted average of the export unit values of these countries. The *level* of this variable in terms of domestic currency is obtained by dividing domestic export unit values in local currency by the real exchange rate. This level is then used to calculate a semi-annual rate of inflation for the same periods as the measure of the rate of expansion of high-powered money. The resulting expression reflects changes in foreign prices as well as changes in nominal exchange rates. Since the final proxy required should reflect only foreign prices we subtract from it a weighted average of semi-annual changes in nominal exchange rates between the home currency and "relevant" foreign currencies. This separation follows from the theoretical framework in which the nominal exchange rate is a choice variable of domestic policy makers whereas foreign price inflation is taken as given by them. The choice of "relevant" foreign currencies and their weights is judgemental and varies from country to country. The weights used appear in part 1 of the appendix.

The divergence between desired and actual employment is proxied by the rate of unemployment except in the case of France for which, due to data problems, vacancies are used instead. Since the original data are quarterly, semi-annual observations are obtained as averages of quarterly observations.[17] To avoid problems of reverse causality and in line with the conceptual framework of section 2, these variables are entered with a one period lag.

The original data on nominal wages are in quarterly levels.[18] Semi-annual increases in wages are obtained by first averaging the levels of the two quarterly observations within each semester and by calculating semi-annual rates of increase between these averages.

4.2 Estimation of reaction functions without foreign reserve money growth

All reaction functions were estimated by ordinary least squares. Most country regressions are based on 30 semi-annual observations. Results are summarized in table 4.2. Constant terms of the reaction functions in equations (13) and (15) like r^* are implicitly incorporated into the regression constants, and white noise shocks like ϵ into the regression residuals.

A quick look at the table suggests that more often than not response coefficients are not significant. In some cases, as for Sweden and the UK, the goodness of fit is very poor and none of the coefficients is significant.[19] The significant coefficients do, however, provide relevant information. It is instructive to focus on the coefficient of one regressor at a time and to compare it across countries.

The response to wage inflation is significant in France, Belgium, Germany, Austria, and Finland. But it is positive in the first two countries and negative in the remaining three. Thus, while France and Belgium accommodate recent wage inflation, monetary authorities in Germany, Austria, and Finland consistently lean against it. By interpreting those coefficients in terms of the conceptual framework of section 2 it is possible to learn something from these findings about the relative emphasis of policy in those countries. Most if not all of them maintained fixed pegs during the sample period. The coefficients of wage inflation are therefore interpretable in terms of equation (13). This equation suggests that countries whose policy makers have a strong concern for employment (large A) will accommodate past wage inflation. Countries with a relatively high concern for price stability (low A) and/or relatively high concern for foreign competitiveness (high B) will lean against wage inflation by reducing monetary growth in reaction to accelerations in wage inflation. These findings are therefore consistent with the view that policy makers in France and Belgium have put a stronger emphasis on employment while policy makers in Germany, Austria, and Finland have shown more concern for price stability and/or external competitiveness.

Turning to the countries with significant foreign inflation coefficients, we note that the US and Spain accommodate foreign inflation, whereas Switzerland and Denmark lean against it. Since they have maintained fixed pegs the coefficients of Spain and Denmark are interpretable in terms of equation (13). The positive Spanish coefficient is consistent with the view that Spanish policy makers were concerned mostly with the maintenance of foreign competitiveness. The negative Danish coefficient is consistent with the view that Danish policy makers were concerned mostly with price stability and/or employment. The interpretation of the US and of the Swiss coefficients is more problematic. Their currencies float and their financial assets are likely to be characterized by perfect substitutability. These coefficients are therefore potentially interpretable in terms of equation (9). But perfect substitutability requires the presence of foreign rates of reserve money expansion (μ^*) as regressors. Those rates do not appear in table 4.2. Below, we discuss the responses to foreign price inflation in the US and in Switzerland.[20]

The coefficient of the real exchange rate is significant and positive in Germany and significant and negative in Finland. In view of equation (13) this is consistent with the conclusion that the negative Finnish coefficient is due to a high concern for international competitiveness. The positive German coefficient is inconsistent with the underlying presumptions of equation (13) which are perfect substitutability and a fixed peg.[21]

The negative and significant coefficient of vacancies in France yields further support to the view that its policy makers emphasize employment considerations. The significantly negative coefficient of unemployment in Italy is not interpretable within the framework of the reaction function in equation (13).

4.3 Reaction functions with foreign reserve money growth

An important implication of the conceptual framework in section 2 is that, under perfect substitutability, monetary reaction functions depend on foreign rates of monetary expansion. To allow for this possibility the rates of reserve money expansion of some key currencies are added as regressors to the equations in table 4.2. To be consistent with the procedure used to calculate foreign price inflation, only the foreign rates of expansion of key currencies that have non zero weights in part 1 of the appendix are entered as regressors.[22] The equations in table 4.2 are then re-estimated by least squares. The results appear in table 4.3.

The addition of foreign rates of monetary expansion to reaction functions is particularly important for countries that are likely to be characterized by perfect or near perfect substitutability. Obvious candidates are the US, the UK, Germany, Japan, Switzerland, and Canada. This conjecture is partially supported because (except for Germany) the addition of foreign reserve expansion results in a substantial improvement in the goodness of

Table 4.2 Policy reaction functions without feedbacks from foreign reserve money growth[a]

(Dependent variable: domestic reserve money growth (μ))

Country	Constant	Wage inflation -lagged (w_{-1})	Foreign inflation (π^*)	Real exchange rate-lagged (r_{-1})	Unemployment lagged (s_{-1})	$\bar{R}^2$	DW
Japan	-0.29 0.115	-0.34 0.573	0.03 0.666	0.00 0.138	0.04 0.249	0.12	2.7
Switzerland	0.13 0.778	1.64 0.148	-0.40* 0.109	-0.00 0.736	0.07 0.490	0.15	1.9
Sweden	-0.08 0.876	-0.16 0.847	-0.22 0.439	0.00 0.710	-0.01 0.711	-0.11	2.5
Denmark	2.12 0.267	-3.81 0.492	-1.85* 0.103	-0.01 0.352	-0.06 0.296	0.03	1.9
Canada	-0.07 0.450	0.05 0.930	-0.04 0.790	0.00 0.394	0.00 0.675	-0.04	2.6
USA	0.07 0.150	-0.32 0.432	0.11** 0.040	-0.00 0.632	-0.00 0.897	0.03	2.9
UK[c]	-0.70 0.936	-1.45 0.511	0.07 0.854	0.00 0.871	0.00 0.791	-0.22	2.8
Austria	0.014 0.882	-0.26** 0.000	-0.12 0.437	0.00 0.639	-0.01 0.127	0.42	2.6
Finland	1.45* 0.068	-2.64** 0.042	-0.21 0.731	-0.11* 0.092	-0.02 0.542	0.15	2.4
Germany	-0.24 0.115	-1.62** 0.031	-0.09 0.248	0.00** 0.240	0.00 0.785	0.21	1.8

Table 4.2 (*continued*)

Country DW	Constant	Wage inflation − lagged (w_{-1})	Foreign inflation (π^*)	Real exchange rate-lagged (r_{-1})	Unemployment lagged (s_{-1})	$\bar{R}^2$	
Belgium	0.03	0.77**	−0.01	−0.00	−0.00	0.19	2.5
	0.823	0.026	0.956	0.818	0.683		
France[b]	−0.06	1.06**	−0.00	0.00	−0.00*	0.22	2.4
	0.776	0.004	0.986	0.640	0.063		
Ireland	0.02	−0.57	0.02	0.00	−0.01	−0.03	2.9
	0.969	0.331	0.940	0.708	0.174		
Netherlands	0.22	0.63	0.33	−0.00	0.00	−0.02	2.6
	0.141	0.352	0.146	0.173	0.363		
Italy	−0.07	−0.18	−0.00	0.00	−0.01*	0.20	2.0
	0.619	0.264	0.955	0.139	0.015		
Norway	0.12	−0.49	0.11	−0.00	−0.02	0.01	3.4
	0.520	0.250	0.755	0.933	0.135		
Spain	0.71	0.08	1.25**	−0.01	0.01	0.10	2.0
	0.546	0.763	0.038	0.435	0.720		

Notes:

[a] The first number in each cell is the coefficient and the second number is its significance level. The typical regression is based on 30 semi-annual observations except for Spain (22), the UK (20), and Switzerland (14).

[b] Vacancies are used instead of unemployment.

[c] μ is calculated from end of period stocks.

* Significant at about the 10 percent level or more but not more than 5 percent.

** Significant at the 5 percent level or more.

Table 4.3 *Policy reaction functions without feedbacks from foreign reserve money growth, least-squares estimation*[a]

(Dependent variable: domestic reserve money growth (μ))

Country	Constant	Wage inflation – lagged (w_{-1})	Foreign inflation (π^*)	Real exchange rate – lagged (r_{-1})	Unemployment – lagged (s_{-1})	Rates of reserve expansion DM	Yen	$	£	$\bar{R}^2$	DW
Japan	-0.15 0.309	-0.55 0.246	0.03 0.635	0.00 0.240	0.00 0.937	0.38** 0.027		0.70** 0.017		0.47	2.4
Switzerland	0.91** 0.001	-0.32 0.437	0.047 0.635	-0.01** 0.001	0.13** 0.002	1.64** 0.003		1.23** 0.021		0.95	1.6
Sweden	-0.11 0.827	-0.05 0.956	-0.17 0.565	0.00 0.753	-0.00 0.927	0.33 0.588	0.62 0.350	-0.16 0.878		-0.12	2.3
Denmark	2.18 0.348	-2.86 0.646	1.78 0.163	-0.15 0.408	-0.05 0.450	1.50 0.459	-0.55 0.788	-1.07 0.762		-0.07	1.8
Canada	-0.16* 0.051	-0.25 0.578	-0.20 0.119	0.00** 0.040	-0.00 0.556	0.10 0.497	0.19 0.284	0.69** 0.036		0.39	2.5
USA	0.03 0.535	-0.11 0.759	0.10** 0.056	-0.00 0.924	0.00 0.980	-0.03 0.794	0.34** 0.005			0.31	2.7
UK[c]	-0.62 0.243	0.28 0.848	0.20 0.477	0.00 0.651	0.00 0.716	-0.27 0.692	1.05 0.143	3.82** 0.001		0.59	2.2
Austria	0.01 0.883	-0.26** 0.000	-0.12 0.466	0.00 0.657	-0.00 0.135	0.00 0.975				0.40	2.6
Finland	1.10 0.160	-2.35* 0.065	-0.36 0.523	-0.01 0.200	0.01 0.685	-0.14 0.858	0.58 0.537	-3.86** 0.011		0.30	2.4
Germany	-0.20 0.205	-0.58 0.692	-0.09 0.366	0.00 0.192	0.00 0.606		0.36 0.261	-0.11 0.802		0.19	1.7

Table 4.3 (*continued*)

Country	Constant	Wage inflation – lagged (w_{-1})	Foreign inflation (π^*)	Real exchange rate – lagged (r_{-1})	Unemployment – lagged (s_{-1})	DM	Yen	$	£	$\bar{R}^2$	DW
Belgium	0.07 0.684	0.62 0.138	-0.01 0.926	-0.00 0.753	-0.00 0.501	-0.11 0.525				0.17	2.4
France[b]	-0.12 0.633	1.12** 0.007	-0.04 0.802	0.00 0.484	-0.00* 0.072	-0.01 0.966		-0.37 0.496	-0.01 0.917	0.17	2.4
Ireland	0.02 0.956	-0.53 0.434	0.01 0.968	0.00 0.741	-0.01 0.198				0.02 0.905	-0.07	2.9
The Netherlands	0.35** 0.032	1.06 0.126	0.29 0.175	-0.00 0.045	0.00 0.392	-0.41* 0.067				0.08	2.5
Italy	-0.08 0.632	-0.17 0.362	-0.01 0.878	0.00 0.158	-0.01** 0.028	-0.01 0.898		-0.09 0.750	0.02 0.715	0.09	2.0
Norway	0.08 0.655	-0.57 0.122	0.26 0.405	0.00 0.980	-0.02 0.121	0.40 0.213		-0.38 0.615	-0.32**	0.33	2.6
Spain	0.65 0.601	0.06 0.857	1.26** 0.044	-0.01 0.484	0.01 0.698	-0.19 0.861				0.05	2.0

Notes:

[a] The first number in each cell is the coefficient and the second number is its significance level. The typical regression is based on 30 semi-annual observations except for Spain (22), the UK (20), and Switzerland (14).

[b] Vacancies are used instead of unemployment.

[c] μ is calculated from end of period stocks.

* Significant at about the 10 percent level or more but not more than 5 percent.

** Significant at the 5 percent level or more.

fit and yields generally significant coefficients on μ^* in those countries. The coefficients on foreign reserves expansion suggest that reserve money growth in the US responds to that of the Yen, in the UK it responds to growth of the dollar, in Japan and Switzerland it respond to those of the Deutschmark and the dollar, and reserve money growth in Canada responds to money growth in the US.

The coefficients of foreign price inflation for Spain and the US which are positive and significant in table 4.2 remain positive and significant in table 4.3 as well. The result for the US is interpretable in terms of equation (9) which corresponds to the case of a flexible rate with perfect substitutability. This equation implies that jointly sufficient conditions for the coefficient of π^* to be positive are a high concern for external competitiveness and $K_2 > 0$. The last condition is satisfied in turn when the direct effect of reserve money growth on domestic prices is large in comparison to its effect on the nominal rate of exchange. The coefficients of π^* in Switzerland and Denmark are now insignificant.

Turning to lagged wage inflation, we observe that all the coefficients that were significant in table 4.2 have, in table 4.3, the same signs that they had in table 4.2. But only the Austrian, Finnish, and French coefficients remain significant. Thus the conclusion that Austria and Finland lean against wage inflation while France accommodates it, is supported by table 4.3 as well. Since Belgium is likely to be characterized by imperfect substitutability it is likely that the more relevant regression for this country (in which w_{-1} is significant) is the one in table 4.2.

The coefficient of the lagged value of the real exchange rate is significant in Switzerland and Canada. The sign of this coefficient is negative in the first case and positive in the second. The significance of the coefficient indicates (as can be seen from equation (9)) that Swiss and Canadian monetary authorities are sensitive to real exchange rate considerations. The negative Swiss coefficient is consistent with a positive value of K_2 and the positive Canadian coefficient with a negative value of K_2. A positive value of K_2 obtains when the direct effect of base expansion on domestic prices dominates its effect on them through the depreciation that it induces in the nominal exchange rate. A negative value of K_2 obtains when the second effect dominates the first one.

The coefficient of lagged unemployment is positive and significant in Switzerland. The coefficient of vacancies is negative and significant in France, as it was in table 4.2. Both results are consistent with the view that monetary policy in these countries is sensitive to employment considerations. A significant and negative coefficient of unemployment for Italy occurs again. It is hard to interpret within the framework of section 2.

The coefficient of base UK money growth is positive and significant in the Norwegian reaction function. All other coefficients in this reaction function are insignificant. The theory from section 2 indicates that we should expect such a result under perfect substitutability provided the Norwegian currency is pegged to sterling. Under the presumption that it pegs to the Deutschmark, the significantly negative coefficient of German reserve money growth in the Dutch reaction function is puzzling.

4.4 Summary

Most of the significant coefficients in both tables 4.2 and 4.3 are consistent with the implications of the conceptual framework in section 2. The conjunction of empirical results with theory often allows us to learn something about the relative importance that monetary authorities in various countries give to alternative objectives. In a small number of cases significant coefficients are not interpretable within the conceptual framework proposed here. This may be due to chance but also to incompleteness of the theory.

Since the main focus of the chapter is on the relationship between accommodative tendencies, on one hand, and central bank independence and types of exchange rate regimes, on the other, a more thorough investigation of the few discrepancies between theory and empirical findings is left for future work.

5 The relationship between accommodation cum activism, and central bank autonomy and the type of exchange rate regime

This section presents cross-sectional evidence on the relation between the response coefficients of the previous section, on one hand, and central bank autonomy (CBA) and the type of exchange rate regime, on the other.

The degree of accommodation is characterized mainly in terms of the response of high-powered money growth to wage inflation and foreign price inflation. Activism is characterized in terms of the response of money growth to the rate of unemployment. The higher algebraically is either one of these three coefficients, the higher the degree of accommodation or of activism of the respective variables by the monetary authorities.

The conceptual framework does not always deliver entirely unambiguous implications for the relationship between the degree of accommodation and CBA. But, to the extent that cross country differences in CBA are reflected mostly as variations in the parameter A – with higher CBA corresponding to a lower A – the accommodation of wage inflation and of unemployment is likely to be stronger in countries with less independent central banks.

How about the type of exchange rate regime? The discussion of section 2 implies that under perfect substitutability there should be no accommodation of wages, foreign prices, and unemployment when the exchange rate is pegged. Nor should there be any response to the real exchange rate in this case. Imperfect substitutability, however, makes the picture murkier. As can be seen from an examination of equation (13) a fixed peg does not necessarily induce zero accommodation in this case. Since the currencies of many of the countries with fixed pegs in the sample are also likely to be characterized by imperfect substitutability, the conceptual framework does not necessarily imply a clear-cut relation between the type of exchange rate regime and the degree of accommodation. Ultimately, therefore, the type of relationship between the degree of accommodation, on one hand, and CBA or the type of exchange rate regime, on the other, has to be settled on empirical grounds.

5.1 Empirical methodology

At first blush an obvious test of the effect of institutional arrangements (like CBA and the exchange rate regime) on the degree of accommodation would be to regress each type of accommodation coefficient on the appropriate institutional indices. But since the significance varies across coefficients and many are statistically insignificant, such a procedure would introduce a lot of noise into the measurement of the dependent variable. An attractive procedure would reflect both the size of the accommodation coefficients and their significance. A natural candidate is the ratio between the magnitude of an estimated coefficient and its variance, as reflected in its t-statistic. We therefore test for potential links between the degree of accommodation and monetary institutions by running cross-sectional regressions of t-statistics of each type of coefficient from the first stage regressions of the previous section on indices of institutional arrangements. The resulting regressions are referred to as "second stage regressions." The chapter focuses on the effect of monetary institutions on the accommodation of wages and foreign prices and on the degree of activism as reflected in the response of monetary policy to unemployment.[23]

Two measures of CBA are used as regressors. One is an aggregate (weighted) index of legal independence (LI), and the other is the political vulnerability (V) of the central bank. The legal measure is taken from Cukierman, Webb, and Neyapti (1992).[24] Political vulnerability of the CB is defined as the fraction of political transitions that is followed within six months by a replacement of the central bank governor. This index is developed in Cukierman and Webb (1995).

Regressors for the type of exchange rate regime are introduced by means of two dummy variables. The first, PU, assumes a value of one if the exchange rate is pegged unilaterally and zero otherwise. The second, PC, assumes a value of one if the exchange rate is pegged cooperatively and zero otherwise. These definitions imply that the coefficient of PU in the second stage regressions measures the differential impact on accommodation between a unilateral peg and a flexible rate and the coefficient of PC measures the differential impact between a cooperative peg and a flexible rate. The classification of countries by type of exchange rate regime appears in part 2 of the appendix. During the sample period Germany was part of the EMS. It is therefore classified as being pegged cooperatively. However, since the Deutschmark floated against other key currencies like the US dollar we also experimented with a classification of Germany as being flexible. Since this reclassification did not affect the qualitative results all the second stage regressions presented here treat the Deutschmark as being pegged cooperatively.

Second stage regressions that relate the degree of accommodation of wage inflation to CBA and to the type of exchange rate regime are summarized in table 4.4. The first two regressions use measures of accommodation obtained from table 4.2 which excludes foreign rates of monetary expansion μ^*.The next two use measures of accommodation from table 4.3 that include foreign rates of monetary expansion. The next two regressions use measures of accommodation from first stage regressions that include μ^* in countries that are likely to be characterized by perfect substitutability and measures of accommodation from first-stage regressions without μ^* in the remaining countries. Some of the second stage regressions in table 4.4 include an index of political vulnerability of the central bank and some do not. The last equation in the table is a replication of the second one without Italy.

5.2 Sensitivity analysis

Equations 5 and 6 in table 4.4 are motivated by the conceptual framework of section 2, which implies that domestic reserve money growth responds to the rates of relevant foreign reserve money growth under perfect substitutability but not under imperfect substitutability. It follows that the measures of accommodation for countries that are likely to be nearer to perfect substitutability should come from table 4.3 while the measures of accommodation for countries that are likely to be characterized by imperfect substitutability should come from table 4.2. Regressions 5 and 6 in table 4.4 implement this idea.

The US, the UK, Japan, Switzerland, Canada, and Germany are classified as possessing perfect substitutability of financial assets. Conventional wisdom implies that in such countries sterilized foreign exchange market

Table 4.4 Second-stage regressions – the effect of central bank independence and type of exchange rate regime on the accommodation of wages[a]

(Dependent variable: t-statistic of lagged wage inflation from first-stage regressions (FSR))

Type of first-stage regression used in second stage	Constant	Legal independence (LI)	Central bank vulnerability (V)	Unilateral peg (PU)	Cooperative peg (PC)	$\bar{R}^2$	DW
1) FSR without foreign reserve expansion	1.72	−4.92*		−2.21**	0.34	0.34	2.5
	0.115	0.051		−0.043	0.695		
2) FSR without foreign reserve expansion	0.69	−3.14	4.56*	2.46*	0.01	0.46	1.8
	0.520	0.177	0.067	0.018	0.987		
3) FSR with foreign reserve expansion	0.90	−3.70*		−1.63*	1.03	0.44	2.6
	0.274	0.054		0.054	0.144		
4) FSR with foreign reserve expansion	0.26	−2.63	2.885	−1.79**	0.823	0.49	2.1
	0.771	0.168	0.146	0.032	0.225		
5) Mixed FSR[b]	0.57	−3.20	3.23	−2.11**	0.63	0.48	2.3
	0.566	0.140	0.148	0.025	0.400		
6) Mixed FSR with lagged foreign reserve expansion[b]	0.78	−3.67*	4.82**	−2.41**	0.19	0.59	2.0
	0.408	0.076	0.030	0.009	0.787		
7) Italy excluded – FSR without foreign reserve expansion	1.01	−3.91*	4.12*	−2.45**	0.35	0.53	1.9
	0.350	0.100	0.089	0.016	0.664		

Notes:
[a] Cross-sectional regressions over 17 countries except for the last regression that excludes Italy. The full list of countries appears in part 1 of the appendix.
[b] The mixed regressions combine the t-statistics from FSR *including* foreign reserve expansion for the US, Japan, Canada, Germany, and Switzerland with t-statistics from FSR *excluding* foreign reserve expansions for the remaining countries.
* Significant at about the 10 percent level or more but not more than 5 percent.
** Significant at the 5 percent level or more.

interventions are ineffective, so that the coefficient θ in equation (5) would be zero. The remaining countries are classified as having imperfect substitutability. This classification is obviously somewhat judgemental. Moreover even for countries like the US and Germany recent evidence does not yield unconditional support for the conventional view that sterilized interventions are ineffective (Dominguez and Frankel, 1993a, 1993b). But most economists would probably agree that sterilized interventions are least likely to be effective in the six countries that are classified here as possessing perfect substitutability of financial assets.

The conceptual framework implies that reserve money growth in one country responds to reserve money growth of some other countries. This may lead to simultaneity bias in the first stage regressions of table 4.3 in which the contemporaneous value of μ^* enters as a regressor. This problem is important for the key currencies in which sterilized intervention is presumed to be ineffective.[25] To examine whether the results of table 4.4 are sensitive to such a potential bias equation 5 is re-estimated, for the countries with perfect substitutability, with accommodation measures from first-stage regression (FSR)[26] in which lagged (rather than contemporaneous) values of μ^* appear as regressors. The results of this experiment appear in equation 6 of table 4.4. All coefficients keep the same sign and, except for that of the cooperative peg, they become larger and more significant.

5.3 Evidence on institutions and wage accommodation

The most striking result is that the unilateral peg dummy is invariably negative and significant. By contrast the cooperative peg dummy is always insignificant. The coefficient of legal independence is always negative and often significant. The coefficient of central bank vulnerability is always positive and sometimes significant. It is also the case that legal independence tends to become insignificant in the presence of the vulnerability index. We decided to try a second-stage regression (SSR) that excludes Italy because of the uninterpretable (to us) negative and significant coefficient of unemployment in the FSR of this country. The exclusion of Italy improves the overall fit and makes the coefficients of legal independence and vulnerability, and the unilateral peg dummy, all significant.

During the sample period the Deutschmark floated against other key currencies like the dollar but was on a fixed peg with other EMS currencies. All the SSRs in table 4.3 treat Germany as having a cooperative peg. In order to examine the sensitivity of the results to this classification the first regression in the table was re-estimated excluding Germany and Italy (not shown). Except for the fact that legal independence became somewhat less significant all the qualitative results remained the same.

It is noteworthy that the mixed second-stage regressions that incorporate our priors about the effectiveness of sterilized interventions in different countries yield a picture similar to the regressions that do not incorporate such priors. Particularly interesting is the fact that equation 6 which incorporates those priors and *also* addresses potential simultaneity problems fits well and yields significant effects for legal independence, political vulnerability of the central bank, and the unilateral peg dummy.

The above findings lead to the following more general conclusions:

1 Accommodation of wages is significantly lower under unilateral pegs than under flexible rates.
2 There is no significant difference in the degree of wage accommodation between countries with cooperative pegs and countries with flexible rates.
3 Accommodation of wages is weaker in countries with more legally independent central banks. The sign of this effect is always the same but it is not always significant.

Accommodation of wages is stronger in countries with more politically vulnerable central banks (V higher). Whenever it is entered in the regressions V has a positive coefficient. But it is not always significant.

5.4 Evidence on institutions, activism and the accommodation of foreign prices

Second-stage regressions of the type that appear in table 4.4 have been estimated also for the responses of monetary policy to unemployment and to foreign price inflation. In the first case the dependent variable is the t-statistic of the coefficient of unemployment from the FSR and in the second it is the t-statistic of the coefficient of foreign price inflation from the FSR. Since the t-statistic is equal to the ratio between a response coefficient and its variance the dependent variable reflects (as in table 4.4) the magnitude as well as the significance of the coefficient.

Most of the effects estimated in these SSRs are insignificant. But several exceptions arise. They are summarized in what follows without presenting the estimation results explicitly. First, the response of monetary policy to unemployment is smaller in countries with unilateral pegs than in countries with flexible rates of exchange. This effect is usually significant. By contrast there is no significant difference in this response between countries with cooperative pegs and flexible rates of exchange. The effect of central bank vulnerability on the response of monetary policy to unemployment is always positive but rarely significant. When a mixed SSR for unemployment (analogous to equation 6 of table 4.4) is estimated the significant effect of the unilateral peg dummy is strengthened and that of CB vulnerability becomes significant.

In summary the evidence indicates that countries on unilateral pegs are less inclined than others to use monetary policy to fight unemployment. The association is weaker than with the tendency to lean against wage inflation, but the two patterns are consistent with the same underlying policy priorities and philosophy. At first blush this appears to be consistent with the hypothesis of Giavazzi and Giovannini (1989) that limiting exchange rate flexibility reduces activism. Our empirical evidence is only partially supportive of this hypothesis, however, since activism is found to be lower only in countries with unilateral pegs but not in countries with cooperative pegs. This difference between cooperative and unilateral pegs is intriguing. It may arise because most of the EMS countries relied on the other members and particularly on Germany to help them maintain their pegs.[27] They felt, therefore, freer to use monetary policy to reduce unemployment. By contrast, countries on unilateral pegs perhaps felt that if they did not take the measures necessary to maintain their pegs no one else would. There is also relatively weak evidence that countries with more politically vulnerable central banks engage in more activist monetary policies.

We turn next to the evidence on the effects of institutional variables on the accommodation of foreign prices. None of the coefficients in the corresponding SSR are significant. But the effects of legal independence and of the two types of pegs are invariably negative. Those results are consistent with the view that countries with more independent central banks are more likely to lean against foreign inflation – as implied by the results of section 2. But the evidence on this is rather weak.

6 Concluding remarks

This chapter has presented evidence from industrialized countries on the relationship between the parameters of monetary reaction functions, on the one hand, and central bank independence and the type of exchange rate regime, on the other. The main results may be summarized as follows:

1 Accommodation of wage inflation is lower in countries with more legally independent central banks.[28] It is also lower in countries with unilateral pegs than in countries with flexible exchange rates.

2 There is no significant difference in the degree of wage accommodation between countries on cooperative pegs and countries with flexible exchange rates.

3 There is a positive, although not always significant, relationship between the degree of wage accommodation and the political vulnerability of the central bank. This result is consistent with the view that legal independence alone does not capture all the dimensions of actual independence. Some of those are reflected in the index of CB vulnerability.

4 Monetary policy in countries with unilateral pegs reacts less strongly to fluctuations in the rate of unemployment than in countries with flexible exchange rates. There is no significant difference in the degree of such policy activism between countries on cooperative pegs and countries with flexible rates of exchange. The first result is consistent with the findings of Alogoskoufis and Smith (1991) and of Alogoskoufis (1992) who find inflation to be less persistent in countries with fixed exchange rates. But the second result indicates that the type of peg matters. Countries with cooperative pegs are not significantly less activists than countries with flexible rates. Our results, thus, partially confirm those of Alogoskoufis and Alogoskoufis and Smith. But they suggest, in addition that *both* central bank independence as well as the type of exchange rate regime affect the degree of wage accommodation.
5 The evidence does not support the view that policy is less activist in countries with more legally independent central banks.
6 The degree of accommodation of foreign price inflation is not significantly related to either CBI or the exchange rate regime. But some countries like Germany and Austria appear to lean against foreign price inflation, while other countries like France and Belgium accommodate it.

An important implication of the conceptual framework underlying the policy reaction functions estimated is that when sterilized interventions are effective, monetary policy should not react to foreign rates of (high-powered) monetary expansion. When sterilized interventions are ineffective policy should *also* react to foreign monetary expansion under flexible rates and *only* to foreign monetary expansion under fixed pegs. Many of the 17 industrialized countries in our sample are likely to be characterized by imperfect substitutability. But those with key currencies like the US, Japan, the UK, and Germany are, by conventional wisdom, characterized by ineffective sterilized interventions. Since the exchange rates of most of these currencies are flexible, a priori considerations imply that their policy reaction functions respond to foreign money growth as well as to other variables. The estimated policy reaction functions usually support this implication.

The conventional view that under fixed pegs policy makers must totally subjugate domestic money supply to the maintenance of the peg is probably not applicable to most of the countries in our sample. It is generally not applicable to the key currencies because most of them are not pegged. It is also not applicable to the other currencies since for most of them sterilized interventions are likely to be effective. As a matter of fact, in view of the theory, evidence of some significant response to variables other than foreign rates of monetary expansion may be taken to indicate that sterilized interventions are effective in the country under consideration or that its exchange rate is not really pegged or both.

In any case these considerations suggest that our focus on reserve money growth as the monetary policy instrument does provide relevant information about the effect of monetary institutions on accommodation and the degree of anti-cyclical activism. Future work may want to experiment with other measures of the stance of monetary policy like net domestic credit as well as with alternative measures of the real exchange rate, of foreign prices, and of the cyclical position of the economy.

Appendix

Part 1 Nominal exchange rate weights used to calculate foreign price inflation

The following weights reflect our judgement about the foreign currencies that policy makers of a given country consider when making monetary policy decisions that affect the nominal exchange rate. Our presumption is that in all the countries policy makers take as reference only key currencies like the dollar, the Deutschmark, the yen and the UK pound. In some countries that have a record of serious pegging to a smaller number of currencies the set is even narrower. Examples are Austria and the Netherlands which peg their currencies to Germany's Deutschmark. For those countries we assign a weight of one to the Deutschmark and a weight of zero to the other key currencies.

	Reference currency			
Country	$	DM	Yen	£
Germany	½		½	
Japan	⅔	⅓		
Finland	¼	½	¼	
Switzerland	⅓	⅔		
Austria		1		
Sweden	¼	½	¼	
Ireland				1
Denmark	¼	½	¼	
Belgium		1		¼
Norway	¼	½		
Spain		1		¼
Italy	⅙	⅔		⅙
France	⅙	⅔		⅙
The Netherlands		1		
Canada	⅔	⅙	⅙	
USA		½	½	
UK	⅓	⅓	⅓	

Part 2 *Classification of countries by type of exchange rate regime for the second stage regressions*

Flexible or dirty float	Pegged unilaterally	Pegged cooperatively
Canada	Austria	Belgium
Japan	Finland	France
Spain	Norway	Denmark
Switzerland	Sweden	Germany*
UK		Ireland
US		Italy
		The Netherlands

* Reclassification of Germany as having a floating rate did not affect the qualitative results of the second stage regressions.

Notes

Cukierman is at Tel-Aviv University and CentER for Economic Research, Tilburg University, Rodriguez and Webb are at the World Bank. The authors acknowledge useful discussions with Joshua Aizenman, Geert Almekinders, Leonardo Leiderman, Allan Meltzer, Assaf Razin, and Peter Wickham. The usual disclaimer applies.

1 This notion of (legal) independence is embedded in most recent indices of central bank independence. Examples are Grilli, Masciandaro, and Tabellini (1991), Cukierman, Webb, and Neyapti (1992), Cukierman (1992, chapter 19), and Eijffinger and Schaling (1993).

2 For non-key currencies imperfect substitutability and effective sterilized interventions are probably the more common case. This situation is often reinforced by the existence of explicit or implicit controls on financial flows. But even for a key currency like the US dollar, recent evidence casts doubt on the conventional view that sterilized interventions are ineffective. Different points of view on this issue can be found in Almekinders and Eijffinger (1991), Dominguez and Frankel (1993a), and Edison, Henderson, and Tryan (1994).

3 See, for example, International Monetary Fund, *International Financial Statistics*, August, 1992, p. 50.

4 A more elaborate formulation in which this is derived as a result appears in chapter 18 of Cukierman (1992). Rogoff's (1985) conservative CB can be thought of as being characterized by a low value of A and, in the wider framework used here, also by a low value of B.

5 The flip coin of this increase in margins is a decrease in real wages which stimulates employment if workers are willing to work at the lower real wage. This is the case, in turn, when labor supply is non-competitive. Details appear in Cukierman (1992, chapter 3, section 6).

6 The underlying concept of relevance is made more precise in the empirical part in section 3.
7 This is an approximation since β is not, in general, constant.
8 Details appear in chapter 3 of Cukierman (1992).
9 In practice, there are limits to this divergence.
10 Formally this reaction function can be obtained as a particular case of the reaction function in equation (9) for the case $\psi = \psi^* = e_p = 0$.
11 Note that the choice of both μ and e determines not only the (new) level of high-powered money but also the composition of CB assets between assets which are denominated in foreign currency and assets that are denominated in domestic currency.
12 This statement obviously excludes the case of a fixed peg under perfect substitutability for which the reaction function does not depend on w_{-1}. See equation (10).
13 It is likely that for non-key currencies, like the Italian lira and the Spanish peseta substitutability is imperfect. But even for key currencies like the US dollar and the Deutschmark the evidence is mixed (Dominguez and Frankel, 1993a and b).
14 The exceptions are Spain, Switzerland, and the UK. Owing to data limitations, the sample periods for these countries are 1979/2 till 1990/2, 1977/2 till 1983/2, and 1980/2 till 1990/2, respectively.
15 For example, the rate of growth corresponding to the first semester of 1975 is calculated as the average of April, May, and June 1975 divided by the average of October, November, and December 1974 (minus one). Similarly, the observation of the second semester of 1975 is obtained as the average of October, November, and December 1975 divided by the average of April, May, and June 1975 (minus one).
16 Further details appear on p. 7 of the July 1991 issue of the IFS and in McGuirk (1986) and Wickham (1987).
17 The data are from the OECD, *Main Economic Indicators – Historical Review*.
18 These are wages in the manufacturing sector and they are obtained from the International Monetary Fund, *International Financial Statistics*.
19 An insignificant coefficient might reflect a lack of any reaction by the country's central bank, but could also reflect a lack of consistency in the strength or direction of responses.
20 In the presence of foreign rates of base expansion the US coefficient remains positive and significant and the Swiss coefficient becomes insignificant.
21 In the regression with μ^* as a regressor this coefficient becomes insignificant.
22 In Germany, for example, the hypothesized reference currencies are the dollar and the yen. Hence only the rates of reserve expansion of those two currencies are added as regressors to the German reaction function.
23 Second-stage regressions have been estimated also for the response to the real exchange rate. But no significant effects of either CBI or the type of exchange rate regime on this response were found.
24 Details on the construction of this index can be found in the article or in chapter 19 of Cukierman (1992).

25 The problem does not arise in the countries with imperfect substitutability since in those countries μ^* is not supposed to enter as a regressor in the FSR in the first place.

26 Those regressions are not shown.

27 Obviously this argument does not apply to Germany. The FSRs for this country show no significant response of monetary policy to unemployment. Moreover, to the extent that there is a response to wage inflation it is of the "leaning against the wind" type.

28 The results for Germany are consistent with casual empirical evidence; when the metalworkers' union in Germany opened the 1995 round of wage negotiations with a demand for a 6 per cent wage raise, the Bundesbank said that anything above 4 per cent would be unacceptable and would lead to monetary tightening. The Bundesbank has a reputation for following such words with actions (*Oxford Analytica*, December 1, 1994).

References

Almekinders, G.J. and Eijffinger, S.C.W. (1991), "Empirical Evidence on Foreign Exchange Market Intervention: Where Do We Stand?" *Review of World Economics*, 127, 645–77.

Alogoskoufis, G.S. (1992), "Monetary Accommodation, Exchange Rate Regimes and Inflation Persistence," *Economic Journal*, 102, 461–80.

Alogoskoufis, G.S. and Smith, R. (1991), "The Phillips Curve, the Persistence of Inflation and the Lucas Critique: Evidence from Exchange-Rate Regimes," *American Economic Review*, 81, 1254–75.

Cukierman, A. (1992), *Central Bank Strategy, Credibility and Independence: Theory and Evidence*, Cambridge, Mass.: MIT Press.

Cukierman, A. and Webb, S. (1995), "Political Influence on the Central Bank – International Evidence," *World Bank Economic Review*, 9, 397–423.

Cukierman, A., Webb, S., and Neyapti, B. (1992), "Measuring the Independence of Central Banks and Its Effect on Policy Outcomes," *World Bank Economic Review*, 6, 353–98.

Dominguez, K.M. and Frankel, J.A. (1993a), *Does Foreign Exchange Intervention Work?* Washington DC: Institute for International Economics.

(1993b), "Does Foreign Exchange Intervention Matter? The Portfolio Effect," *American Economic Review*, 83, 1356–69.

Dornbusch, R. (1982), "Purchasing Power Parity, Exchange Rate Rules and Macroeconomic Stability," *Journal of Political Economy*, 90, 158–65.

Edison, H.J., Henderson, D.W., and Tryan, R.W. (1994), "The Effect of Interventions on the Exchange Rate: A Review of Some Recent Statistical Studies," mimeo, Board of Governors of the Federal Reserve System.

Eijffinger, S.C.W. and Schaling, E. (1993), "Central Bank Independence in Twelve Industrial Countries," *Banca Nazionale del Lavoro Quarterly Review*, 184, 1–41.

Fischer, S. (1977), "Long Term Contracts, Rational Expectations and the Optimal Money Supply Rule," *Journal of Political Economy*, 85, 191–206.

Giavazzi, F. and Giovannini, A. (1989), *Limiting Exchange Rate Flexibility: The European Monetary System*, Cambridge, Mass.: MIT Press.

Grilli, V., Masciandaro, D., and Tabellini, G. (1991), "Political and Monetary Institutions and Public Financial Policies in the Industrial Countries," *Economic Policy*, 13, 341–92.

International Monetary Fund, *International Financial Statistics*, various issues.

McGuirk, A.K. (1987), "Measuring Price Competitiveness for Industrial Country Trade in Manufactures," IMF Working Paper 87–34.

OEDC, Main Economic Indicators, Historical Review.

Rogoff, K. (1985), "The Optimal Degree of Commitment to an Intermediate Monetary Target," *Quarterly Journal of Economics*, 100, 1169–90.

Taylor, J.B. (1980), "Aggregate Dynamics and Staggered Contracts," *Journal of Political Economy*, 88, 1–23.

Wickham, P. (1987), "A Revised Weighting Scheme for Indicators of Effective Exchange Rates," IMF Working Paper 87–87.

Comment

JAKOB DE HAAN

It is often argued that a high level of central bank independence together with some explicit mandate for the central bank to aim for price stability constitute important institutional devices to maintain price stability (see, for example, Alesina and Summers, 1993, and De Haan and Sturm, 1992). The position of the Bundesbank is regularly mentioned as an example par excellence. The German central bank is relatively autonomous; at the same time, Germany has one of the best post-World War II inflation records among OECD countries. As a matter of fact, the statutes of the European Central Bank are largely modeled after the law governing the Bundesbank.

Most observers think that an independent central bank is able to give priority to a low level of inflation, whereas in countries with a more dependent central bank other considerations (like re-election prospects of politicians, promoting a lower level of unemployment) may interfere with the objective of price stability. Indeed, various authors have found empirical support for this hypothesis (see Eijffinger and De Haan, 1996, for a review). The view that, other things being the same, greater central bank independence is conducive to lower inflation rates, raises various questions:

how should central bank independence be measured?;

(how) does central bank independence affect inflation and other macroeconomic variables?; and

why does central bank independence vary across countries?

In close cooperation with various co-authors, Cukierman has dealt with all these issues. In the present chapter, Cukierman *et al.* focus upon the second question, and examine whether accommodation and the degree of policy activism differ systematically across countries with various degrees of central bank independence and different types of exchange rate regimes. They estimate reaction functions for the monetary authorities of 17 industrial countries and employ the *t*-statistics of the coefficient of lagged wage inflation as the dependent variable in so-called second-stage regressions. Their most important conclusion is that wage inflation is less accommodated in countries with more independent central banks, and in countries with unilateral pegs.

Although I admire the approach of the authors, I have some doubts regarding specific parts and the general conclusions of their chapter. In commenting on the chapter, I will also dwell upon the other questions raised above.

The authors discriminate between groups of countries by exchange rate regime: flexible or dirty float, pegged unilaterally (PU), and pegged cooperatively (PC). In the same regression, indicators of central bank independence are included. However, it is possible that central bank independence and exchange rate policies are mutually dependent. In that case, the outcomes of the second stage regressions are difficult to interpret. In principle, central bank independence and exchange rate policies may be positively or negatively related. If a country has, for instance, a dependent central bank, pegging the exchange rate to the Deutschmark may be a good substitute. Indeed, this is the reasoning behind the view that the European Monetary System has functioned as a disciplinary device, lowering disinflation costs.[1] Both central bank independence and pegging the exchange rate may be regarded as (alternative) commitment devices. Alternatively, one could argue that central bank independence and a preference for stable exchange rates are both reflections of underlying societal preferences.[2] In that case a negative correlation is to be expected between central bank independence and exchange rate changes, i.e., the more independent the central bank, the closer it will peg. A negative correlation may also be the outcome of the central banker's preference for low inflation.

Table 4.5 *Exchange rate system and central bank independence (partial correlation)*

	PC	PU	CUK92	CW94	Grilli	Alesina
CUK92	0.05	−0.17				
CW94	0.10	0.11	−0.15			
Grilli	−0.11	0.06	0.87	−0.19		
Alesina	−0.05	−0.18	0.71	0.09	0.74	
ES	0.34	−0.15	0.65	0.10	0.59	0.77

Table 4.5 presents partial correlation coefficients of five measures of central bank independence and the dummy variables PU and PC. The indices for central bank independence are Cukierman's (1992) legal measure (CUK92), the "political vulnerability" index of Cukierman and Webb (1994) (CW94)[3] and the legal measures of Grilli *et al.* (1991), Alesina (1988, 1989), and Eijffinger and Schaling (ES) (1993, 1996). From table 4.5 it follows that there appears to be no strong relationship between the exchange rate dummies and the various indicators for central bank autonomy. This is confirmed by simple OLS regressions (not shown). So, at first glance, there is no problem in including both dummies for the exchange rate system and measure(s) for central bank independence in the second-stage regressions.

Table 4.5 also shows partial correlation coefficients of the various indicators for central bank independence. Note the very low and sometimes even negative correlation between the various measures. I will return to this point below.

Still, one might argue that the classification of countries is too rough. Most ERM countries are in the PC group.[4] However, as follows from table 4.6, which shows all realignments and the cumulative devaluations *vis-à-vis* the Deutschmark, experience differs remarkably across countries. Whereas the Dutch guilder was devalued by only 4 percent, the Italian lira lost almost 50 percent of its value against the Deutschmark. This suggests that the PC dummy may not be appropriate.

An interesting question is whether the divergent experiences of ERM countries is somehow related to central bank independence. Table 4.7 reports some simple OLS regressions of the cumulative devaluations of the ERM currencies divided by the number of months that the currency participated in the ERM between March 1979 and August 1993 and five indices of central bank independence. It follows from table 4.7 that a positive correlation exists between central bank independence and the cumulative devaluations.[5] Only the coefficient of Cukierman's legal index is not

Table 4.6 *Realignments in the ERM*

	France	Italy	The Netherlands	Belgium & Luxembourg	Denmark	Ireland	Spain	Portugal
1979 September 24	−2	−2	−2	−2	−5	−2		
November 30	—	—	—	—	−5	—		
1981 March 23	—	−6	—	—	−5	—		
October 5	−8.5	−8.5	—	−5.5	−5.5	−5.5		
1982 February 22	—	—	—	−8.5	−3	—		
June 14	−10	−7	—	−4.25	−4.25	−4.25		
1983 March 21	−8	−8	−2	−4	−3	−9		
1985 July 22	—	−8	—	—	—	—		
1986 April 7	−6	−3	—	−2	−2	−3		
August 4	—	—	—	—	—	−8		
1987 January 12	−3	−3	—	−1	−3	−3		
1989 June 19	—	—	—	—	—	—		
1990 January 8	—	−3.7	—	—	—	—		
1992 September 14	—	−7	—	—	—	—	—	—
September 17	—	—	—	—	—	—	−5	
November 21	—	—	—	—	—	—	−6	−6
1993 January 30	—	—	—	—	—	−10	—	—
May 15	—	—	—	—	—	—	−6.5	−6.5
Cumulative devaluations	−31	−47	−4	−24	−26	−40	−17.5	−12.5

Source: Based on information provided by De Nederlandsche Bank.

Table 4.7 *OLS regressions of cumulative devaluations and central bank independence (CBI)*

Measure of CBI	Constant	Coefficient	R^2 (adj.)
Alesina (1988, 1989)	0.61 (5.01)	−0.24 (3.55)	0.70
Grilli et al. (1991)	0.90 (7.07)	−0.10 (5.20)	0.79
Cukierman (1992)	0.36 (3.05)	−0.52 (1.46)	0.16
Cukierman and Webb (1994)	−0.04 (0.37)	1.89 (2.14)	0.42
Eijffinger and Schaling (1993, 1996)	0.41 (6.22)	−0.08 (3.67)	0.71

Note: Absolute values of *t*-statistics are shown in parentheses.

significantly different from zero. This may well reflect measurement errors. As Eijffinger and De Haan (1996) have pointed out, there is room for some doubt as to whether Cukierman's index is correct. Table 4.8 contrasts, for instance, the interpretations of the Dutch central bank law ("Bankwet 1948"), which we are most familiar with. In parentheses our numerical codings are presented. It follows from this table that in our view the Dutch central bank is considerably more independent than Cukierman's coding would suggest. This is not to suggest that other legal measures used in table 4.7 are perfect. Eijffinger and De Haan (1996) also criticize the measures proposed by Alesina and Grilli *et al.* With respect to the political vulnerability index, one should also be very careful, especially if there are few changes of central bank governors over the period under consideration. This is, for instance, the case in The Netherlands.

In January 1982, Wim Duisenberg became the new president of De Nederlandsche Bank; he succeeded Jelle Zijlstra who was president from 1967 to 1981. In February 1982 there was a political crisis, which led to a change of government, but this was *after* the entry of the new central bank governor and had nothing to do with it. So the only change that might explain the score of The Netherlands according to this measure (0.10) is the moment at which Zijlstra took over from his predecessor Holtrop. In his memoirs, Zijlstra recollects that his appointment was signed on September 16, 1966, and would be effective as from May 1, 1967. On October 14, 1966, the government fell and was replaced by another coalition, which was wrought and led by Jelle Zijlstra! This interim government was replaced by another one in April 1967, so that Zijlstra could, after all, still become president of De Nederlandsche Bank in May 1967. So it is clear that the score of 0.10 for The Netherlands only mirrors a coincidence.

Given the divergence and noisiness of the various indicators of central bank independence, I decided on a further sensitivity analysis, focusing on rows 1, 2 and 5 of table 4.4 of Cukierman *et al.* What happens if the coeffi-

Table 4.8 *Cukierman's legal variables: the Dutch case*

Variable (see Cukierman, 1992 for description)	Cukierman's coding	Interpretation	Comments (our coding is given in parentheses)
too	0.75	8 > too > 6	board members appointed for seven years; appointment is renewable
app	0.00	CEO appointed by minister of finance	correct, but on the basis of a list, containing only two names, which is drafted by the governing and supervisory boards of the bank (0.75)
diss	0.17	dismissal for policy reasons at executive branch's discretion	only if the minister has given a so-called "instruction," which the governing board rejects, can the board be dismissed; such an instruction has never been given (0.83)
off	1.00	CEO prohibited from holding other office	correct
monpol	0.33	CB has only advisory capacity	incorrect: central bank has full freedom in formulating and implementing monetary policy, except for the (theoretical) possibility pointed out above (1.00)
conf	0.20	government has final authority in case of conflict, but subject to process and protest by central bank	correct, but this process has never occurred, since it is linked with the "instruction" procedure

Table 4.8 (*continued*)

Variable (see Cukierman, 1992 for description)	Cukierman's coding	Interpretation	Comments (our coding is given in parentheses)
adv	0.00	central bank is not given active role in the formulation of government's budget	correct, but one may wonder whether this has anything to do with central bank autonomy; indeed it may be argued that if the CB is involved this may threaten its independence
obj	0.80	price stability mentioned as only goal	the wording of the law also implies external stability
lla	0.67	relatively strict limits (cash amount)	correct; collateral is necessary
lls	0.00	no limits	correct, but this type of credit is not provided
ldec	0.00	executive branch decides the terms	incorrect: the law specifies the terms (0.66)
lwidth	1.00	only central government can borrow	not entirely correct, since Amsterdam and Social Insurance Bank may also borrow
ltype	1.00	limits specified as cash amount	correct as far as article 20 of the Bank Law is concerned; however, additional liquidity may be provided which is limited in terms of a percentage of total government revenues
lmat	0.00	no upper bound	incorrect: maturity is limited to one year
lint	0.00	no interest rate charge	correct
lprim	0.00	not prohibited from buying government securities in primary market	correct

Source: Eijffinger and De Haan (1996).

Table 4.9 *Second-stage regressions – the effects of central bank independence and exchange rate regime on wage accommodation*

(dependent variable: coefficient of lagged wage inflation from first-stage regression of Cukierman *et al.*; estimation by weighted least squares; weights are 1 minus significance levels)

CBI-indicator	Constant	Legal independence	Political vulnerability of CB	PU	PC	R^2
First-stage regressions without foreign reserve expansion (corresponds with row 1 of table 4.4 of Cukierman *et al.*)						
Cukierman	0.66	−0.42		−1.69	−0.47	0.19
	(0.58)	(0.24)		(1.77)	(0.53)	
Alesina	1.80	−0.42		−2.76	−0.68	0.36
	(1.19)	(1.01)		(2.48)	(0.76)	
Grilli *et al.*	1.51	−0.11		−0.82	−0.59	0.16
	(1.06)	(0.84)		(0.76)	(0.73)	
Eijffinger–Schaling	1.31	−0.23		−1.85	−0.45	0.23
	(0.96)	(0.75)		(1.89)	(0.51)	
First-stage regressions without foreign reserve expansion (corresponds with row 2 of table 4.4 of Cukierman *et al.*)						
Cukierman	1.16	0.24	−10.01	−1.99	0.07	0.35
	(1.06)	(0.14)	(1.96)	(2.21)	(0.08)	
Alesina	1.66	−0.21	−6.58	−2.56	−0.19	0.35
	(0.96)	(0.36)	(0.91)	(2.08)	(0.18)	
Grilli *et al.*	1.78	−0.08	−6.15	−1.31	−0.22	0.13
	(1.10)	(0.52)	(0.86)	(1.04)	(0.24)	
Eijffinger–Schaling	1.26	−0.001	−9.66	−2.01	0.05	0.32
	(0.91)	(0.01)	(1.57)	(2.11)	(0.06)	

cients in the first stage regressions are used as dependent variables, instead of the t-statistics? Are the conclusions sensitive with respect to the choice of the indicator of central bank independence?

Table 4.9 reports the outcomes of weighted least squares (WLS) regressions, in which the coefficients of the lagged wage inflation are the dependent variable and the weights are 1 minus the reported significance levels.[6] Using

WLS seems a good alternative to using t-statistics as the dependent variable. As Denmark proved to be an outlier (it has an incredibly high coefficient in the first-stage regression) a dummy is included for this country in all the regressions reported. The qualitative conclusions are, however, not changed if this dummy is not included. The first four rows of table 4.9 can be compared with row 1 of table 4.4 of Cukierman *et al.* The results are, however, strikingly different. The coefficients of the legal measures of central bank independence are never significantly different from zero. In line with the results of Cukierman *et al.*, we find that the coefficient on PU is generally significantly negative and that the coefficient on PC is never significant.

The outcomes of rows 5–8 can be compared with row 2 of table 4.4 of Cukierman *et al.* Again some results are quite different. The coefficient of central bank vulnerability is only significant in combination with Cukierman's legal measure of central bank independence, and it consistently has the "wrong" sign. The coefficient on PU remains significant. Similar results are found for the regressions in which mixed first stage regression coefficients are used as the dependent variable (not shown).[7] Given the foregoing analysis, my conclusions are somewhat different from those of Cukierman *et al.* First, accommodation of wage inflation is lower in countries with a unilateral peg. Second, central bank independence, measured either on the basis of legal independence indices or as the political vulnerability of the central bank, is not related to wage accommodation. Third, central bank independence rather matters in a different way. Countries with a cooperative peg have fewer devaluations if they have an independent central bank.

Notes

1 Although most authors question the view that the EMS has contributed to dis-inflation, Bini Smaghi (1994) concludes that the ERM countries which pegged their exchange rate to the Deutschmark, achieved a larger reduction of inflation than other OECD countries. Disinflation in the ERM countries was more gradual, yet more substantial.

2 For other determinants of central bank independence, see Cukierman (1994). The various hypotheses put forward in that paper are tested by De Haan and Van't Hag (1995).

3 Cukierman and Webb (1994) do not present their estimate of the political vulnerability of the Italian central bank. Consequently, in all tables in this comment where CW94 is taken up, Italy is not included.

4 One may wonder whether The Netherlands should not be included in the group of countries with a unilateral peg, as Dutch monetary authorities have since 1983 strived for a stable guilder–Deutschmark relation. See also Knot and De Haan (1995).

5 The measure of Cukierman and Webb reports the political vulnerability, measured as the fraction of political transitions that are followed promptly by a replacement of the central bank governor. So a higher value of this index implies less independence.
6 I owe this suggestion to Harry Huizinga.
7 These regressions correspond with the results reported in row 5 of table 4.4 of Cukierman et al.

References

Alesina, A. (1988), "Macroeconomics and Politics," *NBER Macroeconomic Annual 1988*, Cambridge: Cambridge University Press.
(1989), "Politics and Business Cycles in Industrial Democracies," *Economic Policy*, 8, 55–89.
Alesina, A. and Summers, L.H. (1993), "Central Bank Independence and Macroeconomic Performance: Some Comparative Evidence," *Journal of Money, Credit, and Banking*, 25, 151–62.
Bini Smaghi, L. (1994), "EMS Discipline: Did it Contribute to Inflation Convergence?" *Banca Nazionale del Lavoro Quarterly Review*, 189, 187–97.
Cukierman, A. (1992), *Central Bank Strategy, Credibility, and Independence*, Cambridge, Mass.: MIT Press.
(1994), "Commitment through Delegation, Political Influence and Central Bank Independence," in J.A.H. de Beaufort Wijnholds, S.C.W. Eijffinger, and L.H. Hoogduin (eds.), *A Framework for Monetary Stability*, Dordrecht/Boston/London: Kluwer Academic Publishers, 55–74.
Cukierman, A. and Webb, S.B. (1994), "Political Influence on the Central Bank – International Evidence," CentER Discussion Paper, Tilburg University, No. 94100, Forthcoming in *World Bank Economic Review*.
Eijffinger, S.C.W. and Haan, J. De (1996), "The Political Economy of Central Bank Independence," *Princeton Special Papers in International Economics,* 19 (May), International Finance Section, Princeton: Princeton University Press.
Eijffinger, S.C.W. and Schaling, E. (1993), "Central Bank Independence in Twelve Industrial Countries," *Banca Nazionale del Lavoro Quarterly Review*, 184, 1–41.
(1996), "The Ultimate Determinants of Central Bank Independence," this volume.
Grilli, V., Masciandaro, D. and Tabellini, G. (1991), "Political and Monetary Institutions and Public Financial Policies in the Industrial Countries," *Economic Policy*, 13, 341–92.
Haan, J. De and Sturm, J.E. (1992), "The Case for Central Bank Independence" *Banca Nazionale del Lavoro Quarterly Review*, 182, 305–27. Reprinted in M. Parkin (ed.), *The Theory of Inflation*, Aldershot: Edward Elgar, 1994.
Haan, J. De and Van 't Hag, G.J. (1995), "Variation in Central Bank Independence across Countries: Some Provisional Empirical Evidence," *Public Choice*, 85, 335–51.
Knot, K.H.W. and De Haan, J. (1995), "Interest Differentials and Exchange Rate Policies in Austria, the Netherlands and Belgium," *Journal of Banking and Finance*, 19, 363–86.

5 Uncertainty, instrument choice, and the uniqueness of Nash equilibrium: microeconomic and macroeconomic examples

DALE W. HENDERSON and NING S. ZHU

1 Introduction

This chapter contains two examples of static, symmetric, positive-sum games with two strategic players and a play by nature: (1) a microeconomic game between duopolists with joint costs facing uncertain demands for differentiated goods and (2) a macroeconomic game between two countries with inflation-bias preferences confronting uncertain demands for money. In both games, each player can choose either of two variables as an instrument. In our terminology, both are linear-reaction-function games because reaction functions are linear in the chosen instruments.

More than a century ago, it was discovered that there are both Cournot (1838) and Bertrand (1883) equilibria for duopoly games with no uncertainty. There are many examples of multiple (Nash) equilibria in linear-reaction-function games with no uncertainty. In the standard differentiated duopoly game with linear demands and independent, quadratic costs, there are four equilibria if each duopolist can choose either price or quantity as an instrument. That is, there are as many equilibria as there are possible pairs of instrument choices. Likewise, in two-player macroeconomic games with quadratic utilities and linear economies there are as many equilibria as there are possible pairs of instrument choices.[1]

The explanation of the existence of multiple equilibria in linear-reaction-function games with no uncertainty is the same as the explanation of a familiar result. Poole (1970) and Weitzman (1974) show that with no uncertainty a single controller is indifferent among instruments. Likewise, with no uncertainty if one player chooses his instrument and sets a value for it, the other is indifferent among instruments. It follows that, for example, if each of two players can choose one of two variables as an instrument, there are four equilibria.[2]

Klemperer and Meyer (1986) modify differentiated duopoly games by introducing uncertainty in the form of a play by nature that is unknown to the duopolists. Introducing uncertainty in this form is of interest in and of itself. However, Klemperer and Meyer find that it results in a game with different qualitative properties: the number of equilibria is smaller than with no uncertainty.

In their main example, Klemperer and Meyer modify the standard differentiated duopoly game by assuming that the demands have a common additive disturbance. This example has the very attractive property that there is a unique equilibrium for every set of parameter values. It also has a somewhat surprising property not emphasized by Klemperer and Meyer. For some parameter values, the symmetric instrument pair chosen in the unique equilibrium is the one that yields lower profits with no uncertainty.

The explanation of the reduction in the number of equilibria with uncertainty is the same as the explanation of another familiar result. Poole (1970) and Weitzman (1974) show that with uncertainty a single controller is not indifferent among instruments. Likewise, with uncertainty if one player chooses his instrument and sets a value for it, the other is not indifferent among instruments. Since players are not indifferent among instruments, the number of equilibria is reduced, perhaps to one.

The two examples in this chapter are designed to shed further light on the implications of introducing uncertainty in the form of a play by nature into linear-reaction-function games for the number of equilibria and the characteristics of these equilibria. The microeconomic example is an extension of the main Klemperer and Meyer (1986) example to the case of joint costs. The macroeconomic example is a two-country version of the Kydland–Prescott (1977) and Barro–Gordon (1983) inflation-bias game with uncertain demands for money similar to the one analyzed by Henderson and Zhu (1990). In the macroeconomic example, each country can choose either its money supply or its interest rate as its instrument.

Our examples yield results similar to those of Klemperer and Meyer in some respects. With no uncertainty there are four equilibria, one for each possible instrument pair. Introducing uncertainty results in a game with fewer equilibria. In some cases in which the equilibrium is unique, the smallest amount of uncertainty causes the players to choose the symmetric instrument pair that is worse for them with no uncertainty. However, our examples yield results different from those of Klemperer and Meyer in an important respect. For some parameter values, introducing uncertainty results in a game with two equilibria.

2 A microeconomic example: differentiated duopoly with uncertain demands

In the microeconomic example, we use a model of duopoly with differentiated goods. First, we lay out a model with linear demands; joint, quadratic costs; and an additive disturbance that affects both demands. Then, we discuss the multiplicity of equilibria with no uncertainty. Finally, we consider the implications of introducing uncertainty in the form of the additive demand disturbance. We analyze both the special case of independent costs for which Klemperer and Meyer (1986) obtain their uniqueness result and the general case of joint costs.

The model

In our model, the symmetric duopolists, nohat and hat, each produce and sell a single differentiated good. Variables with no hats and hats over them are possible instrument variables for nohat and hat, respectively. Prices received (P and $\hat{P}$) are related to quantities sold (Q and $\hat{Q}$) by the inverse demand functions

$$P=a-.5bQ-f\hat{Q}+\eta, \ \hat{P}=a-.5b\hat{Q}-fQ+\eta \tag{1}$$

where η is a disturbance with zero mean and finite variance. The price of each good falls with the quantity of that good sold ($b>0$). We assume that the two goods are substitutes, so the price of each good also falls with the quantity of the other good sold ($f>0$).[3] We also assume that the price of a good falls if the quantity of that good sold increases and the quantity of the other good sold decreases by the same amount ($b>2f$).

We assume that the total costs of the duopolists (C and $\hat{C}$) are the following quadratic functions of their outputs

$$C=gQ+.5kQ^2+uQ\hat{Q}, \ \hat{C}=g\hat{Q}+.5k\hat{Q}^2+u\hat{Q}Q \tag{2}$$

so the duopolists have joint costs.[4] We assume that $0\leq g<a$, but we consider both positive and negative values for k and u.

We assume that the duopolists are involved in a static, positive-sum game with simultaneous play in which nature also makes a play. Each duopolist has two possible instruments, quantity and price. Each must choose an instrument and the value at which to set that instrument before uncertainty is resolved. Since the duopolists are symmetric, we need consider in detail the behavior of only one of them, say nohat.

Nohat's profits when nohat chooses instrument j and hat chooses instrument $\hat{j}$ are represented by $\Pi^{j\hat{j}}(j, \hat{j}; \eta)$. Nohat's profits for the four possible pairs of instrument choices are given by equations (T1.1) through (T1.4) in table 5.1. Nohat's zero-disturbance profits for values of an instrument pair

Table 5.1 *Nohat's profits for four pairs of instrument choices*

$$\Pi^{Q\hat{Q}}(Q,\hat{Q};\eta) = (a-g+\eta)Q-.5(b+k)Q^2-(f+u)\hat{Q}Q, \tag{T1.1}$$

$$\left(\frac{b^2}{2}\right)\Pi^{P\hat{Q}}(P,\hat{Q};\eta) = [b(a+g)+2ak+(b+2k)\eta]P-(b+k)P^2$$
$$+[bfg+(2fk-bu)(a+\eta)]\hat{Q}$$
$$-f(fk-bu)\hat{Q}^2-[f(b+2k)-bu]P\hat{Q} \tag{T1.2}$$
$$-a(bg+ak)-(bg+2ak)\eta-k\eta^2,$$

$$(2b^2)\Pi^{Q\hat{P}}(Q,\hat{P};\eta) = [2ab(b-2f)-2b(bg+2au)-2(2bf-b^2+2bu)\eta]Q$$
$$-b(b^2-4f^2+bk-4fu)]Q^2+4b(f+u)\hat{P}Q, \tag{T1.3}$$

$$\left(\frac{\Delta^2}{2}\right)\Pi^{P\hat{P}}(P,\hat{P};\eta) = \{\Delta bg+[\Delta+2kb+2u(b-2f)](b-2f)(a+\eta)\}P$$
$$-\{2fg\Delta+[4fk-2u(b-2f)](b-2f)(a+\eta)\}\hat{P}$$
$$-b(\Delta+kb-4uf)P^2-4f(kf-bu)\hat{P}^2 \tag{T1.4}$$
$$+2[f(\Delta+2kb)-u(b^2+4f^2)]P\hat{P}$$
$$-g\Delta(b-2f)(a+\eta)-(k+2u)(b-2f)^2(a+\eta)^2,$$

$$\Delta =b^2-4f^2.$$

j and $\hat{j}$ are defined as what nohat's profits would be for values of that instrument pair if the disturbance term were zero and are represented by $\Pi^{ij}(j,\hat{j};0)$. Our assumptions about the parameters of the demand and cost functions imply that nohat's zero-disturbance profits for the instrument pair j and $\hat{j}$ are a concave function of nohat's instrument j for any given value of hat's instrument $\hat{j}$.[5]

The model with no uncertainty

The multiplicity of equilibria: With no uncertainty ($\sigma_\eta^2=0$), we obtain the familiar result that there are four equilibria no matter whether costs are independent ($u=0$) or joint ($u\neq0$). For any given value of a particular instrument variable chosen by hat, the maximum value of nohat's zero-disturbance profits is the same no matter whether nohat chooses Q or P as an instrument because there is a one to one relationship between Q and P:[6]

$$\max_Q[\Pi^{Qj}(Q,\hat{j};0)]=\max_P[\Pi^{Pj}(P,\hat{j};0)] \tag{3}$$

This logic is in accordance with the logic used by Poole (1970) and Weitzman (1974) to establish that with no uncertainty a single controller is indifferent among instruments.

It follows that there are four equilibria in which the instrument pairs are Q and $\hat{Q}$, P and $\hat{Q}$, Q and $\hat{P}$, and P and $\hat{P}$, respectively. We refer to these equilibria as the $Q\hat{Q}$, $P\hat{Q}$, $Q\hat{P}$, and $P\hat{P}$ equilibria. As an example, we establish that there is a $P\hat{Q}$ equilibrium. Begin with nohat's and hat's profits functions when P and $\hat{Q}$ are chosen as instruments. Set both the first derivative of nohat's profit function with respect to P and the first derivative of hat's profit function with respect to $\hat{Q}$ equal to zero. This pair of first-order conditions is a pair of simultaneous linear equations in P and $\hat{Q}$. It remains to demonstrate that the solution to this pair of first-order conditions is an equilibrium. Given the solution for $\hat{Q}$, the solution for P is the best response for nohat given that he chooses P as an instrument. Likewise, given the solution for P, the solution for $\hat{Q}$ is the best response for hat given that he chooses $\hat{Q}$ as an instrument. As we argue in the preceding paragraph, nohat can do no better by choosing Q as an instrument. Likewise, hat can do no better by choosing $\hat{P}$ as an instrument. Therefore, the solution to the pair of first-order conditions when P and $\hat{Q}$ are chosen as instruments is an equilibrium. In a similar manner, it can be established that there are $Q\hat{Q}$, $Q\hat{P}$, and $P\hat{P}$ equilibria.

There is a certain fragility to the set of equilibria. Consider the $P\hat{Q}$ equilibrium. With no uncertainty, nohat is indifferent between using P as an instrument and using Q. Of course, if there is to be a $P\hat{Q}$ equilibrium, he must actually use P. If the game structure were altered so that nohat had even a slight preference for Q, then there would be no $P\hat{Q}$ equilibrium. As we confirm below, with uncertainty nohat is not indifferent between instruments.

The comparison of profits at three points: In this sub-section we compare profits at the symmetric efficient point with those in the $Q\hat{Q}$ (Cournot) and $P\hat{P}$ (Bertrand) equilibria for both the case of independent costs ($u=0$) and the case of joint costs ($u \neq 0$). We use figures 5.1 and 5.2, which are diagrams in $Q\hat{Q}$ space.[7] The comparison is of interest in and of itself, but our main reason for making it is so that we can refer to it in the analysis of the uncertainty case.

The efficient point: As a standard of comparison, we use the symmetric efficient point, the point at which the simple sum of the profits of the duopolists is maximized. We refer to this point as "the" efficient point for short and represent it by point E in figures 5.1 and 5.2. Since the duopolists are symmetric, they produce equal quantities at this point.

At the efficient point, it must be impossible to make either duopolist better off without making the other worse off, and the quantities produced must be equal. Therefore, at E an isoprofit locus for nohat must be tangent to an isoprofit locus for hat on the 45° line

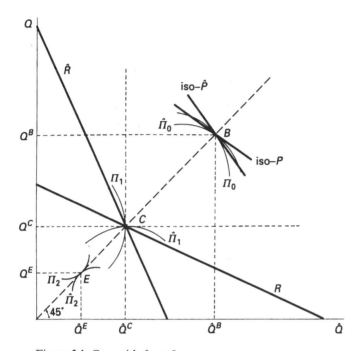

Figure 5.1 Case with $f+u>0$

$$\left[\frac{dQ}{d\hat{Q}}\right]_{d\Pi=0,\,Q=\hat{Q}}=\left[\frac{dQ}{d\hat{Q}}\right]_{d\hat{\Pi}=0,\,Q=\hat{Q}} \tag{4}$$

Since the duopolists are symmetric, at any point on the 45° line the slopes of their isoprofit loci are reciprocals. This fact and equation (4) imply that

$$\left[\frac{dQ}{d\hat{Q}}\right]_{d\Pi=0,\,Q=\hat{Q}}=1 \tag{5}$$

The slope of nohat's isoprofit locus is

$$\left[\frac{dQ}{d\hat{Q}}\right]_{d\Pi=0}=-\frac{\Pi_{\hat{Q}}^{\,Q\hat{Q}}}{\Pi_{Q}^{\,Q\hat{Q}}}=-\frac{-(f+u)Q}{a-g-(b+k)Q-(f+u)\hat{Q}} \tag{6}$$

Therefore, the condition in equation (5) becomes[8]

$$\left[\frac{dQ}{d\hat{Q}}\right]_{d\Pi=0,\,Q=\hat{Q}}=\frac{(f+u)Q}{a-g-(b+k+f+u)Q}=1 \tag{7}$$

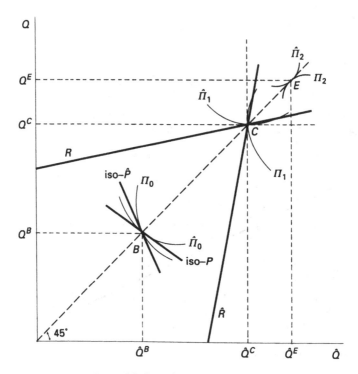

Figure 5.2 Case with $f+u<0$

Solving for Q yields the quantities produced at the efficient point, $Q^E=\hat{Q}^E$

$$Q^E=\hat{Q}^E=\frac{a-g}{b+k+2(f+u)} \tag{8}$$

The $Q\hat{Q}$ equilibrium: In the $Q\hat{Q}$ equilibrium, nohat maximizes profits taking $\hat{Q}$ as given.[9] Given values of $\hat{Q}$ are represented by vertical lines in figures 5.1 and 5.2. When the duopolists choose symmetric instruments, the quantities they produce must be the same. Therefore, in the $Q\hat{Q}$ equilibrium an isoprofit locus for nohat must be tangent to a vertical line at a point on the 45° line as it is at points C (for Cournot) in figures 5.1 and 5.2. This condition is met if and only if

$$\left[\frac{dQ}{d\hat{Q}}\right]_{d\Pi=0,\, Q=\hat{Q}}=\frac{(f+u)Q}{a-g-(b+k+f+u)Q}\rightarrow\pm\infty \tag{9}$$

$f+u$ is always positive when u is zero or positive, and we assume that $f+u\neq0$ if u is negative. It follows that the condition in equation (9) implies that

$$a-g-(b+k+f+u)Q=0 \tag{10}$$

Solving for Q yields the quantities sold in the $Q\hat{Q}$ equilibrium, $Q^C=\hat{Q}^C$

$$Q^C=\hat{Q}^C=\frac{a-g}{b+k+f+u} \tag{11}$$

The $P\hat{P}$ equilibrium: In the $P\hat{P}$ equilibrium, nohat maximizes profits taking $\hat{P}$ as given.[10] Values of $\hat{P}$ are represented by downward-sloping iso-$\hat{P}$ lines in figures 5.1 and 5.2. Solving the second equation in equation (1) for Q yields the equation for iso-$\hat{P}$ lines

$$fQ=a-\hat{P}-.5b\hat{Q} \tag{12}$$

which has the slope $-\dfrac{b}{2f}<-1$ relative to the $\hat{Q}$ axis. When the duopolists choose symmetric instruments, the quantities they produce must be the same. Therefore, in the $P\hat{P}$ equilibrium an isoprofit locus for nohat must be tangent to an iso-$\hat{P}$ line at a point on the 45° line as it is at points B (for Bertrand) in figures 5.1 and 5.2. This condition is met if and only if

$$\left[\frac{dQ}{d\hat{Q}}\right]_{d\Pi=0,\,Q=\hat{Q}}=\frac{(f+u)Q}{a-g-(b+k+f+u)Q}=-\frac{b}{2f} \tag{13}$$

Solving for Q yields the quantities produced in the $P\hat{P}$ equilibrium, $Q^B=\hat{Q}^B$

$$Q^B=\hat{Q}^B=\frac{a-g}{b+k+\left[1-\dfrac{2f}{b}\right](f+u)} \tag{14}$$

The reaction functions and the isoprofit loci: The reaction function for nohat represented by R in figures 5.1 and 5.2 gives the optimal Q for each value of $\hat{Q}$ when Q and $\hat{Q}$ are the instruments. The equation for R is obtained by setting $\Pi^{Q\hat{Q}}_{\hat{Q}}$, which is given by the denominator of the last term in equation (6), equal to zero and solving for Q to obtain

$$(b+k)Q=(a-g)-(f+u)\hat{Q} \tag{15}$$

R has a positive intercept but may have a negative or positive slope as in figures 5.1 and 5.2, respectively, depending on whether $f+u\gtrless0$.

At their intersections with R, isoprofit loci for nohat have slopes approaching plus or minus infinity with respect to the $\hat{Q}$ axis and slopes of zero with respect to the Q axis

$$\left[\frac{dQ}{d\hat{Q}}\right]_{d\Pi=0,\ \Pi_Q^{Q\hat{Q}}=0} = -\left[\frac{\Pi_{\hat{Q}}^{Q\hat{Q}}}{\Pi_Q^{Q\hat{Q}}}\right]_{\Pi_Q^{Q\hat{Q}}=0} \to \pm\infty,$$

$$\left[\frac{d\hat{Q}}{dQ}\right]_{d\Pi=0,\ \Pi_Q^{Q\hat{Q}}=0} = -\left[\frac{\Pi_Q^{Q\hat{Q}}}{\Pi_{\hat{Q}}^{Q\hat{Q}}}\right]_{\Pi_Q^{Q\hat{Q}}=0} = 0 \tag{16}$$

Expressions for $\Pi_Q^{Q\hat{Q}}$ and $\Pi_{\hat{Q}}^{Q\hat{Q}}$ are given in equation (6). $\Pi_{\hat{Q}}^{Q\hat{Q}} \neq 0$ by assumption, and $\Pi_Q^{Q\hat{Q}}=0$ on R. At their intersections with R, isoprofit loci for nohat are concave or convex to the Q axis as in figures 5.1 and 5.2, respectively, depending on whether $f+u \gtrless 0$.[11]

$$\left[\frac{d\left(\left[\frac{d\hat{Q}}{dQ}\right]_{d\Pi=0}\right)}{dQ}\right]_{\Pi_Q^{Q\hat{Q}}=0} = -\frac{\Pi_{QQ}^{Q\hat{Q}}}{\Pi_{\hat{Q}}^{Q\hat{Q}}} = -\frac{b+k}{f+u} \tag{17}$$

Thus, at their intersections with R, isoprofit loci for nohat are concave to the Q axis if R is downward sloping and are convex to the Q axis if R is upward sloping.

The $P\hat{P}$ equilibrium is the point on the 45° line at which an isoprofit locus for nohat is tangent to an iso-$\hat{P}$ line and an isoprofit locus for hat is tangent to an iso-P line. The $P\hat{P}$ equilibrium must lie to the northeast or southwest of the $Q\hat{Q}$ equilibrium as in figures 5.1 and 5.2, respectively, depending on whether $f+u \gtrless 0$.

The comparison: The ranking of the quantities produced in the $Q\hat{Q}$ and $P\hat{P}$ equilibria and at the efficient point depends on the sign of $f+u$, but the ranking of profits does not.[12] It follows from the graphical analysis above that if $f+u>0$, then the $P\hat{P}$ equilibrium lies to the northeast of the $Q\hat{Q}$ equilibrium which lies to the northeast of the efficient point as in figure 5.1 so that

$$Q^E = \hat{Q}^E < Q^C = \hat{Q}^C < Q^B = \hat{Q}^B \tag{18}$$

but that if $f+u<0$, then the $P\hat{P}$ equilibrium lies to the southwest of the $Q\hat{Q}$ equilibrium which lies to the southwest of the efficient point as in figure 5.2, so that

$$Q^B = \hat{Q}^B < Q^C = \hat{Q}^C < Q^E = \hat{Q}^E \tag{19}$$

These rankings follow from equations (8), (11), and (14) and our assumption that $b>2f$.

Q and $\hat{Q}$ are smaller or larger at the efficient point than at the $Q\hat{Q}$ equilibrium and the $P\hat{P}$ equilibrium depending on whether the spillover effects of quantity increases are negative or positive and depending on whether the spillover effects of price increases are positive or negative, respectively. One duopolist's instrument is said to have a positive spillover effect or a negative spillover effect depending on whether an increase in that instrument raises or lowers the other duopolist's profits.[13] $-(f+u)\hat{Q}$ and $-(f+u)Q$ are

the spillover effects of Q on $\hat{\Pi}$ and $\hat{Q}$ on Π, respectively, and $\left[1-\dfrac{2f}{b}\right](f+u)\hat{Q}$

and $\left[1-\dfrac{2f}{b}\right](f+u)\,Q$ are the spillover effects of P on $\hat{\Pi}$ and $\hat{P}$ on Π respec-

tively. Q and $\hat{Q}$ are positive, so the spillover effects of Q and $\hat{Q}$ are negative or positive and the spillover effects of P and $\hat{P}$ are positive or negative depending on whether $f+u \gtreqless 0$.

If the duopolists cooperate, they take account of spillover effects and attain the efficient point. However, if they behave non-cooperatively, they do not take these effects into account. For example, if $f+u>0$ so that the spillover effects of Q and $\hat{Q}$ are negative and the spillover effects of P and $\hat{P}$ are positive, nohat does not take into account the fact that an increase in his quantity lowers hat's profits or the fact that an increase in his price raises hat's profits. As a result, he chooses a larger quantity or a lower price than he would at the efficient point. Of course, if he is to obtain a lower price he must sell a larger quantity.

Q and $\hat{Q}$ are larger or smaller in the $P\hat{P}$ equilibrium than in the $Q\hat{Q}$ equilibrium depending on whether the quantities of the two goods are strategic substitutes or strategic complements. The quantities of the two goods are said to be strategic substitutes or strategic complements depending on whether an increase in one quantity lowers or raises the marginal profit of increasing the other quantity, that is, depending on whether $\Pi_{Q\hat{Q}}^{Q\hat{Q}}=f+u \gtreqless 0$. If hat chooses $\hat{P}$ instead of $\hat{Q}$ as an instrument, then when nohat increases Q, hat must reduce $\hat{Q}$ in order to keep $\hat{P}$ from falling. If the two quantities are strategic substitutes, a decrease in $\hat{Q}$ raises nohat's marginal profit, so the value of Q at which nohat's marginal profit is zero is larger. For analogous reasons, if nohat chooses P instead of Q as an instrument, the value of $\hat{Q}$ at which hat's marginal profit is zero is larger. Therefore, Q and $\hat{Q}$ are larger in the $P\hat{P}$ equilibrium than in the $Q\hat{Q}$ equilibrium.

Profits at the efficient point are always higher than profits in the $Q\hat{Q}$ equilibrium which are always higher than profits in the $P\hat{P}$ equilibrium

$$\Pi^B=\hat{\Pi}^B<\Pi^C=\hat{\Pi}^C<\Pi^E=\hat{\Pi}^E \tag{20}$$

Profits increase, remain unchanged, or decrease with increases in $Q = \hat{Q}$ depending on whether $Q = \hat{Q} \lessgtr Q^E = \hat{Q}^E$.[14] The $P\hat{P}$ equilibrium is always farther from the efficient point than the $Q\hat{Q}$ equilibrium along the 45° line.

The implications of introducing an additive demand disturbance
Preliminaries: In this section we consider the implications of introducing uncertainty into our differentiated duopoly game with joint costs in the form of an additive disturbance term that affects both demand functions ($\sigma_\eta^2 > 0$). Klemperer and Meyer (1986) discovered that with uncertainty of this form there is only one equilibrium in a differentiated duopoly game with independent costs. They obtain their result because with this kind of uncertainty nohat is not indifferent between choosing Q or P as an instrument for a given value of hat's instrument. The logic they use to establish this result is in accordance with the logic used by Poole (1970) and Weitzman (1974) to establish that with uncertainty a single controller is not indifferent among instruments. There is an important similarity between the case of independent costs considered by Klemperer and Meyer and the case of joint costs considered here: the number of equilibria is smaller with uncertainty than without it. However, there is also an important difference between the two cases: with independent costs, there is only one equilibrium for all parameter values, but with joint costs, whether there is one equilibrium or two depends on parameter values.

Recall that we assume that demands are linear, that costs are quadratic, and that the only kind of uncertainty is an additive disturbance that enters both demand functions. These assumptions have the familiar implication that nohat's expected profits for values of an instrument pair j and $\hat{j}$ can be written as the sum of nohat's zero-disturbance profits for those values of that instrument pair and a linear function of the variance of the disturbance

$$E\Pi^{ij}(j,\hat{j};\eta) = \Pi^{ij}(j,\hat{j};0) + \ell^{ij}(\sigma_\eta^2) \tag{21}$$

It is important to note that the linear function $\ell^{ij}(\sigma_\eta^2)$ depends only on which instrument pair is chosen and not on the values at which the instruments are set.

Consequently, the maximized value of nohat's expected profits for instrument j given a value of instrument $\hat{j}$ can be written as the sum of the maximized value of nohat's zero-disturbance profits for instrument j given that value of instrument $\hat{j}$ and the same linear function of the variance of the disturbance

$$\max_j[E\Pi^{ij}(j,\hat{j};\eta)] = \max_j[\Pi^{ij}(j,\hat{j};0)] + \ell^{ij}(\sigma_\eta^2) \tag{22}$$

where $max_j[E\Pi^{ij}(j,\hat{j};\eta)]$ represents the maximized value of nohat's expected profits for the instrument j given a value for the instrument $\hat{j}$, and

$max_{\hat{j}}[\Pi^{ij}(j,\hat{j};0)]$ represents the maximized value of nohat's zero-disturbance profits for the instrument j given a value for the instrument $\hat{j}$.

Evaluating $\ell^{Q\hat{Q}}(\sigma_\eta^2)$, $\ell^{P\hat{Q}}(\sigma_\eta^2)$, $\ell^{Q\hat{P}}(\sigma_\eta^2)$ and $\ell^{P\hat{P}}(\sigma_\eta^2)$, using equations (T1.1), (T1.2), (T1.3), and (T1.4) and inserting them into the appropriate version of equation (22) yield

$$max_Q[E\Pi^{Q\hat{Q}}(Q,\hat{Q};\eta)]=max_Q[\Pi^{Q\hat{Q}}(Q,\hat{Q};0)],$$

$$max_P[E\Pi^{P\hat{Q}}(P,\hat{Q};\eta)]=max_P[\Pi^{P\hat{Q}}(P,\hat{Q};0)]-2k\left(\frac{1}{b}\right)^2\sigma_\eta^2,$$

$$max_Q[E\Pi^{Q\hat{P}}(Q,\hat{P};\eta)]=max_Q[\Pi^{Q\hat{P}}(Q,\hat{P};0)],$$

$$max_P[E\Pi^{P\hat{P}}(P,\hat{P};\eta)]=max_P[\Pi^{P\hat{P}}(P,\hat{P};0)]-2(k+2u)\left(\frac{1}{b+2f}\right)^2\sigma_\eta^2. \quad (23)$$

Recall that the maximized value of nohat's zero-disturbance profits depends only on which instrument is chosen by hat and not on which instrument is chosen by nohat as stated in equations (3). Equations (23) and equations (3) together imply that

$$max_Q[E\Pi^{Q\hat{Q}}(Q,\hat{Q};\eta)]-max_P[E\Pi^{P\hat{Q}}(P,\hat{Q};\eta)]=2k\left(\frac{1}{b}\right)^2\sigma_\eta^2,$$

$$max_Q[E\Pi^{Q\hat{P}}(Q,\hat{P};\eta)]-max_P[E\Pi^{P\hat{P}}(P,\hat{P};\eta)]=2(k+2u)\left(\frac{1}{b+2f}\right)^2\sigma_\eta^2. \quad (24)$$

Our analysis of instrument choice is based on equations (24). If hat chooses $\hat{Q}$ as an instrument, nohat's expected profit is higher when Q or P is chosen as an instrument depending on whether k is positive or negative, that is, depending on whether nohat's marginal cost is increasing or decreasing in his own output. If hat chooses $\hat{P}$ as an instrument, nohat's expected profit is higher when Q or P is chosen as an instrument depending on whether

$$k+2u\gtrless0 \quad (25)$$

The Klemperer and Meyer result: Klemperer and Meyer (1986) consider the case of independent costs ($u=0$) and find that there is always a unique equilibrium. In this case, if hat chooses $\hat{P}$ as an instrument, nohat's expected profit is higher when Q or P is chosen as an instrument depending on whether k is positive or negative according to the condition in equation (25). It follows that no matter whether hat chooses $\hat{Q}$ or $\hat{P}$ as an instrument, nohat's expected profit is higher when Q or P is chosen as an instrument depending on whether k is positive or negative. A similar argument can be used to establish that in the case of independent costs no matter whether nohat chooses Q or P as an instrument, hat's expected profit

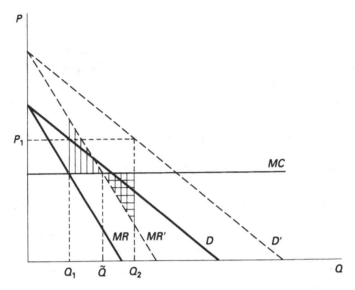

Figure 5.3 Independent costs: u=0, $k=0$

is higher when $\dot{Q}$ or $\hat{P}$ is chosen as an instrument depending on whether k is positive or negative. Therefore, if k is positive, there is a unique equilibrium in which Q and $\hat{Q}$ are chosen as the instruments, and if k is negative there is unique equilibrium in which P and $\hat{P}$ are chosen as the instruments.

The Klemperer and Meyer result can be explained graphically using figure 5.3.[15] No matter whether hat chooses $\hat{Q}$ or $\hat{P}$ as an instrument, nohat faces a residual demand curve. The slope and location of the residual demand curve are different depending on which instrument hat chooses, and the location of the residual demand curve depends on the value at which hat's instrument is set. However, the slope and location of the residual demand curve do not affect the argument made below, so D and MR can be thought of as representing the zero-disturbance residual demand curve and residual marginal revenue curve, respectively, for a particular value of either of hat's possible instruments. As a benchmark, we consider the case of constant marginal costs ($k=0$) represented by MC in figure 5.3. Nohat's profits in the zero-disturbance equilibrium are represented by the difference between the area under MR and the area under MC between zero and Q_1.

Suppose nohat's residual demand curve shifts up from D to D'. If nohat chooses Q as an instrument, profits increase by the amount of the difference between the areas under MR and MR' between the origin and Q_1. If nohat chooses P as an instrument, the change in profits has three components: (1) an increase equal to the increase that occurs when nohat chooses Q as an instrument; (2) an increase equal to the difference between the areas under MR' and MC between Q_1 and $\tilde{Q}$, the *ex post* optimal quantity, represented by the lined triangle in figure 5.3; and (3) a decrease equal to the difference between the areas under MR' and MC between $\tilde{Q}$ and Q_2, the quantity at which $P=P_1$, represented by the hatched triangle in figure 5.3. Nohat prefers Q as an instrument, is indifferent between Q and P, or prefers P as an instrument depending on whether the lined triangle is smaller than, equal to, or larger than the hatched triangle.

The lined triangle is the same size as the hatched triangle if marginal cost is constant, the case represented by MC in figure 5.3. The two triangles are similar.[16] Furthermore, $\tilde{Q}-Q_1=Q_2-\tilde{Q}.Q_2-Q_1$ is the increase in Q required to keep $P=P_1$. $\tilde{Q}-Q_1$ is the increase in Q required to keep marginal revenue constant. Since the residual demand curve is linear, $\tilde{Q}-Q_1$ is half of Q_2-Q_1. It follows that the lined triangle is smaller or larger than the hatched triangle depending on whether marginal cost is rising ($k>0$) or falling ($k<0$). Thus, nohat prefers Q as an instrument if $k>0$ and prefers P as an instrument if $k<0$.

There is a striking result not emphasized by Klemperer and Meyer. As shown above, in the case of independent costs ($u=0$) with no uncertainty, profits are larger in the $Q\hat{Q}$ equilibrium than in the $P\hat{P}$ equilibrium. In the presence of the smallest amount of uncertainty with $k<0$, there is a unique equilibrium in which P and $\hat{P}$ are chosen as the instruments. That is, for some parameter values, with the smallest amount of uncertainty the symmetric instrument pair chosen in the unique equilibrium is the one that yields lower profits with no uncertainty.

Joint costs: In the case of joint costs considered in this chapter, for some parameter values there is a unique equilibrium but for others there are two equilibria. The crucial difference between the case of independent costs and the case of joint costs is that in the latter, each duopolist's marginal cost depends on the output of the other.

If hat chooses $\hat{Q}$ as an instrument, the results for nohat's instrument choice are the same with joint costs as with independent costs: nohat prefers Q or P as an instrument depending on whether k is greater than or less than zero. A shift in D leaves nohat's marginal cost curve unaffected even though $\hat{Q}$ enters nohat's marginal costs because $\hat{Q}$ is kept fixed. Therefore, the graphical analysis above for the case of independent costs applies.

However, if hat chooses $\hat{P}$ as an instrument, the results for nohat's instrument choice are different with joint costs than with independent costs according to the condition in equation (25). Suppose nohat's costs

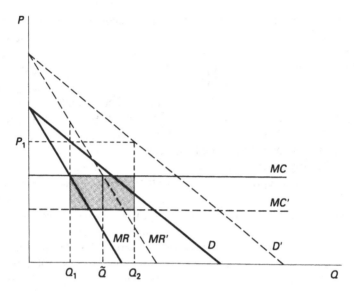

Figure 5.4 Joint costs: $u<0$, $k=0$

rise with the square of own output ($k>0$). If each duopolist's costs rise with the product of outputs ($u>0$), nohat definitely prefers Q as an instrument according to the condition in equation (25). However, if each duopolist's costs fall with the product of outputs ($u<0$), nohat prefers Q or P as an instrument depending on whether $k+2u\gtreqless0$. Now suppose that $k<0$. If $u<0$, nohat definitely prefers P as instrument. However, if $u>0$, nohat prefers P or Q as an instrument depending on whether $k+2u\lesseqgtr0$. It can be shown that if nohat chooses P as an instrument, the analysis of this paragraph applies *mutatis mutandi* to hat's instrument choice. It follows that there is a unique equilibrium or two equilibria depending on whether

$$k(k+2u)\gtreqless0 \tag{26}$$

The logic behind the results of the preceding paragraph can be explained graphically using figure 5.4 drawn for the case in which $u<0$, $k=0$, and hat chooses $\hat{P}$ as an instrument. Suppose nohat's residual demand curve shifts from D to D'. Recall that the same disturbance affects the demand curve of each duopolist. In order to keep $\hat{P}$ from rising, hat must raise $\hat{Q}$. The increase in $\hat{Q}$ lowers nohat's marginal cost from MC to MC'. This shift down in the marginal cost schedule in figure 5.4 is the only difference between figures 5.3 and 5.4. Since we know that with $k=0$ and independent costs, nohat is indifferent between P and Q as instruments because the lined triangle is the same size as the hatched triangle in figures 5.3, we can focus on the additional changes in nohat's profits that arise in the case of joint costs. If nohat chooses Q as an instrument, the additional increase in nohat's profits is equal to the difference between the areas under MC and MC' between the origin and Q_1. If nohat chooses P as an instrument, the additional increase in profits has two components: (1) the additional increase that would occur if nohat chose Q as an instrument and (2) the additional increase corresponding to the difference between the areas under MC and MC' between Q_1 and Q_2 represented by the shaded area in figure 5.4. It follows that nohat's profits are higher if P is chosen as an instrument.

Since with $u<0$ and $k=0$ nohat prefers P as an instrument, it makes sense that nohat will also prefer P as an instrument if $u<0$ and k is positive but small enough that $k+2u<0$ as stated in equation (25). Since nohat prefers Q as an instrument with $u>0$ and $k=0$, it makes sense that nohat will also prefer Q as an instrument if $u>0$ and k is negative but small enough in absolute value that $k+2u>0$ as stated in equation (25).

What conclusions can be drawn regarding the number of equilibria in a differentiated duopoly game with joint costs? If $k(k+2u)>0$, there is a unique equilibrium in which either Q and $\hat{Q}$ (if $k>0$, $k+2u>0$) or P and $\hat{P}$ (if $k<0$, $k+2u<0$) are chosen as instruments. However, if $k(k+2u)<0$, there are two equilibria, one in which Q and $\hat{Q}$ are chosen as instruments and one in which P and $\hat{P}$ are chosen as instruments. That is, for some parameter values there is only one equilibrium, but for others there are two.

It should come as no surprise that with joint costs just as with independent costs, for some parameter values there is a unique equilibrium in which the symmetric instrument pair chosen is the one that yields lower profits with no uncertainty. For example, as shown above, with no uncertainty, profits are always higher in the $Q\hat{Q}$ equilibrium than in the $P\hat{P}$ equilibrium. In the presence of the smallest amount of uncertainty with $k<0$ and $k+2u<0$, there is a unique equilibrium in which P and $\hat{P}$ are chosen as the instruments.

3 A macroeconomic example: inflation bias and uncertain money demands

In the macroeconomic example, we use a two-country version of the Kydland–Prescott (1977) and Barro-Gordon (1983) inflation-bias model similar to the one in Henderson and Zhu (1990). First, we lay out a model with (log) linear relations summarizing private sector behavior, quadratic inflation-bias preferences for countries, and an additive velocity disturbance that affects both money demands. Then, we discuss the multiplicity of equilibria with no uncertainty. Finally, we consider the implications of introducing uncertainty in the form of the additive velocity disturbance.

The Model

Private sector behavior: We use a model with two countries, nohat and hat.[17] Each country specializes in the production of a different good, and the natural rates of output in the two countries are the same when they are measured in the same good. All the variables of the model are logarithms except for the interest rates. Variables with hats over them are hat country variables. Time subscripts are suppressed wherever possible.

According to the production functions, outputs $(y, \hat{y})$ are increasing functions of employments $(n, \hat{n})$:

$$y = \bar{y} + (1-\alpha)n, \ \hat{y} = \bar{y} + (1-\alpha)\hat{n} \tag{27}$$

where $0 < \alpha < 1$ and $\bar{y} = -\ln(1-\alpha)$. Units are defined so that the natural rate of employment is equal to zero in each country, so $\bar{y}$ is the natural rate of output in each country.

In order to maximize profits, firms employ labor up to the point at which marginal products of labor are equal to real product wages

$$w - p = -\alpha n, \ \hat{w} - \hat{p} = -\alpha\hat{n} \tag{28}$$

Marginal products decrease as employments increase. Real product wages are nominal wages $(w, \hat{w})$ minus product prices $(p, \hat{p})$. Equations (28) can be solved for output prices

$$p = w + \alpha n, \ \hat{p} = \hat{w} + \alpha\hat{n} \tag{29}$$

Before markets meet each period, workers and firms enter into wage contracts that specify nominal wages and employment rules. We explain how nominal wages are determined later when we discuss the game between the countries; at this point we take them as given. Workers agree to supply whatever quantity of labor firms want at the nominal wages specified in the contracts.

Consumer price levels $(q, \hat{q})$ are given by

$$q = (1-\beta)p + \beta(e+\hat{p}) = p + \beta z$$

$$\hat{q} = \beta(p-e) + (1-\beta)\hat{p} = \hat{p} - \beta z \tag{30}$$

where $0 < \beta < 1$ is the average propensity to import in each country, the exchange rate (e) is the nohat currency price of hat currency, and the relative price of the foreign good or real exchange rate (z) is

$$z = e + \hat{p} - p \tag{31}$$

Each country's money is held only by the residents of that country. Money markets are in equilibrium when money supplies $(m, \hat{m})$ satisfy simple quantity-theory equations

$$m+v+\bar{y}=p+y, \ \hat{m}+v+\bar{y}=\hat{p}+\hat{y} \tag{32}$$

For algebraic simplicity, the expected value of the logarithm of velocity has been set equal to $\bar{y}$ in each country. The world velocity disturbance (v) is identically and independently distributed with a zero mean.

Residents of each country may hold bonds denominated in both currencies. They regard bonds denominated in the two currencies as perfect substitutes, so they will hold positive amounts of both kinds of bonds only when the nominal interest rate on nohat-currency bonds (i) is equal to the nominal interest rate on hat-currency bonds ($\hat{i}$) plus the expected rate of depreciation

$$i=\hat{i}+e_{+1}-e \tag{33}$$

where a variable with $+1$ subscript is the value of that variable expected to prevail next period based on today's information. In what follows we refer to nominal interest rates simply as interest rates. The expected real interest rates for residents of the two countries are

$$r=i-q_{+1}+q, \ \hat{r}=\hat{i}-\hat{q}_{+1}+\hat{q} \tag{34}$$

Log-linearizing the demands for the two goods in the neighborhood of the natural rates of output yields

$$y=\bar{y}+\delta z+(1-\beta)\epsilon(y-\bar{y})+\beta\epsilon(\hat{y}-\bar{y})-(1-\beta)\gamma r-\beta\gamma\hat{r}$$

$$\hat{y}=\bar{y}-\delta z+\beta\epsilon(y-\bar{y})+(1-\beta)\epsilon(\hat{y}-\bar{y})-\beta\gamma r-(1-\beta)\gamma\hat{r} \tag{35}$$

Demands for both goods increase with both outputs. Residents of each country increase spending by the same fraction ($0<\epsilon<1$) of increases in output. The marginal propensity to import is equal to the average propensity to import of β in each country. Demands for both goods decrease with expected real interest rates (r, $\hat{r}$). Residents of each country decrease spending by the same amount (γ) for each percentage point increase in the expected real interest rate available to them. Depreciation of the real exchange rate shifts world demand from foreign goods to home goods.[18]

We assume that countries care about employment (n, $\hat{n}$) and inflation (π, $\hat{\pi}$), where

$$\pi=q-q_{-1}, \ \hat{\pi}=\hat{q}-\hat{q}_{-1} \tag{36}$$

so we solve the model for these variables. Since the countries are symmetric, we need explain in detail the solution for only one country, say nohat. The solutions are different when different variables are chosen as policy instruments. Each country can choose either the money supply or the interest rate as an instrument, so there are four regimes: the $m\hat{m}$, $i\hat{i}$, $m\hat{i}$, and $i\hat{m}$

regimes. We also calculate the inflation–employment tradeoffs faced by the countries. The tradeoff faced by a country depends not on which variable it chooses as its instrument but on which variable the other country chooses as its instrument.

In the $m\hat{m}$ regime, the reduced forms for employments can be obtained by substituting equations (27) and (29) into equations (32)

$$n=m+v-w, \; \hat{n}=\hat{m}+v-\hat{w} \tag{37}$$

Nohat employment rises one for one with the nohat money supply and is unaffected by the hat money supply. These results depend crucially on two key features of our quantity-theory formulation: the nohat interest rate does not enter nohat money demand, and the real income elasticity of nohat money demand is equal to one. These features imply that increases in the nohat money supply must be matched by increases in nohat nominal income. Nohat nominal income increases one for one with increases in nohat employment and is unaffected by increases in the hat money supply.

Obtaining solutions for inflation rates takes somewhat longer. According to equations (30), each country's consumer price level can be written as a weighted sum of that country's product price and the real exchange rate. Product prices are obtained by substituting equations (37) into equations (29)

$$p=\alpha(m+v-w)+w, \; \hat{p}=\alpha(\hat{m}+v-\hat{w})+\hat{w} \tag{38}$$

Increases in m raise n thereby lowering the nohat marginal product of labor, so p must rise to reduce the nohat real product wage.

The real exchange rate is obtained in several steps. Subtracting the second equation in equations (35) from the first and solving for z yields

$$2\delta z=[1-(1-2\beta)\epsilon][(y-\bar{y})-(\hat{y}-\bar{y})]+(1-2\beta)\gamma(r-\hat{r}) \tag{39}$$

Subtracting the second equation in equations (34) from the first and making use of equations (30), (31), and (33) yield

$$r-\hat{r}=(1-2\beta)(z_{+1}-z)=-(1-2\beta)z \tag{40}$$

where $z_{+1}=0$ because we assume that there are no speculative bubbles.[19] Substituting equation (40) into equation (39) and solving for z yield

$$z=\left(\frac{\rho}{1-\alpha}\right)[(y-\bar{y})-(\hat{y}-\bar{y})],$$

$$\rho=\frac{(1-\alpha)[1-(1-2\beta)\epsilon]}{2\delta+(1-2\beta)^2\gamma} \tag{41}$$

Substituting equations (37) into equations (27) and substituting the resulting equations into equation (41) yield

$$z=\rho[(m+v-w)-(\hat{m}+v-\hat{w})] \tag{42}$$

Increases in a country's money supply raise its employment and, therefore, its output. Increases in nohat output and decreases in hat output increase the difference between the excess supply of the nohat good and the excess supply of the hat good, so the nohat currency must depreciate in real terms.

The reduced forms for price levels and inflation rates are obtained by substituting equations (38) and (42) into equations (30)

$$\pi=q=w+(\alpha+\beta\rho)(m+v-w)-\beta\rho(\hat{m}+v-\hat{w}),$$

$$\hat{\pi}=\hat{q}=\hat{w}-\beta\rho(m+v-w)+(\alpha+\beta\rho)(\hat{m}+v-\hat{w}) \tag{43}$$

where we have set last period's price levels equal to zero ($q_{-1}=\hat{q}_{-1}=0$) so that price levels and inflation rates are the same thing in the current period. Increases in the nohat money supply raise the price of nohat output and cause real depreciation of the nohat currency, so they increase nohat inflation and decrease hat inflation.

For the $m\hat{m}$ regime we collect together the reduced forms for employments and inflations and present the inflation–employment tradeoffs

$$n^{m\hat{m}}=m+v-w,$$

$$\hat{n}^{m\hat{m}}=\hat{m}+v-\hat{w}, \tag{44}$$

$$\pi^{m\hat{m}}=w+(\alpha+\beta\rho)(m+v-w)-\beta\rho(\hat{m}+v-\hat{w}),$$

$$\hat{\pi}^{m\hat{m}}=\hat{w}-\beta\rho(m+v-w)+(\alpha+\beta\rho)(\hat{m}+v-\hat{w}), \tag{45}$$

$$\tau^{m\hat{m}}=\frac{\pi^{m\hat{m}}_m}{n^{m\hat{m}}_m}=\alpha+\beta\rho, \quad \hat{\tau}^{m\hat{m}}=\frac{\hat{\pi}^{m\hat{m}}_{\hat{m}}}{\hat{n}^{m\hat{m}}_{\hat{m}}}=\alpha+\beta\rho \tag{46}$$

where n^{ij}, $\hat{n}^{ij}$, π^{ij}, and $\hat{\pi}^{ij}$ represent the solutions for n, $\hat{n}$, π, and $\hat{\pi}$ under the $j\hat{j}$ regime, respectively, and where τ^{ij} represents the inflation–employment tradeoff for nohat when hat chooses $\hat{j}$ as its instrument and $\hat{\tau}^{ij}$ represents the inflation–employment tradeoff for hat when nohat chooses j as its instrument.

It is useful to derive solutions for (expected) real interest rates in the $m\hat{m}$ regime. Adding the two equations in equations (35) and rearranging yield

$$r+\hat{r}=-\left(\frac{2\phi}{1-\alpha}\right)[(y-\bar{y})+(\hat{y}-\bar{y})],$$

$$\phi=\left(\frac{1-\epsilon}{2\gamma}\right)(1-\alpha). \tag{47}$$

Eliminating z from equation (40) using equation (41) yields

$$r - \hat{r} = -\left(\frac{2\theta}{1-\alpha}\right)[(y-\bar{y})-(\hat{y}-\bar{y})],$$

$$\theta = \left(\frac{1-2\beta}{2}\right)\rho \tag{48}$$

Using equations (47) and (48) to solve for r and in terms of $y-\bar{y}$ and $\hat{y}-\bar{y}$, and using equations (27) and (37) to eliminate $y-\bar{y}$ and $\hat{y}-\bar{y}$ yield

$$r = i - \pi_{+1} = -(\theta+\phi)(m+v-w)+(\theta-\phi)(\hat{m}+v-\hat{w}),$$

$$\hat{r} = \hat{i} - \hat{\pi}_{+1} = (\theta-\phi)(m+v-w)-(\theta+\phi)(\hat{m}+v-\hat{w}) \tag{49}$$

Increases in the sum of and the difference between nohat's output and hat's output increase the sum of and the difference between excess supplies of the two goods, respectively. Therefore, it is logical that $r+\hat{r}$ is negatively related to the sum of outputs and that $r-\hat{r}$ is negatively related to the difference between outputs as shown in equations (47) and (48), respectively.

r can be expressed as half the sum of $r+\hat{r}$ and $r-\hat{r}$. Increases in m lower r because they increase both the sum of outputs and the difference between outputs. $\hat{r}$ can be expressed as half the difference between $r+\hat{r}$ and $r-\hat{r}$. Under our assumption that $\theta>\phi$, an increase in m raises $\hat{r}$ because the decrease in $r-\hat{r}$ caused by the increase in the difference between outputs is greater in absolute value than the decrease in $r+\hat{r}$ caused by the increase in the sum of outputs.

A decrease in i with no change in $\hat{i}$ is achieved by increasing m and increasing $\hat{m}$ by less. $\hat{m}$ must increase because an increase in m with $\hat{m}$ held constant causes r to fall and $\hat{r}$ to rise. However, the increase in $\hat{m}$ must be less than the increase in m because equal increases in m and $\hat{m}$ lower both r and $\hat{r}$. We assume that π_{+1} and $\hat{\pi}_{+1}$ are unaffected by changes in m and $\hat{m}$, so changes in r and $\hat{r}$ are reflected completely in changes in i and $\hat{i}$, respectively.

For what follows it is helpful to use equations (49) to obtain expressions for $m+v-w$ and $\hat{m}+v-\hat{w}$ in terms of $i-\pi_{+1}$ and $\hat{i}-\hat{\pi}_{+1}$

$$m+v-w = -\left(\frac{\theta+\phi}{4\theta\phi}\right)(i-\pi_{+1})-\left(\frac{\theta-\phi}{4\theta\phi}\right)(\hat{i}-\hat{\pi}_{+1}),$$

$$\hat{m}+v-\hat{w} = -\left(\frac{\theta-\phi}{4\theta\phi}\right)(i-\pi_{+1})-\left(\frac{\theta+\phi}{4\theta\phi}\right)(\hat{i}-\hat{\pi}_{+1}), \tag{50}$$

In an $i\hat{i}$ regime, the reduced forms for employment and inflation rates and the inflation–employment tradeoffs are

$$n^{ii} = -\left(\frac{\theta+\phi}{4\theta\phi}\right)(i-\pi_{+1}) - \left(\frac{\theta-\phi}{4\theta\phi}\right)(\hat{i}-\hat{\pi}_{+1}),$$

$$\hat{n}^{ii} = -\left(\frac{\theta-\phi}{4\theta\phi}\right)(i-\pi_{+1}) - \left(\frac{\theta+\phi}{4\theta\phi}\right)(\hat{i}-\hat{\pi}_{+1}), \tag{51}$$

$$\pi^{ii} = -\left(\frac{\theta+\phi}{4\theta\phi}\right)\left[\alpha+\beta\rho\left(\frac{2\phi}{\theta+\phi}\right)\right](i-\pi_{+1})$$

$$-\left(\frac{\theta+\phi}{4\theta\phi}\right)\left[\alpha-(\alpha+\beta\rho)\left(\frac{2\phi}{\theta+\phi}\right)\right](\hat{i}-\hat{\pi}_{+1})+w,$$

$$\hat{\pi}^{ii} = -\left(\frac{\theta+\phi}{4\theta\phi}\right)\left[\alpha-(\alpha+\beta\rho)\left(\frac{2\phi}{\theta+\phi}\right)\right](i-\pi_{+1})$$

$$-\left(\frac{\theta+\phi}{4\theta\phi}\right)\left[\alpha+\beta\rho\left(\frac{2\phi}{\theta+\phi}\right)\right](\hat{i}-\hat{\pi}_{+1})+\hat{w} \tag{52}$$

$$\tau^{ii} = \frac{\pi_i^{ii}}{n_i^{ii}} = \alpha+\beta\rho\left(\frac{2\phi}{\theta+\phi}\right), \quad \hat{\tau}^{ii} = \frac{\hat{\pi}_i^{ii}}{\hat{n}_i^{ii}} = \alpha+\beta\rho\left(\frac{2\phi}{\theta+\phi}\right) \tag{53}$$

The solutions for employments and inflation rates are obtained by using equations (50) to eliminate $m+v-w$ and $\hat{m}+v-\hat{w}$ in equations (44) and (45).

The important thing to note here is that nohat's inflation–employment tradeoff is flatter when hat is fixing $\hat{i}$ than when hat is fixing $\hat{m}$; that is $\tau^{ii} < \tau^{m\hat{m}}$ if $\theta > \phi$. As explained above, a reduction in i with $\hat{i}$ held constant is achieved by increasing m and increasing $\hat{m}$ by less. Therefore, when hat is fixing $\hat{i}$, the increase in π accompanying an increase in n is less because the increase in $\hat{m}$ partially offsets the real depreciation of nohat's currency caused by the increase in m.

In an $m\hat{i}$ regime, the solutions for employment and inflation rates and the inflation–employment tradeoffs are

$$n^{m\hat{i}} = m+v-w,$$

$$\hat{n}^{m\hat{i}} = \left(\frac{\theta-\phi}{\theta+\phi}\right)(m+v-w) - \left(\frac{1}{\theta+\phi}\right)(\hat{i}-\hat{\pi}_{+1}), \tag{54}$$

$$\pi^{m\hat{i}} = \left[\alpha+\beta\rho\left(\frac{2\phi}{\theta+\phi}\right)\right](m+v-w) + \left(\frac{\beta\rho}{\theta+\phi}\right)(\hat{i}-\hat{\pi}_{+1})+w,$$

$$\hat{\pi}^{m\hat{i}} = \left[\alpha-(\alpha+\beta\rho)\left(\frac{2\phi}{\theta+\phi}\right)\right](m+v-w) - \left(\frac{\alpha+\beta\rho}{\theta+\phi}\right)(\hat{i}-\hat{\pi}_{+1})+\hat{w}, \tag{55}$$

$$\tau^{mi} = \frac{\pi_m^{mi}}{n_m^{mi}} = \alpha + \beta\rho\left(\frac{2\phi}{\theta+\phi}\right), \quad \hat{\tau}^{mi} = \frac{\hat{\pi}_i^{mi}}{\hat{n}_i^{mi}} = \alpha + \beta\rho \tag{56}$$

The solutions for employment and inflation rates are obtained by solving the second equation in equations (49) for $\hat{m} + v - \hat{w}$ and using the result to eliminate this variable in equations (44) and (45).

In an $i\hat{m}$ regime, the reduced forms for employment and inflation are completely symmetric to the reduced forms in a mi regime. Nohat and hat variables are simply interchanged.

The important thing to note here is that a country's choice of instrument does not affect its own inflation–employment tradeoff, but it does affect its opponent's. No matter which instrument nohat chooses, it faces the steep tradeoff, $\tau^{m\hat{m}} = \tau^{i\hat{m}} = \alpha + \beta\rho$, when hat fixes $\hat{m}$ and the tradeoff, $\tau^{i\hat{i}} = \tau^{mi}$

$$= \alpha + \beta\rho\left(\frac{2\phi}{\theta+\phi}\right), \text{ when hat fixes } \hat{i}.$$

Countries' utility functions: The countries' period utility functions are[20]

$$U = \Psi n - .5\pi^2, \quad \hat{U} = \Psi\hat{n} - .5\hat{\pi}^2 \tag{57}$$

Each country's period utility is increasing in its employment and decreasing in squared deviations of its inflation from zero. Wage setters want zero employment, and they set the nominal wages, w and $\hat{w}$ to achieve their goals. Why do countries want higher employment than their wage setters? At least two answers have been given: one is that income taxes may distort the labor–leisure decision, making the "natural rate" of employment too low, and another is that monopolistic unions may seek real wages that are too high for the employment of the entire labor force. Expressions for period utilities in terms of instruments, wages, expected inflations, and the disturbance are given in equations (T2.1) through (T2.4) in table 5.2 where w, $\hat{w}$, π_{+1}, and $\hat{\pi}_{+1}$ have been omitted from the lists of arguments in the utility functions for brevity.

The model with no uncertainty

The multiplicity of equilibria: With no uncertainty ($\sigma_v^2 = 0$) there is a multiplicity of equilibria in the macroeconomic example, just as in the microeconomic example. The method of proof used in the macroeconomic example is analogous to the method used in the microeconomic example. However, there is an important difference. In the microeconomic example, each duopolist must take into account only the behavior of the other duopolist. All that either of the duopolists needs to know about the other agent is summarized in the demands and costs. In contrast, in the macroeconomic

Table 5.2 *Nohat's utility for four pairs of instrument choices*

$$
\begin{aligned}
U^{m\hat{m}}(m,\hat{m};v) = &[\Psi - w(\alpha + \beta\rho)](m+v-w) + w\beta\rho(\hat{m}+v-\hat{w}) \\
&-.5(\alpha+\beta\rho)^2(m+v-w)^2 -.5(\beta\rho)^2(\hat{m}+v-\hat{w})^2 \\
&+\beta\rho(\alpha+\beta\rho)(m+v-w)(\hat{m}+v-\hat{w}) -.5w^2,
\end{aligned}
\tag{T2.1}
$$

$$
\begin{aligned}
(\theta+\phi)^2 U^{i\hat{m}}(i,\hat{m};v) = &-(\theta+\phi)[\Psi - w(\alpha+\beta\rho)](i-\pi_{+1}) \\
&+(\theta+\phi)\{\Psi(\theta-\phi) - w[\alpha(\theta+\phi)-(\alpha+\beta\rho)2\phi]\}(\hat{m}+v-\hat{w}) \\
&-.5(\alpha+\beta\rho)^2(i-\pi_{+1})^2 \\
&-.5[\alpha(\theta+\phi)-(\alpha+\beta\rho)2\phi]^2(\hat{m}+v-\hat{w})^2 \\
&+(\alpha+\beta\rho)[\alpha(\theta+\phi)-(\alpha+\beta\rho)2\phi](i-\pi_{+1})(\hat{m}+v-\hat{w}) \\
&-.5(\theta+\phi)^2 w^2,
\end{aligned}
\tag{T2.2}
$$

$$
\begin{aligned}
(\theta+\phi)^2 U^{m\hat{i}}(m,\hat{i};v) = &(\theta+\phi)\{(\theta+\phi)\Psi - w[\alpha(\theta+\phi)+\beta\rho(2\phi)]\}(m+v-w) \\
&-w(\theta+\phi)\beta\rho(\hat{i}-\hat{\pi}_{+1}) -.5[\alpha(\theta+\phi)+\beta\rho(2\phi)]^2(m+v-w)^2 \\
&-.5(\beta\rho)^2(\hat{i}-\hat{\pi}_{+1})^2 \\
&-\beta\rho[\alpha(\theta+\phi)+\beta\rho(2\phi)](m+v-w)(\hat{i}-\hat{\pi}_{+1}) -.5(\theta+\phi)^2\hat{w}^2,
\end{aligned}
\tag{T2.3}
$$

$$
\begin{aligned}
16\theta^2\phi^2 U^{i\hat{i}}(i,\hat{i};v) = &-4\theta\phi\{\Psi(\theta+\phi) - w[\alpha(\theta+\phi)+\beta\rho(2\phi)]\}(i-\pi_{+1}) \\
&-4\theta\phi\{\Psi(\theta-\phi) - w[\alpha(\theta+\phi)-(\alpha+\beta\rho)(2\phi)]\}(\hat{i}-\hat{\pi}_{+1}) \\
&-.5[\alpha(\theta+\phi)+\beta\rho(2\phi)]^2(i-\pi_{+1})^2 \\
&-.5[\alpha(\theta+\phi)-(\alpha+\beta\rho)2\phi]^2(\hat{i}-\hat{\pi}_{+1})^2 \\
&-[\alpha(\theta+\phi)+\beta\rho(2\phi)] \\
&\times[\alpha(\theta+\phi)-(\alpha+\beta\rho)2\phi](i-\pi_{+1})(\hat{i}-\hat{\pi}_{+1}) -8\theta^2\phi^2 w^2.
\end{aligned}
\tag{T2.4}
$$

example each country must take into account not only the behavior of the other country but also the behavior of the wage setters and the values of expected inflation in both countries. As in the microeconomic example, since the players are symmetric we need consider in detail the behavior of only one of them, say nohat.

If hat chooses $\hat{j}$ as an instrument and sets it at a particular value, wage setters set w and $\hat{w}$ at particular values, and π_{+1} and $\hat{\pi}_{+1}$ are given, the maximum value of nohat's zero-disturbance utility is the same no matter which variable it chooses as an instrument

$$
\max_m[U^{m\hat{j}}(m,\hat{j};0)] = \max_i[U^{i\hat{j}}(i,\hat{j};0)]
\tag{58}
$$

For given values for $\hat{j}$, w, $\hat{w}$, π_{+1}, and $\hat{\pi}_{+1}$, there is a one to one relationship between m and i.

It follows that there are four equilibria in which the instrument pairs are m and $\hat{m}$, i and $\hat{m}$, m and $\hat{i}$, and i and $\hat{i}$ respectively. We refer to these equilibria as the $m\hat{m}$, $i\hat{m}$, $m\hat{i}$, and $i\hat{i}$ equilibria, respectively. As an example, we establish that there is an $i\hat{m}$ equilibrium conditional on values for w, $\hat{w}$, π_{+1}, and $\hat{\pi}_{+1}$. The determination of the equilibrium values of w, $\hat{w}$, π_{+1}, and $\hat{\pi}_{+1}$ is explained below. Begin with the expressions for nohat's and hat's utility when i and $\hat{m}$ are chosen as instruments, where the expression for nohat is equation (T2.2) in table 5.2 and the expression for hat is analogous to equation (T2.3) in table 5.2. Set both the first derivative of nohat's utility function with respect to i and the first derivative of hat's utility function with respect to $\hat{m}$ equal to zero. This pair of first-order conditions is a pair of simultaneous linear equations in i and $\hat{m}$. It remains to demonstrate that the solution to this pair of first-order conditions is an equilibrium. Given the solution for $\hat{m}$, the solution for i is the best response for nohat given that it chooses i as an instrument. Likewise, given the solution for i, the solution for $\hat{m}$ is the best response for hat given that it chooses $\hat{m}$ as an instrument. As we argue in the preceding paragraph, nohat can do no better by choosing m as an instrument. Likewise, hat can do no better by choosing $\hat{i}$ as an instrument. Therefore, the solution to the pair of first-order conditions when i and $\hat{m}$ are chosen as instruments is an equilibrium. In a similar manner, it can be established that there are $m\hat{m}$, $m\hat{i}$, and $\hat{i}$ equilibria conditional on values for w, $\hat{w}$, π_{+1}, and $\hat{\pi}_{+1}$.

The comparison of utilities at five points: In this sub-section, we compare utilities at the symmetric efficient point with those in the four non-cooperative equilibria, the $m\hat{m}$, $i\hat{m}$, $m\hat{i}$, and $\hat{i}$ equilibria.

The efficient point: As in the microeconomic example, we use as a standard of comparison the symmetric efficient point, the point at which the simple sum of the utilities of the countries is maximized subject to the constraint that employment is zero, and refer to it as "the" efficient point.

Setting up the maximization problem and deriving the first-order conditions are straightforward exercises, but little insight is gained by performing them. It is obvious from inspection of the countries' utility functions that if employment is constrained to be equal to zero, then in order to maximize the sum of their utilities the countries should choose their policy instruments so that their inflation rates are equal to zero.

The four non-cooperative equilibria: Now we derive expressions for countries' utilities in the four non-cooperative equilibria, the $m\hat{m}$, $i\hat{m}$, $m\hat{i}$, and $\hat{i}$ equilibria. As part of the derivation, we explain how w, $\hat{w}$, π_{+1}, and $\hat{\pi}_{+1}$ are determined.

The first-order conditions for the countries are

$$U_j^{jj} = \Psi n_j^{jj} - \pi \pi_j^{jj} = 0, \quad \hat{U}_j^{jj} = \Psi \hat{n}_j^{jj} - \hat{\pi} \hat{\pi}_j^{jj} = 0 \qquad (59)$$

and the reduced forms for n, $\hat{n}$, π, and $\hat{\pi}$ for each instrument pair are given above.

Equilibrium inflation rates are obtained by solving equations (59) for π and $\hat{\pi}$

$$\pi^{ij}= \Psi\left[\frac{\pi_j^{ij}}{n_j^{ij}}\right]^{-1} =\frac{\Psi}{\tau^{ij}},\ \hat{\pi}^{ij}= \Psi\left[\frac{\hat{\pi}_j^{ij}}{\hat{n}_j^{ij}}\right]^{-1} =\frac{\Psi}{\hat{\tau}^{ij}}, \tag{60}$$

If the instruments chosen imply flat inflation–employment tradeoffs, inflation must be high in both countries; if the instruments chosen imply steep tradeoffs, inflation can be low.

Wage setters know the equilibrium values of π and $\hat{\pi}$ and the reduced forms for n, $\hat{n}$, π, and $\hat{\pi}$, so they can set money wages, w and $\hat{w}$, just high enough that both countries will give them the zero employment they want. Let j and $\hat{j}$ be the instruments the countries have chosen. For given values of π_{+1} and $\hat{\pi}_{+1}$, the wage setters can calculate the values of w, $\hat{w}$, j, and $\hat{j}$ that are consistent with the conditions that π and $\hat{\pi}$ be equal to the equilibrium values given in equations (60) and with the two additional conditions that n and $\hat{n}$ be equal to zero. Wage setters then set w and $\hat{w}$ equal to the values they have calculated. Given these values of w and $\hat{w}$, the countries must set j and $\hat{j}$ equal to the values calculated by wage setters in order to achieve the equilibrium values of π and $\hat{\pi}$.

Only i and $\hat{i}$ depend on the given values of π_{+1} and $\hat{\pi}_{+1}$. We assume that the private sector expects that the countries' preferences will be the same in all future periods and, therefore, sets π_{+1} and $\hat{\pi}_{+1}$ equal to the values of π and $\hat{\pi}$ given by equations (60) in each period.

The equilibrium utilities for the countries are

$$U^{ij}(j,\hat{j};0)=-.5\left[\frac{\Psi}{\tau^{ij}}\right]^2,\ \hat{U}^{ij}(j,\hat{j};0)=-.5\left[\frac{\Psi}{\hat{\tau}^{ij}}\right]^2 \tag{61}$$

where $U^{ij}(j,\hat{j};0)$ and $\hat{U}^{ij}(j,\hat{j};0)$ represent the zero-disturbance utilities of nohat and hat when nohat chooses j and hat chooses $\hat{j}$. Each country's utility depends on its inflation–employment tradeoff, a tradeoff imposed on it by the other country's choice of instrument, and on the employment weight in its own utility function but not on the employment weight in the other country's utility function.[21] For a given value of its employment weight, the steeper a country's inflation–employment tradeoff, the lower its inflation rate and the higher its utility.

The implications of introducing an additive disturbance to money demands

In this section we consider the implications of introducing uncertainty into our monetary policy game in the form of an additive velocity disturbance that affects both money demands ($\sigma_v^2>0$). For some parameter values there is a unique equilibrium but for others there are two equilibria.

Recall that we assume that countries' preferences are quadratic, that the behavior of the private sector can be summarized by (log) linear equations, and that the only kind of uncertainty is an additive velocity disturbance that affects both money demands. These assumptions have the familiar implication that nohat's expected utility for values of an instrument pair j and $\hat{j}$ can be written as the sum of nohat's zero-disturbance utility for those values of that instrument pair and a linear function of the variance of the disturbance

$$E[U^{i\hat{j}}(j,\hat{j};v)]=U^{i\hat{j}}(j,\hat{j};0)+\ell^{i\hat{j}}(\sigma_v^2) \tag{62}$$

where the linear function $\ell^{i\hat{j}}(\sigma_v^2)$ depends only on which instrument pair is chosen and not on the values at which the instruments are set.

Consequently, the maximized value of nohat's expected utility for instrument j given a value of instrument $\hat{j}$ can be written as the sum of the maximized value of nohat's zero-disturbance utility for instrument j given that value of instrument $\hat{j}$ and the same linear function of the variance of the disturbance

$$\max_j E[U^{i\hat{j}}(j,\hat{j};v)]=\max_j[U^{i\hat{j}}(j,\hat{j};0)]+\ell^{i\hat{j}}(\sigma_v^2) \tag{63}$$

Evaluating $\ell^{m\hat{m}}(\sigma_v^2)$, $\ell^{i\hat{m}}(\sigma_v^2)$, $\ell^{mi}(\sigma_v^2)$, and $\ell^{ii}(\sigma_v^2)$ using equations (T2.1), (T2.2), (T2.3), and (T2.4) and inserting them into the appropriate version of equation (63) yield

$$\max_m[EU^{m\hat{m}}(m,\hat{m};v)]=\max_m[U^{m\hat{m}}(m,\hat{m};0)]-.5\alpha^2\sigma_v^2,$$

$$\max_i[EU^{i\hat{m}}(i,\hat{m};v)]=\max_i[U^{i\hat{m}}(i,\hat{m};0)]-.5\left[\alpha-(\alpha+\beta\rho)\left(\frac{2\phi}{\theta+\phi}\right)\right]^2\sigma_v^2$$

$$\max_m[EU^{m\hat{i}}(m,\hat{i};v)]=\max_m[U^{m\hat{i}}(m,\hat{i};0)]-.5\left[\alpha+\beta\rho\left(\frac{2\phi}{\theta+\phi}\right)\right]^2\sigma_v^2$$

$$\max_i[EU^{i\hat{i}}(i,\hat{i};v)]=\max_i[U^{i\hat{i}}(i,\hat{i};0)] \tag{64}$$

Students of Poole (1970) will find it natural to begin the analysis of the effects of a velocity disturbance with the case in which hat chooses $\hat{i}$.[22] If hat chooses $\hat{i}$, nohat is better off choosing i for all values of the parameters. Recall that the maximized value of nohat's zero-disturbance utility depends only on which instrument is chosen by hat and not on which instrument is chosen by nohat as stated in equations (58). Equations (64) and (58) together imply that

$$\max_i[EU^{i\hat{i}}(i,\hat{i};v)]-\max_m[EU^{m\hat{i}}(m,\hat{i};v)]=.5\left[\alpha+\beta\rho\left(\frac{2\phi}{\theta+\phi}\right)\right]^2\sigma_v^2>0 \tag{65}$$

The only way that both i and $\hat{\imath}$ can be kept constant is if nohat offsets the effect of the velocity disturbance on the nohat money market and hat offsets the effect of the velocity disturbance on the hat money market. Thus, if nohat chooses i, a velocity disturbance has no effect on either target variable. However, if nohat chooses m, a positive velocity disturbance has the same effect as an increase in m of equal size. With $\hat{\imath}$ fixed, an increase in m increases n and π.

Unfortunately, when hat chooses $\hat{m}$, the results are not so clear cut. If hat chooses $\hat{m}$, nohat is better off choosing i if and only if

$$\max_i[EU^{i\hat{m}}(i,\hat{m};v)] - \max_m[EU^{m\hat{m}}(m,\hat{m};v)]$$

$$= -.5\left\{\left[\alpha-(\alpha+\beta\rho)\left(\frac{2\phi}{\theta+\phi}\right)\right]^2 - \alpha^2\right\}\sigma_v^2 \tag{66}$$

$$= .5\left[\alpha-(\alpha+\beta\rho)\left(\frac{2\phi}{\theta+\phi}\right)+\alpha\right]\left[(\alpha+\beta\rho)\left(\frac{2\phi}{\theta+\phi}\right)\right]\sigma_v^2>0$$

that is, if and only if

$$\alpha-(\alpha+\beta\rho)\left(\frac{2\phi}{\theta+\phi}\right)>-\alpha \tag{67}$$

If nohat chooses m, the effects of an increase in v are the same as the effects of an increase in m and $\hat{m}$ by equal amounts. The increase in π is

$$\pi_v^{m\hat{m}}=\alpha \tag{68}$$

from equations (45). If nohat chooses i, the change in π is

$$\pi_v^{i\hat{m}}=\alpha-(\alpha+\beta\rho)\left(\frac{2\phi}{\theta+\phi}\right)\gtreqless 0 \tag{69}$$

by analogy with equations (55). The total effect of an increase in v on π in an $i\hat{m}$ regime may be positive or negative and can be written as the sum of two effects: (1) the increase in π resulting from an increase in v under an $m\hat{m}$ regime which is equal to α and (2) the decrease in π caused by the decrease in m required to keep i constant which is equal to $-(\alpha+\beta\rho)\left(\dfrac{2\phi}{\theta+\phi}\right)$. The second effect is the product of the decrease in m required to keep i constant which is equal to $-\dfrac{2\phi}{\theta+\phi}$ from equations (49) and the change in π caused by a change in m which is equal to $\alpha+\beta\rho$ from equations (45). The interpretation of the condition in equation (67) is that if hat chooses $\hat{m}$, nohat is better off choosing i if and only if the change in π when it chooses i is greater in algebraic value than the negative of the change in π when it chooses m.

Hat and nohat are symmetric. Therefore, if nohat chooses i, hat is better off choosing $\hat{i}$ for all parameter values. However, if nohat chooses m, hat is better off choosing $\hat{i}$ if and only if the condition in equation (67) is fulfilled. It follows that there is a unique equilibrium with i and $\hat{i}$ chosen as instruments if and only if the condition in equation (67) is fulfilled. However, if this condition is not fulfilled there are two equilibria, one with i and $\hat{i}$ chosen as instruments and another with m and $\hat{m}$ chosen as instruments.

It is interesting that the condition in equation (67) is independent of the parameter δ, the parameter which determines the amount by which the demand for nohat's good rises and the demand for hat's good falls when nohat's currency depreciates in real terms. Multiplying through the condition in equation (67) by $\theta + \phi$, rearranging, and using the definition of θ given in equation (48) above yields

$$2(\alpha\theta - \beta\rho\phi) = 2\rho\left[\alpha\left(\frac{1-2\beta}{2}\right) - \beta\phi\right] > 0 \qquad (70)$$

where ρ and θ are the only parameters that depend on δ.

4 Conclusions

If there is no uncertainty and players can choose among instruments, there are multiple (Nash) equilibria in static, two-person, non-cooperative, positive-sum games with linear reaction functions. In this chapter we confirm this assertion by providing a microeconomic example in which each duopolist can choose either price or quantity as an instrument and a macroeconomic example in which each of two countries can choose either a money supply or an interest rate as an instrument. Once one player has chosen his instrument and set a value for it, the other is indifferent between instruments. Therefore, there are four equilibria, one for each possible instrument pair.

In the microeconomic example, the equilibrium payoff of each player depends on the instruments chosen by both. However, in the macroeconomic example, the equilibrium payoff of each player depends only on the instrument chosen by the other because of the behavior of wage setters.

We proceed to introduce uncertainty into both of our examples in the form of a play by nature represented by an additive disturbance. Introducing uncertainty in this form is of interest in its own right. However, we introduced it because we hoped that doing so would yield unique equilibria in our two examples. Our hope was based on Klemperer and Meyer (1986). They introduce an additive disturbance into the linear demand curves in a differentiated duopoly game in which the duopolists face independent, quadratic costs and find that the number of equilibria is reduced from four to one. The number of equilibria is reduced because with uncertainty even when one player has chosen his instrument and set a value for it, the other is not indifferent between instruments.

In our examples, introducing uncertainty reduces the number of equilibria, but sometimes to two instead of one. Furthermore, in both the Klemperer and Meyer example and in our examples with unique equilibria, for some parameter values with the smallest amount of uncertainty the symmetric instrument pair chosen in the unique equilibrium is the one that yields the lower payoff with no uncertainty. Further analysis of the implications of introducing uncertainty into deterministic games for the number of equilibria and for the characteristics of these equilibria seems to be in order.

Notes

We would like to thank Marc Dudey for suggesting the set up for the microeconomic example and Stephen Salant and Russell Cooper for helping us to master some concepts in game theory. Useful comments were provided by Harald Uhlig, our discussant, and others attending the conference entitled "Positive political economy: theory and evidence" at the CentER for Economic Research of Tilburg University; by Jon Faust; and by David Bowman, Andrew Levin, and others attending a seminar at the Board of Governors of the Federal Reserve System. The contribution reflects the views of the authors and should not be interpreted as reflecting either the views of the Board of Governors of the Federal Reserve System or other members of its staff, or the views of the World Bank, its Executive Board of Directors, its member countries, or other members of its staff.

1 Giavazzi and Giovannini (1989) and Canzoneri and Henderson (1988) compare an equilibrium in which each of two countries chooses its money supply as its instrument with an equilibrium in which one chooses its money supply and the other chooses the exchange rate. Turnovsky and d'Orey (1986), Canzoneri and Henderson (1989), and Henderson and Zhu (1990) compare the four equilibria which are possible when each of two countries can choose either its money supply or its interest rate as its instrument. Tabellini (1987) compares the two equilibria which are possible when the monetary authority can choose either the money supply or its interest rate as its instrument and the fiscal authority chooses government expenditure as its instrument.

2 In linear-reaction-function games, there can be multiple equilibria only if there are two or more possible pairs of instrument choices. However, in non-linear-reaction-function games, there can be multiple equilibria even if there is only one possible pair of instrument choices as explained in, for example, Cooper and John (1988).

3 The case in which the two goods are complements so that the price of each good rises with the quantity of the other good sold ($f<0$) is considered in Henderson and Zhu (forthcoming).

4 These cost functions are special cases of the general quadratic cost functions

$$C=gQ+h\hat{Q}+.5kQ^2+uQ\hat{Q}+.5x\hat{Q}^2, \quad \hat{C}=g\hat{Q}+hQ+.5k\hat{Q}^2+uQ\hat{Q}+.5xQ^2 \quad \text{(F4.1)}$$

With $x\neq0$, the analysis is only a little more complicated, but with $h\neq0$, the analysis is considerably more complicated. Yohe (1979) uses models with general quadratic cost functions like those in equations (F4.1).

5 That is

$$\Pi^{P\hat{Q}}(P,\hat{Q};\eta)=\Pi^{Q\hat{Q}}[Q^{P\hat{Q}}(P,\hat{Q};\eta),\ \hat{Q};\eta],\Pi^{Q\hat{P}}(Q,\hat{P};\eta)=\Pi^{Q\hat{Q}}[Q,\hat{Q}^{Q\hat{P}}(Q,\hat{P};\eta);\eta],$$
$$\Pi^{P\hat{P}}(P,\hat{P};\eta)=\Pi^{Q\hat{Q}}[Q^{P\hat{P}}(P,\hat{P};\eta),\ \hat{Q}^{P\hat{P}}(P,\hat{P};\eta);\eta] \quad \text{(F5.1)}$$

where $Q^{P\hat{Q}}(\cdot)$ is obtained by solving the first equation in equations (1) for Q, $\hat{Q}^{Q\hat{P}}(\cdot)$ is obtained by solving the second equation in equations (1) for $\hat{Q}$, and $Q^{P\hat{P}}(\cdot)$ and $\hat{Q}^{P\hat{P}}(\cdot)$ are obtained by solving equations (1) simultaneously for Q and $\hat{Q}$. The expressions for $Q^{P\hat{Q}}$, $\hat{Q}^{Q\hat{P}}$, $Q^{P\hat{P}}$, and $\hat{Q}^{P\hat{P}}$ are

$$Q^{P\hat{Q}}(P,\hat{Q};\eta)=\left(\frac{2}{b}\right)(a-P-f\hat{Q}+\eta), \ \hat{Q}^{Q\hat{P}}(Q,\hat{P};\eta)=\left(\frac{2}{b}\right)(a-\hat{P}-fQ+\eta),$$

$$Q^{P\hat{P}}(P,\hat{P};\eta)=\left(\frac{2}{\Delta}\right)[(b-2f)a-bP+2f\hat{P}+(b-2f)\eta],$$

$$\hat{Q}^{P\hat{P}}(P,\hat{P};\eta)=\left(\frac{2}{\Delta}\right)[(b-2f)a-b\hat{P}+2fP+(b-2f)\eta],$$

$$\Delta=b^2-4f^2 \quad \text{(F5.2)}$$

6 Of course, if nohat could use his instrument choice to affect hat's instrument choice, he would no longer be indifferent between instruments.

7 Throughout this note we refer to results for symmetric duopolists whose products are substitutes ($f>0$) or complements ($f<0$). Singh and Vives (1984), Vives (1985), and Cheng (1985) analyze the case of constant marginal costs. Singh and Vives and Vives establish algebraically and Cheng establishes graphically that profits are higher or lower in the $Q\hat{Q}$ equilibrium than in the $P\hat{P}$ equilibrium depending on whether the products are substitutes or complements. Xiang (1993) analyzes the case of independent variable marginal costs. In Henderson and Zhu (forthcoming) we generalize the analyses of these authors to the case of joint costs. In the text of the current contribution we apply a slightly modified version of Cheng's graphical technique to derive results for substitutes with joint costs. The slight modification of Cheng's technique is that we operate in $Q\hat{Q}$ space rather than in $P\hat{P}$ space as Cheng did.

8 In algebraic terms, necessary and sufficient conditions for being at the efficient point are obtained by setting $\hat{Q}$ equal to Q in the expression for nohat's profits in equation (T1.1) and differentiating. The first derivative of the resulting expression must be equal to zero

$$\frac{d[(\Pi^{Q\hat{Q}})_{Q=\hat{Q}}]}{dQ}=a-g-[b+k+2(f+u)]Q=0 \quad \text{(F8.1)}$$

as it is if the condition in equation (7) is met. The second derivative must be negative

$$\frac{d^2[(\Pi^{Q\hat{Q}})_{Q=\hat{Q}}]}{dQ^2}=-[b+k+2(f+u)]<0 \tag{F8.2}$$

as it is if the parameters of the model are chosen appropriately. Note that equation (F8.2) implies that $b+k+2(f+u)>0$, so equation (F9.1) implies that $Q^E=\hat{Q}^E>0$ if and only if $a-g>0$.

9 In algebraic terms, necessary and sufficient conditions for being at the $Q\hat{Q}$ equilibrium are obtained by differentiating the expression for nohat's profits in equation (T1.1) with respect to Q and setting $\hat{Q}$ equal to Q in the resulting expressions. The first-order condition is that

$$[\Pi_Q^{Q\hat{Q}}]_{Q=\hat{Q}}=a-g-(b+k+u)Q=0 \tag{F9.1}$$

as it is when the condition in equation (10) is met. The second-order condition is that

$$\Pi_{QQ}^{Q\hat{Q}}=-(b+k)<0 \tag{F9.2}$$

which implies that $b+k=0$. Since we must have $b+k+2(f+u)>0$ in order for the efficient point to be a constrained maximum, $b+k+f+u>0$. Since we must have $a-g>0$ in order for outputs to be positive at the efficient point, equation (F9.1) implies that $Q^C=\hat{Q}^C>0$.

10 In algebraic terms, the version of the necessary and sufficient conditions for being at the $P\hat{P}$ equilibrium that is most useful for present purposes can be derived by differentiating the expression for nohat's profits as a function of Q and $\hat{Q}$ in equation (T1.1) with respect to P using the chain rule. The first-order condition is that

$$[\Pi_P^{P\hat{P}}]_{Q=\hat{Q}}=\frac{2b}{\Delta}\left\{a-g-\left[b+k+\left(1-\frac{2f}{b}\right)(f+u)\right]Q\right\}=0 \tag{F10.1}$$

as it is when the condition in equation (13) is met. The second-order condition is that

$$\Pi_{PP}^{P\hat{P}}=-(b+k)\left(\frac{4b^2}{\Delta^2}\right)-(f+u)\left(\frac{16bf}{\Delta^2}\right)=-\left(\frac{4b}{\Delta^2}\right)[b(b+k)-4f(f+u)]<0 \tag{F10.2}$$

$\Delta=b^2-4f^2$

which implies that $b(b+k)-4f(f+u)>0$. Since we must have $b+k+2(f+u)>0$ in order for the efficient point to be a constrained maximum,

$b+k+\left(1-\frac{2f}{b}\right)(f+u)>0$. Since we must have $a-g>0$ in order for outputs to

be positive at the efficient point, equation (F10.1) implies that $Q^B=\hat{Q}^B>0$.

11 The change in the slope of an isoprofit locus with respect to the Q axis is

$$\frac{d\left(\left[\frac{d\hat{Q}}{dQ}\right]_{d\Pi=0}\right)}{dQ}=-\left[\frac{1}{\Pi_{\hat{Q}}^{Q\hat{Q}}}\right]^3[\Pi_{QQ}^{Q\hat{Q}}(\Pi_{\hat{Q}}^{Q\hat{Q}})^2-2\Pi_{Q\hat{Q}}^{Q\hat{Q}}\Pi_Q^{Q\hat{Q}}\Pi_{\hat{Q}}^{Q\hat{Q}}+\Pi_{\hat{Q}\hat{Q}}^{Q\hat{Q}}(\Pi_Q^{Q\hat{Q}2})] \tag{F11.1}$$

and the result in equation (17) follows because $\Pi_Q^{Q\hat{Q}}=0$ on R.

12 Recall that we assume throughout that $f>0$. Our result that the ranking of profits in the $Q\hat{Q}$ and $P\hat{P}$ equilibria is independent of the sign of $f+u$ given that $f>0$ does not conflict with the standard result that the ranking of profits in the $Q\hat{Q}$ and $P\hat{P}$ equilibria with independent costs depends on the sign of f as shown for example in Singh and Vives (1984).

13 For a concise statement of the standard definitions of positive spillover effect, negative spillover effect, strategic substitutes, and strategic complements see Cooper and John (1988).

14 When $\hat{Q}$ is kept equal to Q and the conditions in footnote 8 are met, nohat's profit function is concave in Q and has a unique maximum at $Q^E=\hat{Q}^E$.

15 Figure 5.3 is constructed in the same way as the figures used by Klemperer and Meyer (1986) to illustrate their result.

16 They are formed by two parallel lines cutting two intersecting straight lines on opposite sides of their intersection.

17 Our model is identical to the one used in chapter 2 of Canzoneri and Henderson (1991). Deterministic and stochastic special cases of this model are used in Canzoneri and Henderson (1989) and Henderson and Zhu (1990), respectively. A similar model with no capital mobility is used in Canzoneri and Henderson (1988).

18 It is assumed (1) that trade is balanced in zero-disturbance equilibrium and (2) that the response of home spending, measured in home goods, to changes in the real exchange rate is the same as the response of foreign spending, measured in foreign goods. These two assumptions are sufficient to ensure that the responses of demands for the two goods to changes in the real exchange rate are equal and opposite in sign.

19 For proof that the assumption that there are no speculative bubbles implies that $z_{+1}=0$ see Appendix A of Canzoneri and Henderson (1991).

20 In the example in Henderson and Zhu (1990) we assume that the countries' period utility functions are
$$U=-\Psi(n-\check{n})^2-.5\pi^2, \quad \hat{U}=-\Psi(\hat{n}-\check{n})^2-.5\hat{\pi}^2 \tag{F20.1}$$
where $\check{n}$ is a bliss level of employment above the natural rate of zero.

21 Suppose, for example, that the weight on employment in hat's utility function is $\hat{\Psi}>\Psi$. $\hat{\pi}$ will be greater than π, but nohat will be unaffected, as long as hat continues to choose the same instrument. The differential between inflation rates is matched exactly by an exchange rate change.

22 Turnovsky and D'Orey (1989) analyze instrument selection in a two-country model and obtain results similar to the ones reported in this section.

References

Barro, Robert and Gordon, David (1983), "Rules, Discretion and Reputation in a Model of Monetary Policy," *Journal of Monetary Economics*, 12, 101–21.

Bertrand, Joseph (1883), "Revue de la *Theorie Mathematique de la Richesse Sociale* et des *Recherches sur les Principes Mathematiques de la Theorie des Richesses*," *Journal des Savants*, 499–508.

Canzoneri, Matthew and Henderson, Dale (1988), "Is Sovereign Policymaking Bad?" *Carnegie-Rochester Series on Public Policy*, 28, 93–140.

(1989), "Optimal Choice of Monetary Policy Instruments in a Simple Two-Country Game," in Frederick van der Ploeg and Aart de Zeeuw (eds.), *Dynamic Policy Games in Economics*, Amsterdam: North-Holland Publishing Company, 223–40.

(1991), *Monetary Policy in Interdependent Economies: A Game Theoretic Approach*, Cambridge, Mass.: MIT Press

Cheng, Leonard (1985), "Comparing Bertrand and Cournot Equilibria: A Geometric Approach," *Rand Journal of Economics*, 16, 146–52.

Cooper, Russell and John, Andrew (1988), "Coordinating Coordination Failures in Keynesian Models," *Quarterly Journal of Economics*, 100, 441–63.

Cournot, Augustin (1838), *Recherches sur les Principes Mathematiques de la Theorie des Richesses*, Paris: L. Hachette.

Giavazzi, Francesco and Giovannini, Alberto (1989), "Monetary Policy Interactions Under Managed Exchange Rates," *Economica*, 56, 199–213.

Henderson, Dale and Zhu, Ning (1990), "Uncertainty and the Choice of Instruments in a Two-Country Policy Game," *Open Economies Review*, 1, 39–65.

(forthcoming), "Price and Quantity Competition in Differentiated Duopoly: How Cost Assumptions Matter," mimeo.

Klemperer, Paul and Meyer, Margaret (1986), "Price Competition vs. Quantity Competition: The Role of Uncertainty," *Rand Journal of Economics*, 17, 618–38.

Kydland, Finn and Prescott, Edward (1977), "Rules Rather than Discretion: The Inconsistency of Optimal Plans," *Journal of Political Economy*, 85, 473–91.

Poole, William (1970), "Optimal Choice of Monetary Policy Instruments in a Simple Stochastic Macro Model," *Quarterly Journal of Economics*, 84, 197–216.

Singh, Nirvikar and Vives, Xavier (1984), "Price and Quantity Competition in a Differentiated Duopoly," *Rand Journal of Economics*, 15, 546–54.

Tabellini, Guido (1987), "Optimal Monetary Instruments and Policy Games," *Ricerche Economiche*, 41, 315–25.

Turnovsky, Stephen and d'Orey, Vasco (1986), "Monetary Policies in Interdependent Economies with Stochastic Disturbances: A Strategic Approach," *Economic Journal*, 96, 696–721.

(1989), "The Choice of Monetary Instrument in Two Interdependent Economies Under Uncertainty," *Journal of Monetary Economics*, 23, 121–33.

Vives, Xavier (1985), "On the Efficiency of Bertrand and Cournot Equilibria with Product Differentiation," *Journal of Economic Theory*, 36, 166–75.

Weitzman, Martin (1974), "Prices vs. Quantities," *Review of Economic Studies*, 41, 477–91.

Xiang, Pinggui (1993), "Strategic Delegation," Ph. D. dissertation, University of Iowa.

Yohe, Gary (1979), *A Comparison of Price Controls and Quantity Controls*, New York: Garland Publishing Inc.

Comment

HARALD UHLIG

Here is a short summary of the chapter. Klemperer and Meyer (1986) examined a standard oligopoly game in which there are four (different) Nash equilibria, depending on whether an oligopolist fixes his price or his quantity: $(P; \hat{P})$, $(Q; \hat{P})$, $(P; \hat{Q})$, $(Q; \hat{Q})$. These four Nash equilibria arise because the oligopolist can pick the same desired point on his residual demand curve by fixing the price or fixing the quantity. Klemperer and Meyer introduce demand uncertainty into this game and show how only one Nash equilibrium remains because that uncertainty breaks the indifference between fixing P or fixing Q.

Henderson and Zhu build their chapter on this argument. First, they show how in the standard oligopoly game, more than one Nash equilibrium can survive if cost functions take a more general form, thus extending the Klemperer–Meyer result. They then apply these insights to a game between two monetary policy makers, which is a version of the game in Canzoneri and Henderson (1991): nominal wages are fixed by the private sector at the beginning of a period, aiming at the natural rate of employment. The two monetary authorities then choose whether to fix the money supply (m) or to fix the nominal interest rate (i). A worldwide velocity shock is then realized, and the remaining monetary policy variables are determined along with employment, prices, and output. Without velocity uncertainty, there are four Nash equilibria as in the duopoly situation: $(m; \hat{m})$, $(m; \hat{i})$, $(i; \hat{m})$, and $(i; \hat{i})$. With velocity uncertainty, there are sometimes one and sometimes two Nash equilibria. The $(i; \hat{i})$ equilibrium is always there, whereas the $(m; \hat{m})$ equilibrium can also remain for certain parameters. The $(i; \hat{i})$-equilibrium, as it turns out, is often Pareto dominated (from the point of view of the two monetary authorities) by the $(m; \hat{m})$-choice: if $(i; \hat{i})$ is the only equilibrium, the monetary authorities find themselves essentially in a prisoner's dilemma.

I liked this contribution and I especially liked the monetary policy game part. For my tastes the chapter focuses too much on the somewhat exotic questions about the numbers of equilibria in oligopoly games rather than the more interesting issues in monetary policy that arise here. There is a lot

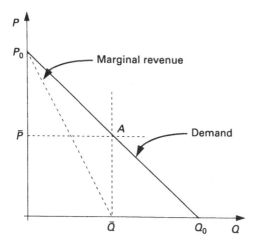

Figure 5.5 Monopolistic price–quantity choice: the textbook certainty case

of interesting economics in the paper, but the authors have somehow chosen to hide it a bit!

In my comments, I will therefore focus mainly on the monetary economics part. Before doing so, however, it is worthwhile to shed a bit more light on the Klemperer–Meyer argument. Since an oligopolist reacts to his residual demand curve the way a monopolist would, it suffices to consider the problem of a monopolist with, say, zero marginal costs of production and a linear and downward-sloping demand curve. In other words, consider figure 5.5, which shows a standard textbook example.

In that example, the monopolist finds its revenue-maximizing choice by equating marginal revenues to zero and then picking either $\bar{P}$ or $\bar{Q}$ to get to point A on the demand curve: the monopolist is perfectly indifferent between these two choices.

Introduce uncertainty. For the sake of the argument here, I will deviate slightly from the contribution and suppose that the randomness in the demand function $D(P)$ takes the form

$$D(P)=Q_0-(Q_0/(P_0+\epsilon))P, \text{ with } \epsilon \text{ random, as in figure 5.6.}$$

The monopolist needs to fix either price or quantity before the demand uncertainty is realized. If he fixes the quantity at $\bar{Q}$, he will get one of the three prices P_ℓ, $\bar{P}$, or P_h If he fixes $\bar{P}$ he will get one of the three quantities Q_ℓ, $\bar{Q}$, or Q_h However, it is clear that is the optimal choice no matter which one of the three demand curves is realized. Thus, if the monopolist prefers

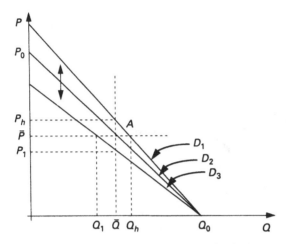

Figure 5.6 Uncertainty in the maximal price

to fix $\bar{Q}$ rather than $\bar{P}$ the indifference is broken. For the oligopoly game, the number of Nash equilibria is reduced from four to one.

This is not the end of the story, however. Consider figure 5.7. There the randomness takes the form

$$D(P) = Q_0 + \epsilon - \frac{Q_0^{+\epsilon}}{P_0}P, \text{ with } \epsilon \text{ random.}$$

Here, of course, the monopolist is better off fixing $\bar{P}$ rather than $\bar{Q}$. Again, there will only be one equilibrium in the duopoly game. Unfortunately, the "surviving" equilibrium is a different one from the one surviving in figure 5.6. The upshot is, it matters a lot exactly how the uncertainty is introduced.

Figures 5.6 and 5.7 actually just scratch the surface of all the possibilities. Consider figure 5.8, where the demand curves take the form

$$D(P) = Q_0 - \frac{Q_0}{P_0}P + \epsilon, \text{ with } \epsilon \text{ random.}$$

While it may be interesting to figure out whether the monopolist prefers to fix $\bar{P}$ or $\bar{Q}$ it actually turns out that the best thing for him to do is to fix the supply schedule S. Depending on the realization of the shock, he will end up with one of the three quantity-price pairs (Q_ℓ, P_ℓ), $(\bar{Q}, \bar{P})$, or (Q_h, P_h), which are *ex post* revenue maximizing. Once one opens the Pandora's box of admitting supply curves, possibly subject to some restrictions, all kinds of things may happen. Plus, there are lots of interesting questions one may wonder about. For example, could some additional agency, by injecting the "right" kind of noise, force the oligopolists into Bertrand competition

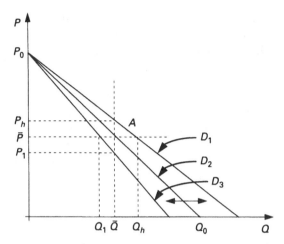

Figure 5.7 Uncertainty in the maximal quantity

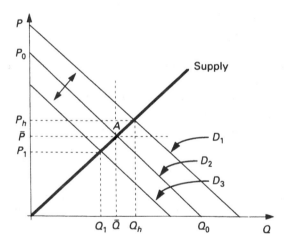

Figure 5.8 Uncertainty in the market size

rather than Cournot competition, say? Note, in particular, that the
Bertrand equilibrium dominates the Cournot equilibrium from a social
welfare point of view for the case of perfect substitutes, but is Pareto-
dominated, if one only takes the objective functions of the two oligopolists
into account. Thus, one needs to be careful not to judge the ranking of the
equilibria from the perspective of the players only. The chapter does not
deal at all with these issues. Instead, it concentrates too much on general-
izing the cost function, for my taste.

On to the monetary model. Take the home country ("nohat"). Given nominal wages w as well as the money supply m, quantity theory, the labor market and the production function result in the equations

$$m+v=s+y \quad w-s=-\alpha n \quad y=\bar{y}+(1-\alpha)n$$

where v is velocity, s is the nominal product price, y is output, n is labor and α is a parameter (the capital share).

Given the three equations above, labor is $n=m+v-w$ and s and y can be computed as well. Symmetrically, these variables can be determined for the foreign country ("hat"). Since consumers consume goods from both countries, one can finally compute inflation rates

$$\pi=w+(\theta+\frac{\alpha}{2})n-(\theta-\frac{\alpha}{2})\hat{n}$$

$$\hat{\pi}=\hat{w}+(\theta+\frac{\alpha}{2})\hat{n}-(\theta-\frac{\alpha}{2})n$$

and short-term nominal interest rates

$$i=-w-(\theta+\phi)n+(\theta-\phi)\hat{n}$$

$$\hat{i}=-\hat{w}-(\theta-\phi)\hat{n}+(\theta-\phi)n$$

for some constants $\theta>\phi>0$. If (one of) the policy makers sets the nominal interest rate rather than the money supply, one has to start from the last two equations and solve for m and $\hat{m}$. Policy makers care about $U=\psi n-0.5\pi^2$ and $\hat{U}=\psi\hat{n}-0.5\hat{\pi}^2$. Wage setters, knowing this, set wages so that policy makers end up choosing $n=\hat{n}=0$, on average, at least.

One should note a particular feature of this model: a rise in m yields a corresponding rise in n and thus a rise in π and i, but a fall in $\hat{\pi}$ and $\hat{i}$: an inflation at home is exported as deflation abroad. While the theoretical underpinnings are certainly fine, I wonder how well this feature is supported by the empirical facts, and thus, whether this is a wise modeling choice or not. Furthermore, it is not clear how the stated equations could (at least approximately) be derived from a fully specified model with agents optimizing some utility function. It is therefore hard to go from model implications to welfare implications, which is necessary to arrive at normative statements about monetary policy. Micro foundations are implicit rather than explicit and the equations could be treated as a quiz for graduate students: "Which fully specified model leads to these reduced form equations?" I believe that such a fully specified model can indeed be found and I would favor more explicitness. This is, however, a feature of much of the literature in this field, and the chapter at hand is not to be blamed in particular.

I also wish the chapter had spent more time explaining why it is particularly interesting to choose velocity to be random. Why not, for example, total factor productivity or the discount factor for future periods in the utility function of agents? As pointed out above for the Klemperer–Meyer analysis, the way uncertainty is introduced matters a lot! I do think that there actually are good reasons to choose velocity for this exercise. Perhaps the major reason why money targeting has not worked quite so well in the last decade and why almost all central banks have silently given up doing so is precisely that velocity seemed to be shifting too much to allow for reliable monetary policy. On the other hand, short-term nominal interests are an instrument which central banks seem to be able to move quite well. It is no surprise then, that the federal funds rate is the best indicator for US monetary policy, as Bernanke and Blinder (1992) have shown. The arguments in the chapter show why all this is a plausible outcome. It should have linked up to that debate a bit, since doing so is practically a free lunch here!

The analysis proceeds by first considering the case with no velocity shocks: $v \equiv 0$. In that case, given that the foreign country fixes $\hat{i}$ say, the monetary authority in the home country is indifferent between fixing i or m. However, it matters whether the foreign monetary authority has fixed $\hat{m}$ or $\hat{i}$: if $\hat{i}$ is fixed, for example, an increase in m leads to home inflation, and foreign deflation, putting upward pressure on $\hat{i}$. Since $\hat{i}$ is fixed, $\hat{m}$ has to expand leading to some additional foreign inflation, imported as deflationary pressure, partially offsetting the home inflationary effects of the rise in m. Thus, if the foreign monetary authority fixes $\hat{i}$ rather than $\hat{m}$ the effect on inflation by the home monetary authority is smaller and thus the temptation to use the short-run Phillips curve tradeoff is greater. As a result, wage setters must set a high wage w so as to force policy makers, whose objective function is quadratic in the inflation rate but linear in labor, into choosing $n = \hat{n} = 0$ on average anyhow. Thus, setting interest rates rather than money supplies leads to higher inflation but the same employment and thus to a worse outcome from the point of view of the policy makers. It seems self-evident that this is also the less preferred outcome from some social planners' perspective, but, as pointed out above, one should be wary of making welfare conclusions in the absence of a welfare function.

From the monetary policy makers' perspective, the game looks similar to the following game:

		foreign	
		$\hat{m}$	$\hat{i}$
home	m	1;1	0;1
	i	1;0	0;0

There are four Pareto-ranked Nash equilibria.

Introduce velocity uncertainty. Since surprise velocity acts like a surprise injection of money, a policy maker will usually prefer to fix the nominal interest rate and let the market determine the money supply in a velocity-compensating manner. Thus, the policy makers loosen ϵ slightly, say, if they fix the money supply rather than the nominal interest rate. The game turns into the prisoner's dilemma:

foreign

		$\hat{m}$	$\hat{i}$
home	m	$1-\epsilon; 1-\epsilon$	$-\epsilon; 1$
	i	$1; -\epsilon$	$0;0$

Indeed, $(i; \hat{i})$ is the only equilibrium and it is dominated by the strategy pair $(m; \hat{m})$ Actually, $(m; \hat{m})$ can also be an equilibrium, depending on the parameters: of course, the payoffs must then be different from the ones above, and the intuition changes, too.

I wish the chapter had spent a bit more effort in clearly drawing out these conclusions and their intuitive explanations, since I think that they are actually the most interesting results of the analysis. The result hinges on making velocity random rather than something else. If it is the discount factor between periods instead which is random, then monetary policy makers may prefer to fix the money supply so as to let interest rates adjust endogenously to the randomly changing rates of time preference. Something similar may be true for productivity shocks which are so popular in the real business cycle literature. Even if the argument seems tiring now: the way uncertainty is introduced here matters greatly for the conclusions one draws.

What have we learned? We have learned that introducing uncertainty can reduce the number of equilibria sometimes to one and sometimes to two. That is fine, but one probably needs to be a game theorist to find this very exciting. We have also learned that introducing uncertainty into a version of the well-studied Canzoneri–Henderson model can lead policy makers to select the worst outcome (from the point of view of the monetary policy makers but perhaps also from the point of view of the society at large). This result comes about because policy makers prefer to fix nominal interest rates rather than money supply in the presence of velocity uncertainty, since the money supply can then adjust endogeneously to the "equivalent" velocity shock. If policy makers do so, however, they end up affecting inflation less for the reasons explained above. This forces wage setters and, thus monetary policy makers, into effecting high nominal wages and high inflation, so that monetary policy makers are no longer tempted by the short-run Phillips curve. Do we believe this argument? Sometimes, it seems to me to be a bit like a somersault backwards but it is certainly an argument worth thinking about, since it comes about not by clever construction but as an unintended result in a reasonable modification of a reasonable model. I find this exciting and interesting.

To sum up: this is a nice contribution about lively monetary economics, that everybody should read.

References

Bernanke, Ben S. and Blinder, Alan S. (1992), "The Federal Funds Rate and the Channels of Monetary Transmission," *American Economic Review*, 82, 901–21.

Canzoneri, Matthew and Henderson, Dale (1991), *Monetary Policy in Interdependent Economies: A Game Theoretic Approach*, Cambridge, Mass: MIT Press.

Klemperer, Paul and Meyer, Margaret (1986), "Price Competition vs. Quantity Competition: The Role of Uncertainty," *Rand Journal of Economics*, 17, 473–91.

6 New empirical evidence on the costs of European Monetary Union

HÉLÈNE ERKEL-ROUSSE and JACQUES MÉLITZ

1 Introduction

Work on the costs of European Monetary Union (EMU) has mostly centered on the shocks affecting the member countries. Except for efforts to apply large-scale macroeconomic models,[1] this research has usually tried to distinguish between common and idiosyncratic or symmetric and asymmetric shocks.[2] Only the idiosyncratic or asymmetric ones spell any cost of monetary union. Recently Bayoumi and Eichengreen (1992) have taken a different tack: they try to distinguish between two shocks within each individual country and subsequently analyze the association of each separate shock between countries. The two shocks in their analysis are demand and supply ones. We shall extend Bayoumi and Eichengreen's analysis by trying to identify more shocks than they do. By isolating a separate shock representing the effect of a surprise in monetary policy (which could also come from abroad or from the demand for money), we hope to see whether monetary policy can deal with asymmetric shocks in the short run. If surprises in monetary policy merely affect prices rather than volumes in the short run, then the sacrifice of monetary policy independence would not seem very costly. Similarly, if we can identify a separate shock which represents unexpected fiscal policy and trace its effects, then we may be able to see if fiscal policy independence would help reduce the cost of monetary union. In sum, the identification of shocks provides an opportunity to carry the analysis of the costs of monetary union much further than the mere question of the degree of asymmetry between the shocks.

Our first task will be to explain the basic philosophy underlying our work (section 2). Next, we will present our theoretical model (section 3). This model is an open economy version of IS–LM with a Phillips curve. It admits five shocks, three of which pertain directly to the real exchange rate and net exports. These are shocks to the price of imported raw materials, the relative velocity of money at home and abroad, and net foreign demand (the difference between foreign demand for home goods and home demand

162

for foreign goods). The remaining two shocks concern home absorption and supply. The relative velocity shock incorporates unexpected monetary policy, the absorption one unexpected fiscal policy.

The section following the theoretical model (section 4) presents our data and econometric method. First, we discuss the data, the order of integration of the series, and the tests of cointegration. Next, we explain precisely what we did in order to extract the shocks. Our method was pioneered by Blanchard and Quah (1989), later repeated by Bayoumi and Eichengreen, and extended by others.[3] It consists of using the structural VAR approach based on a long run identifying scheme. However, as we try to identify five different shocks, we naturally require more theoretical restrictions than do either Blanchard and Quah or Bayoumi and Eichengreen (both of whom only needed to identify two). Our study will concern only six EU countries – France, Germany, Italy, The Netherlands, Spain and the United Kingdom – since we were not able to obtain long enough quarterly series for any of the rest, and we needed quarterly series in order to have an adequate sample size, if nothing else.[4] It is only because they use annual series that Bayoumi and Eichengreen are able to discuss more EU countries. We shall present our results in a separate section (section 5) which centers on the evidence bearing on the costs of monetary union.

One general caveat is in order. The only wide experimentation with VAR models thus far in connection with aggregate economic performance relates to the US. Serious evaluations of Blanchard and Quah's proposal for identifying shocks have depended heavily on these earlier experiments. There is no similar breadth of experience with applications of the same methods to the European aggregates, while the results in Europe could differ sharply because of the smaller size and greater openness of the economies. To make matters worse, we are concerned with cross-country evidence. For all these reasons, we shall emphasize our logic and bases for inference as much as what we find.

2 Basic principles

What does a country sacrifice when it gives up a separate currency – apart from any matter of political prestige? According to the literature on optimum currency areas, the costs of monetary union consist of the inability to use independent monetary policy in order to achieve optimal adjustment to shocks. Thus, we must look for higher adjustment costs. Suppose then that we know the structure of the shocks affecting macroeconomic performance in all individual countries and that this knowledge extends to the covariances of the shocks affecting the individual countries. There are still two reasons why we cannot infer the loss of welfare caused by monetary union (apart from issues of social preferences, including the social discount rate). One is that a country may still be able to respond to shocks without a separate currency. The other is that a union member might not be able to do anything about the shocks anyhow. Both of these reasons are important.

To all evidence, the individual countries of Western Europe – certainly the large ones – will retain more influence over domestic fiscal policy after entry into EMU than exists in any other monetary union today – far more such influence than the Canadian provinces possess, for example, to say nothing of the American states. Studies always show that the mobility of labor in the EU is lower than within national borders.[5] Thus, member countries' capacity to tax will be correspondingly higher. Supporters of EMU also differ widely in their preferred degree of centralization inside the EU. It is therefore important not to identify the costs of European Monetary Union with those of surrendering all independent macroeconomic management, but to maintain a clear distinction between EMU and a European Union with all power over fiscal policy concentrated at the center.

As regards monetary policy independence today, imagine a progressive sub-division of a country into smaller and smaller regions. As the regions get smaller, the variance of the shocks hitting them must rise in many individual cases and become more distinct from the variance hitting the aggregate of the rest, since the smaller the regions the more specialized many of them will be. Does this mean that the costs of monetary union correspondingly rise with smaller size? To say so would be almost paradoxical. Yet the paradox is revealing and the answer is clear: with smaller size also comes lower capacity to wield the instruments of macroeconomic policy in any meaningful way. A very small economy has little autarky with respect to macroeconomic policy. As reflected in the literature on optimum currency areas, successively smaller regions also become increasingly open and price takers. The mere covariance of the shocks between different countries therefore cannot instruct us adequately about the costs of monetary union. We must take separate account of the degree of sacrifice of macroeconomic influence.

In order to heed these problems, we shall need to distinguish and analyse more shocks than demand and supply ones. While the cross-country relationships between the shocks will provide relevant information, so will other evidence about the shocks, as we will see. The variance decomposition of the influences of the shocks on real variables at home will prove particularly useful in interpreting the costs of monetary union.

3 The model

Since we will want the smallest possible framework in order to increase the chances of a successful application of a structural VAR, the model we will propose will be somewhat unfamiliar. Rather than proceed directly to this model, therefore, we will start with a larger one which is more easily recognizable. The larger model we have in mind is an open economy version of IS–LM with a Phillips curve. It can be expressed, in general functional form, as follows

$$A=f_A(Y, R-\Delta p^e_{+1}, U_A) \qquad \text{Absorption} \qquad (1)$$

$$X=f_x(Y, Y^*, \frac{P}{EP^*}, U_x) \qquad \text{Net exports} \qquad (2)$$

$$\bar{Y}=f_{\bar{Y}}(K, N, Q, U_s) \qquad \text{Supply} \qquad (3)$$

$$Y=A+X+\Delta\bar{Y} \qquad \text{Output} \qquad (4)$$

$$\Delta P=f_P(\Delta P_{-1}, \Delta(EP^*), A+X-\bar{Y}) \qquad \text{Phillips curve} \qquad (5)$$

$$Q=f_Q(Q_{-1}, U^*_Q) \qquad \text{Imported raw materials} \qquad (6)$$

$$P^*=f_{P^*}(P^*_{-1}, U^*_Q, U^*_{MS}, U^*_{MD}) \qquad \text{Price of foreign output} \qquad (7)$$

$$R^*=f_{R^*}(R^*_{-1}, U^*_{MS}, U^*_{MD}) \qquad \text{Foreign interest rate} \qquad (8)$$

$$R=R^*+\Delta e^e_{+1}+U_{MS} \qquad \text{Interest rate parity} \qquad (9)$$

$$\frac{M}{P}=f_{MD}(Y, R, U_{MD}) \qquad \text{Demand for money} \qquad (10)$$

$$\frac{P}{EP^*}=f_{P/EP^*}(X, U^*_Q, U^*_{MS}, U^*_{MD}, U_{MD}) \qquad \text{Real exchange rate} \qquad (11)$$

Much of the notation is familiar enough not to need explanation. All the U variables refer to shocks. Equation (1) pertains to home absorption A, equation (2) to net exports X, $\bar{Y}$ in equation (3) refers to supply of output, and Q in this equation to imported raw materials. Equations (1) through (5) represent the IS and the Phillips curves. Equation (4) may appear to be a definition, but is instead a statement about production. In fact, this statement deviates from the typical textbook which says that output only responds to demand shocks in the current period, while supply shocks affect output (through prices) after a lag. This idea of strictly lagged influences of supply shocks involves a strong restriction that we do not wish to impose (compare Gali (1992), who adopts the same view). Our alternative hypothesis is that a positive (negative) supply shock will cause firms to raise (lower) capacity and thereby affect current output (through demand for capacity). Based on the last equation (or (4)), firms will also respond to positive (negative) demand shocks, in the textbook manner, by raising (lowering) output without changing capacity. Correspondingly, equation (5), which represents the Phillips curve, allows for contemporary effects on prices of, both, differences between demand $(A+X)$ and supply $(\bar{Y})$, and changes in import prices (EP^*).

Equations (6), (7), and (8) introduce various shocks from abroad: one to the foreign price of imported raw materials, U_Q^*, and two more to the prices of other imports besides raw materials and the foreign nominal interest rate. We label these last two shocks U_{MS} and U_{MD} on the view that foreign monetary policy (MS for money supply) or foreign money demand (MD) will be heavily responsible. Equation (9) states interest rate parity on the basis of one-period-ahead forecasts of the rate of appreciation of the exchange rate Δe_{+1}^e (where e is the log of the exchange rate E) in conformity with the general presentation of the model in interval time. Since we suppose that the authorities fix U_{MS} (possibly at zero, as in the case of no money-supply surprises), quite significantly, our formulation considers that the domestic monetary authorities set the money interest rate R and not the money stock M. Being unanticipated, U_{MS} enters separately in equation (9). Equation (10) concerns the demand for money or the LM curve. The last equation, (11), which serves to determine E, notably ties the real exchange rate to the current account balance X as well as a number of shocks. Finally, the two expected variables, p_{+1}^e and e_{+1}^e, can be interpreted as the mathematical expectations of p and e in the next period.

But while the model may be small, it is extremely large for the application of a VAR. There are probably too many shocks: eight of them altogether. Therefore we proceeded to reduce the model by eliminating the real interest rate as a separate influence in the absorption equation. One interpretation would be that $R-\Delta p_{+1}^e$ does not affect demand. But a better interpretation, we think, would be the presence of a strong positive association between $R-\Delta p_{+1}^e$ and the real exchange rate P/EP^* which is reinforced by the responses of the monetary authorities to other shocks and therefore the behavior of U_{MS}. On this next view, the impact of P/EP^* in the demand equation really comprises that of $R-\Delta p_{+1}^e$.

Having eliminated $R-\Delta p_{+1}^e$, we may reformulate the model as follows

$$y-x=\alpha_0+(u_s-\alpha_1 u_q^*)-\alpha_2(p-e-p^*)+u_a \tag{12}$$

$$x=\beta_0-\beta_1(\alpha_0+u_a)-(\beta_2-\beta_1\alpha_2)(p-e-p^*)+u_x \quad \beta_2>\beta_1\alpha_2 \tag{13}$$

$$\Delta p_q^*=\Delta p_{q,-1}^*+u_q^* \tag{14}$$

$$p-e-p^*=(p-e-p^*)_{-1}+\lambda_1 x \pm \lambda_2 u_q^*+u_v \tag{15}$$

$$\Delta p=\Delta p_{-1}+\delta_0 u_q^*-\delta_1 u_v+\delta_2(u_a+u_x-u_s) \tag{16}$$

Small Roman letters serve to indicate logarithms of the previous capitals except in the case of x, which now stands for the log of the ratio of exports to imports, and that of p_q^*, a new symbol representing the log of the foreign price of imported raw materials. Greek letters refer to (positive) coefficients. We thus adopt a loglinear form. Because of this loglinear choice, we subdivide Y multiplicatively between the ratio of exports to imports and the rest, rather than additively, as before, between A, X, and $\Delta \bar{Y}$. The sign of the influence of the real exchange rate in equation (12), relating to all output except for net exports,[6] echoes the previous idea that $p-e-p^*$ may reflect the implicit joint effect of $R-\Delta p_{+1}^e$ and thus may bear a negative impact on home investment. Equation (13), in turn, derives from

$$x=\beta_0-\beta_1 a-\beta_2(p-e-p^*)+u_x \qquad (13a)$$

where a is the (logarithmic) reflection of home absorption and equals $y-x-u_s+\alpha_1 u_q^*$.

The biggest contraction of the model of all comes from the compression of the previous shocks U_{MS}^*, U_{MD}^*, U_{MS}, and U_{MD} into a single one, u_v (v for velocity). This new shock then is supposed to embrace all influences of monetary policies and demands for money at home and abroad on the real exchange rate. We term this shock a relative-velocity one because of its presumed monetary origins. Thus, two countries in a monetary union would experience identical u_v shocks. Furthermore, any unexpected change in competitiveness resulting from wage contracts at home, for example, would not be reflected in u_v but u_s. The endogenous variables become simply output, the ratio of exports to imports, the foreign price of imported raw materials, the real exchange rate, and the price of home output.

Once we rewrite equations (12) through (16) in reduced form, we can undertake the necessary steps to convert the system into a VAR model and then proceed to apply Blanchard and Quah's method of imposing long-run restrictions in order to identify the shocks. The particular restrictions we shall use are in the same spirit as theirs. Demand influences have no effect on output in the long run: therefore, neither u_a nor u_x has any long-run effect on y. Similarly, nominal variables have neutral effects in the long run: thus u_v should leave the real exchange rate unchanged in the long run (as this shock strictly reflects nominal conditions at home and abroad). But if u_v does not affect $p-e-p^*$, it cannot affect either the current account, x, or output, y. This already yields us five separate long-run restrictions in the VAR. A sixth one derives from the Phillips curve: it says that the difference between demand and supply, or the excess demand, determines the pressure on prices. If so, the respective effects of u_a+u_x and u_s on Δp should be of equal and opposite strength (as equation (16) asserts). Imposing this last condition only in the long run allows short-run deviations and therefore restricts the dynamics less than a similar short-run application would.

We simplified further by treating the vector autoregression Δp_q^* of the variable of equation (14) as directly yielding the import-price shock (while testing the assumption with exogeneity tests). Consequently, the identification of the shocks became much easier in the VAR. As we shall show later on, the preceding six long-run identification conditions suffice.

4 The series and methodology

The series

All of our statistical series come from the OECD. Our figures for output (GDP), the price level (the price of GDP), exports and imports are seasonally adjusted and drawn from the *Quarterly National Accounts*. The price of imported raw materials comes from the *International Trade and Competitiveness Indicators*, the exchange rates from the *Main Economic Indicators*. As mentioned before, given our decision to use quarterly data, we limit ourselves to six EMS countries: France, Germany, Italy, The Netherlands, Spain, and the UK. The sample period runs from 1970.1 to 1992.4 – 92 observations per individual country. In order to construct real exchange rates, we must pay separate attention to the prices of foreign competitors, or in terms of our earlier notation, P^* times E. We do so by collecting quarterly data for the price of GDP from as many OECD members as possible and then constructing weighted averages for P^* for each of our six EMS country members on the basis of the prices of all the rest (notably comprising the US, Japan, and Canada – among others – as well as the other five countries in the EU). The weights depend on the import shares recorded in the OECD model INTERLINK. We construct E in the same way: that is, on the basis of the bilateral exchange rates with the same set of foreign trade partners and the same weights.

Continuing the study until the end of 1992 means dealing with the German unification shock. This poses important problems for 1990–1992 German data, to which there is no easy solution. We opted in favor of calculating German output and prices since the third quarter of 1990 by extending the earlier West German data on the basis of the pan-German growth rates. German output following unification is then the West German output in 1990.2 times one plus the compounded quarterly rate of growth of output in East and West therefrom; and the German price level obtains the same way. As a result of this procedure, the poor output performance of the eastern region in 1990–1992 shows up in our data as a deceleration of German output growth, and therefore as a negative shock. Had we simply switched instead to the data for pan-German output in 1990.3, the contribution of East Germany to output would have signified more growth (as we are using output aggregates), and the effect of unification on output would then have shown up as a positive shock. This consideration explains our choice, since we tend to think of unification as a negative output shock with inflationary implications (thus a negative *supply* shock). On the other hand, as regards the ratio of exports to imports, we did simply switch from the West German to the pan-German data in 1990.3. Consequently, we display a sharp deterioration of the German current account at the time of unification, implying a negative net foreign demand shock u_x (in terms of our notation in equation (13)). Had we used the West German current account data instead, we would have exhibited a marked *increase* in the trade surplus following unification in light of the massive transfer of goods from the western to the eastern region of the country. The West German data thus become particularly misleading regarding trade relations with the rest of the world after unification, and it is extremely important to view the current account of Germany on a pan-German basis from that time on. With respect to the price of imported raw materials (P_Q^*) and the home price of foreign goods (P^*E), we simply extended the previous West German series and therefore, quite specifically, kept the same weights of foreign prices throughout (whether they be those of the OECD, as in the case of P_Q^*, or ours, as in the case of P^*E).[7]

Integration and cointegration

The passage into logs yields y, x, Δp, Δp_q^*, and $p-e-p^*$. Subsequently, we must check for the order of integration of the series for $y-x$, x, Δp, Δp_q^*, and $p-e-p^*$. We did so for $\Delta p - \Delta p_q^*$ as well in order to be able to substitute this variable for Δp, as turns out to be useful later on. To check for the order of integration, it is important to choose the length of the lags carefully, since totally different results can obtain depending on lag lengths. We must also pay attention to the possibility of I(2) or second-order integration. The procedure we used (prescribed by Jobert (1992)) is to choose an appropriate lag length based on various criteria, and then carry out a whole battery of augmented Dickey–Fuller tests in a particular sequential order depending on the significance of constants and deterministic time trends in earlier steps. We performed Schmidt–Phillips tests as well. These tests lead to an acceptance of I(0) for Δp, Δp_q^* and $\Delta p - \Delta p_q^*$, but as we might expect, adjusted output, $y-x$, and the real exchange rate, $p-e-p^*$, are clearly I(1). The only ambiguity concerns the export–import ratio x, which appears I(0) for one country (the UK), I(1) for another (Spain), but could be either one for the rest depending on the test. Since we aim to construct some cross-country aggregates and to make cross-country comparisons, we have strong reason to prefer adopting the same order of integration for all the countries. I(1) then seems to be the superior choice on general principles (better to err by treating I(0) series as I(1) than doing the reverse), and it suits us better as well since $y-x$ is I(1) and we shall need to add up $y-x$ and x in order to obtain y later on. The hypothesis I(2) can be uniformly rejected.

Given the clear presence of a unit root in adjusted output $(y-x)$ and the real exchange rate, cointegration between these two variables and between them and the rest becomes a plain possibility, in which case, of course, the Vector Error Correction Model (VECM) would be more appropriate than a VAR. Tests of cointegration require first finding the optimal number of lags (using a VECM). Based on the usual criteria, this number turns out to be one or two depending on the country. In testing for cointegration, we chose two lags everywhere, and subsequently resorted to tests of maximum eigenvalue and trace. But since questions of cointegration did not determine our final choice of the number of quarterly lags, we also duplicated our tests of cointegration based on our preferred choice of lags and got essentially the same results.

The only significant cointegrating relationships that emerged from these tests, according to the thresholds in the tables of Osterwald-Lenum (1992) (which modify those of Johansen and Juselius (1990)), are between Δp and Δp_q^* and the alternative pair $\Delta p - \Delta p_q^*$ and Δp_q^*. This is clearly true everywhere except the UK. But it also holds there as well if we apply stringent enough significance tests to deny the presence of a second cointegrating relationship (at the 2.5 percent level). Since Δp, Δp_q^* and $\Delta p - \Delta p_q^*$ are I(0), the cointegration of either Δp and Δp_q^* or $\Delta p - \Delta p_q^*$ and Δp_q^* poses no problem and we were able to pursue the rest of the analysis with a VAR (compare Karras, 1994).

Identification

Based on the previous analysis, the model we will investigate will be

$$z(t) = C(L)e(t) \tag{17}$$

where the vector $z(t) \equiv [\Delta(y\text{-}x)(t), \Delta x(t), \Delta p(t), \Delta(p-e-p^*)(t), \Delta p_q^*(t)]'$ (alternatively with $((\Delta p - \Delta p_q^*)(t))$ instead of $\Delta p(t)$) is a stationary process, L is the lag operator, $C(L)$ is a 5×5 matrix of lagged polynomials, and $e(t) \equiv [e_a(t), e_x(t), e_s(t), e_v(t), e_{q*}(t)]'$ is assumed to be a serially uncorrelated vector of structural disturbances relating to absorption, the ratio of exports to imports, supply, relative velocity, and the foreign-currency price of imported raw materials, in that order. Under usual assumptions, $z(t)$ has a moving-average, Wold representation such that

$$z(t) = E(L)v(t) \tag{18}$$

where $E(L)$ is an invertible 5×5 matrix of lagged polynomials, $E(0)$ is the identity matrix of order 5, and $v(t)$ is the vector of innovations of the elements of $z(t)$. As $E(L)$ is invertible, equation (18) can be estimated in the autoregressive VAR form, $E(L)^{-1}z(t)=v(t)$, which yields an estimate of the matrix $E(L)$.

The critical next step is to assume that the vector of innovations can be expressed as a linear combination of the structural shocks

$$v(t)=Se(t) \tag{19}$$

where S is an invertible matrix. From (17), (18), and (19), we have

$$C(L)=E(L)\,S \tag{20}$$

Thus, if we can succeed in determining the matrix S, we can identify the structural shocks in equation (19) and $C(L)$ can be derived.

The identification of S results from a set of restrictions. Since S is a 5×5 matrix, 25 restrictions on its components are necessary. Equation (19) implies a strict relation between the variance–covariance structure of the innovations or $V(v(t))$ and that of the structural shocks or $V(e(t))$: namely

$$V(v(t))=SV(e(t))\,S' \tag{21}$$

where the estimated residuals of the VAR, of course, provide convergent estimators of $V(v(t))$.

According to a conventional normalization, the five diagonal elements of the $V(e(t))$ matrix are set equal to one. It is also commonly assumed (rather heroically) that the covariances of the structural shocks are all equal to zero. From these conventions, $V(e(t))$ is the identity matrix of order 5 and equation (21) reduces to

$$V(v(t))=SS' \tag{22}$$

Based on the perfectly symmetric nature of $V(v(t))$, we can then deduce 15 non-linear and independent constraints on the components of S. Four additional restrictions derive in our case from the idea that the price of imported raw materials p_q^* is exogenous, which means that the other four structural shocks in the analysis have no influence upon this price. This last assumption can be written as

$$S_{5i}=0 \qquad \forall i=1 \text{ to } 4 \tag{23}$$

Exogeneity tests clearly support this assumption except in the case of Spain where it can only be accepted at the 1 percent significance level (rather than the 5 percent). With regard to the remaining six identifying restrictions $(25-15-4=6)$, we depend on our theoretical hypotheses about the long-run effects of shocks.

Specifically, the use of these next theoretical ideas can be explained as follows. Let the matrix of long run structural coefficients $C(1)$ be

$$C(1) \equiv \begin{bmatrix} c_{ya} & c_{yx} & c_{ys} & c_{yv} & c_{yq^*} \\ c_{xa} & c_{xx} & c_{xs} & c_{xv} & c_{xq^*} \\ c_{pa} & c_{px} & c_{ps} & c_{pv} & c_{pq^*} \\ c_{va} & c_{vx} & c_{vs} & c_{vv} & c_{vq^*} \\ c_{q^*a} & c_{q^*x} & c_{q^*s} & c_{q^*v} & c_{q^*q^*} \end{bmatrix} \qquad (24)$$

where the coefficient c_{ij} is the long run response of the variable i ($i = \Delta(y\text{-}x)$, Δx, Δp or $\Delta p - \Delta p_q^*$, $\Delta(p - e - p^*)$, Δp_q^*) to the structural shock j ($j = e_a$, e_x, e_s, e_v, e_{q^*}). Our previous theoretical assumptions would say

$$C(1) \equiv \begin{bmatrix} c_{ya} & c_{yx} & c_{ys} & 0 & c_{yq^*} \\ -c_{ya} & -c_{yx} & c_{xs} & 0 & c_{xq^*} \\ c_{pa} & c_{px} & -(c_{pa} + c_{px}) & c_{pv} & c_{pq^*} \\ c_{va} & c_{vx} & c_{vs} & 0 & c_{vq^*} \\ c_{q^*a} & c_{q^*x} & c_{q^*s} & c_{q^*v} & c_{q^*q^*} \end{bmatrix} \qquad (25)$$

The twin conditions $c_{xa} = -c_{ya}$ and $c_{xx} = -c_{yx}$ follow from the supposed absence of any long-run influence of demand shocks on output y. The condition $c_{vv} = 0$ is, practically speaking, our definition of the relative-velocity shock e_v and implies c_{yv} and $c_{xv} = 0$ as well. $c_{ps} = -(c_{pa} + c_{px})$ expresses the Phillips curve hypothesis that inflation depends on excess demand. The last row of the matrix, which relates to effects on Δp_q^*, should obviously contain four zeros. But this last property of $C(1)$ is already contained in the construction of S via equation (23) and the exogeneity of Δp_q^*. Given equation (20), the preceding six long-run theoretical conditions imply six corresponding restrictions on the product $E(1)S$, which can serve in identifying S. The count is right: with 25 conditions, S is just-identified.

5 The results

We used the method of seemingly unrelated regressions in order to estimate the matrix of coefficients in the VAR rather than OLS because of the exogenous nature of the import price of raw materials. At first we experimented with a uniform number of lags in these matrices in all six countries, and once having identified the matrix S, we compared the influence of the structural shocks with our theoretical specification. Bayoumi and Eichengreen did the same. But whereas they merely looked for two particular signs of influence (positive effects of demand shocks and negative effects of supply shocks on inflation), we had many more signs to check. Our five shocks yield 15 different effects on three variables of major policy interest: output y, inflation Δp, and the current account x. Of these 15 effects, 13 have a specific sign on the basis of our theoretical model (equations (12) through (16)) – that is, they do so if we consider the situation prior to complete adjustment when many of those influences go to zero.[8] Not surprisingly, our estimates never satisfy all 13 corresponding conditions (prior to complete adjustment). But occasionally, they obey as many as ten of them. Following an examination of the robustness of the results based on a wide range of specifications (concerning lag length, Δp or $\Delta p - \Delta p_q^*$ as a dependent variable, etc.), we decided eventually to adhere to as uniform a specification as possible on condition of having at least a majority of correct signs. The country estimates we then choose yield ten correct signs (out of the 13) in two country cases, nine correct signs plus one ambiguous one in another, eight correct ones in two others, and seven correct signs plus two ambiguous ones in one case. The specifications giving rise to these results differ only as regards the presence of either three or four lags in the autoregressive VAR and ΔP or $\Delta p - \Delta p_q^*$ as a dependent variable.

We may begin the discussion of the empirical results with a cursory look at the variance decompositions of the forecast errors in output (y), the current account (x), and inflation (Δp), which we will examine more closely later on. A glance at table 6.1 shows that the shock-and-response structures differ widely between the countries. It will not be surprising, in this light, to find that the cross-country associations between the shocks are very low except in the instance of the import price of raw materials.

In order to measure these associations, we constructed a foreign shock pertaining to each country which consisted of a weighted-average of the other five (with fixed weights based on national output relative to the aggregate output of all six in marks during the middle of the sample, or in 1978–82). Next, we calculated covariances between the home and foreign shock (cov (e_h, e^*)) for each country and each shock. The ratio of the covariance to the variance (cov(e_h, e^*)/$V(e_h)$) served as our measure of association. This measure has the desirable property of reflecting amplitude as well as direction. The measure is also particularly desirable in our case because of our use of a weighted-average foreign shock, which makes the correlation coefficient a bit awkward since the latter becomes impossible to divorce from the composition of the variances between the foreign countries, whereas, in principle, a correlation is meant to be distinct from variances.

Table 6.2 shows the only strong association between the shocks to concern the import price of raw materials, e_{q^*}, as we mentioned before. In the case of the other shocks, the ratios of the covariance to the variance are generally small and mostly close to zero. Even the association between the e_{q^*} shocks is weaker than we might expect, being only around 0.4 to 0.6. Since these expectations rest on annual oil prices, we also examined the associations between the annual averages of the shocks e_{q^*} and found them to be indeed much higher: in the 0.60–0.80 range.

Table 6.1 *Decomposition of forecast errors*

Shock	Absorption	Net foreign demand	Supply	Relative velocity	Import price of raw materials
GERMANY (Δp; 3 lags)					
Output					
6 quarters	4	51	6	28	12
30 quarters	7	31	1	29	32
Net exports					
6 quarters	0.2	40	49	0.5	10
30 quarters	0	66	22	0.3	12
Inflation					
6 quarters	17	12	31	33	7
30 quarters	16	15	30	32	7
FRANCE (Δp; 3 lags)					
Output					
6 quarters	57	17	24	0.5	2
30 quarters	46	35	15	3	1
Net exports					
6 quarters	5	30	63	0.3	2
30 quarters	8	42	41	1	8
Inflation					
6 quarters	3	2	2	83	10
30 quarters	4	2	2	80	12
UNITED KINGDOM (Δp; 4 lags)					
Output					
6 quarters	39	1	49	5	6
30 quarters	28	1	43	6	22
Net exports					
6 quarters	9	19	61	10	3
30 quarters	2	16	38	24	21
Inflation					
6 quarters	7	1	3	50	39
30 quarters	6	2	2	37	53
ITALY (Δp; 3 lags)					
Output					
6 quarters	46	4	15	2	33
30 quarters	40	5	12	13	30
Net exports					
6 quarters	2	40	43	2	14
30 quarters	1	38	45	1	16

Table 6.1 (continued)

Shock	Absorption	Net foreign demand	Supply	Relative velocity	Import price of raw materials
ITALY (continued)					
Inflation					
6 quarters	26	7	3	40	24
30 quarters	18	5	5	35	38
SPAIN ($\Delta p - \Delta p_q^*$; 3 lags)					
Output					
6 quarters	29	2	66	0.4	2
30 quarters	18	14	62	2	4
Net exports					
6 quarters	28	58	8	3	3
30 quarters	48	20	25	1	6
Inflation					
6 quarters	14	15	15	17	39
30 quarters	12	13	30	9	36
NETHERLANDS ($\Delta p - \Delta p_q^*$; 3 lags)					
Output					
6 quarters	1	3	87	3	7
30 quarters	1	4	90	3	2
Net exports					
6 quarters	77	9	7	0.4	7
30 quarters	88	2	4	0.1	7
Inflation					
6 quarters	19	5	2	68	6
30 quarters	20	6	2	66	6

The only other column of table 6.2 deserving comment is the relative-velocity one, essentially because the contribution of the e_v shock to the variance decompositions proved to be much more stable than those of e_a, e_x, and e_s (in the first three columns) in the earlier trials.[9] Table 6.3, which concerns bilateral relations with Germany, facilitates the interpretation of the e_v column of table 6.2 (though table 6.2 remains our basic point of reference, since we posit a monetary union between all six countries rather than alternatives ones between Germany and one of the other countries, each taken in turn). This next table shows a positive association between the e_v shocks in Germany and The Netherlands but a negative one between those in Germany and every other country. This result conforms to the usual impression that positive news about the mark leads the guilder also to move up but the franc, the pound, the lira, and the peseta to move down.

Table 6.2 *Ratios of covariance to variance*

	Absorption	Net foreign demand	Supply	Relative velocity	Import-price of raw materials
Germany	0.08	0.03	−0.06	−0.09	0.58
France	−0.03	0.07	−0.04	0.03	0.44
United Kingdom	0.12	−0.07	−0.02	−0.04	0.58
Italy	0.12	−0.04	−0.02	−0.08	0.40
Spain	−0.06	0.05	−0.05	0.01	0.46
Netherlands	−0.02	0.03	0.00	−0.03	0.50

Table 6.3 *Ratios of covariance to variance in relation to Germany alone*

	Absorption	Net foreign demand	Supply	Relative velocity	Import-price of raw materials
Germany	1	1	1	1	1
France	0.04	0.06	−0.08	−0.07	0.53
United Kingdom	−0.06	−0.00	−0.09	−0.19	0.72
Italy	0.43	0.04	−0.07	−0.17	0.51
Spain	0.05	0.11	−0.07	−0.04	0.45
Netherlands	−0.11	−0.05	0.17	0.34	0.69

The general upshot of this analysis is a view of great disparities between the six countries – greater than any similar impression gained through previous two-part classifications of shocks: between demand and supply or between symmetric and asymmetric. From the perspective of the associations between shocks, therefore, the costs of monetary union seem very high.[10]

But the analysis can go on to consider the two earlier questions we raised about the possible ability of countries to parry shocks through independent fiscal policy within a monetary union and their possible ability to attenuate the impact of shocks through monetary policy outside a monetary union. The first question – regarding fiscal policy – requires focus on the impact of absorption shocks as such, since fiscal policy essentially affects absorption. If absorption shocks explain a great deal of the forecast errors in output or net exports or both, then presumably fiscal policy could be helpful in stabilizing output or the current account in a monetary union. More specifically, it could be so as long as the absorption shocks become effective in a reasonable time, since any stabilization policy must aim at a fairly short-term impact.

If we read the first numerical column of table 6.1 in this light, we find that the retention of fiscal policy would be important for all countries except Germany, since in all of the other cases, the e_a shock contributes a lot to explaining news about output or net exports or both within a six-quarter horizon. As a matter of fact, even the German lack of interest in keeping the fiscal policy instrument can be contested, because of aforementioned instability in the distinction between absorption and net foreign demand shocks in the analysis (see note 9). Since the short-run effects of the foreign demand shocks are considerable in Germany according to table 6.1, it could then be that some of the influence of these shocks in the table should be attributed to absorption shocks instead.

The issue of the value of independent monetary policy requires us to shift our attention to the relative velocity shock. The results concerning this shock are more interesting than those about e_a since the contributions of the e_v shocks to the variance decompositions are far more stable. With the possible exception of the United Kingdom (where the e_v shock has some short-run significance in explaining output and net export performance, if we take the two together), according to table 6.1, Germany represents the only country where the e_v shocks are an important source of unexpected real behavior in the short run. The relative-velocity shock explains a good deal of the surprises in output performance in Germany over a six-quarter horizon. By comparison, in the case of France, Italy, Spain, and The Netherlands, this shock accounts for almost none of the unexpected short run behavior of output or the current account. On this evidence, these four countries would lose little by surrendering their monetary policy independence. Indeed, this last conclusion can be reinforced, since the argument cannot be questioned on the grounds that the influence of the e_v shocks merely evaded us, as in all four countries the e_v shocks have important effects on inflation – exceptionally so in the case of France and The Netherlands.[11] The evidence would then say that monetary policy feeds directly into prices rather than volumes in the four countries. All four countries seem to offer textbook examples of cases where monetary policy has no value as a stabilization device.

6 Conclusion

We have provided a different reading of the evidence about the costs of European Monetary Union. Our decomposition of five shocks in six member countries of the EU (the only six for which we had the required data) shows the association between individual shocks to be much lower than has often been recorded. But we also pursued the analysis to examine the impact of monetary and fiscal policy on economic performance.

Independent monetary policy might be of little value outside of monetary union, and independent fiscal policy could serve to mitigate costs of adjustment later on, inside a monetary union.[12] In pursuing the analysis thus far, we responded to some important concerns about European Monetary Union which have often been slighted in empirical work. Our conclusions on the basis of these added considerations lead to a different assessment. Major doubts arise about the costs of monetary union except for Germany and possibly the United Kingdom.

Once again, we should emphasize in closing that our empirical results regarding the individual European economies must be viewed with caution because of a scarcity of experience with similar study methods in the European context. We are very much inclined to underline the methodological interest of our work quite apart from our specific results. Decompositions of the shocks affecting individual economies can potentially provide major evidence about the costs of monetary union, going far beyond the question of the cross-country associations between shocks.

Notes

Centre de Recherche en Economie et Statistique (CREST), Paris, France. We wish to thank Bertrand Candelon of the University of Paris I for generously furnishing us his computer programs, and Jean-François Jacques of CREST for similar help. We are also grateful to our discussant, Daniel Gros, the participants at the conference on "Positive political economy: theory and evidence" held at Tilburg University on January 23–4, 1995, Matthew Canzoneri, Benoît Coeuré, and Axel Weber for valuable comments.
  1 See Commission of the European Communities (1990) and Minford, Rastogi, and Hughes Hallett (1993).
  2 Sometimes this work has been done at the national level and has distinguished between shocks affecting two-country sums and two-country differences. See, in particular, Cohen and Wyplosz (1989). Sometimes the work has been done at the industry level and the distinction has been between shocks affecting an entire industry in the EC and others hitting only the firms in the industry in one particular country. See Bini-Smaghi and Vori (1993) and Helg, Manasse, Monacelli, and Rovelli (1994).
  3 See, in particular, Gali (1992).
  4 See Canova, Faust, and Leeper (1993) who also argue that a high frequency of observations may be important because of the assumption of the independence of the structural shocks in the statistical analysis.
  5 See, for example, Eichengreen (1990) and de Grauwe and Vanhaverbeke (1991). Low labor mobility in the EU is typically invoked as a major argument against EMU. But it is also true that such low mobility would make fiscal policy more effective.
  6 Since net exports enter positively in $y - x$ through y but negatively through $-x$, they may be supposed not to be concerned in the equation at all (just as they

clearly were not in equation (1) before). This matters because we shall need to assume that u_a and u_x are uncorrelated in our econometric work.

7 There was some problem with the published quarterly Dutch data as well, which only begin in 1977. However, we were able to obtain earlier Dutch figures directly from the OECD, and when we converted these to a 1980 base – the same base year we used for all the other countries in our study – we found no break in any of the individual Dutch series.

8 Quite specifically, the signs of those influences are as follows, where parenthetical zeros serve to indicate the cases of a tendency for the influence to vanish in the long run

	e_a	e_x	e_s	e_v	e_{q^*}
x	+(0)	+(0)	+	−(0)	−
y	−	+	?	−(0)	?
Δp	+(0)	+(0)	−(0)	−(0)	+(0)

9 Indeed, the estimates of the absorption and net foreign demand shocks proved particularly unstable. At first we thought that we had not provided adequate grounds for distinguishing the two. Therefore, we experimented with the very strong identifying condition that e_x has no immediate influence on absorption, in accordance with equations (12) and (13) of our theoretical model. This means imposing an additional zero in the e_x column (along y-x the row) of the matrix S and correspondingly dropping one of our earlier identifying restrictions. We picked the absence of the long-run influence of e_x on either x or y-x as the condition to drop. However, the same instability in the estimates of e_a and e_x remained. Therefore, we stuck to the previous long run theoretical restrictions, which we prefer (as a bit less confining).

10 It should be noted that the low cross-country correlations largely result from the fact that the identification method supposes no covariance between the structural shocks within each country. If instead of looking at the cross-country associations between the structural shocks themselves, we were to examine the cross-country correlations between the components of output, inflation, and the current account – or the macroeconomic variables of primary interest – that are attributable to the separate shocks, then the similitudes between the macroeconomic experiences of the six countries would re-emerge in the analysis. Many high correlations would appear (compare Mélitz and Weber (1995)).

11 The Spanish case might seem a bit questionable, but our conclusions about the impact of the shocks e_v in the Spanish example (as to relative effects on inflation and real performance) proved quite robust under alternative specifications (which we rejected because of fewer theoretically correct signs).

12 Interestingly enough, the very presence of highly asymmetric shocks amplifies the argument for independent fiscal policy by diminishing the problem of non-cooperative behavior.

References

Bayoumi, Tamim and Eichengreen, Barry (1992), "Shocking Aspects of European Monetary Unification," CEPR Discussion Paper, No. 643.

Bini-Smaghi, Lorenzo and Vori, Silvia (1993), "Rating the EC as an Optimal Currency Area," Banca d'Italia Temi di Discussione, No. 187.

Blanchard, Olivier and Quah, Danny (1989), "The Dynamic Effects of Aggregate Demand Supply Disturbances," American Economic Review, 79, 655–73.

Canova, Fabio, Faust, Jon and Leeper, Eir (1993), "Do Long-Run Identifying Restrictions Identify Anything?" mimeo, Washington DC: Board of Governors of the Federal Reserve System.

Cohen, Daniel and Wyplosz, Charles (1989), "The European Monetary Union: An Agnostic Evaluation," CEPR Discussion Paper, No. 306.

Commission of the European Communities (1990), "One Market, One Money," European Economy, 44.

De Grauwe, Paul and Vanhaverbeke, Wim (1991), "Is Europe and Optimum Currency Area? Evidence from Regional Data," CEPR Discussion Paper, No. 555.

Eichengreen, Barry (1990), "One Money for Europe? Lessons from the U.S. Currency and Customs Union," Economic Policy, 10, 117–87.

Gali, Jordi (1992), "How Well Does the IS–LM Curve Fit Postwar US Data?" Quarterly Journal of Economics, 107, 709–38.

Helg, Rodolfo, Manasse, Paolo, Monacelli, Tommaso, and Rovelli, Riccardo (1994), "How Much (A)symmetry in Europe? Evidence from Industrial Sectors," IGIER (Università Bocconi) Working Paper, No. 70.

Jobert, Thomas (1992), "Test de racine unitaire: une stratégie et sa mise en oeuvre," Université de Paris I, Cahiers Ecomath 92.44.

Johansen, Søren and Juselius, Katarina (1990), "Maximum Likelihood Estimation and Inference on Cointegration – With Applications to the Demand for Money," Oxford Bulletin of Economics and Statistics, 52, 169–210.

Karras, Georgios (1994), "Sources of Business Cycles in Europe: 1960–1988. Evidence from France, Germany, and the United Kingdom," European Economic Review, 38, 1763–78.

Mélitz, Jacques and Weber, Axel (1996), "The Costs/Benefits of a Common Monetary Policy in France and Germany and Possible Lessons for Monetary Union," CEPR Discussion Paper, No. 1374.

Minford, Patrick, Rastogi, A., and Hughes Hallett, Andrew (1993), "The Price of EMU Revisited," in Anthony Courakis and George Tavlas (eds.), Financial and Monetary Integration, Cambridge: Cambridge University Press.

Osterwald-Lenum, Michael (1992), "A Note with Quantiles of the Asymptotic Distribution of the Maximum Likelihood Cointegration Rank Test Statistics," Oxford Bulletin of Economics and Statistics, 54, 461–72.

Comment

DANIEL GROS

The chapter promises in its title (new) empirical evidence on the costs of EMU. My comments will be directed at this claim. I should emphasize at the outset that I symphasize with the agenda of the authors and that I agree with them that the existing evidence on the costs of EMU is rather weak. So this contribution is certainly a step in the right direction, but I would have liked to see more movement. Why is the existing evidence on the correlation of shocks unsatisfactory? Not only for the reason explained by the authors – with which I agree – but also because of another fundamental problem: the existing empirical literature on the costs of EMU mostly just measures correlations and variances of shocks to certain macro-variables such as output or the exchange rate. It assumes implicitly that any shocks would be a valid reason to adjust the exchange rate. But this is not the case!

The usual story, first told by Mundell, is quite simple: there is a shock to (an unexpected fall in) the demand for the goods exported by the country under consideration. This shock requires a change in the real exchange rate to preserve internal and external balance. If the nominal exchange rate cannot move, the adjustment has to come from wages and prices, but this will be too slow; hence there will be unemployment. The story is clear so far in that a shock of this type requires an exchange rate adjustment.

However, there remain potentially other shocks that are independent of policy and require an exchange rate adjustment from the point of view of the individual country concerned. But, in the case of these other shocks it is much more questionable whether greater exchange rate flexibility would be beneficial from an overall point of view. Imagine the case of a country that experiences a sudden fall in domestic demand because households suddenly save more. A depreciation would shift demand toward domestic goods and increase exports, thus reducing the unemployment that would otherwise result from the drop in demand. However, the "gain" in demand of the country experiencing the shock would come at the expense of the rest of the world. The country that depreciates would only export its unemployment problems. From a global point of view little would be gained from exchange rate flexibility in this case.

This argument that at the global level the effects of exchange rate change on demand net out to zero does not apply to shocks that affect trade directly. If demand shifts from one country to another, an exchange rate adjustment is required from the point of view of both. Hence fluctuations in exports are the main source of shocks that should be taken into account to ascertain the importance of exchange rate flexibility from a global point of view. Other sources of shocks that would be legitimate reasons to adjust the exchange rate would be shocks to the terms of trade and natural resource price variables considered in the chapter by Erkel-Rousse and Mélitz. But shocks to domestic demand or fiscal policy should not be considered legitimate sources of exchange rate variability, although in reality they contribute to it.

The chapter does not address this line of reasoning directly, but it represents already a big improvement compared with the existing literature which focuses only on correlations of output and exchange rates without any idea of where the shocks come from.

Let me now turn to the specific approach used in the chapter. I will start with a few general comments:

1 Like all VARs one cannot really go back from the results to one specific model. The authors have shown that the standard model they use leads to the VAR they finally estimate (given the constraints they impose). But does the reduced form actually make sense? It would be useful to have an idea of the sign and approximate magnitude of the coefficients. Are they estimated with any precision? (The authors should thus present the elements of $C(L)$ of equation (17) as estimated by them with some confidence bounds.)

2 A specific example of the general problem mentioned above is the "competitiveness shock," which is the sum of two monetary policy shocks and a shock to the foreign price level. What happens when EMU comes? Does a part of that shock disappear?

3 Supply and demand are identified by the length of time they affect output. This is a standard assumption, but not self-evident. Perhaps one should just say that there are short-run and long-run shocks.

4. The real interest rate is eliminated from the model (i.e., from the absorption equation). This is very unsatisfactory if one thinks about the recent experience in Europe, especially the ERM crises of 1993 that were caused by the perception that the interest hikes of the BUBA would have an unacceptably large negative impact on output and employment in France. The observation that French real interest rates were much higher than German ones was also widely cited during that crisis.

5. A key issue is robustness. This requires much more work by the authors. What happens if you change one of the 25(!) identifying restrictions.

Fifteen restrictions come from the assumptions that all shocks are mutually uncorrelated. Is this really acceptable? For example, the competitiveness shock contains (apart from monetary policy shocks) the foreign price level which should be correlated with the price of raw materials. The treatment of the post-unification German data also raises concerns. The easiest way out would be to use data only up to 1990.[1]

6. The interpretations of the results given by the authors, which concentrates on the absorption shocks, are difficult to accept as it stands because this shock (as others) comprises truly exogenous shocks and policy responses. The variance of e_a could thus be low because final policy was used to keep absorption constant, as suggested by Jürgen von Hagen in the discussion. How could one get around this problem? I would propose a two stage procedure: use the existing results in a second stage that looks at the correlation of shocks to absorption and the fiscal policy instrument.

I cannot say a lot about the *empirical results*.

(a) I share the impression of the authors that there is a great diversity of experience in these results. But perhaps the diversity is too large to be believable. For example, if one compares France and the UK the role of fiscal policy, or rather the absorption shock, for output and the trade balance in the UK is completely different. The e_a shock affects output but not the trade balance in the UK, whereas for France the opposite holds.

(b) What is the power of fiscal policy to affect output? This could be a key issue for EMU because fiscal policy is the only macroeconomic policy instrument that remains. Since fiscal policy is in the absorption shock, one should look at the first column of table 6.1. Here I agree with the authors when they say that for Spain and the UK fiscal policy appears to be important in the short run for output (and inflation).

(c) In the light of the fact that very few systematic relationships have been detected in the quarterly data, one has to ask: why use quarterly data? The authors present anyway only the results for the six-quarter (1½ years) and 30-quarter (five years) horizons. At this point one could have used annual data.

All in all this chapter remains a refreshing departure from the usual approach to analyse the costs of losing the exchange rate instrument.

Note

1 The author has since argued in a subsequent communication that there is no problem because there is no correlation between innovations in the growth rate of the price of imported raw materials and the price ratio p/ep*.

II

Exchange rate policy and redistribution

7 Exchange rate anchors and inflation: a political economy approach

SEBASTIAN EDWARDS

1 Introduction

For many developing and Eastern European countries, the 1980s and early 1990s were years of macroeconomic upheaval. The debt crisis generated serious dislocations throughout the Latin American region: balance of payments deficits soared and inflation increased rapidly. In the former communist countries, on the other hand, the fall of the Berlin Wall was accompanied by serious macroeconomic disequilibria, large public sector deficits and very high inflation rates. During the last few years, most countries in these regions have embarked on major structural reforms and have struggled to regain macroeconomic stability.

Much of the policy discussion in these countries has centered on the most effective way of implementing stabilization programs. A particularly important question relates to the role of nominal exchange rate anchors as a device for reducing inflation and maintaining stability over the longer run. A number of authors have argued that fixed nominal exchange rates provide an effective constraint on the behavior of monetary authorities, introducing the financial discipline required for achieving price stability. Others, however, have pointed out that in a world of very high capital mobility, fixed exchange rates are ineffective anchors that introduce unnecessary rigidities and do not allow countries to react optimally to external shocks. This discussion has been particularly heated in the case of Russia. Jeffrey Sachs,[1] for instance, has argued that a pegged exchange rate should be a fundamental element in any plan aimed at stabilizing the Russian economy, and has strongly criticized the IMF for not endorsing this position. Bruno (1991) has also supported the view that, to the extent that fiscal fundamentals are in place, pegging the exchange rate facilitates the reduction of inflation in transitional economies.

Some authors, however, have argued that, in the presence of price and wage inertia, a stabilization program based on a nominal exchange rate anchor will result in an increasing degree of real exchange rate overvaluation and, as a consequence, will eventually generate a speculative attack and a collapse of the parity. This suggests that a fixed exchange rate could be adequate at the early stages of a stabilization program, but that at some point the exchange rate regime should become more flexible – see, for instance, Dornbusch and Werner (1994) and Edwards (1995).

The crisis of the Exchange Rate Mechanism of the EEC in September 1992 introduced new doubts on the ability of fixed – or semi-fixed – nominal exchange regimes to act as effective constraints on inflation over the long run. Svensson (1993), for example, has argued that "fixed exchange rates are not a short cut to price stability." Also, the Mexican peso crisis of 1994 has generated renewed skepticism on the ability of predetermined exchange rate regimes to impose long term price stability.[2]

In a way it is ironic that more than twenty years after the collapse of the Bretton Woods system, policy makers and academics are again discussing the merits of pegged exchange rates as a way to achieve and maintain stability. This revival of interest in fixed nominal rates has been deeply influenced by the modern credibility and time consistency literature, which argues that, in the absence of commitment technologies, opportunistic governments will abuse their discretion and will move the economy to a high-inflation equilibrium. The fact that in the 1990s a large number of countries – eighty-eight in 1992, according to the IMF – still have some kind of fixed exchange rate regime has added an important empirical twist to the question of optimal exchange rate regimes.

Three fundamental and related issues have dominated recent policy discussions on the relationship between nominal exchange rates and macroeconomic stability: (a) Why have some countries adopted fixed exchange rate regimes, while others have opted for more flexible systems?; (b) do fixed exchange rate regimes impose an effective constraint on monetary behavior and, thus, result in lower inflation rates over the long run?; and (c) are exchange-rate-based stabilization programs superior to money-based stabilization programs? The first two issues deal with the long run, while the third one deals with short-run and transitional consequences of stabilization programs.

The purpose of this chapter is to deal, from a political economy perspective, with questions (a) and (b): the choice of exchange rate regime and the effectiveness of fixed exchange rate constraints as a way to generate a low inflation equilibrium over the long run.[3] The chapter is organized as follows: section 2 deals with the choice of exchange rate regime. A simple model of an economy with policy makers that behave strategically is presented, and its implications are tested using a large cross-country data set. In section 3, I move a step further and examine whether those countries that have chosen a fixed exchange rate regime have indeed been able to constrain, in an *ex ante* fashion, monetary behavior and, thus, have had a lower rate of inflation. In section 4, I present some concluding remarks, including some discussion on directions for future research.

2 The political economy of exchange rate regimes

Much of the recent enthusiasm for fixed nominal exchange rates is intellectually rooted on the modern credibility and time-consistency literature. According to this approach, governments that have the *discretion* to alter the nominal exchange rate will tend to abuse their power, introducing an inflationary bias into the economy.[4] The reason for this is that under a set of plausible conditions, such as labor market rigidities that preclude the economy from reaching full employment, it will be optimal for the government to "surprise" the private sector with unexpected devaluations.[5] By engineering these unexpected devaluations, the government expects to induce a reduction in real wages and, thus, an increase in employment and a boost in output. Naturally, in equilibrium the public will be aware of this incentive faced by the authorities, and will react to it by anticipating the devaluation surprises, hence rendering them ineffective. As a consequence of this strategic interaction between the government and the private sector, the economy will reach a high inflation plateau. What is particularly interesting about this result is that this inflationary bias will be present even if it is explicitly assumed that the government has an aversion for inflation – which in most models is fueled by the devaluation. This is because the government perceives that the marginal benefits of higher inflation – associated with the increase in employment once nominal wages have been set – outweigh its marginal costs.[6]

An important feature of the simple credibility literature is that under most circumstances policy *commitment* is welfare-superior to *discretionary* policy. If the government can credibly commit itself to low (or no) inflation, society will be better off: employment will be the same as in the discretionary policy case, but inflation will be lower. The problem, however, is that governments have a hard time making *credible* commitments. In the absence of effective constraints that will tie the government's hands, any promise of low inflationary policy will not be credible and, thus, will be self-defeating.

A key policy implication of this literature is that defining (and implementing) constraints – either institutional or reputational – that make government commitments *credible* will result in an improvement in society's welfare. It has been argued that the adoption of a fixed exchange rate will constrain the ability of governments to surprise the private sector through unexpected devaluations. Promises of fiscal discipline will become *credible* and private sector actions will not elicit successive rounds of inflationary actions.

In spite of its appeal, this view, in its simplest incarnation, has some problems. First, in simple settings exchange rate policy has a very limited role. In fact, its only effect is to alter the domestic rate of inflation and, through it, the government perceives it as altering real wages. However, in most modern exchange rate models, nominal devaluations can also help accommodate shocks to real exchange rate fundamentals, helping to avoid real exchange rate (RER) misalignment, or affecting real variables such as output or employment.[7] Second, in economies with stochastic shocks, contingent exchange rate rules can, at least in principle, be superior to fixed rates (Flood and Isard, 1989). Third, it is not clear why a country that can credibly commit itself to unilaterally fixing the exchange rate, cannot commit itself to maintaining a monetary anchor.[8]

In more general frameworks, policy makers face a tradeoff regarding exchange rate policy: while exchange rate flexibility has an inflationary bias, it also allows the country to reduce output and employment variability. This is accomplished by smoothing, via exchange rate adjustments, the consequences of terms of trade shocks. In this type of model it is not possible to rank a priori fixed and flexible (or active) exchange rate regimes.

In evaluating the desirability of alternative exchange rate regimes – adjustable or fixed – it is important to have an idea of the authorities' proclivity towards inflation. If given discretion to adjust the exchange rate, how tempted will they be to "abuse" that discretion? This is largely a (difficult) empirical issue which will depend on the specific economic, social and especially political characteristics of the country. Recent work on the political economy of inflation can, in fact, provide some clues to this question. For example, it has been found that there is a close relationship between the degree of political instability and polarization, on the one hand, and the reliance on the inflation tax, on the other: societies that are politically more unstable and/or polarized will tend to have a higher proclivity toward inflation.[9] Recently, Edwards and Tabellini (1994) have measured the degree of political instability as the perceived probability of a transfer of political power. According to their index, Asian nations tend to have a lower degree of political instability than that observed in other developing countries and, especially, in Latin America. This suggests that Asian countries, as a group, face a smaller temptation to abuse their exchange rate discretion and, then, the benefits associated with fixed rates will tend to be smaller than in other regions.

2.1 A simple framework

Consider the case of a small country whose authorities have to decide whether to adopt a fixed or a flexible exchange rate regime. Assume, as in much of modern theories of macroeconomic policy, that in making this decision the authorities take into account the expected value of a loss function under the two alternative regimes. Consider the case where the loss function is quadratic and depends on inflation (θ) squared and on squared deviations of unemployment (u) from a target value (u^*).[10] The model is given by equations (1) through (5)

$$L=E(\pi^2+\mu(u-u^*)^2); \; \mu>0 \tag{1}$$

$$u=u'+\theta\,(\pi-\omega)+\psi(x-x'); \; E(x)=x', \; V(x)=\sigma^2 \tag{2}$$

$$u^*>u' \tag{3}$$

$$\omega=E(\pi)+\alpha E(x-x') \tag{4}$$

$$\pi=\beta d+(1-\beta)\omega \tag{5}$$

Equation (1) is the loss function. Equation (2) states that the observed rate of unemployment (u) will be below the natural rate (u') if inflation exceeds wage increases – $(\pi-\omega)>0$–, and if external shocks (x) exceed their mean (x'). Variable x can be interpreted as a composite of terms of trade and world interest rate shocks. It is assumed to have a variance equal to σ^2. Equation (3) establishes that the target rate of unemployment u^* exceeds the natural rate u'. Equation (4) says that agents are rational in setting wage increases. Under rational expectations this means that they take into account the expected behavior of inflation and the expected external shocks. Finally equation (5) defines inflation as a weighted average of the rate of devaluation d and the rate of wage increases ω. Under fixed rates d is by definition equal to zero, while under flexible rates the authorities have to decide an optimal rule for d.[11]

The solution of this type of model depends crucially on the sequence in which decisions are made. Assume that workers determine ω before they observe x, d, or π. The government, on the other hand, sets its exchange rate policy after both ω and x are observed. The government's objective is to set its exchange rate policy so as to minimize the value of the loss function (1). Naturally, and by definition, the solution in the case of fixed exchange rates is trivial: $d=0$. It is straightforward to show that in this case

$$\pi=0 \tag{6'}$$

$$u=u'+\psi(x-x') \tag{6''}$$

The solution is slightly more complicated under flexible exchange rates. In this case the authorities have to determine the optimal exchange rate adjustment rule. The solution to this problem is given by

$$d=\Delta\{(\beta^2(1+\mu\theta^2)-\beta)\omega-\theta\beta\mu(u'-u^*)-\mu\theta\beta\psi(x-x')\} \tag{7}$$

where, $\Delta=\{\beta^2(1+\mu\theta^2)\}^{-1}$.

Under most plausible conditions $(\beta^2(1+\mu\theta^2)-\beta)>0$. According to equation (7) the authorities will accelerate the rate of devaluation if the rate of wage adjustment increases. This, however, will be done in less than in a one to one fashion. Also, if the unemployment target (u^*) goes up, the rate of devaluation will increase, while it will decline if there is a positive external shock. From here it follows that the expected rate of devaluation is

$$E(d)=-\theta\mu(u'-u^*) \tag{8}$$

The final solution for d, π, and u under flexible exchange rates are given by

$$d=\Delta\{\beta^2(1+\theta^2\mu)\theta\mu(u^*-u')-\mu\theta\beta\psi(x-x')\} \tag{8'}$$

$$\pi^{\text{flex}}=\pi^{\text{fixed}}+\theta\mu(u^*-u')-\beta^2\mu\theta\psi\Delta(x-x') \tag{8''}$$

$$u^{\text{flex}}=u^{\text{fixed}}-\theta^2\beta^3\psi\Delta(x-x') \tag{8'''}$$

Equation (8″) establishes that due to the unemployment objective, inflation under flexible rates will tend to exceed its equilibrium level under fixed rates. On the other hand, unemployment under flexible rates will be higher (lower) than under fixed rates if there are negative (positive) external shocks.

In selecting the exchange rate regime, the authorities will compare the expected value of the loss function under both regimes

$$K=E\{L^{\text{flex}}-L^{\text{fixed}}\} \tag{9}$$

If $K>0$, a fixed exchange rate regime will be adopted. It is easy to see that

$$K=E\{(\pi^{\text{flex}})^2+\mu(u^{\text{flex}}-u^*)^2-\mu(u^{\text{fixed}}-u^*)^2\} \tag{10}$$

This expression is intuitively appealing. It states that the selection of the exchange rate regime will depend on the square of inflation under flexible rates – remember that inflation is zero in the fixed rate regime – and on the difference between the squared deviations of unemployment from their respective targets. After some manipulations, equation (10) can be rewritten as

$$K=(\theta\mu)^2(u^*-u')^2-\gamma\sigma^2 \tag{11}$$

where γ is a positive function of Δ, β, μ, θ, and ψ. This expression says that in order for K to be positive, and thus for fixed rates to be preferred, the country's "inflationary bias" – measured by (u^*-u') – has to be "large enough." More specifically, it has to exceed the external shocks variance term. On the other hand, if σ^2 is high enough, K can be negative indicating that flexible rates are preferred. According to this framework, then, the selection of exchange rate regime will be affected by the relative magnitude of external shocks and by the country's propensity toward inflation. As pointed out by Persson and Tabellini (1990) among others, the latter will tend to depend on political economy considerations, including the degree of instability and political polarization of the country.

An important difficulty in the empirical evaluation of this (and related) models is how to *measure* a country's inflationary bias – term $(u^* - u')$. This is particularly problematic in multi-country studies, since very few nations have reliable series on unemployment. Cukierman, Edwards, and Tabellini (1992), Edwards and Tabellini (1994), and I assume that countries with more unstable political systems have a higher propensity to follow inflationary policies. I also assume that there is some degree of persistency in attitudes toward inflation, and that countries with a history of high inflation will have a higher inclination toward inflation.

2.2 Empirical results

In this sub-section I use a cross-country data set to analyze why some countries have adopted fixed exchange rate regimes while others have opted for more flexible systems. I estimate a number of probit equations to investigate whether, among other variables, a country's political structure – and in particular its degree of political instability – helps explain the selection of exchange rate regime. The analysis is based on the model sketched in the preceding section, which suggests that countries with a greater "inflationary propensity" and less volatile external shocks will tend to select a fixed exchange rate regime.

The data set is comprised of 70 advanced and developing countries. Two alternative dependent variables were used. The first is a dummy variable that takes a value of one if the country in question had a fixed exchange rate between 1979 and 1985 (D79–85), and a value of zero otherwise. The second is a dummy variable that takes the value of + if the country had a fixed exchange rate during 1979 and 1992 (D79–92), and zero otherwise. The IMF classification was used to separate countries between fixers and non-fixers. Table 7.1 contains the list of the countries in the sample.

Three types of variables were used as requested in the analysis. The first captures countries' inflationary bias; the second measures the magnitude of external shocks; and the third refers to structural variables, including the degree of development of the country in question. In an effort to relate the selection of the exchange rate regime to long-run structural variables, and

Table 7.1 *Countries included in the data set*

High-income countries	
Australia	Japan
Austria	The Netherlands
Belgium	New Zealand
Denmark	Norway
Finland	Spain
France	Sweden
Germany	Canada
Ireland	United Kingdom
Italy	United States
Others	
Bolivia	Jamaica
Botswana	Kenya
Brazil	Lesotho
Burundi	Mauritius
Cameroon	Mexico
Central African Rep.	Morocco
Chad	Nicaragua
Chile	Nigeria
Colombia	Pakistan
Congo	Paraguay
Dominican Republic	Peru
Ecuador	Philippines
El Salvador	Portugal
Ethiopia	Rwanda
Gabon	Sierra Leone
Ghana	Somalia
Greece	South Africa
Honduras	Sri Lanka
India	Sudan
Indonesia	Tanzania
Iran	Thailand
Ivory Coast	Togo

to avoid simultaneity problems, most regressors used in the analysis were defined over a number of years preceding the period under analysis. In most cases averages for 1970–82 were used. However, when, variables for 1979–92 were used the results reported here were basically unaffected.

Inflationary "inclination." As pointed out above, an index of political instability was used as a proxy for the degree of inflationary bias of the country in question. The index was taken from Cukierman, Edwards, and Tabellini (1992) who constructed it as the estimated probability of government change during 1971–82. They obtained the estimated probability from a probit analysis where actual government changes were regressed against political, economical, and institutional variables. Countries with a more unstable political system will have a higher temptation to inflate and, thus, a higher incentive to "tie their own hands" by choosing a pegged exchange rate regime. Thus, the coefficient of this variable is expected to be positive in the probit analysis. As is explained in greater detail below, in order to analyze the robustness of the results alternative indices of political instability were also used.

External shocks. Four alternative indices were used to measure the extent of external shock variability. (a) Coefficient of variation of real exports growth for 1970–82. This variable was constructed with raw data obtained from the International Monetary Fund's *International Financial Statistics* (IFS). (b) Coefficient of variation of real bilateral exchange rate changes for 1970–82. This index was constructed from data obtained from the IFS. (c) Average change in terms of trade. This index was constructed with data obtained from the World Bank. (d) Coefficient of variation of terms of trade changes. It is expected that the coefficient of these variables in the probit regressions will be negative.

In principle, the actual importance of external shocks should also depend on the degree of openness of the economy – more open countries are more "vulnerable" to external disturbances. In order to consider this effect I added an interactive term between external variability and the degree of openness. The latter was defined as the ratio of imports plus exports to GNP, and was constructed from data obtained from the IFS.

Structural variables. In addition to the variables on inflationary bias and external shocks, a number of variables that capture the structural characteristics of the economy were incorporated into the analysis. (a) Log of income per capita measured in 1989 dollars. This variable captures the degree of development, and was taken from the *World Development Report.* If, as it has sometimes been claimed, less advanced countries do not have the institutional and administrative ability to implement a flexible exchange rate regime, its coefficient should be negative.[12] (b) Proportion of the population living in urban areas. A number of authors have argued that in countries with larger shares of urban population there is a greater propensity for political instability and upheaval (Cukierman, Webb, and Neyapti, 1992). Consequently, the expected sign of this coefficient is positive. This variable was obtained from the *World Development Report.* (c)

Share of agriculture in GDP. This variable is related to the degree of "vulnerability" of the economy to external shocks and was taken from the *World Development Report*. Since agricultural commodity prices are particularly variable, countries with a larger share of agriculture in GDP will tend to be more severely affected by external shocks, and thus we can expect negative coefficients for this variable. (d) Current account balance. In principle, countries with a history of current account imbalances will be, with other things given, more reluctant to adopt a fixed exchange rate regime. The balance was defined as a proportion of GDP – a positive number is a surplus – and the data were taken from the IFS. Its coefficient is expected to be positive. (e) Past average rate of inflation. Countries with a long history of inflation will face greater difficulties in maintaining a fixed rate and, thus, will tend not to choose that type of system. In order to avoid simultaneity problems, the log of inflation for 1965–80 was used. The data were taken from the World Bank's *World Development Report*. It's coefficient is expected to be negative in the probit analysis.

Table 7.2 contains the main results from the probit analysis. The results are presented for the complete data set, as well as for LDCs only. Estimates using D79–85 as a dependent variable yielded very similar results, and are not reported here due to space considerations.

All the coefficients of the variables measuring inflationary bias are significantly negative. This contradicts the intuition provided earlier, and highlights the difficulties encountered in defining the authorities' incentive to "tie their own hands" for empirical purposes. It is interesting to note that the negative coefficient is consistent with an alternative interpretation. A particularly attractive one is related to the political costs of implementing exchange rate changes. According to this view, suggested by Collins (1994) and Edwards and Tabellini (1991) among others, changing the exchange rate (and, in particular, devaluing) will result in a reduced probability that the current government (or coalition) will remain in office. This argument explains why the coefficient of political instability can be negative.[13]

The coefficients associated with the indices of external shock volatility are also negative, as expected, and significant in a number of the regressions. What is particularly interesting is that the coefficients of the interactive term between the external shock and openness are positive and, in most equations, significantly so. This suggests that as countries are more open, the importance of the external disturbance in deciding the selection of the exchange rate regime loses importance.

The estimated coefficients of the current account balance have the expected signs and are statistically significant. These results suggest that countries with a *history* of current account deficits have a greater

Table 7.2 *Probit regression results: D79–92 as dependent variable (t-statistics in parentheses)*

Equation sample	I All	II All	III All	IV All	V All	VI LDCs	VII LDCs	VIII LDCs
Constant	-4.443 (-1.539)	-5.266 (-2.189)	-8.012 (-2.257)	0.614 (0.561)	-0.873 (-0.079)	0.617 (0.557)	-7.988 (-1.906)	-11.598 (-1.978)
Log of political instability	-0.851 (-2.729)	-0.809 (-2.814)	-1.323 (-2.687)	-0.634 (-2.740)	-0.763 (-3.101)	-0.655 (-2.460)	-0.686 (-2.009)	-1.196 (-1.994)
Export growth variability (CVX)	-0.302 (-1.842)	—	—	-0.011 (-0.590)	—	-0.011 (-0.557)	-0.193 (-0.953)	—
Real exchange rate variability (RERV)	— (-1.270)	-0.033 (-2.541)	-0.397 (-1.774)	—	-0.090	—	—	-0.476 (-1.978)
RERV*openness	0.004 (1.452)	—	0.006 (2.770)	—	0.002 (2.157)	—	0.002 (0.954)	0.007 (1.938)
CVX*openness	1.131 (2.958)	1.005 (2.883)	1.476 (2.770)	—	—	—	1.606 (2.613)	1.939 (2.147)
Log of GNP per capita	-0.058 (-2.794)	-0.050 (-2.799)	-0.070 (-2.617)	—	—	—	-0.071 (-2.711)	-0.095 (-2.458)
Urban	0.034 (1.320)	0.038 (1.680)	0.093 (2.382)	—	—	—	0.049 (1.590)	0.122 (2.141)
Agriculture	-1.464 (-2.083)	-0.827 (-1.327)	-1.206 (-1.658)	-0.915 (-2.175)	-0.715 (-1.859)	-0.954 (-2.059)	-1.127 (-1.646)	-0.539 (-1.619)
Log of lagged (−1) inflation	0.044 (1.559)	—	0.154 (1.904)	—	—	—	0.024 (0.447)	0.152 (1.466)
Current account								
N	61	64	60	70	63	51	44	45
Log likelihood	-22.61	-25.88	-16.91	-33.58	-27.98	-26.20	-15.93	-11.29
Chi-square	28.79	27.73	41.10	16.59	21.16	12.51	24.59	34.18

Table 7.3 *Probit regression results: D79–92*
as dependent variable: CADEF as independent
variable (t-statistics in parentheses)

Equation sample	IX All
Constant	−7.473 (−1.932)
Log of political instability	−1.173 (−2.690)
Real exchange rate variability (RERV)	−0.355 (−2.953)
RERV*openness	0.005 (3.065)
Log of GNP per capita	1.556 (2.768)
Urban	−0.084 (−2.815)
Agriculture	0.106 (2.528)
Log of lagged (−1) inflation	−1.181 (−1.491)
CADEF	−2.051 (−2.394)
N	61
Log likelihood	−15.50
Chi-square	44.67

probability of selecting a more flexible exchange rate regime. In order to explore this issue further, I defined a dummy variable (CADEF) that takes the value of + if the average current account *deficit* during the 1979–92 period was larger than 2.5 percent of GDP and zero otherwise. As can be seen from table 7.3, when this variable was added to the probit analysis its coefficient turned out to be negative and significant at the conventional level. Somewhat puzzling, and contrary to simple intuition, the coefficient of log of per capita income is significantly positive. This indicates that, with other things given, there is a higher probability that more advanced countries will have a fixed exchange rate.[14] The coefficient of historical inflation is significantly negative, as expected.

Table 7.4 *Probit regression results: D79–92 as dependent variable:*
CADEF, TP, NPC, MAJ, and COAL as independent variables (t-statistics
in parentheses)

Equation sample	X All	XI All
Constant	−5.276 (−1.598)	−16.131 (−1.440)
Real exchange rate variability (RERV)	−0.285 (−2.798)	−0.075 (−2.188)
RERV*openness	0.004 (2.790)	0.011 (2.132)
Log of GNP per capita	1.512 (2.529)	4.451 (1.989)
Urban	−0.088 (−2.769)	−0.223 (−1.958)
Agriculture	0.100 (2.676)	0.288 (2.224)
Log of lagged (−1) inflation	−0.887 (−1.101)	−1.280 (−0.945)
CADEF	−1.264 (−1.772)	−3.452 (−1.873)
TP	−5.918 (−2.053)	−17.230 (−1.893)
NPC	—	−2.899 (−1.863)
MAJ	—	−1.031 (−0.415)
COAL	—	0.164 (0.073)
N		61
Log likelihood		−15.50
Chi-square		44.67

Two important questions are whether these results are sensitive to the
definition (and measurement) of political instability, and whether other
variables that capture the structural features of the political system are
important in helping explain the selection of exchange rate regime. These
issues are addressed in table 7.4, where an alternative index of political

instability is used and where additional politically based variables are added to the analysis. The new index of political instability (TP) measures the frequency with which *political power* is transferred from the ruling party (or coalition) to the opposition. The main difference between this index and that used in tables 7.2 and 7.3, then, is that changes in the head of government within the same political party, are not recorded as a transfer of power.[15] The data were taken from Edwards and Tabellini (1994). Table 7.4 also includes a probit regression with three additional politics-related regressors. These indicators capture the degree of political strength or weakness of the executive. (a) The first one (MAJ) measures whether the party or parties in office have the absolute majority of seats in the lower house of parliament.[16] (b) The second one is the number of political parties in the ruling coalition (NPC). (c) Finally, the third one (COAL) reflects whether the government is indeed a coalition. The indicator takes, each year, the value of zero for dictatorships, one for single party governments, and two for coalition governments. As in the case of other regressors, these indices are expected to measure the political history of the country, and are averaged for the period 1970–82. The sources of the primary data are given in Edwards and Tabellini (1994).

As can be seen from table 7.4, the coefficient of the alternative index of political instability (TP) is significantly negative. Of the other three indices, only NPC is significant, with a negative sign. This provides some preliminary support to the notion that countries with weaker political systems have a lower probability of adopting fixed exchange rate regimes.

3 Fixed nominal exchange rates and macroeconomic discipline: some cross-country evidence

As was pointed out in the introduction to this chapter, a second important question is whether fixed exchange rate regimes indeed introduce macroeconomic (financial and fiscal) discipline and, thus, result in lower levels of inflation. It has often been argued that the comparative inflation record of countries with alternative exchange regimes supports this contention. For instance, according to the IMF, "the inflation performance of the countries that have operated under a fixed exchange rate regime has been, on the whole, superior to that of the group operating under more flexible arrangements" (Aghevli *et al.*, 1991, p. 13). A serious problem with this line of argument – and one acknowledged in the IMF document – is that the direction of causality is not clear: is it that those countries that have operated under fixed rates for a long period of time have lower inflation, or is it that those countries with lower inflation have been able to maintain a fixed rate? The IMF document by Aghevli *et al.* (1991) states this problem as follows: "[A]n examination of countries that maintained pegged exchange rate arrangements over a given period neglects the experience of countries that initially adopted a pegged arrangement but were forced to abandon it . . ." (p. 13). The problem, of course, is that these simple descriptive analyses focus on the *ex post* performance of peggers and non-peggers.

An essential question in this debate refers to whether a nominal fixed exchange rate regime indeed provides *ex ante* constraints to fiscal and credit policy. In analyzing this issue, two basic alternative forms of fixed rates should be distinguished. The first and most common system is one where a country *unilaterally* declares that it is pegging its currency to another country's currency. Usually, under this type of regime there is no *institutional* impediment to alter the exchange rate. Under these circumstances the adoption of fixed exchange rates amounts to a declaration of good intentions; the authorities can alter the exchange rate at will. The public can, in fact, see this type of regime as a commitment with escape clauses. If the contingencies under which such escape clauses are used are perceived as being too permissive, the commitment itself will be very weak and will have little effectiveness. An alternative line of argument emphasizes the role of *reputation*. By choosing a highly visible variable (the exchange rate) as the anchor, the authorities are placing their reputations at stake in a very obvious fashion; if the peg is altered, the authorities could incur heavy political costs. According to this line of reasoning one would expect that the reputational constraint is more important in countries with a more stable political system. This is because in unstable political regimes the probability of government change is high, and thus the costs associated with being thrown out of office for incompetence reasons is very low (see Edwards and Tabellini, 1991).

The second basic type of fixed exchange rate regime corresponds to a system where the authorities enter some type of multilateral arrangement that makes the alteration of the peg costly. There are a number of such regimes that attempt to preclude or limit exchange rate flexibility. Among them, some of the best known are the French Zone African Monetary Unions before 1994, the ERM of the EMS and, before 1971, the Bretton Woods system. Naturally, the degree of commitment associated with this type of system will depend on the costs related to changing the parity. In the pre–1971 Bretton Woods regime, for example, this was not very costly; all it took was for a country to declare that it was facing a situation of "fundamental disequilibrium." In the case of the African Franc Zone, on the other hand, the alteration of the parity was for a long time virtually impossible.[17] Moreover, as the September 1992 ERM crisis has shown, even in the presence of this type of institutional constraints exchange rate crises can (and do) occur.

In this section I investigate empirically whether the adoption of a fixed exchange rate has indeed resulted in *ex ante* financial discipline in a large cross section of developing nations. I do this by analyzing whether those countries that had a fixed rate *at the beginning of the 1980s* have done better throughout the decade than those with a more flexible regime. By considering all those countries that had a fixed rate at the beginning of the decade of the 1980s, an effort is made to isolate the role of *initial conditions*.

3.1 Fixed exchange rates and inflation in the 1980s: preliminaries

Table 7.5 contains data on a number of key macroeconomic variables for the 1980s for 37 developing countries that according to the IMF had a fixed exchange rate with respect to the US dollar in December 1979. A number of interesting features emerge from this table. First, out of the 37 countries with a fixed rate in late 1979, only 11 maintained the parity throughout the 1980s. This makes the rather obvious (but not always recognized) point that adopting a fixed parity at a particular moment in time is no guarantee that the rate will in fact not be altered in the future. Second, the countries that *did* in fact maintain a fixed exchange rate throughout the 1980s correspond, in a large proportion, to very small countries, including a substantial set of Caribbean nations. It is unclear, however, whether this fact introduces some bias into our sample. Third, during the 1980s (or sub-period with available data) the countries that had a fixed rate in 1979 experienced non-trivial levels of inflation: 23.4 percent yearly average. This figure is significantly higher than the average inflation for those countries in this sample table that actually maintained a fixed nominal rate relative to the US dollar throughout the period. Fourth, as can be seen in the last two columns, in those countries where the fixed rate was abandoned, the rate of growth of monetary aggregates – money and domestic credit – was very high, greatly exceeding what is compatible with the maintenance of a fixed parity. The average annual inflation for this second group was only 5.5 percent.[18]

It may be tempting at this point, and in consideration of the information in table 7.5, to argue that fixed exchange rate arrangements have no *ex ante* effects on financial discipline and inflationary performance. This, however, is an incorrect inference for at least two reasons: first, this analysis has not inquired into the fate of those countries that did *not* adopt a fixed rate in the early 1980s. They may, in fact, have fared much worse than those nations in table 7.5. Second, we have not controlled for other determinants of inflation. In the sub-section that follows I take these two factors into account in trying to explain the determinants of inflation for a cross section of countries.

Modern analyses on the determinants of inflation have emphasized the

Table 7.5 *Macroeconomic performance of 1979 exchange rate fixers during the 1980s (percentages)*

Country	Avg. annual devaluation	Avg. annual inflation	Avg. change in REER*	Avg. growth of dom. credit	Avg. growth of money
Chile	24.1	20.3	6.9	—	—
Costa Rica	28.3	25.6	4.8	21.5	24.8
Dom. Rep.	26.3	24.6	4.2	19.4[1]	24.3[1]
Ecuador	42.7	36.4	7.9	42.4[2]	28.4[2]
El Salvador	12.4	18.5[1]	—	11.7	11.3
Guatemala	17.5	11.8[1]	—	13.0	15.7
Haiti	0.0	5.2[1]	—	8.5[1]	12.1[1]
Honduras	0.0	6.2[1]	—	13.9	12.0
Nicaragua	252.9	304.4[2]	−14.6	—	—
Panama	0.0	1.8	—	1.8	2.6
Paraguay	25.9	20.2[2]	8.2	24.1[2]	23.1[2]
Venezuela	27.9	23.3	7.5	22.3	18.3
Bahamas	0.0	5.5	0.6	11.3	9.2
Barbados	0.0	5.7	—	13.2	10.5
Dominica	0.0	4.7[1]	—	13.2	10.5
Grenada	0.0	5.4[1]	−1.5[1]	13.5	6.6
Jamaica	16.3	14.8	—	10.6	18.8
Surinam	0.0	12.4[2]	—	27.3[1]	24.8[1]
Trinidad & Tobago	5.9	11.0	—	—	5.4[1]
Iraq	0.5	—	—	—	—
Oman	1.1	—	—	17.4	9.7
Yemen P.D.R.	1.6[1]	6.1[5]	—	14.8[2]	9.1[2]
Syrian A.R.	11.1	22.1[1]	—	19.2[3]	17.6[3]
Egypt	11.1	16.9	—	21.6	14.0
Yemen A.R.	8.8[1]	—	—	28.1[1]	16.1[1]
Laos	61.0[2]	—	—	—	—
Nepal	9.7	10.1	—	22.0[1]	16.9[1]
Pakistan	8.3	7.0	—	14.6	14.3
Djibouti	0.0	—	—	—	—
Burundi	6.3	7.6	2.6	11.3[1]	8.8[1]
Ethiopia	0.0	4.4	—	12.4	12.9
Liberia	0.0	3.9[1]	—	12.7[1]	14.8[1]
Libya	0.2	—	—	21.0[1]	2.2[1]
Rwanda	2.7	4.3	—	27.8[1]	3.3[1]
Somalia	74.2[1]	45.6[2]	—	43.3[1]	54.5[1]
Sudan	24.6	36.2[1]	—	33.4[1]	37.2[1]
Romania	6.8	4.0[4]	—	7.4[4]	7.8[4]
AVERAGE	19.1	23.4	2.5	18.4	15.5

Notes:
* A positive number denotes a real devaluation.
[1] 1980–89   [2] 1980–88   [3] 1980–87   [4] 1980–86   [5] 1980–85
Source: IMF, *International Financial Statistics*, various issues.

fact that inflation is a tax on money holdings.[19] From a modern public finance perspective the share of the inflation tax on total government revenue will depend on the country's structural, political, and institutional characteristics. The higher the costs of administering a "regular" tax system, the higher the reliance on the inflation tax will tend to be. The reason for this is that, although inflation is a highly distortionary tax, it is very easy to collect. Variables that capture the cost of running a regular tax system will thus be important determinants of the variability of inflation across countries (Edwards and Tabellini, 1991).

Recent inflation theories have also predicted that, with other things given, countries that are politically more unstable will tend to rely more heavily on inflationary finance. There are two reasons for this: first, in politically unstable countries there are few incentives to implement an efficient tax system (i.e., one that does not rely heavily on inflation). This is because there is a higher probability that the benefits of the more efficient tax regime will be reaped by the government's opponent.[20] Second, in more politically unstable countries, reputational constraints are less binding.[21] Finally, the degree of reliance on inflationary finance will also depend on institutional arrangements. In this chapter, we are interested in determining whether from an *ex ante* perspective the exchange rate regime affects macroeconomic and inflationary performance. Does the *adoption* of a fixed exchange rate introduce financial discipline?[22]

3.2 A simple analytical framework

In this sub-section I develop a simple framework for analyzing the *ex ante* effects of fixed exchange rates on macroeconomic discipline. Consider the case of a small country with a pegged exchange rate. In contrast with the simple monetary approach to the balance of payments, I assume that this fixed parity can be abandoned through a stepwise devaluation. I also assume that adjusting the parity entails a (political) cost for the government in office.[23] In every period the authorities have to decide how expansive domestic credit policy will be. A more expansive policy has the benefit of reducing the rate of unemployment; on the costs side, however, it increases the probability of devaluation. The objective function of the government is a weighted average of utility when the pegged rate is maintained (W^p), and utility in the case there is a devaluation crisis (W^c). The weights are related to the probability of devaluation (q):

$$W = (1-q) \ W^p + q W^c \tag{12}$$

Utility under fixity depends on the inflation rate (π) and, quadratically, on unemployment (u). Utility under crisis depends, in addition, on the cost of devaluation C. This cost, in turn, is a function of a number of factors, including the structural degree of political instability. If the country in question is inherently very unstable, C will tend to be small. In a very stable setting, on the other hand, a major event such as a devaluation will result in high political costs

$$W^p = -(\vartheta u^2 + \varphi \pi) \tag{13}$$

$$W^c = -(\vartheta u^2 + \varphi \pi) - \epsilon C \tag{14}$$

The probability of devaluation is associated with the probability that the stock of international reserves (R) will fall below a minimum level $(\underline{R})$. This probability, in turn, depends on a number of factors, including the initial level of reserves R' (negatively); the rate of growth of domestic credit λ (positively); and the rate of growth of the demand for domestic credit ς (negatively).

$$q = \text{Prob } (R \leq \underline{R}) = P(R', \lambda, \varsigma, C) \tag{15}$$

Equation (16) describes the behavior of unemployment. It states that if the rate of growth of domestic credit λ exceeds the rate of growth of its demand ς, actual unemployment (u) will be below its natural rate (u').

$$u = u' - \zeta(\lambda - \varsigma) \tag{16}$$

Maximizing equation (12) with respect to λ yields the optimal domestic credit policy. The differential between the optimal λ and ς can be interpreted as the degree of financial discipline imposed by the pegged exchange rate regime. If $\lambda = \varsigma$, there is "perfect discipline"; this is the textbook case corresponding to the monetary approach to the balance of payments. If, however, $\lambda > \varsigma$ the monetary authority has fallen victim to expansionary "temptation." After some manipulations it is easy to show that:

$$\lambda = \varsigma + \tau \tag{17}$$

where τ is greater than or equal to zero, and is given by (sub-indexes refer to partial derivatives)[24]

$$\tau = (1/\zeta)u' - (\varphi/2\vartheta^2\zeta^2)\pi_\lambda - (C\epsilon/2\vartheta^2\zeta^2)\,q_\lambda \tag{18}$$

The first term is positive, and captures the fact that an "overly" expansive domestic credit policy can reduce the level of unemployment. The next two terms, on the other hand, are the costs of expansive credit policy. The term $(\varphi/2\vartheta^2\zeta^2)\pi_\lambda$ represents the direct inflation effect, and measures the direct impact of expansive credit policy on inflation. This will tend to moderate the employment-motivated expansionary bias. Term $(C\epsilon/2\vartheta^2\zeta^2)q_\lambda$ captures the effect of expansionary credit policies on the probability of an exchange rate crisis. Since $q_\lambda > 0$ – a more expansionary credit policy increases the probability of an exchange rate devaluation crisis – this term is positive and exercises a compensatory effect over the employment-expansion bias. This is the *fixed exchange rate discipline* effect. Notice that the coefficient of q_λ depends positively on the cost of abandoning the peg (C). The higher this cost, the more important will be the fixed rate's disciplinary effect. In the extreme case where $C=0$ – there are no costs associated with devaluations – a fixed exchange rate will impose no discipline over macroeconomic policy. Then, to the extent that C is related to the political structure of the country, we will expect that the degree of political instability will influence the *ex ante* disciplinary effects of fixed rates. This implication of the model is tested empirically in the following sub-section.

3.3 Empirical results

In this section I use the data set from the previous section to investigate the *ex ante* effect of fixed exchange rates on inflation and monetary policy. Two alternative dependent variables were used: a measure of the excess supply for credit – calculated as the rate of growth of domestic credit minus real income growth – and the average rate of inflation for 1982–90.

The following variables were used as regressors in the cross-country regressions:[25] (a) The log of income per capita measured in 1989 dollars. This variable captures the ability of running a "regular" tax system; its coefficient is expected to be negative. (b) Proportion of the population living in urban areas. Since it is easier to reach urban taxpayers, its coefficient is expected to be negative. (c) Share of agriculture in GDP. This variable is also related to the cost of administering a non-inflationary tax system. Its coefficient is expected to be positive. (d) Dummy variables for Asian, Latin American, and industrial countries. (e) The index of political instability used in the preceding section. And (f), a dummy variable that captures the exchange regime *at the beginning of the period*. This variable takes the value of one if the country in question had a fixed exchange rate during 1979–80, and zero otherwise. In order to analyze the channels through which political instability affects macroeconomic policy, an interactive term defined as the exchange regime dummy variable times political instability was also included in some of the regressions.

Table 7.6 contains the basic results. As can be seen they are quite satisfactory. All coefficients have the expected signs and a large number of them are statistically different from zero at standard significance levels. What is particularly important, and to some extent even striking for the purpose of our discussion is that these results provide preliminary evidence suggesting that, with other things given, countries that had a fixed exchange rate at the

Table 7.6 *Regression results: inflation and excess credit as dependent variables (t-statistics in parentheses)*

Equation sample dependent variable	XII All inflation	XIII LDCs inflation	XIV LDCs inflation	XV LDCs inflation	XVI All excess credit	XVII All excess credit	XVIII LDCs excess credit	XIX LDCs excess credit
Constant	-0.840 (-0.990)	1.243 (2.191)	-0.288 (-0.313)	-0.023 (-0.023)	0.002 (0.140)	0.004 (0.246)	0.012 (0.734)	0.010 (0.651)
Log of GNP per capita	0.978 (0.832)	-1.480 (-1.573)	0.216 (0.172)	0.437 (0.326)	0.006 (0.310)	0.009 (0.423)	0.000 (0.008)	-0.003 (-0.126)
Urban	1.90E-04 (0.040)	-9.10E-04 (-0.151)	-7.50E-04 (-0.123)	-1.76E-03 (-0.273)	-6.00E-05 (-0.729)	-7.00E-05 (-0.830)	-9.00E-05 (-0.800)	-9.00E-05 (-0.850)
Agriculture	0.017 (2.686)	—	0.014 (2.065)	0.015 (2.086)	5.00E-05 (0.466)	5.00E-05 (0.504)	2.00E-05 (0.177)	1.00E-05 (0.093)
Latin America	0.615 (3.209)	0.471 (2.165)	0.588 (2.688)	0.714 (3.143)	0.006 (2.187)	0.007 (2.318)	0.008 (2.235)	0.006 (1.957)
Asia	-0.241 (-1.090)	-0.505 (-1.959)	-0.372 (-1.436)	-0.324 (-1.122)	-0.005 (-1.419)	-0.005 (-1.357)	-0.006 (-1.274)	-0.007 (-1.618)
Industrial countries	-0.409 (-1.306)	—	—	—	-0.006 (-1.152)	-0.005 (-0.936)	—	—
Pol. inst.	0.974 (2.157)	1.730 (2.524)	1.624 (2.428)	—	0.011 (1.606)	—	—	0.018 (1.834)
d79-80	-0.372 (-2.589)	-0.488 (-2.604)	-0.468 (-2.507)	-0.695 (-2.587)	-0.005 (-2.235)	-0.007 (-2.100)	-0.008 (-1.875)	-0.006 (-2.221)
d79-80* Pol. inst.	—	—	—	0.515 (0.585)	—	0.004 (0.442)	0.002 (0.148)	—
N	69	52	51	51	69	69	51	51
R^2	0.433	0.419	0.470	0.407	0.266	0.237	0.229	0.284

Table 7.7 *Regression results: determinants of inflation in developing countries: average inflation as dependent variable (t-statistics in parentheses)*

Equation sample	XX LDCs
Constant	0.082 (0.242)
Political instability	1.179 (1.964)
Exchange rate regime (ERR)	−0.359 (−1.424)
ERR*inflation 1965–80	−0.707 (−2.543)
GNP per capita	2.478 (1.722)
Agriculture	−7.7E-05
Latin America	0.011 (1.810)
Asia	0.619 (3.339)
N	52
R^2	0.467

beginning of 1980 have been financially more responsible – in the sense of having a lower average rate of inflation and of domestic credit growth than those with a more flexible exchange rate regime.[26] The results reported in this table also support the view that the extent of political instability plays an important role in explaining inflation. Interestingly enough, political instability appears to enter additively, rather than multiplicatively, in the excess credit and inflationary regressions.

In order to test whether financial history matters, an interactive term between the exchange rate regime dummy and the rate of inflation during 1965–80 was added to the regression. The results obtained appear in table 7.7. The coefficient of the interactive term (Exchange regime)×(Inflation 65–80) is positive and marginally significant, tending to confirm the hypothesis that the financial discipline effect of a fixed exchange rate is higher in countries with a history of price stability. As past inflation becomes higher and higher, the discipline *ex ante* effect of fixed rates on financial stability becomes weaker and weaker. In fact, according to these point estimates, at levels of 30 percent of historical inflation, fixed rates lose their *ex ante* discipline effect.

To sum up, the evidence presented here suggests that, with other things given, the adoption of a fixed exchange rate regime has indeed been associated with financial discipline and lower inflation. What is particularly interesting is that this result holds even after we have controlled for other determinants of inflation, including the perceived degree of political instability and some important structural characteristics. A crucially important result from this analysis is that the discipline effect of fixed exchange rates depends on the inflationary history of the country. Nations with a history of stability are in fact those that will probably gain the most from a fixed exchange rate regime. It is important to note, however, that the fact that the regional dummies for Latin America and Asia are significant in almost every regression suggests that there are elements determining inflation and government financial discipline not fully captured by this analysis.

4 Concluding remarks

Recently, fixed exchange rates have become increasingly popular in some policy circles. Some authors have argued that a return to limited flexibility (or plain fixed parities) would provide a credible *nominal anchor* to the developing countries that will help them (rapidly) achieve stability and low inflation.

In this chapter I have investigated several aspects of the new nominal exchange rate anchor view. I first analyzed whether the selection of the exchange rate regime responds to political and external sector determinants. The results reported in section 2 provide some support to that view.

In section 3, I concentrated on the longer run effects of fixed exchange rates on financial discipline, macroeconomic policy, and inflation. The empirical analysis reported in that section supported the contention that political instability and the exchange rate regime affect, in an *ex ante* way, macroeconomic discipline. However, history also matters. As reputation for macroeconomic stability – which we measured by past inflation – becomes weaker, the constraining effect of the fixed exchange rate begins to disappear rapidly. This result provides some important, but qualified, support for the modern credibility-based views of inflationary finance. This, of course, does not mean that fixed rates are superior to adjustable pegs. While the evidence supports the view that fixed rates help reduce the inflationary bias of the payments system, it also indicates that this positive effect is stronger in those countries that may need it the least: those nations that already have a history of stable prices. That is, the evidence indicates that fixed exchange rates reduce the ability to abuse discretion in those nations where this temptation is weaker.

Notes

This is a revised version of a paper presented at a conference on "Positive political economy: theory and evidence," organized by the CentER for Economic Research, Tilburg University, The Netherlands, January 23–4, 1995. I thank Daniel Lederman and Fernando Losada for their help.

1 "Reformers' Tragedy," *New York Times*, January 23, 1994.
2 On Mexico's exchange rate policy see, for example, Dornbusch and Werner (1994).
3 Issues related to the third question have been addressed by a number of authors. See, for example, Calvo and Vegh (1994), Edwards (1993), and Kiguel and Liviatan (1992).
4 This approach contrasts with two earlier strands in the literature: one that emphasized structural features of different countries in determining optimal currency areas (Mundell, 1961), and one that made a distinction between monetary and real shocks in assessing the optimal degree of flexibility of exchange rates (McKinnon, 1963).
5 This assumes that wages are set before the government implements the exchange rate policy, but after it has been announced.
6 See Persson and Tabellini (1990).
7 See, for example, Edwards (1988).
8 By "unilaterally" I mean that the fixed rate is not enforced by a multilateral institutional arrangement such as the European Monetary System (EMS) or the African Monetary Union.
9 For recent work on the political economy of inflation, see Persson and Tabellini (1990).
10 This type of approach has been taken, with some variants, by a number of authors. See, for example, Persson and Tabellini (1990), Devarajan and Rodrik (1992) and Frankel (1995).
11 A limitation of this approach is that it assumes that fixed rates are irrevocable. The case of a pegged but adjustable regime can be handled by assuming that the fixed rule has embodied escape clauses. See Flood and Isard (1989).
12 See Aghevli *et al.* (1991). For a critical view see Collins (1994).
13 Edwards (1996) presents a formal model of this reasoning.
14 This somewhat counter-intuitive result is the consequence of controlling for other variables. A univariate probit yields a significantly negative coefficient for the log of per capita income.
15 In the case of non-democratic regimes, a change in the head of state that does not imply a return to democracy is not recorded as a transfer of power.
16 In the case of dictatorships it is assumed that they do have absolute majority.

17 Until now the only way for a country to effectively alter the parity has been to abandon the union.

18 This discrepancy in the two averages neatly captures the selectivity bias in those studies that look at the performance of fixed rate countries from an *ex post* perspective.

19 This, of course, is not a new idea. However, it is a notion that from time to time has been ignored by many analysts.

20 For a model along these lines see Cukierman, Edwards, and Tabellini (1992).

21 Persson and Tabellini (1990); Edwards and Tabellini (1991).

22 Other studies have inquired as to whether the degree of independence of the central bank affects a country's proclivity toward inflation. An inherent difficulty in that line of analysis, however, is that it is not easy to measure the degree of central bank independence. On these issues see Canzoneri *et al.* (1992).

23 Cooper (1971) pointed out that the majority of the finance ministers that implemented major devaluations in the developing nations were ousted a few months later.

24 In this model there is no benefit of having a rate of expansion of domestic credit below its rate of demand growth. Thus, τ is constrained from below at 0.

25 See Cukierman, Edwards, and Tabellini (1992) for a formal model that argues for the inclusion of these regressors in empirical analyses on inflation.

26 This result still holds if we use the average rate of growth of money as the dependent variable.

References

Aghevli, Bijan, Khan, Mohsin, and Montiel, Peter (1991), "Exchange Rate Policy in Developing Countries: Some Analytical Issues," International Monetary Fund, Occasional Paper No. 78.

Bruno, Michael (1991), "High Inflation and the Nominal Anchors of an Open Economy," *Princeton Essays in International Finance*, No. 174.

Calvo, Guillermo and Vegh, Carlos (1994), "Stabilization Dynamics and Backward-Looking Contracts," *Journal of Development Economics*, 43, 1, 59–84.

Canzoneri, Matthew, Grilli, Vittorio, and Masson, Paul (eds.) (1992), *Establishing a Central Bank: Issues in Europe and Lessons from the US*, New York: Cambridge University Press.

Collins, Susan (1994), "On Becoming More Flexible: Exchange Rate Regimes in Latin America and the Caribbean," paper presented at the VII IASE/NBER Meetings, Mexico, November.

Cooper, Richard (1971), "Currency Devaluation in Developing Countries," *Princeton Essays in International Finance*, No. 86.

Cukierman, Alex, Edwards, Sebastian, and Tabellini, Guido (1992), "Seignorage and Political Instability," *American Economic Review*, 82, 537–55.

Cukierman, Alex, Webb, Steve, and Neyapti, Bilip (1992), "Measuring the Independence of Central Banks and Its Effect on Policy Outcomes," *World Bank Economic Review*, 6, 353–90.

Devarajan, Shantanayan and Rodrik, Dani (1992), "Do the Benefits of Fixed Exchange Rates Outweight Their Costs? The CFA Zone in Africa," in Ian Goldin and Alan Winters (eds.), *Open Economies: Structural Adjustment and Agriculture*, Cambridge: Cambridge University Press.

Dornbusch, Rudiger and Werner, Alejandro (1994), "Mexico: Stabilization and No Growth," *Brookings Papers on Economic Activity*, 1.

Edwards, Sebastian (1988), *Exchange Rate Misalignment in Developing Countries*, Baltimore: Johns Hopkins University Press.

(1989), *Real Exchange Rates, Devaluation and Adjustment*, Cambridge, Mass.: MIT Press.

(1993), "Exchange Rates as Nominal Anchors," *Welwirtschaftliches Archiv*, 129, 1, 1–32.

(1995), "Exchange Rates, Inflation and Disinflation: Latin American Experiences," in Sebastian Edwards (ed.), *Capital Controls, Exchange Rates and Monetary Policy in the World Economy*, New York: Cambridge University Press.

(1996), "Exchange Rates and the Political Economy of Macroeconomic Discipline," *American Economic Review, Papers and Proceedings*, forthcoming.

Edwards, Sebastian and Tabellini, Guido (1991), "Explaining Inflation and Fiscal Deficits in Developing Countries," *Journal of International Money and Finance*, 10, supplement, 16–40.

(1994), "Political Instability, Political Weakness and Inflation," in Chris Sims (ed.), *Advances in Econometrics*, New York: Cambridge University Press.

Flood, Robert and Isard, Peter (1989), "Monetary Policy Strategies," *International Monetary Fund Staff Papers*, 36, 3, 612–32.

Flood, Robert and Marion, Nancy (1991), "Exchange Rate Regime Choice," International Monetary Fund, Working Paper.

Frankel, Jeffrey (1995), "Monetary Regime Choices for a Semi-Open Country," in Sebastian Edwards (ed.), *Capital Controls, Exchange Rates and Monetary Policy in the World Economy*, New York: Cambridge University Press.

Kiguel, Miguel and Liviatan, Nissan (1992), "The Business Cycle Associated With Exchange Rate Based Stabilizations," *World Bank Economic Review*, 6, 2, 279–305.

McKinnon, Ronald (1963), "Optimum Currency Areas," *American Economic Review*, 53, 717–25.

Mundell, Robert (1961), "A Theory of Optimum Currency Areas", *American Economic Review*, 51, 657–65.

Persson, Torsten and Tabellini, Guido (1990), *Macroeconomic Policy, Credibility and Politics*, New York: Harwood Academic Publishers.

Sargent, Thomas (1986), "Stopping Moderate Inflation: The Methods of Poincare and Thatcher," in Rudiger Dornbusch and Mario Simonsen (eds.), *Inflation, Debt and Indexation*: Cambridge, Mass.: MIT Press.

Svensson, Lars (1993), "Fixed Exchange Rates as a Means to Price Stability: What Have We Learned?" NBER Working Paper No. 4504.

World Bank, *World Development Report*, various years.

Comment

CASPER DE VRIES

1 Introduction and summary

How does a foreign exchange rate regime affect inflation and why is a particular regime adopted? In his contribution Edwards sets out to disentangle
the answers to these two interrelated questions. To this end a small theoretical frame of reference is developed first. The authorities are assumed to
minimize a weighted average of the inflation volatility and the squared
deviations from an unemployment target. The minimization is subject to a
rational expectations model for a small open economy that exhibits a short-
run Phillips curve tradeoff. The economy is subject to external shocks. The
solution of the minimum problem yields a bivariate system that explains the
regime, i.e., fix or float, as a linear function of the squared average inflation
rate and the volatility of external shocks. And the average inflation rate is
obtained as a function of the regime and the unemployment target. In the
later part of the chapter the second equation is given further underpinning
by allowing for imperfectly credible fixings.

The empirical analysis is divided into two parts whereby the two equations are analysed separately, each purporting to answer one of the questions that motivated the chapter. Due to the dichotomous nature of the
regime variable, a probit regression is used in analyzing the regime equation
while OLS with a dummy for the regime is used for the inflation equation.
In order to conduct these regressions, an impressive cross-country data set
has been collected. In addition to the variables suggested by the backbone
model, a number of interesting structural variables like current account
data and indexes of political instability are added. Edwards nicely circumvents the selection bias problem in the inflation equation due to regime
changes, by using *ex ante* regime dummies.

The qualitative results of the empirical analysis are supportive of the
theory, but the evidence is not overwhelming. This is in line with other
research in the area. For example, Eichengreen (1994) investigates the
output stability and transmission of external shocks during the gold standard, interwar period, Bretton Woods, and the recent float and finds some
episodes which lend credence to the basic predictions of the

Mundell–Fleming theory. The problem with using episodic averages and variances is that, even if fiscal policy could be effective in stabilizing output under fixed exchange rates, the timing is essential, and we know that policy often turned out to be procyclical rather than countercyclical. An interesting exercise for the future may therefore be the pooling of cross-section and time series data.

2 Rational expectations, political economy, and inflation

The model laid out by Edwards has central bankers, endowed with an objective function, choosing between regimes subject to the constraints that are imposed by a small rational expectations model for the macro economy. But with an electorate that holds rational expectations over the actions of the government it elects, the utility function of the authorities reflects the preferences of the public. And the authorities have no freedom to choose but to implement the regime and its consequences which are demanded by the voters. The regressions thus reflect both the preference structure of the public, the importance of external shocks and the validity of the macro model being entertained by the public.

What is missing on the theory side is an analysis of why the authorities have an incentive to implement the public's desires. Explicit investigation of the political economy aspect may, however, be rewarding because it can suggest specific alternatives against which one can test. For example, a political economy analysis of the special interest group of central bankers may explain why the "wrong" regime is implemented. The central bank may have a preference for a (temporary) fixing, because this keeps them busy. Combatting the inflationary pressures on the exchange rate through official intervention, capital controls, etc. yields more arguments for supporting bureaucracies than a free float. A political economy argument as to why the government officials may prefer semi-fixed exchange rates is provided in chapter 9 in this volume by Minford. The public being aware of this "preference reversal" fuels inflation through its wage demands. Thus, high inflation rates may go hand in hand with managed exchange rates.

Another explanation for the mostly insignificant coefficients on the inflation rate in the regime regressions is based on the inability of the officials to time their decisions correctly. As many others, Edwards assumes that the exchange rate policy is implemented after wages are set and the external shock is realized. One could debate whether this timing is also observed in practice. If the sequencing is reversed, then minimization of the loss function entails that the exchange rate is used to counter external shocks. But another feature of this solution is that the depreciation rate is independent from the employment objective, and therefore it is never optimal to fix. It follows that the decision to fix is likely to be unrelated to the variables from the theoretical model, see the t-values on the inflation and volatility variables to the other variables in table 7.2 of Edwards.

3 The regression analysis

The way in which I summarize the theoretical model in the introduction emphasizes the bivariate nature of the two reduced-form equations. The dependent variable from the one equation appears as an explanatory variable in the other equation. This suggests running a two-stage estimation procedure with a dichotomous endogenous variable as explained in Maddala (1983, chapters 5.1 and 8.7). Instead, Edwards runs two separate regressions by instrumenting the variables. This is achieved by using in the regime regression inflation and other explanatory variables from a period that antedates the period over which the regime variable is constructed, while in the inflation equation, the dependent variable is advanced to a period after the period from which the regime dummy is constructed. On the one hand, the latter procedure nicely circumvents the problem of selectivity bias. It is in line with the credibility-building argument developed in the amended model in the second part of the chapter. On the other hand, it goes against the spirit of the sequencing which presumes that the government responds optimally with its choice of regime after wages are set and shocks have been realized.

The instrumental variables procedure by which inflation, as an explanatory variable, is lagged in the first equation and is advanced in the second equation, when it is the dependent variable, does not necessarily eradicate the simultaneity bias. The reasoning is as follows. In the first equation, lagged inflation is assumed to be correlated with current inflation, but to be independent from the error term. This implies for the second equation that the explanatory dummy on regimes, which is contemporaneously correlated with inflation, can be correlated with the residual, because the dependent variable, i.e., inflation, is correlated with its lagged value.

Another remark concerns the use of coefficients of variation as measures for the volatility of external shocks. Because for some of these variables, such as the real bilateral exchange rate changes and the terms of trade changes, the period average is likely be close to zero, the coefficient of variation can be very high. Thus one should be careful when interpreting the (relative) magnitudes of the estimated coefficients. Note that the estimates on these volatility measures are indeed very small. The question is why not just use the variance? This would also be in line with the theory.

4 Conclusion

Other quibbles, e.g., concerning the definition of the regime dummy in a multilateral world with several large countries, are always possible. But then again, the complementary set to a positive investigation is always infinitely larger than the original set. Thus the commentator in an exchange of positive political arguments has to safeguard against emptiness. Therefore, I stop here by noting that Edwards has delivered an admirable positive analysis of the motives for and consequences of regime choices.

References

Eichengreen, B. (1994), "History of the International Monetary System: Implications for Research in International Macroeconomics and Finance," in F. van der Ploeg (ed.), *The Handbook of International Macroeconomics*, Oxford: Basil Blackwell, 153–91.

Maddala, G. (1983), *Limited-Dependent and Qualitative Variables in Econometrics*, Cambridge: Cambridge University Press.

8 Why capital controls? Theory and evidence

GIAN MARIA MILESI-FERRETTI

1 Introduction

The last decade has been characterized by a financial liberalization process that has led several industrialized and developing countries to dismantle or drastically reduce restrictions on international capital mobility. In the countries belonging to the European Monetary System, capital controls were gradually dismantled during the 1980s and abolished by 1990. In several developing countries, barriers to international capital movements are being reduced, as domestic investors are allowed to purchase foreign assets and non-residents to invest in domestic financial markets. The removal of restrictions to capital mobility was undertaken with the primary purpose of improving economic efficiency through better resource allocation and a more efficient functioning of financial markets. The liberalization of capital flows would also allow domestic investors to better hedge against macroeconomic risks through international portfolio diversification. The process of financial liberalization was further stimulated by the realization that the technological progress in telecommunications together with the growing integration of financial markets made it more difficult for authorities to effectively monitor capital flows.

Two recent developments, however, have contributed to give prominence once again to the debate on the usefulness of restrictions on international capital flows. The first is the series of speculative attacks on currencies belonging to the European Monetary System and to the European Free Trade Area, beginning in September 1992, that brought abruptly to an end a period of exchange rate stability in Europe. The demise of the EMS has led some economists to suggest that introducing some friction in foreign exchange markets may help to prevent the occurrence of speculative attacks that are not motivated by economic fundamentals (See, for example, Eichengreen and Wyplosz, 1993). The second development is the process of capital inflows in developing countries that are liberalizing their economic systems and opening their domestic financial markets to foreign investment. The size of capital inflows has led to concerns that unfettered capital mobility may jeopardize macroeconomic stability by weakening the control of authorities over domestic monetary conditions.[1]

This contribution surveys the theoretical arguments and the empirical literature on costs and benefits of capital controls, and presents some evidence on the determinants of restrictions to capital mobility. The review of the theoretical literature, an extension of the one presented in Alesina, Grilli, and Milesi-Ferretti (1994), discusses several political economy arguments. The empirical analysis extends previous results on the determinants of capital controls presented in Alesina, Grilli, and Milesi-Ferretti (1994) and Grilli and Milesi-Ferretti (1995) by focusing on a wider set of countries and foreign exchange restrictions. This analysis is conducted with a medium- to long-run perspective – it uses low frequency (annual) data for the period 1966–89 for a sample of 61 industrialized and developing countries. The data on foreign exchange restrictions are taken from the IMF's publication *Exchange Arrangements and Exchange Restrictions* and are of a binary nature – they simply indicate whether a restriction is in place for a given country in a given year. Two important and related issues are not discussed in the chapter. The first is the issue of the *effectiveness* of capital controls, which is discussed in Mathieson and Rojas-Suarez (1993). This requires data at a higher frequency, as well as attention to the details of restrictions and the timing of policy measures that an aggregate study like the present one cannot provide. The second is the issue of the *intensity* of controls, that the binary nature of our data prevents us from addressing. Potential proxies for the intensity of capital controls are onshore–offshore interest rate differentials, deviations from covered interest rate parity, and black market premia.

The empirical analysis examines whether the presence or absence of capital controls in a given country can be related to its economic, political, and structural features. For example, capital controls may facilitate the taxation of domestic capital, as well as the extraction of seigniorage through the inflation tax. The incentive to use them should therefore be higher in countries with a larger share of government and with a less developed tax system. Also, capital controls can allow a country to pursue for a certain time an independent monetary policy. The incentive of the government to impose capital controls for this reason should then depend on the degree of control the government has over monetary policy, and therefore on the degree of central bank independence. As for distributional considerations, capital controls may be favored by more labor-oriented governments because they facilitate the taxation of domestic capital – provided they are effective in curtailing capital flight. Overall, the chapter is related to the literature on endogenous macroeconomic policy formation that links economic policy choices to various structural, institutional and political features of an economy.[2]

The rest of the chapter is organized as follows. Section 2 reviews the literature on the determinants of capital controls. Section 3 describes the capital controls data, and section 4 presents an empirical analysis of the determinants of capital controls and other foreign exchange restrictions in a sample of industrial and developing countries. Section 5 contains some concluding remarks.

2 Determinants of foreign exchange restrictions: a review of the theory

In order to discuss the literature on foreign exchange restrictions, it is useful to provide a classification of the main motivations to impose such restrictions. Mathieson and Rojas-Suarez (1993) classify these motivations as follows:

1 limitation of volatile short-term capital flows (avoiding balance of payments crises etc.);
2 retention of domestic savings;
3 help for stabilization and structural reform programs;
4 fiscal and distributional aspects.

We also consider an additional motivation:

5 welfare consequences of external indebtedness.[3]

Clearly, the relevance of these motivations depends on the ability of the government to impose effective capital controls. This ability has probably weakened over time, for two reasons. The first is the endogenous "erosion" of existing barriers, as agents find ways to circumvent official restrictions. The second has to do with structural change and technological progress in financial markets, that facilitate international capital movements and make them harder to monitor. As mentioned in the introduction, the nature of our data makes it impossible to account for these factors; they should be taken into account, however, when weighing the arguments in favor or against financial liberalization.[4]

2.1 Volatility of short-term capital flows and stability of foreign exchange markets

Foreign exchange markets are very liquid and react quickly to shocks. Because of factors such as price and wage rigidities and investment irreversibility, the real economy has a slower speed of adjustment than financial markets. Authors such as Tobin (1978) and Dornbusch (1986) argue that this differential speed of adjustment, together with exogenous "excess volatility" in financial markets, may induce excess exchange rate volatility (overshooting, bubbles, etc.), with negative effects on real economic activity. Tobin proposed to "throw sand in the wheels" of short-run capital flows through a uniform tax on all foreign exchange transactions, thereby discouraging very short-term capital flows, but with negligible effects on long-run ones.[5] Dornbusch (1986) suggests the adoption of measures such as dual exchange rate systems, that are able to shield, at least partially, the real economy from the vagaries of short-term financial markets behavior.

Tornell (1990) provides an analytical exposition of the argument in favor of "Tobin taxes." In his model, "rumors" unrelated to economic fundamentals cause volatility in the rate of return on financial investment, which is reflected in the required return on real investment. As a result, investment in real capital, which is irreversible, is discouraged, because investors prefer to wait for the resolution of uncertainty. An appropriately designed tax on international financial transactions can reduce the variance of domestic interest rates, while leaving its mean unchanged. This will induce more investment in irreversible real capital. Empirical studies, such as Giavazzi and Pagano (1988), show that capital controls in the EMS did indeed reduce the volatility of domestic interest rates with respect to "offshore" rates, even though they did not keep domestic rates below offshore rates for prolonged periods of time. Interest rate variability is particularly damaging in countries with a large short-term public debt, or where long-term public debt instruments are indexed to short-term interest rates.[6]

With pegged exchange rates, short-term capital flows may cause not only high interest rate variability, but also large variations in foreign exchange reserves and the collapse of the peg. The recent turbulence experienced in the European Monetary System and in countries that unilaterally pegged their rate to the ECU or the D-Mark proves this point very effectively. The sheer size of foreign exchange markets makes it very difficult for central banks to resist a speculative attack. According to their proponents, effective capital controls can at least mitigate these undesirable effects in the short run. The early literature on speculative attacks (Krugman, 1979; Flood and Garber, 1984) shows how balance of payments crises can occur because fundamentals are out of line, as is the case when two macroeconomic policy objectives (say, domestic credit expansion and fixed exchange rates) are mutually inconsistent. In order to justify the imposition of controls using this line of argument, however, one would need to motivate explicitly the adoption of policy measures that are inconsistent with the exchange rate peg in the long run. Furthermore, as shown by Wyplosz (1986), controls would simply postpone the depletion of foreign exchange reserves that would occur gradually through the current account.

However, the possibility of self-fulfilling speculative attacks against a fixed exchange rate, not motivated by market fundamentals, provides another justification for the imposition of some form of exchange restriction: the exchange-rate peg can collapse even when current fundamentals are consistent with the peg (Obstfeld, 1986, 1988). Loosely speaking, these attacks can occur because economic agents anticipate that, in the event of a collapse in the peg, the monetary authority would choose a more expansionary monetary policy, although it does not do so as long as the peg is maintained. This line of argument has been adopted recently by Eichengreen and Wyplosz (1993).

Overall, the analysis would suggest that governments with stronger "credibility problems" would be more likely targets of speculative attacks and may therefore be more likely to impose capital controls. But if agents are forward-looking, would the expectation of a future imposition of controls trigger a change in their behavior? Dellas and Stockman (1993) show that a speculative attack on a pegged currency can occur precisely because of self-fulfilling expectations of the imposition of capital controls, even if there is no expectation of changes in monetary policy. It is also necessary to take into account the impact of imposing capital controls on the credibility of the policy itself. The imposition of capital controls allows the government to pursue "inconsistent" policies for a while. If private agents do not fully know government preferences, this may raise the probability that the government will indeed behave inconsistently, implying a worsening of credibility rather than an improvement.[7]

2.2 *Retention of domestic savings*

If the private return from holding domestic instruments is below the social return, for example because of the existence of positive externalities from domestically invested capital, such as knowledge spillovers, there may be a rationale for limiting capital outflows and/or for encouraging capital inflows. A related argument is that a government may be willing to adopt measures that stimulate savings if the latter are prevented from flowing abroad by low capital mobility or by capital controls. For example, a panel study of OECD countries by Jappelli and Pagano (1994) finds that savings are higher in countries with restrictions on household borrowing. In order to be effective in raising savings these restrictions require the presence of capital controls.

Finally, capital inflows may be discouraged by countries that wish to limit foreign ownership of domestic factors of production, for political or ideological reasons. These limitations, however, would prevent a country from using external finance and from benefiting from technological transfers through foreign direct investment.

2.3 Help for stabilization and structural reform programs

Free capital flows can be destabilizing when a country implements a stabilization or a structural reform plan. There is an extensive literature on the optimal sequencing of external sector liberalization. Authors such as Frenkel (1982), Edwards (1984, 1989), and Van Wijnbergen (1990) have stressed the effects of liberalizing the capital account on the real exchange rate. In the context of a stabilization plan accompanied by trade liberalization, an early opening of the capital account can cause a real appreciation, because of the high interest rates typically associated with a stabilization plan, and more real exchange rate volatility. Both of these effects would make trade liberalization more problematic. In practice, political economy arguments may push the government toward an early liberalization of the capital account, since this type of reform is likely to encounter less domestic opposition. An early capital account liberalization can contribute to make other distortions more evident, thus favoring further economic reform.[8]

The credibility of the stabilization plan plays a key role in determining the consequences of free capital mobility. Lack of credibility of the stabilization plan may cause capital flight and a balance of payments crisis, making the plan failure more likely. If the plan is credible, the high real interest rates typically associated with a stabilization program may cause temporary large capital inflows. If these inflows are sterilized, interest rates remain high, thereby encouraging further inflows, and the central bank incurs a quasi-fiscal cost, because the return on foreign exchange reserves is below the return on domestic assets.[9] If no sterilization occurs, the increase in the money supply can jeopardize the control of inflation. Finally, letting the nominal exchange rate appreciate may hamper a trade reform aiming at lower barriers to imports.[10]

The appropriate response to a surge in capital inflows cannot be determined without a close examination of the causes of the inflow, and may differ depending on the *composition* of inflows. Clearly, portfolio investment is more "reversible" than foreign direct investment. From a political economy point of view, one should consider the relation between political stability, government preferences and credibility. Again, governments with lower initial credibility may be those with stronger incentives to introduce capital controls (see 2.1 above). Overall, this motivation for the introduction of capital controls may have greater relevance for developing countries.

2.4 Fiscal and distributional aspects

Capital controls limit the ability of individuals to avoid the inflation tax on domestic money holdings by holding foreign currency assets and deposits:

hence they have a direct impact on the "tax base" of the inflation tax. Drazen (1989) emphasizes that capital controls allow the imposition of measures such as high reserve requirements that raise the demand for money and therefore the inflation tax base. He also argues that these measures may be detrimental in the long run, because they may discourage capital accumulation by raising the interest rates that banks charge on loans.[11] In order to maintain seigniorage revenue following the dismantling of barriers to trade and capital flows, Brock (1984) argues that the central bank can impose a reserve requirement on foreign capital inflows and a prior import deposit.

Capital controls are often accompanied by various types of financial market restrictions, such as controls on interest rates. Giovannini and De Melo (1993) focus on a sample of developing countries and relate capital controls with government revenue from financial repression, measured by comparing the domestic and foreign cost of borrowing of the government, and show that this source of revenue can be substantial. Work by Goldsmith (1969), McKinnon (1973), and more recently by Roubini and Sala-i-Martin (1992, 1995) and King and Levine (1993) relates financial development to macroeconomic performance. The argument is that an underdeveloped and repressed financial system allows the government to finance public expenditure more easily when the tax system is inefficient, but may constitute an obstacle to growth. Similarly, when taxes are very distortionary and domestic debt is large, capital controls may allow the government to reduce the cost of financing its debt (Aizenman and Guidotti (1994)).[12] This is equivalent to a form of seigniorage on government liabilities.

Giovannini (1988) and Razin and Sadka (1991) focus on the taxation of capital and on capital flight, and argue that capital controls may be justified by the difficulty of taxing foreign-source income. In Giovannini's paper, the distortions introduced by capital controls (a tax on foreign assets) may be smaller than those implied by the impossibility of taxing foreign-source income. Razin and Sadka model capital controls as a quantitative restriction on foreign asset holdings, and show that when taxing foreign-source income is impossible, it may be optimal to impose a restriction on capital exports in order to generate "overinvestment" domestically.

A recent paper by Bartolini and Drazen (1997) nicely illustrates an important point: namely, capital flows are determined not only by current policies, but by the expectation of future policies as well. In a model in which capital controls are motivated by the need to raise revenue from domestic capital, the removal of restrictions on capital outflows can signal that the government does not need or want to rely on capital taxation as a source of revenue. When uncertainty over government types is large enough, this signal may trigger a capital inflow. Indeed, in many episodes

of capital account liberalization the removal of restrictions on capital outflows was followed by an increase in capital inflows. In the context of countries experiencing a sustained capital inflow (section 2.3), this paper also
suggests that removing restrictions to capital outflows may not necessarily
reduce net capital inflows.

The link between the distributional aspects of tax policy and capital controls is studied by Alesina and Tabellini (1989). The authors view capital
controls as way of limiting holdings of foreign assets that are non-taxable.
Individuals would accumulate foreign assets to avoid the risk of future
taxation. In their model there are two social groups, "workers" and
"capitalists", and two parties, each representing a social group. The
workers' source of income is labor (they cannot own domestic capital),
while the capitalists' income comes from capital holdings. Under reasonable assumptions about initial endowments and distribution it is shown
that fear of a future workers' government may induce capitalists to export
capital. Among other things, the paper shows that once homogeneity
among private agents is removed, distributional reasons become an important consideration in the evaluation of foreign exchange restrictions.
Epstein and Schor (1992) present a Keynesian macroeconomic model that
implicitly comprises three social groups – labor, industry, and the financial
sector. They argue that capital controls favor labor at the expense of the
financial sector, while the effects on industry are uncertain. In their model,
effective capital controls allow expansionary domestic monetary policy to
lower real interest rates and thereby to increase capacity utilization and
reduce unemployment. The industry sector gains from controls if the profit
rate increases with capacity utilization, and loses otherwise. Finally, the
financial sector is hurt by the reduction in interest rates. The authors
present some cross-sectional empirical evidence in support of their model
(see also section 4).

Overall, this section suggests that capital controls are more likely to be
imposed in countries with a less-developed tax system, with a large share
of government in relation to GDP and by countries more ideologically ori-
ented toward the taxation of capital.

2.5 Welfare consequences of foreign indebtedness

This argument has been put forward by Harberger (1986). He points out
that individual borrowers do not internalize the impact of their foreign borrowing decision on the overall "country risk" and therefore on the rate of
return charged to domestic borrowers on international capital markets. The
presence of this externality is driven by the wedge between the marginal
social cost of foreign borrowing (that includes the marginal cost of default-

ing for the country) and its average cost. Harberger suggests the imposition of a tax on foreign borrowing proportional to the premium over LIBOR on the country's foreign borrowing (which is related to the size of the externality), analogously to an optimal congestion toll.

We now turn to the empirical analysis, that attempts to examine whether theoretical predictions on determinants of foreign exchange restrictions find support in the data.

3 The data on capital controls

The data on restrictions to international capital flows adopted in this study come from the International Monetary Fund's annual report *Exchange Arrangements and Exchange Restrictions*. The report has been issued since 1950, and provides a description of the exchange rate system and of exchange rate restrictions for individual country members. Since the 1967 issue (covering 1966) the Report also includes a summary table specifying whether given forms of exchange arrangements and restrictions are adopted by member countries. The data presented in this table were used to construct dummy variables taking the value of one when a restriction was in place for a given year in a given country, and zero otherwise. This study focuses on three forms of exchange restrictions. The first is "restriction on payments for capital transactions." This restriction refers exclusively to resident-owned funds. The second restriction is "separate exchange rate(s) for some or all capital transactions and/or some or all invisibles." This restriction reflects mainly multiple currency practices, as well as the use of a unitary rate for transactions with a certain group of countries and another different unitary rate for transactions with other countries. Both these restrictions can broadly be interpreted as a form of control on capital flows.

The third restriction ("restriction on payments for current transactions") refers to limitations on current account transactions. It has been included in the study because current account transactions can be used to (partially) evade restrictions on capital transactions through practices such as leads and lags in export billing, overinvoicing of imports, and underinvoicing of exports, etc.

The problem with the use of these dummy variables to measure restrictions on international capital flows is that they provide no measure of the *intensity* of controls. Although there have been attempts to construct indices of the degree of capital controls, it is difficult to find a measure which is comparable across countries and that is available for a sufficiently long period of time. To some degree, the current account restrictions dummy variable can proxy for the intensity of controls.

Alternative measures of the degree of intensity of capital controls have

Table 8.1 *Foreign exchange restrictions*

Type of restrictions	1969	1979	1989
Number of countries	58	61	61
(1) Restrictions on cap. acct. trans.	44	43	45
Industrial	17	14	11
Developing	27	29	34
(2) Restrictions on curr. acct. trans.	32	27	30
Industrial	9	4	2
Developing	23	23	28
(3) Multiple currency practices	11	15	14
Industrial	4	3	1
Developing	7	12	13
(1) & (2) Total	32	27	30
Industrial	9	4	2
Developing	23	23	28
(1) & (3) Total	8	11	13
Industrial	3	2	0
Developing	5	9	13
(1), (2), & (3) Total	7	10	11
Industrial	2	2	0
Developing	5	8	11

been adopted in previous studies. Among these, one can cite onshore–off-shore interest differentials (see, for example, Giavazzi and Pagano, 1988), the size of the black market premium, and deviations from covered interest rate parity (Dooley and Isard, 1980; Ito, 1983). These measures can be used to gauge the effectiveness of controls, and are more suited to empirical analysis that uses higher frequency data. A comparison of findings using different measures of controls is a topic for future research.

Examination of the dummy variables for the sample of countries under examination reveals several interesting regularities, summarized in table 8.1.[13] The most common form of restriction is the first (capital controls).

Of the 61 countries in our sample, 34 had capital controls in place throughout the period, while five never had controls. Also, while the number of industrial countries with capital account restrictions decreases, the number of developing countries increases.

Current account restrictions are in place throughout the period in 19 countries, while they are never in place in 15 countries. Interestingly, current account restrictions are in place in countries that have restrictions on capital account transactions as well (compare row (2) with the rows (1) and (2)).

Once again, the number of countries with this type of restrictions is falling among industrial countries and rising among developing countries.

Multiple currency practices are the least common form of restriction. Only four countries had them in place throughout the period, while they were never in place in 27 countries.[14] Also, most countries using separate exchange rates for capital transactions have restrictions on capital and current account transactions as well (row (1), (2), and (3)).

Before turning to the empirical evidence, it is important to point out its limitations. Given the nature of our measures of foreign exchange restrictions, the analysis focuses on medium- and long-run aspects, and is less suitable for the study of the interaction between foreign exchange market instability, speculative attacks, and capital controls.[15] The second limitation is that the imposition and removal of capital account restrictions is typically undertaken together with other macroeconomic and structural reform measures. For example, capital controls may be a complement to measures of financial repression designed to facilitate the financing of government spending when the tax system is relatively inefficient. This makes it more difficult to evaluate the consequences of measures such as capital account liberalization per se. The empirical evidence in this chapter refers exclusively to the determinants of controls: Grilli and Milesi-Ferretti (1995) also discuss the macroeconomic effects of foreign exchange restrictions.

4 Determinants of capital controls

The review of the literature in section 2 broadly suggests several potential determinants for capital controls:

1 Tax system and size of government. In a country with an underdeveloped tax system and a narrow tax base for income taxation, capital controls may facilitate the taxation of domestic capital, as well as the collection of revenue through the inflation tax. Taxing domestic assets only would lead to capital flight and a reduction in the domestic capital stock. A related argument is that the incentive to impose controls for fiscal reasons is likely to be larger, the larger the share of government.

2 Distributional considerations. Governments attempting to redistribute resources from capital to labor may want to impose capital controls in order to avoid capital flight. It should also be noted that the distributive implications of controls may differ in the short and in the long run: higher taxes on capital will discourage capital accumulation and may therefore reduce productive capacity and wages in the long run.

3 Independence of monetary policy. When monetary policy is not a "choice variable" for the government because of the independence of the

central bank, the incentive to increase seigniorage revenue by raising money demand is reduced, because monetary policy is decided autonomously.[16]

4 External sector and exchange rate management: capital controls can make it easier – *ceteris paribus* – to manage the exchange rate, and may be imposed in order to limit the loss of foreign currency when the current account is in deficit.

5 Credibility of government policy. Capital flight and speculative attacks are more likely to occur when the credibility of the government's policy stance is in doubt.

Previous research on the determinants of controls is presented in Epstein and Schor (1992) and Alesina, Grilli, and Milesi-Ferretti (1994) for OECD countries, and by Grilli and Milesi-Ferretti (1995) for industrial and developing countries. Epstein and Schor present some cross-sectional evidence that controls have been more frequent in countries with a larger share of left-wing vote and a less independent central bank. Alesina *et al.* and Grilli and Milesi-Ferretti provide an analysis of determinants and effects of capital controls based on panel data, and find evidence that both fiscal and external sector variables help explain the presence of capital controls.

The empirical investigation of the determinants of foreign exchange restrictions looks at the empirical support for existing theories, but is not based on a formal model. The main reason for this approach is the difficulty in providing a unified framework that is able to encompass the set of economic, political and institutional considerations we want to take into account. The sample includes 61 industrial and developing countries (listed in the appendix). These are countries for which data on central bank independence are currently available. We plan to expand the sample in the future so as to include a wider set of developing countries. The dependent variables in the analysis are the dummy variables describing foreign exchange restrictions. The explanatory variables are economic, political, and structural variables taken from various sources, described in detail in the appendix. The sample period is 1966–89.

With regard to general public finance motivations, countries with an inefficient tax system may be more likely to impose capital controls and current account restrictions in order to facilitate the taxation of imports and exports, tax capital, and extract revenue through financial repression. The sophistication of the tax system is positively correlated with the level of development. Furthermore, richer countries are more likely to have at their disposal alternative redistribution channels that are less distortionary than controls. We therefore introduce the level of income per capita (GDP) as an explanatory variable for the presence of capital controls. As pointed out by Lans Bovenberg in his discussion, it should be taken into account that this variable can also proxy for other variables, such as the degree of sophistication of financial markets.[17] Finding a good proxy for the latter for the countries in our sample would be an important extension of this study. There is another channel through which the level of per capita income matters: namely, the negative impact of lower interest rates on savings may be smaller in poorer countries, where the rate of intertemporal substitution is low, making governments less reluctant to impose restrictions on capital outflows. The need to raise revenue for the government is enhanced when its size is "large" relative to the size of the economy: we therefore include among the regressors the share of government consumption in GDP (GCONS), lagged one period in order to limit endogeneity problems.

Given that capital controls can facilitate the imposition of financial repression measures and thereby lower the cost of debt service, the initial level of government debt could be introduced into the regression. One would expect countries with higher domestic public debt to have an incentive to impose capital controls (see, for example, Aizenman and Guidotti, 1994). However, data on domestic public debt are not available for the first years of this sample for a large number of countries. Furthermore, there is a reverse causality problem: since countries with capital controls have lower real interest rates on government debt (Grilli and Milesi-Ferretti, 1995) public debt accumulates more slowly.

The control that the government acquires over monetary policy by imposing controls depends, among other things, on the degree of independence of the central bank. We therefore included among our regressors two variables measuring the independence of the central bank, TURNOVER and LEGAL, taken from Cukierman, Webb, and Neyapti (1992). The first variable (LEGAL) measures the legal independence of the central bank – higher numbers imply a more independent central bank. According to Cukierman *et al.* (1992), this is a good measure of central bank independence for industrial countries. The second variable (TURNOVER) measures the turnover of central bankers, which is considered to be negatively correlated with the degree of independence of the central bank. According to the source, this is a good measure of central bank independence for developing countries. Both measures change every ten years for most countries, and are constant across time for the rest. We expect inflation to be lower in countries with a more independent central bank.[18] With regard to distributional motivations, capital controls may facilitate the taxation of domestic capital if they succeed in preventing capital flight. Alesina and Tabellini (1989) and Epstein and Schor (1992) argue that in the presence of distributional conflict between "labor" and "capital" (and/or financial interests) capital controls are likely to be imposed by left-wing governments, traditionally closer to labor. In order to capture the impact

of the political leaning of the government on the decision whether to introduce or remove capital controls, we use two dummy variables, LEFT and
NODEM. The first variable takes the value of one when a democratic left-
wing government is in power, and zero otherwise. Epstein and Schor (1992)
use instead the average share of the left-wing vote in their cross-sectional
analysis. The second variable takes the value of one when a non-democratic government is in power, and zero otherwise. We expect the coefficient on
the first variable to be positive, while there is no *a priori* presumption on the
sign of the second dummy variable.

With regard to government credibility, a more independent central bank
can increase the credibility of monetary policy.[19] In general, credibility is
likely to be higher when the government is "stable." Possible proxies for
government stability include the number of government changes in a given
period, the number of coups, as well as variables that characterize the
nature of the government's support in parliament (a majority government
is more likely to be stable than a coalition government). We therefore introduce three measures of political stability. The first is the dummy variable
MAJ, that takes the value of one when a (democratic) majority government
is in power, and zero otherwise. The second is the country-specific variable
TCHANGE, that equals the number of government changes during the
period 1950–82. The third variable, COUP, equals the number of successful coups during the period 1950–82.[20] In general, we might expect unstable governments to be more likely to impose capital controls, in order to
prevent capital flight.

Finally, three external sector variables are included among the determinants of controls. The first is a dummy variable (EXR) taking the value of
one when the exchange rate is fixed or managed, and zero when the exchange
rate is floating. Theory suggests that capital controls are more likely to be in
place when the exchange rate is pegged or managed. The second variable is
the (lagged) value of the ratio of the current account balance to GDP
(CAY). We expect countries that experienced current account difficulties to
be more likely to impose controls. The third variable, OPEN, measures the
degree of openness of the economy, and is given by the sum of imports and
exports over GDP. The sign on this variable is a priori ambiguous. On the
one side, monitoring capital flows is more difficult in a very open economy,
suggesting that the expected sign should be negative. On the other side, the
effects of external shocks on the domestic economy are larger, the more open
is the economy, so that the incentive to insulate it from foreign shocks
through foreign exchange restrictions is stronger. All three external sector
variables raise the issue of the direction of causality: it can be argued that
the size of current account imbalances and the degree of openness of the
economy are themselves affected by foreign exchange restrictions. We there-

fore use lagged values of both CAY and OPEN. Models of speculative attacks suggest that the level of foreign exchange reserves is an important determinant of controls – countries may have an incentive to impose controls if their level of reserves is too low. As an alternative to the current account variable, we also considered the ratio of foreign exchange reserves to total imports, although we do not report the results.[21]

We followed two estimation methods. We first used annual data and estimated the probability that the different forms of foreign exchange restrictions described in section 3 are in place as a function of the independent variables discussed above, using both a logit and a probit model; since results using either estimation method were analogous, only the logit regressions are reported. We subsequently calculated five-year non-overlapping averages of each variable, in order to reduce serial correlation problems and smooth out the effects of temporary shocks, and studied the determinants of controls using simple regression analysis.

Results for the logit model of capital account restrictions are presented in table 8.2.[22] An asterisk indicates statistical significance of a coefficient at the 10 percent confidence level, and two asterisks at the 5 percent level. The first column refers to the whole sample, with pooled cross-section/time series data. A time trend is also in the regression, in order to control for the fact that, if there is a tendency to remove capital account restrictions over time, the income variable (also a trending one) may simply capture a trend toward liberalization.[23] The second column describes results obtained by adding time dummies to the regressors. The third and fourth columns show results for the sub-periods 1970–9 and 1980–9.

The variables capturing the degree of central bank independence, LEGAL and TURNOVER, are significant and have the expected sign: capital controls are less likely to be in place in countries with a legally independent central bank and with a lower turnover of central bankers.[24] As expected, countries with lower income per capita and a higher ratio of government consumption to GDP are more likely to have capital controls in place. As mentioned above, a "fiscal" explanation of this finding would be that capital controls help raise revenue from financial repression, and that poorer countries with inefficient tax systems are more likely to rely on these forms of taxation to finance government spending. The need to raise revenue is greater, the larger the size of government.

With regard to political variables, the logit analysis shows evidence that left-wing governments are more likely to impose capital controls; this result is consistent with theories of income distribution that emphasize how capital controls facilitate the taxation of domestic capital, and more generally of wealth. There is no clear evidence on the relation between political instability and controls – the coefficients on the majority (MAJ) and coup

Table 8.2 Determinants of capital controls, whole sample

(Annual data, estimation by logit*)

	1966–89 No time dummies	1966–89 Time dummies	1970–9 Time dummies	1980–9 Time dummies
Constant	5.687 (2.93)**	5.767 (2.80)**	−1.137 (−0.37)	23.807 (5.05)**
TCOUP	0.059 (0.91)	0.063 (0.96)	0.146 (1.26)	−0.113 (−0.95)
TCHANGE	0.043 (3.43)**	0.040 (3.14)*	0.069 (2.98)**	−0.011 (−0.63)
LEGAL	−3.172 (−5.01)**	−3.296 (−5.14)**	−4.649 (−4.33)**	−3.170 (−2.82)**
TURNOVER	2.430 (4.10)**	2.547 (4.21)**	3.613 (3.96)**	8.701 (3.69)**
MAJ	0.160 (0.71)	0.115 (0.50)	0.708 (1.99)**	−0.814 (−1.64)**
LEFT	0.733 (3.63)**	0.697 (3.39)**	0.694 (1.93)*	1.539 (4.27)**
NODEM	0.417 (1.32)	0.313 (0.97)	0.963 (1.94)*	−1.209 (−1.66)*
EXR	0.684 (3.12)**	0.732 (3.22)**	0.274 (0.78)	1.539 (3.55)**
LRGDP	−0.764 (−3.19)**	−0.814 (−3.31)**	0.146 (0.40)	−2.949 (−5.53)**
CAY{1}	−0.082 (−3.99)**	−0.084 (−3.85)**	−0.077 (−2.32)**	−0.059 (−1.75)*
GCONS{1}	0.086 (3.73)**	0.086 (3.71)**	0.071 (2.14)**	0.157 (3.28)**
OPEN{1}	−0.015 (−5.05)**	−0.015 (−5.16)**	−0.009 (−2.50)**	−0.032 (−5.21)**
AFRICA	2.637 (3.41)**	2.645 (3.41)**	1.888 (2.18)**	
WESHEM	−1.793 (−5.59)**	1.824 (−5.59)**	−2.829 (−4.97)**	−1.799 (−3.15)**
IND	1.214 (2.79)**	1.310 (2.96)**	0.399 (0.60)	4.011 (4.01)**
Usable obs.	1171	1171	509	481
Deg. of fr.	1154	1131	469	442
Cases corr.	938	941	410	396
Average lik.	0.66	0.66	0.68	0.70

Note: * t-statistics in parentheses.

(TCOUP) dummies are not statistically significant, although there is some evidence that countries with frequent government changes are more likely to impose controls.

The external sector variables are all statistically significant at the 5 percent confidence level: countries with a flexible exchange rate and without current account imbalances are less likely to have capital controls in place. Interestingly, the sign on the OPEN coefficient is negative – capital controls are less likely to be in place if the ratios of exports and imports to GDP are high. As can be seen from columns 3 and 4, results are generally robust across sub-periods. If the current account variable is replaced by the lagged ratio of foreign exchange reserves to total imports, we find a positive correlation, instead of the expected negative one (results not reported). One possible reason for this finding is that a decline in reserves may be followed by an intensification of already existing controls that our binary variable would not capture. Another explanation is reverse causality – countries with controls are more likely to peg their exchange rate and have more reserves. Even though the reserves variable is lagged, this reverse causality cannot be ruled out because of the persistence of controls. Incidentally, the same argument applies to the other lagged explanatory variables.

Table 8.3 presents results for industrial and developing countries separately. The results for industrial countries are in line with those for the whole sample. The degree of legal independence of the central bank, the level of income per capita, the share of government consumption in GDP, the ratio of the current account balance to GDP, the openness of the economy and the exchange rate regime all contribute to explaining the presence or absence of controls. The degree of central bank independence remains significant even when using other indices, such as those reported in Grilli, Masciandaro, and Tabellini (1991) and Eijffinger and Schaling (1993, 1996).

As for developing countries, the coefficients on the level of output and the exchange rate regime dummy are statistically insignificant, while the other determinants are analogous to those for industrial countries. Overall, the logit analysis on the two separate groups of countries cannot detect systematic effects of political variables on controls.

Tables 8.4 and 8.5 present the results for the determinants of current account restrictions and multiple currency practices, respectively, for the whole sample and for industrial and developing countries separately. For current account restrictions, output, the share of government consumption, and openness are all statistically significant, with the expected sign. Somewhat surprisingly, the current account variable is not significant for the whole sample, but only for the sub-set of industrial countries, for which the fit of the model is better. Central bank independence seems to matter for developing countries, but not for industrial ones.

Table 8.3 *Determinants of capital controls, industrial and developing countries*

(Annual data, estimation by logit*)

	Indust. 1955–89 Time dummies	Indust. 1966–89 Time dummies	Devel. 1966–89 Time dummies
Constant	130.032 (8.66)**	124.229 (7.17)**	−0.996 (−0.45)
TCOUP			0.346 (3.75)
TCHANGE	−0.091 (−3.72)**	−0.079 (−2.91)**	−0.077 (−2.65)**
LEGAL	−9.199 (−7.11)**	−9.300 (−6.13)**	
TURNOVER			2.254 (3.89)
MAJ	−0.966 (−2.14)**	−0.381 (−0.76)	−0.130 (−0.32)
LEFT	0.361 (1.08)	−0.014 (−0.04)	0.472 (1.28)
NODEM			−0.149 (−0.34)
EXR	4.721 (7.38)**	4.932 (6.84)**	0.023 (0.07)
LRGDP	−13.87 (−8.94)**	−13.17 (−7.40)**	0.327 (1.16)
CAY{1}	−0.548 (−6.25)**	−0.506 (−5.54)**	−0.039 (−1.59)
GCONS{1}	0.439 (5.57)**	0.341 (4.35)**	0.069 (2.77)**
OPEN{1}	−0.074 (−7.60)**	−0.072 (−6.54)**	−0.019 (−5.05)**
AFRICA			3.173 (4.05)**
WESHEM			−2.639 (−6.41)**
Usable obs.	630	463	733
Deg. of fr.	586	430	696
Cases corr.	550	403	610
Average lik.	0.78	0.77	0.71

Note: * t-statistics in parentheses.

The fit for the multiple exchange rates model is somewhat poorer for the aggregate sample. For industrial countries, the coefficient on central bank independence is significant and has the expected negative sign, and the coefficient on GCONS is positive and significant. Interestingly, the signs on all three external sector variables are reversed with respect to the capital controls logit model. While the sign on the OPEN variable was a priori uncertain, it is hard to find an explanation for the positive correlation between the multiple currency practices dummy and the current account balance or for the negative correlation of the former with the exchange rate regime dummy. For developing countries, instead, the signs on the external sector variables are the same as in the capital controls model, but only openness is statistically significant. The coefficients on GCONS and GDP are significant, but the latter has the wrong sign.

We also calculated five-year non-overlapping averages of all variables

Table 8.4 *Determinants of current account restrictions*
(Annual data, estimation by logit*)

	Whole sample, 1966–89 Time dummies		Indust., 1966–89 Time dummies		Devel., 1966–89 Time dummies	
Constant	9.975	(4.604)**	58.058	(6.875)**	7.292	(3.271)**
TCOUP	−0.228	(−3.943)**			0.026	(1.125)
TCHANGE	0.090	(6.686)**	0.063	(2.914)**	−0.137	(−2.031)**
LEGAL	0.937	(1.207)	1.192	(0.804)		
TURNOVER	1.563	(2.821)**			2.190	(3.939)**
MAJ	0.884	(3.417)**	0.635	(1.489)	0.463	(1.255)
LEFT	0.280	(1.161)	−0.252	(−0.527)	0.745	(2.155)**
NODEM	1.417	(4.525)**			0.766	(2.026)**
EXR	−0.476	(−2.065)**	0.683	(1.255)	−0.378	(−1.270)
LRGDP	−1.548	(−5.997)**	−6.886	(−7.107)**	−1.056	(−3.983)**
CAY{1}	0.005	(0.266)	−0.170	(−2.006)**	0.028	(1.164)
GCONS{1}	0.098	(3.842)**	0.247	(2.966)**	0.103	(3.690)**
OPEN{1}	−0.030	(−7.417)**	−0.081	(−4.805)**	−0.030	(−6.930)**
AFRICA	2.388	(4.981)**			2.516	(5.108)**
WESHEM	0.007	(0.026)			−0.508	(−1.587)
IND	0.289	(−0.610)				
Usable obs.	1173		465		733	
Deg. of fr.	1134		432		697	
Cases corr.	975		425		605	
Average lik.	0.69		0.80		0.68	

Note: * t-statistics in parentheses.

and regressed the frequency of capital controls, current account restrictions, and multiple exchange rate practices on a similar set of explanatory variables. Among the explanatory variables, the only variable which is not an average is the (log of) the level of income (GDP), which is the level of income at the beginning of each five-year period (1965–85). The results of these regressions are presented in tables 8.6, 8.7 and 8.8 for the whole sample only, for the periods 1965–89 and 1970–89.[25] For each period, the first regressions control for fixed time effects, while the second control for both time and country effects.

Before turning to the results, it should be noted that the low (or zero) time variability of the central bank independence data implies that the coefficients on LEGAL and TURNOVER will not be very significant in the

Table 8.5 *Determinants of multiple exchange rates*

(Annual data, estimation by logit*)

	Whole sample, 1966–89 Time dummies		Indust., 1966–89 Time dummies		Devel., 1966–89 Time dummies	
Constant	−5.591	(−3.388)	−8.800	(−0.848)	−10.203	(−5.416)**
TCOUP	−0.097	(−1.771)*			0.121	(5.418)**
TCHANGE	0.074	(6.575)**	0.134	(4.864)**	−0.203	(−2.664)**
LEGAL	−1.638	(−2.237)**	−5.324	(4.864)**		
TURNOVER	0.850	(1.717)*			−0.427	(−0.809)
MAJ	0.209	(0.890)	1.944	(3.977)**	0.470	(1.247)
LEFT	0.033	(0.153)	0.395	(0.788)	−0.532	(−1.655)*
NODEM	−0.106	(−0.364)			−0.204	(−0.491)
EXR	−0.069	(−0.332)	−1.234	(−2.185)**	0.284	(1.015)
LRGDP	0.236	(0.209)	−0.637	(−0.641)	0.757	(3.207)**
CAY{1}	0.020	(1.239)	0.213	(2.735)**	−0.005	(−0.292)
GCONS{1}	0.076	(4.846)**	0.268	(2.843)**	0.114	(5.465)**
OPEN{1}	−0.003	(−1.458)	0.085	(7.382)**	−0.037	(−6.047)**
AFRICA	0.128	(0.429)			0.470	(1.468)
WESHEM	2.046	(7.052)**			2.236	(6.057)**
IND	−0.610	(−1.512)				
Usable obs.	1173		465		724	
Deg. of fr.	1134		432		688	
Cases corr.	952		426		574	
Average lik.	0.64		0.80		0.65	

Note: * t-statistics in parentheses.

regressions including fixed country effects. The results for capital account restrictions show that the share of government, the degree of openness, and the level of income per capita are the most significant determinants of controls. The fit of the current account restrictions regressions is better – the R^2 is 0.50 in the regressions without country effects, and 0.76 in the regressions with country-specific fixed effects. The size of government seems to be the most robust determinant; the level of income is significant only when country-specific effects are not included. As in the logit model, the ratio of the current account balance to GDP is not significant. As for multiple currency practices, the size of government is again significant, while the level of income is significant only in the regressions including country effects, where GCONS and OPEN are the other significant determinants. Overall the fit of the regression is not remarkable unless country effects are included.

Table 8.6 *Determinants of capital controls*

(Five-year averages, OLS*)

	1966–89 Time dummies	1966–89 Fixed effects	1970–9 Time dummies	1970–89 Fixed effects
Constant	1.766 (3.82)**			1.742 (3.51)**
LEGAL	−0.718 (−3.15)**	0.842 (1.30)**	0.687 (−2.75)**	0.308 (1.71)**
TURNOVER	0.488 (2.77)**	0.379 (2.13)**	0.664 (3.18)**	0.519 (2.02)**
LEFT	0.126 (1.50)	0.010 (0.15)	0.206 (2.25)**	0.032 (0.40)
MAJ	−0.003 (−0.04)	−0.004 (−0.06)	−0.060 (−0.69)	0.101 (−1.20)
NODEM	0.020 (0.21)	−0.086 (−0.06)	−0.046 (−0.44)	−0.189 (−1.97)**
LRGDP	−0.134 (−2.44)**	−0.340 (−2.22)**	−0.129 (−2.15)**	−0.255 (−1.65)
GCONS	0.597 (1.35)	2.389 (4.19)**	0.501 (1.09)	2.261 (4.11)**
CAY{1}	−0.015 (−2.31)**	−0.005 (−0.87)	−0.014 (−2.07)**	0.001 (0.20)
EXR	0.179 (2.28)**	0.066 (1.03)	0.150 (1.91)*	0.081 (1.18)
OPEN{1}	−0.003 (−5.00)**	−0.002 (−0.89)	−0.003 (−4.88)**	−0.004 (−2.24)**
IND	0.252 (2.11)**		0.224 (1.66)	
WESHEM	−0.329 (−3.42)**		−0.303 (−2.78)**	
AFRICA	0.084 (1.02)		0.124 (1.33)	
Usable obs.	220	220	184	184
Deg. of fr.	202	153	167	118
R^2	0.25	0.69	0.25	0.67
Mean. dep. var.	0.72	0.72	0.74	0.74
St. err. dep. var.	0.43	0.43	0.42	0.42

Note: * *t*-statistics in parentheses.

Table 8.7 *Determinants of current account restrictions*

(Five-year averages, OLS*)

	1966–89 Time dummies	1966–89 Fixed effects	1970–89 Time dummies	1970–89 Fixed effects
Constant	1.820 (4.27)**		1.961 (4.46)**	
LEGAL	−0.050 (−0.29)	−0.549 (−0.48)	0.030 (0.18)	2.572 (−2.91)**
TURNOVER	0.429 (2.48)**	0.479 (3.36)**	0.496 (2.59)**	0.593 (2.62)**
LEFT	−0.020 (−0.30)	0.026 (0.42)	0.021 (0.32)	0.066 (1.23)
MAJ	0.153 (1.94)*	0.105 (1.44)	0.064 (0.81)	0.034 (0.59)
NODEM	0.189 (1.75)*	0.048 (0.54)	0.099 (0.88)	0.107 (1.32)
LRGDP	−0.182 (−3.63)**	−0.165 (−1.10)	−0.195 (−3.67)**	−0.052 (−0.43)
GCONS	0.502 (1.21)	2.635 (5.44)**	0.459 (1.09)	2.394 (4.98)**
CAY{1}	−0.002 (−0.48)	0.006 (1.26)	−0.002 (−0.35)	0.012 (2.97)**
EXR	−0.039 (−0.52)	0.088 (1.37)	−0.099 (−1.31)	0.031 (0.51)
OPEN{1}	−0.002 (−5.18)**	−0.002 (−1.41)	−0.002 (−4.53)**	−0.004 (−2.67)
IND	0.012 (0.10)		−0.026 (−0.20)	
WESHEM	−0.192 (−1.97)**		−0.123 (−1.15)	
AFRICA	0.131 (1.63)		0.142 (1.61)	
Usable obs.	221	221	185	185
Deg. of fr.	203	154	168	119
R^2	0.50	0.76	0.56	0.85
Mean. dep. var.	0.45	0.45	0.46	0.46
St. err. dep. var.	0.47	0.47	0.47	0.47

Note: * t-statistics in parentheses.

Table 8.8 *Determinants of multiple exchange rates*

(Five-year averages, OLS*)

	1966–89 Time dummies	1966–89 Fixed effects	1970–89 Time dummies	1970–89 Fixed effects
Constant	−0.173 (−0.39)		−0.117 (−0.27)	
LEGAL	−0.280 (−1.56)		−0.383 (−2.03)**	
TURNOVER	−0.271 (1.30)	0.349 (0.34)	0.347 (1.81)*	−0.198 (−0.16)
LEFT	−0.031 (−0.43)	0.352 (1.72)**	0.010 (0.13)	0.608 (2.94)**
MAJ	−0.013 (−0.16)	−0.069 (−1.18)	−0.065 (−0.85)	−0.044 (−0.72)
NODEM	−0.088 (−0.92)	0.107 (1.51)	−0.170 (−1.80)*	0.052 (0.73)
LRGDP	0.031 (0.59)	−0.056 (−0.73)	0.036 (0.69)	−0.077 (−0.94)
GCONS	1.373 (2.11)**	−0.383 (−2.91)**	1.041 (1.47)	−0.362 (−2.38)**
CAY{1}	0.005 (0.80)	2.793 (5.10)**	0.006 (1.00)	2.564 (4.35)**
EXR	0.020 (0.26)	0.006 (1.21)	0.004 (0.05)	0.007 (1.26)
OPEN{1}	−0.001 (−0.95)	−0.037 (−0.65)	−0.000 (−0.98)	−0.082 (−1.19)
IND	−0.016 (−0.13)**	−0.003 (−2.20)**	−0.028 (−0.24)	−0.004 (−2.36)**
WESHEM	0.345 (3.12)**		0.427 (3.48)**	
AFRICA	0.001 (0.01)		0.109 (0.89)	
Usable obs.	221	221	185	185
Deg. of fr.	203	154	168	119
R^2	0.16	0.69	0.22	0.70
Mean. dep. var.	0.25	0.25	0.25	0.25
St. err. dep. var.	0.40	0.40	0.40	0.40

Note: * t-statistics in parentheses.

Overall, results confirm those of the logit regressions for the regressions with time effects only. Adding country-specific effects improves the fit of the regressions considerably. This finding is not surprising, and suggests that other country-specific characteristics, not included in this study, are important determinants of foreign exchange restrictions. An interesting issue to explore is whether our dummies for foreign exchange restrictions help explain the behavior of key macroeconomic variables such as inflation, budget deficits, real interest rates, and economic growth. Results presented in Grilli and Milesi-Ferretti (1995) show, for example, a strong positive correlation between inflation and seigniorage, on the one hand, and foreign exchange restrictions, on the other hand.

Notwithstanding the limitations inherent in our measures of foreign exchange restrictions, the empirical analysis lends support to theories emphasizing the importance of fiscal and external sector motivations in the imposition of controls. Somewhat surprisingly, political variables do not appear to be very significant. This can be due to several reasons. For example, the dummy variables used in this study provide a rather coarse characterization of the political system. The lack of systematic correlation between foreign exchange restrictions measures and political variables could also be due to the binary nature of control measures, that cannot capture the intensity of controls. Exploring the importance of these issues is a subject for future research.

5 Concluding remarks

The results presented in the previous section are encouraging, especially given the binary nature of the dependent variable. Although the empirical analysis is "model-free," and therefore does not allow any formal test of a theory of capital controls, we have established empirical regularities regarding the imposition or removal of foreign exchange restrictions that are consistent with theoretical predictions. In particular, this study finds that capital controls are more likely to be in place in countries where monetary policy is more firmly under government's control, because the central bank is not independent. Also, they are more likely to be imposed in poorer countries, and in countries with a larger government. An explanation for the latter finding is that capital controls appear to have strong fiscal implications, working through their impact on the use of seigniorage as a source of revenue and through their effects on the real return on domestic government debt. Finally, external sector variables are also significantly correlated with controls – these are less likely to be imposed in economies that are very open, that have a flexible exchange rate system and no current account difficulties. As for other foreign exchange restrictions, such as multiple currency practices and restrictions on current account transactions, results suggest a similar set of determinants, although the correlation with external factors is not as clear-cut as it is for capital account restrictions.

Further research should aim at measuring the intensity of capital controls through better measures than the dummy variable used in this chapter, as well as shedding light on the issue of the effectiveness of capital controls, which is not addressed in this study.

Appendix

1 List of countries

1	United States*	32	Honduras
2	United Kingdom*	33	Mexico
3	Austria*	34	Nicaragua
4	Belgium*	35	Panama
5	Denmark*	36	Peru
6	France*	37	Uruguay
7	Germany*	38	Venezuela
8	Italy*	39	Bahamas
9	The Netherlands*	40	Barbados
10	Norway*	41	Israel
11	Sweden*	42	Egypt
12	Canada*	43	India
13	Japan*	44	Indonesia
14	Finland*	45	Malaysia
15	Greece*	46	Nepal
16.	Iceland*	47	Pakistan
17	Ireland*	48	Philippines
18	Malta	49	Singapore
19	Portugal*	50	Thailand
20	Spain*	51	Botswana
21	Turkey	52	Zaire
22	Yugoslavia	53	Ethiopia
23	Australia*	54	Ghana
24	New Zealand*	55	Kenya
25	South Africa	56	Morocco
26.	Argentina	57	Nigeria
27	Bolivia	58	Tanzania
28	Brazil	59	Uganda
29	Chile	60	Zambia
30	Colombia	61	Western Samoa
31	Costa Rica		

* Countries marked with an asterisk were classified as industrial countries in the regressions of section 4.

2 Variables used in the regressions in section 4

Dependent Variable(s)

CAPCONTR: Dummy variable taking the value of one when capital controls are in place, zero otherwise. Capital controls defined as "Restrictions on payments on capital transactions." *Sources:* IMF's *Exchange Arrangements and Exchange Restrictions*, various issues.

CURRCONTR: Dummy variable taking the value of one when restrictions on current account transactions are in place, zero otherwise. Current account restrictions defined as "Restrictions on payments for current transactions." *Sources:* IMF's *Exchange Rate Arrangements and Exchange Restrictions*, various issues.

MULTER: Dummy variable taking the value of one when multiple exchange rate practices are in place and zero otherwise. Multiple exchange rate practices defined as: "Separate exchange rate(s) for some or all capital transactions and/or some or all invisibles." *Source:* IMF's *Exchange Rate Arrangements and Exchange Restrictions*, various issues.

Explanatory variables

LRGDP: (Log of) real GDP per capita. *Source:* Summers and Heston (1991) and subsequent PWT 5.5 update.

GCONS: Ratio of government consumption to GDP. *Source:* Summers and Heston (1991) and PWT 5.5 update.

OPEN: Ratio of the sum of imports and exports to GDP. *Source:* Summers and Heston (1991) and PWT 5.5 update.

CAY: Ratio of current account deficit to GDP. *Source:* IMF's *International Financial Statistics*, various issues.

EXR: Dummy variable taking the value of one during periods of fixed or managed exchange rates and zero during periods of freely floating exchange rates. *Source:* IMF's *Exchange Arrangements and Exchange Restrictions*, various issues.

LEGAL: Index of legal central bank independence. Higher numbers correspond to more CB independence. *Source:* Cukierman (1992).

TURNOVER: Actual turnover of central bankers per year. *Source:* Cukierman (1992).

LEFT: Dummy variable taking the value of one when a democratic left-wing government is in power, and zero otherwise. *Source:* Banks, various issues.

MAJ: Dummy variable taking the value of one when a majority government is in power, and zero in the case of a coalition or minority government. *Source:* Banks, various issues.

NODEM: Dummy variable taking the value of one when a totalitarian government is in power, and zero otherwise. Source: Banks, various issues.

TCHANGE: Total number of government changes for a given country in the period 1950–82. *Source:* Taylor and Jodice (1983).
TCOUP: Total number of successful coups for a given country in the period 1950–82. *Source:* Taylor and Jodice (1983).

Notes

This chapter is based on a research project on capital controls undertaken with Vittorio Grilli of the Italian Treasury. I am grateful to my discussant Lans Bovenberg and to conference participants for useful comments and suggestions. The chapter reflects the views of the author and not necessarily those of the International Monetary Fund.

1 The recent Mexican crisis (December 1994) is a good example.
2 For related work see, for example, Roubini and Sachs (1989), Grilli, Masciandaro, and Tabellini (1991), and Alesina and Roubini (1992). On the specific issue of capital controls, see Epstein and Schor (1992).
3 I am grateful to Sebastian Edwards for pointing this out to me.
4 Some studies have suggested that the actual degree of capital mobility in countries that impose capital controls is indeed quite high. See, for example, Haque and Montiel (1990).
5 For a related argument, see also Harberger (1986).
6 Giavazzi and Giovannini (1989) underline the asymmetry between strong- and weak-currency countries in an exchange rate regime such as the EMS: as long as the burden of adjustment falls on the weak-currency countries, the other countries are "isolated" from the effects of interest rate variability. Giavazzi and Pagano (1990) relate the likelihood of a "confidence crisis" to public debt management.
7 For a similar argument based on signalling, see Bartolini and Drazen (1997). Lane and Rojas-Suarez (1992) analyze the impact of capital controls on the credibility of a commitment to keep the exchange rate within pre-specified bands.
8 I am grateful to Lans Bovenberg for this point.
9 For an illustration of the "perils of sterilization", see Calvo (1991).
10 For an analysis of policy response to capital inflows following stabilization, see, for example, Calvo, Leiderman, and Reinhart (1993). Among the policy responses being discussed, one can mention fiscal restraint, the removal of restrictions on capital outflows, and the imposition of "Tobin taxes" on short-run capital inflows.
11 On the relation between reserve requirements and the inflation tax, see also Brock (1984).
12 Using an overlapping-generations framework, Sussman (1991) also suggests that capital controls (in the form of a tax on interest-bearing foreign assets, accompanied by a tax on domestic assets) reduce debt service and increase the demand for money.
13 A similar table for a larger sample of countries but not including current account restrictions is presented in Mathieson and Rojas-Suarez (1993).

14 The only industrial country with separate exchange rates in 1989 is Belgium. Several industrial countries, among them Belgium and Italy, dismantled remaining foreign exchange restrictions the following year.

15 On this topic, see Eichengreen, Rose, and Wyplosz (1994).

16 Epstein and Schor (1992) argue that central bank independence reflects "the power of financial sector interests," who are against limitations to capital mobility.

17 Furthermore, there is an endogeneity problem in using real income as an explanatory variable. An alternative specification of the logit model would include only the initial level of income as an explanatory variable. Results, not reported, are analogous to those presented later. Alesina, Grilli and Milesi-Ferretti (1994) also use the share of agricultural value added over value added in services as a proxy of development. This variable, however, is not available on a consistent basis for some developing countries in our sample.

18 The inclusion of variables measuring central bank independence raises the issue of whether the metric with which independence is measured is the appropriate one. We do not explore this issue further in this chapter.

19 I am grateful to Sylvester Eijffinger for this point.

20 This is the time period covered in the Taylor and Jodice (1983) study from which the data on coups and government changes are drawn. The use of an average value over a long time period can be interpreted as a measure of the average probability of the event occurring in a given year.

21 I am grateful to Sebastian Edwards for suggesting the use of this variable.

22 The whole sample covers the years 1966–89, because the data on restrictions to capital account transactions for developing countries are available only after that date.

23 We also introduce the initial level of income (coefficient not reported) in order to control for the fact that the coefficient on the income variable reflects both a cross-section and a time-series component, while the trend captures only the latter.

24 Note that a high turnover of central bankers indicates less independence. One needs to take into account the possibility that the inverse correlation between the capital control dummy and the degree of central bank independence captures reverse causality (when capital controls are in place, the government is less likely to want an independent central bank). Given the fact that central bank statutes are changed very infrequently, we tend to favor the first interpretation.

25 For the foreign exchange restrictions variables, data for 1965 are unavailable. For the five-year period 1965–9 we therefore use the average value for the period 1966–89. The results for the period 1970–89 are presented because for four developing countries the observations on capital controls start only between 1968 and 1971.

References

Aizenman, J. and Guidotti, P. (1994), "Capital Controls, Collection Costs, and Domestic Public Debt," *Journal of International Money and Finance*, 13, 41–54.

Alesina, A., Grilli, V., and Milesi-Ferretti, G. M. (1994), "The Political Economy of

Capital Controls," in L. Leiderman and A. Razin (eds.), *Capital Mobility: The Impact on Consumption, Investment and Growth*, Cambridge: Cambridge University Press for CEPR.

Alesina, A. and Roubini, N. (1992), "Political Cycles in OECD Economies," *Review of Economic Studies*, 59, 663–88.

Alesina, A. and Summers, L. (1993), "Central Bank Independence and Economic Performance: Some Comparative Evidence," *Journal of Money, Credit and Banking*, 25, 151–62.

Alesina, A. and Tabellini, G. (1989), "External Debt, Capital Flight and Political Risk," *Journal of International Economics*, 27, 199–220.

Banks, A., *Political Handbook of the World*, various issues.

Bartolini, L. and Drazen, A. (1997), "Capital Account Liberalization as a Signal," *American Economic Review*, forthcoming.

Brock, P. (1984), "Inflationary Finance in an Open Economy," *Journal of Monetary Economics*, 14, 37–53.

Calvo, G. (1991), "The Perils of Sterilization," *IMF Staff Papers*, 38, 921–6.

Calvo, G., Leiderman, L., and Reinhart, C. (1993), "Capital Inflows and Real Exchange Rate Appreciation in Latin America: The Role of External Factors," *IMF Staff Papers*, 40, 108–51.

Cuddington, J. (1986), "Capital Flight: Estimates, Issue and Explanations," *Princeton Essays in International Finance*, No. 162.

Cukierman, A. (1992), *Central Bank Strategy, Credibility, and Independence*, Cambridge, Mass.: MIT Press.

Cukierman, A., Edwards, S., and Tabellini, G. (1992), "Seigniorage and Political Instability," *American Economic Review*, 82, 537–55.

Cukierman, A., Webb, S. B. and Neyapti, B. (1992), "Measuring the Independence of Central Banks and its Effect on Policy Outcomes," *World Bank Economic Review*, 6, 353–98.

Dellas, H. and Stockman, A. (1993), "Self-Fulfilling Expectations, Speculative Attacks and Capital Controls," *Journal of Money, Credit and Banking*, 25, 721–30.

Dooley, M. and Isard, P. (1980), "Capital Controls, Political Risk and Deviations from Interest-Rate Parity," *Journal of Political Economy*, 88, 370–84.

Dornbusch, R. (1986), "Special Exchange Rates for Capital Account Transactions," *World Bank Economic Review*, 1, 1–33.

Drazen, A. (1989), "Monetary Policy, Capital Controls and Seigniorage in an Open Economy," in M. De Cecco and A. Giovannini (eds.), *A European Central Bank?* Cambridge: Cambridge University Press, 13–32.

Edwards, S. (1984), "The Order of Liberalization of the External Sector in Developing Countries," *Princeton Essays in International Finance*, 156.

(1989), "On the Sequencing of Structural Reform," NBER Working Paper, No. 3138.

Edwards, S. and van Wijnbergen, S. (1986), "Welfare Effects of Capital and Trade Account Liberalization," *International Economic Review*, 141–48.

Eichengreen, B., Rose, A., and Wyplosz, C. (1994), "Is There a Safe Passage to

EMU? Evidence from the Markets and a Proposal," in J. Frankel and A. Giovannini (eds.), *The Micro-Structure of Foreign Exchange Markets*, University of Chicago Press.

Eichengreen, B. and Wyplosz, C. (1993), "The Unstable EMS," *Brookings Papers on Economic Activity*, 1, 51–143.

Eijffinger, S. and Schaling, E. (1993), "Central Bank Independence in Twelve Industrial Countries," *Banca Nazionale del Lavoro Quarterly Review*, 184, 1–41.

(1996), "The Ultimate Determinants of Central Bank Independence," this volume.

Epstein, G. and Schor, J. (1992), "Structural Determinants and Economic Effects of Capital Controls in OECD Countries," in T. Banuri and J. Schor (eds.), *Financial Openness and National Autonomy: Opportunities and Constraints*, Oxford: Clarendon Press, 136–61.

Flood, R. and Garber, P. (1984), "Collapsing Exchange Rate Regimes: Some Linear Examples," *Journal of International Economics*, 17, 1–13.

Frenkel, J. (1982), "Comment to McKinnon," *Carnegie-Rochester Conference Series*, 17, 199–201.

Giavazzi, F. and Giovannini, A. (1989), *Limiting Exchange Rate Flexibility: The European Monetary System*, Cambridge, Mass.: MIT Press.

Giavazzi, F. and Pagano, M. (1988), "Capital Controls in the EMS," in D.E. Fair and C. De Boissieu (eds.), *International Monetary and Financial Integration: The European Dimension*, Dordrecht: Martinus Nijhoff, 261–89.

(1990), "Confidence Crises and Public Debt Management," in R. Dornbusch and M. Draghi (eds.), *Public Debt Management: Theory and History*, Cambridge: Cambridge University Press.

Giovannini, A. (1988), "Capital Controls and Public Finance: The Experience of Italy," in F. Giavazzi and L. Spaventa (eds.), *High Public Debt: The Italian Experience*, Cambridge: Cambridge University Press, 177–211.

Giovannini, A. and De Melo, M. (1993), "Government Revenue from Financial Repression," *American Economic Review*, 83, 953–63.

Goldsmith, R. W. (1969), *Financial Structure and Development*, New Haven: Yale University Press.

Grilli, V. (1986), "Buying and Selling Attacks on Fixed Exchange Rate Systems," *Journal of International Economics*, 20, 143–56.

Grilli, V., Masciandaro, D., and Tabellini, G. (1991), "Political and Monetary Institutions and Public Financial Policies in the Industrial Countries," *Economic Policy*, 13, 341–92.

Grilli, V. and Milesi-Ferretti, G. M. (1995), "Economic Effects and Structural Determinants of Capital Controls," *IMF Staff Papers*, 42, September, 54–88.

Haque, N. and Montiel, P. (1990), "Capital Mobility in Developing Countries: Some Empirical Tests," IMF Working Paper 90/117.

Harberger, A. C. (1986), "Welfare Consequences of Capital Inflows," in A. Choksi and D. Papageorgiou (eds.), *Economic Liberalization in Developing Countries*, Oxford: Basil Blackwell, 157–78.

Ito, T. (1983), "Capital Controls and Covered Interest Rate Parity," NBER Working Paper No 1187, August.

Jappelli, T. and Pagano, M. (1994), "Savings, Growth and Liquidity Constraints," *Quarterly Journal of Economics*, 109, 83–110.

Khan, M. and Haque, N. (1985), "Foreign Borrowing and Capital Flight," *IMF Staff Papers*, 32, 606–28.

King, R. and Levine, R. (1993), "Finance, Entrepreneurship and Growth: Theory and Evidence," *Journal of Monetary Economics*, 32, 3, 513–42.

Krugman, P. (1979), "A Model of Balance of Payments Crises," *Journal of Money, Credit and Banking*, 11, 3, 311–25.

Lane, T. and Rojas-Suarez, L. (1992), "Credibility, Capital Controls and the EMS," *Journal of International Economics*, 32, 321–37.

Mathieson, D. J. and Rojas-Suarez, L. (1993), "Liberalization of the Capital Account: Experiences and Issues," IMF Occasional Paper, No. 103, March.

McKinnon, R. I. (1973), *Money and Capital in Economic Development*, Washington, DC: The Brookings Institution.

(1982), "The Order of Economic Liberalization: Lessons from Chile and Argentina," *Carnegie-Rochester Conference Series*, 17, 159–86.

Obstfeld, M. (1986), "Rational and Self-Fulfilling Balance-of-Payments Crises," *American Economic Review*, 76, 72–81.

(1988), "Comments to Giovannini," in F. Giavazzi and L. Spaventa (eds.), *High Public Debt: The Italian Experience*, Cambridge: Cambridge University Press, 212–16.

Razin, A. and Sadka, E. (1991), "Efficient Investment Incentives in the Presence of Capital Flight," *Journal of International Economics*, 31, 171–81.

Roubini, N. and Sachs, J. (1989), "Political and Economic Determinants of Budget Deficits in Industrial Democracies," *European Economic Review*, 33, 903–33.

Roubini, N. and Sala-I-Martin, X. (1992), "Financial Repression and Economic Growth," *Journal of Development Economics*, 39, 5–30.

(1995), "A Growth Model of Inflation, Tax Evasion and Financial Repression," *Journal of Monetary Economics*, 35, 2, 275–301.

Summers, R. and Heston, A. (1991), "The Penn World Table (Mark 5): An Expanded Set of International Comparisons, 1950–88," *Quarterly Journal of Economics*, 106, 2, 327–68.

Sussman, O. (1991), "Macroeconomic Effects of a Tax on Bond Interest Rates," *Journal of Money, Credit and Banking*, 23, 352–66.

Taylor, C. L. and Jodice, D. (1983), *World Handbook of Social and Political Indicators*, New Haven: Yale University Press.

Tobin, J. (1978), "A Proposal for International Monetary Reform," *Eastern Economic Journal*, 4.

Tornell, A. (1990), "Real vs. Financial Investment: Can Tobin Taxes Eliminate the Irreversibility Constraint?" *Journal of Development Economics*, 32, 419–44.

Van Wijnbergen, S. (1990), "Capital Controls and the Real Exchange Rate," *Economica*, 57, 15–28.

Wyplosz, C. (1986), "Capital Controls and Balance of Payments Crises," *Journal of International Money and Finance*, 5, 167–79.

Comment

LANS BOVENBERG

This is a nice chapter for at least two reasons. First, it combines theory with empirical results. Second, it uses an eclectic approach, i.e. it does not rely on a single, often narrow, theory to explain the world but rather draws on a number of theories.

1 Theory

Of course, the chapter also has its weaknesses. Let me start with the theoretical section, which is actually very similar to that in Alesina, Grilli, and Milesi-Ferretti (1994). It would be nice if the introduction made it clear how this contribution differs from previous papers by the author and made it clearer what the specific contribution of this particular chapter is. In this connection, the existing literature on the political economy of capital controls should be referred to, for example, an article by Epstein and Schor (1992).

The theory section describes a number of arguments in favor of capital controls. For an IMF official, this is not easy to accept because the IMF tends to promote free international capital flows and thus typically argues in favor of removing these controls. Indeed, the theoretical section does reflect some tension between, on the one hand, providing arguments in favor of such controls, and, on the other hand, counseling against capital controls by pointing out that capital controls tend to be counterproductive. If countries believed this counsel, they would almost never use them.

More generally, the theory section could be better integrated with the empirical section. To illustrate, the theoretical section deals with the speculative attack literature and explains how capital controls can be imposed in order to stem short-term capital flows. The empirical part, in contrast, focuses on long-term issues as it uses low-frequency data, i.e. annual data. Indeed, the beginning of the empirical section mentions only the structural, i.e.. the long-term reasons for adopting capital controls.

2 Political economy

After reading the theoretical section, I was a bit disappointed. The reason is that the introduction of the chapter promises the reader a focus on political-economy arguments for capital controls. However, the theoretical section deals mainly with rather familiar economic arguments. Interestingly enough, political arguments can point in quite different directions.

Take the example of the optimal sequencing of reforms. Traditonal welfare theory argues that governments should first liberalize goods and labor markets (i.e., the real sector) before liberalizing international capital flows (i.e., the financial sector). If they do the reverse, they run the danger that capital flows exacerbate distortions in the domestic markets and in international trade.

Interestingly enough, in liberalizing their economies, many governments start with liberalizing international capital flows. Examples are the Thatcher government in 1979 and the New Zealand government in the beginning in the 1980s. Why did these countries start their market-oriented reforms this way? Do government officials fail to read the articles of academic economists? Well, when I worked for the International Monetary Fund, I found out that these officials actually do read the literature and even understand parts of it. Nevertheless, they believed their governments had no other choice than to liberalize international capital flows first. The reason is that governments encounter less political resistance against liberalizing financial markets than they do against liberalizing labor and commodity markets.

After liberalizing international capital flows, the distortions in the domestic markets become much more visible. Hence, the political task of liberalizing these markets becomes easier. Moreover, once the spirit of free international capital flows is out of the bottle, it becomes very difficult to put that spirit back in that bottle as institutions develop. In this way, market-oriented governments can use capital-market liberalization strategically. In particular, a government favoring free markets commits subsequent governments, which may have other views, to free markets. It is clear, then, that the primary purpose of the removal of capital controls in these countries was not so much to enhance the efficiency of financial markets but rather to create the political momentum to liberalize the entire economy.

This is, of course, not the whole story on the political economy of capital controls and capital market liberalization. Letting commodity market liberalization lag capital market liberalization too much can be dangerous – even from a political point of view. In particular, with a rigid real sector and a lot of barriers in international commodity trade, capital flows can result in rather large swings in the real exchange rate, threatening the competitive position of tradable industries. This raises protectionist pressure. Indeed, in this way, more open capital markets can result in more closed commodity markets.

This type of reasoning suggests that the political-economic literature can contribute to our understanding of why and how countries liberalize. Of course, one cannot do all this in just one chapter. However, I would like to have seen some more discussion of these political issues.

3 Empirical analysis

Let me turn now to the empirical analysis, starting with the specification of the left-hand variable, i.e., official capital controls. As the authors stress, a shortcoming of the binary IMF data they use is that these data measure neither the intensity nor the effectiveness of the controls. Hence, the authors would be well advised to supplement their information with other information, such as deviations from covered interest parity or information on black-market premia. This also would help to find out whether countries imposed implicit or informal controls rather than explicit or formal controls.

I was also wondering why the chapter does not distinguish between controls on outflows and controls on inflows. Motivations for controls on outflows tend to be quite different from those for controls on inflows. Most of the arguments mentioned here involve restrictions on outflows. However, the variables measuring capital controls include also controls on inflows.

Real GDP

Let me turn now to the right-hand variables. An important explanatory variables is real GDP. This variable picks up the impact of various omitted variables. Unfortunately, it is not clear which ones. The first omitted variable is technological progress in financial markets. More modern financial markets make capital controls not only less effective but also less attractive because these developments reduce the base of the inflation tax.

The second omitted variable one could call technological progress in economic ideas. Governments believe more and more that the IMF is right: capital controls are often counterproductive.

The third omitted variable is the availability of alternative redistributive instruments. Whereas capital controls can be used as such an instrument, developed economies tend to have more efficient redistributive instruments, such as social security and progressive taxation.

The last omitted variable is the extent to which capital ownership is spread among the population. In developed economies, workers – through, for example, pension funds – tend to have more claims on the capital stock. Hence, capital taxation becomes a less attractive instrument for redistributing income in favor of labor.

Central bank independence

The second important explanatory variable is central bank independence. The chapter uses the argument that capital controls are more atrractive if governments control monetary policy. In my view, both the absence of capital controls and central bank independence are driven by the same fundamental forces, namely a belief in the importance of gaining credibility in financial markets. In other words, central bank independence is not exogenous but rather a function of another more fundamental factor.

There is also reverse causation here. With free international capital flows, credibility becomes a more important commodity (so as to stem capital outflows). Hence, an independent central bank becomes more attractive as a device to gain that credibility.

Political leaning of governments

This brings me to the third explanatory variable: the political leaning of the government. The chapter uses the left/right distinction but does not find a strong effect. This is not surprising because the left–right distinction is more about objectives than instruments. To illustrate, socialist governments in Australia and New Zealand liberalized their economies after conservative governments had left a legacy of heavily regulated economies. Indeed, these left-wing governments believed that capital controls would be ineffective instruments for redistribution – this is especially so if the poor hold relatively more nominal claims, including cash, or if workers hold capital through funded pension funds.

Fiscal variables

Another important explanatory variable is the size of government as measured by the tax to GDP ratio. Here I was wondering whether spending minus taxes would not be a better measure for the need to raise revenues through capital controls. Of course, we have the problem of reverse causation here. Tax revenues are endogenous: the more effective capital controls, the higher tax revenues can be.

Another variable the author may want to include is the level of public debt. This determines not only the need to raise revenues but also the desire to restrict capital outflows in order to keep interest rates low and stable.

Another measure for the attractiveness of capital controls from a fiscal perspective is the size of the tax base. I wonder why the author did not include a measure for the base of the inflation tax, such as the monetary base, estimates for the black or informal economy, or proxies for the inefficiency of the financial system.

In describing capital controls as an instrument for fiscal policy, the chapter very much focuses on the use of capital controls to raise revenue from capital taxes and the inflation tax. The focus on the inflation tax seems appropriate only in the context of LDCs. However, in developed countries with modern financial sectors, the inflation tax tends to be rather small. In developed countries, capital controls may facilitate the taxation not only of capital but also of labor. The experience of the Scandinavian countries illustrates this. The removal of capital controls forced these countries to cut taxes on capital in order to prevent capital flight. However, low taxes on capital also eroded the base of the tax on labor income because many agents, especially the self-employed, started to classify their labor income as capital income so as to benefit from the low rate. Through this channel, capital controls may be an important instrument for raising revenue – not only from capital taxes but also from labor taxes.

Finally, capital controls are less important if countries can coordinate in taxing capital, for example through the exchange of information. This suggests that the absence of international fiscal coordination may be an important determinant of capital control.

9 The political economy of the Exchange Rate Mechanism

PATRICK MINFORD

1 An open economy model

The model, set out in table 9.1, is a distillation of the dependent economy model of Swan (1963); its derivation is based on Minford (1992) and is explained fully in the appendix. The time horizon is the "intermediate run," where capital is, at least to some degree, fixed.

(1) is the supply curve of traded goods; (2) is the demand curve for traded goods; (3) and (4) equate the implied demand for non-traded goods with the output of these, by market-clearing through p_{NT}; (5) is the overall output identity; (6) is the national budget constraint in the absence of long-term loans – it forces the current account of the balance of payments into balance. For convenience, it ignores the payment of net interest to foreign residents that would result from the integral of past current account deficits (this would in fact lower domestic demand pro tanto), but our focus here is on the effects of the ERM and this element depends on demand policies pursued by the government – a separate issue, so we omit it (or equivalently, treat it as exogenous); (7) is the open economy supply curve. Its derivation assumes that non-traded goods are more labor intensive than traded goods and have a higher elasticity of labor demand to the product real wage.

To pay for the cost of the subsidy, we assume the government raises either a tax on non-traded goods or a general consumption (or income) tax, following the normal assumption that it is impossible for the government to levy non-distorting taxes. Notice too that there is no way that the effect of I^{ue} on wages can be undone by the tax/subsidy system; if, for example, a subsidy was paid to labor, this would have to be financed by a general tax of the same size, producing an exact offset. Since the share of traded goods in total GDP is t, the government budget constraint can be written

$$tS = G + (1-t)N$$

Table 9.1 *The open economy model*

$$y_T = a_0e + a_1(I^{ue} - G) + a_2N + (a_1 + a_2)S + y_T^* + u \qquad (1)$$
$$D_T = tD + be \qquad (2)$$
$$D_{NT} = D - D_T \qquad (3)$$
$$D_{NT} = y_{NT} \qquad (4)$$
$$y = y_{NT} + y_T \qquad (5)$$
$$D = y \qquad (6)$$
$$y = h_0e + (h_1 + h_2)(I^{ue} - G) - h_1N + h_2S + y^* + u \qquad (7)$$

Notes: y=output; $y^*(y_T^*)$=the natural rate of output (traded output) in the absence of subsidies; D=demand (in real terms); p=log of prices; I=inflation (with superscript 'ue' it is unexpected and with 'e' expected); T, NT (subscripts)=traded, non traded sectors; e = the real exchange rate, i.e., $p_{NT}-p_T$; u=random error term reflecting trading conditions in traded sector; S=subsidy rate on traded output; N=tax rate on non-traded output; G=general tax rate on consumption (or income). $t(=y^*/y_T^*)$, the natural share of traded output in GNP, is less than 1. The natural rate for the real exchange rate, e, is zero without subsidies.

It is shown in the appendix that it makes no substantive difference whether G or N or some combination is chosen to finance subsidies. Hence we assume for simplicity that the government chooses to levy the general tax, $G=tS$.

We treat inflation, I, as policy determined, specifically by use of the exchange rate instrument. Since p_T equals world traded goods prices converted into home currency, the log of domestic prices, p, is given by

$$p = tp_T + (1 - t)p_{NT} + G \qquad (1)$$

Its rate of change can be set by manipulating the exchange rate, after allowing for the changes in the real variables of the state, viz. the real exchange rate, the subsidy rate, and the traded sector shock. We assume in what follows that $I=I^*$ (the government's target for inflation) corresponds to no devaluation of the parity. Without any substantive change in the following argument, however, this assumption allows for both movements within the parity margins and in extremes a revaluation of the parity, precisely because of this dependence of inflation on real variables, as well as on the exchange rate. The appendix expands on these issues but notice that I^* merely affects the nominal equilibrium, whereas the argument of the chapter concerns the real equilibrium, which depends on unexpected movements in I.

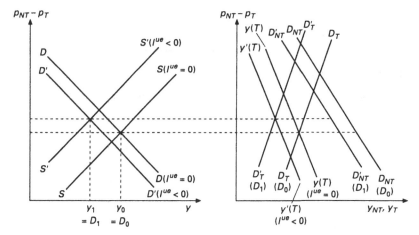

Figure 9.1 The model's response to unexpected inflation (zero subsidies assumed)

Note: In the right quadrant, traded supply and demand and nontrader demand are shown; aggregate demand (D) must vary to ensure $y_T = D_T$, as illustrated for two values of I^{ue}. In the left quadrant, the DD curve shows the resulting locus of aggregate demand points for which there is current account balance; SS shows the supply-side locus. At their intersection $D = y$ and hence the non-traded market clears.

2 The model's equilibrium

We begin by computing the model's equilibrium, treating I^{ue} and S as exogenous. The model is illustrated in figure 9.1 for a given I^{ue} (and zero S). As I^{ue} changes, total demand (D) has to change also from DO to $D1$ as shown. The equilibrium expressions are given in the appendix as (A. 12–14).

Unexpected inflation raises the real exchange rate and lowers both total and traded output because of this rise in the real exchange rate. A subsidy raises traded output but lowers total output because of the resulting distortion to relative prices.

A helpful way to think about the model is to treat non-traded goods as pure services and let their price, p_{NT}, be the (log of the) wage level, W. Then in figure 9.1 the vertical axis measures a transform of the real wage (given by $W - p = W - tp_T - (1 - t)W = t([W - p_T])$. An unanticipated inflation ($I^{ue} > 0$) would then shift the supply curve of labor (and of total output), in the left-hand quadrant outwards, expanding the economy in the usual Phillips curve fashion. A subsidy to the traded goods sector paid for by a rise in general taxation lowers real wages and so shifts this same supply curve inwards; hence, though the traded sector expands, it must do so at the expense of a greater contraction in the non-traded sector.

3 The political economy of subsidy and devaluation

We assume that the government's objective function, as discussed in the appendix, is to maximize

$$U = -0.5\{[ty^* - y_T]^2 + kS^2 + j[I - I^*]^2\} \text{ for } y_T < y_T^*$$

and

$$0.5(kS^2 + j[I - I^*]^2) \text{ for } y_T \geq y^*_T \tag{2}$$

and subject to $I \leq I^*$ for u other than $u-$ (this being the "ERM constraint" of no devaluation except in bad times – see appendix for more detail). Notice that this will probably imply a setting of I^* greater than that of foreign traded-goods inflation, because, as explained in the appendix, this will appropriately restrict exchange rate movements within the margins.

y^*_T is the natural rate of traded goods output; maintaining this level is the objective of vested interests in those industries. For $y_T \geq y^*_T$ the government is assumed to have satisfied the vested interests involved. Inflation enters for conventional reasons, the target being set at I^* – in line with the no-devaluation condition. Because of the distortion created by the subsidy-cum-tax, S, and its effect on overall output and consumer welfare, the government also experiences a cost in raising it. We set out the government's maximizing solution in table 9.2.

The solution for I and I^e depends on the distribution of u. To illustrate, we choose a three-valued distribution:

$$u_- = -1 \text{ (bad times) with probability } \pi_-$$

$$u_0 = 0 \text{ (normal times) with probability } \pi_0$$

and $$u_+ = +1 \text{ (good times) with probability } \pi_+.$$

We assume that the units of y_T are such that for $u_+ = +1$, y_T is greater than y^*_T. We will take it that $\pi_+ = \pi_-$ i.e., the distribution of u is symmetric.

In this case, $I_+ = I^*$ for $u_+ = +1$

$$I_0 = I^* \text{ for } u_0 = 0 \tag{3}$$

and $$I_- = (jk + q_1^2 k + q_2^2 j)^{-1} ([kj + q_2^2 j]I^* + kq_1^2 I^e + kq_1 q_3)$$

for $$u_- = -1 \tag{4}$$

$$I^e = \pi_- I_- + (1 - \pi_-)I^* \text{ can be found by substitution as}$$

Table 9.2 *The government's first order conditions*

When $y_T \geq y_T^*$, the government (trivially) maximizes by setting $S=0$ and $I=I^*$

The first-order conditions when $y_T < y_T^*$ yield

$$I - I^* = [y_T^* - y_T](q_1/j) \text{ for } u = u_-$$

and $I = I^*$ for u not equal to u_- (1)

$$S = [y^*_T - y_T](q_2/k) \tag{2}$$

Hence for $u = u_-$

$$S = (q_2 j/q_1 k)I \tag{3}$$
$$I = (jk + q_1^2 k + q_1^2 j)^{-1}[(kj + q_2^2 j)I^* + kq_1^2 I^e - kq_3 q_1 u)] \tag{4}$$
$$q_1 = (th_0 + a_0 + b)^{-1}\{(a_1 + a_2)th_1 + a_2 th_2 + a_1 b\}$$
$$q_2 = (th_0 + a_0 + b)^{-1}\{ba_0\}$$

and

$$q_3 = (th_0 + a_0 + b)^{-1}\{t(h_0 + a_0) + b\}$$

and for u not equal to u_-

$$I = I^* \tag{5}$$
$$S = (k + q_2^2)^{-1}\{q_1 q_2 [I^e - I^*] - q_2 q_3 u\} \tag{6}$$

$$I^e = I^* (jk + kq_1^2 [1 - \pi_-] + jq_2^2)^{-1} \pi_- kq_1 q_3 \tag{5}$$

Clearly, for any symmetric distribution of u, the distribution of I is skewed rightward from I^*, so that its mean, I^e, lies above its mode, I^*.

Hence, we obtain here the "peso problem" result, that I^* is less than I^e. It follows of course that in both good and normal times I^{ue} will be negative. In normal times there will be target inflation, I^* (with rising wages being partly offset by some rise of the exchange rate within its margins) and a positive subsidy, S. In (presumably rare) good times, inflation will also be on target (with similarly rising wages again being partly offset by a rising exchange rate) but the subsidy will in principle be lifted (in practice with bureaucratic lags, given that the good times only last briefly, this may not occur; S should be interpreted no doubt as planned subsidies).

Figure 9.2 illustrates the equilibrium inflation rate under different shocks (with their attached probabilities) and their relation to the expected inflation rate; the resulting subsidy rate is proportional to any reduction in traded output below its natural rate. Target inflation, I^*,

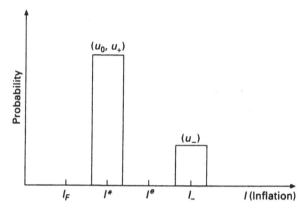

Figure 9.2 One inflation distribution illustrated

Notes: Real exchange rate is defined as the domestic level multiplied by MERM and divided by the GNP weighted price level of the G7 countries (own country excluded where relevant). MERM is the effective exchange rate index constructed by the IMF from weights derived from its multilateral exchange rate model. Data are taken from the IMF, International Financial Statistics. The data for 1991 are partly estimated.

typically exceeds foreign (traded goods) inflation, I_F (that is, I_T absent any exchange rate change) – hence one would observe long periods of relatively fixed exchange rates combined with domestic inflation in excess of foreign inflation.

4 Interpretation

In concrete terms what we visualize occurring is that wage bargainers, setting wages for a coming contract period, persistently expect a large devaluation with some positive probability. But it rarely comes, and in both good and normal times there is no depreciation. When bad times strike, the parity "collapses," and the real exchange rate drops below equilibrium as inflation exceeds expected inflation. The subsidy is subject to upward pressure from the poor trading conditions.

The model has used undated variables and its structure is "intermediate term." Therefore it is best interpreted as applying over a "period" of three to five years. u can be thought of as the average of a series of random drawings within that period, each drawing taking place over a sub-period, the length of the wage contract.

5 Conclusion

What we have here is a stylized model, which nevertheless seems to capture some key elements of the ERM experience: a prevalence of overvaluation and of subsidies among countries pegging to the DM – in particular those for whom the probability of devaluation has remained significant (or, equivalently, have not "achieved credibility" or have not completely "tied their hands"). While clearly this model cannot offer a complete account of overvaluation and subsidies within the EEC, it would seem that this political open economy theory promises a useful contribution to such an account and could be the basis of proper empirical investigation.

Appendix: The derivation and solution of the open economy model

Derivation

The labor market equates labor supply with labor demand (which reacts to unanticipated inflation, following either Lucas's (1972) lagging information or Phelps and Taylor's (1977) framework)

$$L = l_s(w-p+I^{ue}) = -l_{dN}(w-p_{NT}+N) - l_{dT}(w-p_T-S) \tag{A1}$$

while the price level is given by

$$p = tp_T + (1-t)p_{NT} + G \tag{A2}$$

L=log of employment; w=log of nominal wages; l_s=labor supply elasticity; l_{dN} (l_{dT})=labor demand response of non-traded (traded) sector (percent of total labor force laid off in response to a 1 percent rise in real product wage). Hence $l_{dN}=\epsilon_N(1-t)$, $l_{dT}=\epsilon_T t$, where ϵ is a sector's labor demand elasticity. It is assumed, following Minford (1992), that $\epsilon_N>\epsilon_T$, that the traded sector is more capital intensive than the non-traded and consequently exhibits less flexibility of manning for a given capital stock (its marginal product declines more rapidly). We assume in (A1) that the marginal product of labor in the traded sector is independent of the traded sector shock, u.
It follows that

$$w-p = -(1-l_N-l_T)I^{ue} - l_N N + l_T S - (l_N+l_T)G + (t-v)e \tag{A3}$$

where $l_N = \epsilon_N(1-t)/\Sigma, l_T = \epsilon_T t/\Sigma$, $v = t(l_s+\epsilon_T)/\Sigma$,

$$\Sigma = l_s + \epsilon_N(1-t) + t\epsilon_T$$

so that $t-v=t(1-t)(\epsilon_N-\epsilon_T)>0$

Since output, $y/y^*=\sigma L+u/y^*$, we obtain

$$y=h_0e+(h_1+h_2)(I^{ue}-G)-h_1N+h_2S+y^*+u \qquad (A4)$$

where $h_0=\sigma y^*l_s t(1-t)(\epsilon_N-\epsilon_T)/\Sigma(>0)$, $h_1=\sigma y^*l_s\,\epsilon_N(1-t)/\Sigma$;

$h_2=\sigma y^*l_s\epsilon_T t/\Sigma$. (It follows that $h_0=th_1-(1-t)h_2$.)

Similarly, we find $y_T/y_T^*=-\sigma_T\epsilon_T t(w-p_T-S)+u/y_T^*$ as

$$y_T=-a_0e+a_1(I^{ue}-G)+a_2N+(a_1+a_2)S+y_T^*+u \qquad (A5)$$

where $a_0=\sigma_T y^*_T t(1-t)\epsilon_T(\epsilon_N+l_s)/\Sigma$; $a_1=\sigma_T y^*_T l_s t\epsilon_T/\Sigma$;

$a_2=\sigma_T y^*_T t(1-t)\epsilon_N\epsilon_N/\Sigma$. (Hence $a_0=a_1(1-t)+a_2$.)

Note that $\sigma_T<\sigma<1$ (because as output expands the marginal product of labor is declining in general and declining faster than average in the traded sector).

Solution

We can solve for e by noting that the model's equilibrium imposes $D_T=y_T$, so that

$$e=\{[a_1-t(h_1+h_2)][I^{ue}-G]+(a_2+th_1)N+(a_1+a_2-th_2)S$$

$$+(1-t)u\}/(th_0+a_0+b) \qquad (A6)$$

It follows, substituting for e, that

$$y=y^*+[th_0+a_0+b]^{-1}\{[h_1(a_1+a_2)+b(h_1+h_2)+a_2h_2](I^{ue}-G)$$

$$-[(1-t)(h_1\,(a_1+a_2)+a_2h_2)+h_1b](N)$$

$$+[th_1(a_1+a_2)+h_2(b+th_2)](S)$$

$$+[h_0(1-t+t^2)+t(a_0+b)](u)\} \qquad (A7)$$

Doing the same with y_T yields

$$y_T=y^*_T+(th_0+a_0+b)^{-1}\{[(a_1+a_2)th_1+a_2th_2+a_1b][I^{ue}-G]$$

$$-\{t(1-t)[h_1(a_1+a_2)+a_2h_2]-a_2b\}(N)$$

$$+[(a_1+a_2)(t^2h_1+b)+a_2t^2h_2](S)$$

$$+[t(h_0+a_0)+b](u)\}$$ (A8)

Possible tax-subsidy combinations

Suppose there is a negative I^{ue} (for reasons discussed in the text) and it is desired to counteract its effects on the traded sector by some given subsidy to it, S. There is an apparent choice of tax instruments, G (a general tax on both sectors) and N (a tax on the non-traded sector only). The government budget constraint in general is

$$tS=G+(1-t)N$$ (A9)

However, G is an equal tax on both sectors

$$G=tG+(1-t)G$$

So that we can rewrite (A9) as

$$t(S-G)=(1-t)(N+G)$$ (A10)

This states that net support to the traded sector, $S-G$, must be paid for by total tax on the non-traded sector, $N+G$. Since it is net support that determines the size of the traded sector (and other effects on the economy), it turns out that for a given desired expansion of the traded sector it makes no difference whether a subsidy is financed by N or G; if financed by G then S, the gross subsidy, must simply be bigger. For convenience we assume that S is financed by G (implying net support to the traded sector of $S-G=(1-t)S$, since $G=tS$).

Setting $G=tS$ we can simplify the solution of the model as follows

$$e=(th_0+a_0+b)^{-1}\{[a_1-t(h_1+h_2)]I^{ue}+(a_0+th_0)S+(1-t)u\}$$ (A11)

$$y=y^*+(th_0+a_0+b)^{-1}\{[h_1(a_1+a_2)+b(h_1+h_2)+a_2h_2]I^{ue}$$

$$-bh_0S+[h_0(1-t+t^2)+t(a_0+b)]u\}$$ (A12)

$$y_T=ty^*+(th_0+a_0+b)^{-1}\{[(a_1+a_2)th_1+a_2th_2+a_1b]I^{ue}$$

$$+ba_0S+[t(h_0+a_0)+b]u\}$$ (A13)

Note that $a_1-t[h_1+h_2]<0$ because it can be rewritten as $(-l_st/\Sigma)(\sigma y^*\epsilon -\sigma_Ty^*_T\epsilon_T)$, where $\epsilon=t\epsilon_T+(1-t)\epsilon_N$ is the elasticity of demand for labor overall; $\sigma>\sigma_T$, $\epsilon>\epsilon_T$ and $y^*>y^*_T$ by construction. All the reduced-form coefficients in the solution are therefore unambiguously signed.

The authorities' objective function

In general one would write the objective of the authorities as to protect the traded sector from injury so that $[ty^* - y_T]$ is zero or as small as possible, to reduce inflation as close to zero as possible and minimize distortions to the general economy.

From the viewpoint of social welfare, the effect of I^{ue} is self-correcting in the sense that it is the result of a private sector mistake. Sooner or later the private sector can find a way around it. Ultimately, if all else fails, it can write contracts contingent on u. By contrast, S is a government-created distortion which the private sector cannot eliminate; it is a constraint on private sector choice. Hence, strictly speaking, S is the only distortion created by government actions.

Of course I^{ue} has effects in the period we are considering, so that the private sector does not succeed in avoiding them. The government may well be concerned about these effects when $I^{ue} < O$ but it is of course already being forced by the traded sector's complaints to mitigate them by raising a subsidy. We assume that this action is adequate (if not excessive) to satisfy its more general concern about these effects.

We write the government's utility function therefore as

$$h = -0.5[(y^*_T - y_T)^2 + kS^2 + j[I - I^*]^2] \text{ for } y^*_T > y_T$$

and

$$-0.5(kS^2 + j[I - I^*]^2) \text{ for } y^*_T \leq y_T$$

(When the traded sector is uninjured, the government is assumed not to be under any pressure to help, or else to be able to resist it.)

The government's instruments are I and S; it is assumed to be able to set policy contingent on the value of u, the shock (or equivalently to remaximize whenever there is a new reading on u).

The ERM constraint

Nothing we have said up to now distinguishes this economy by exchange rate status; we could let I be determined by the money supply (exchange rate floating) or by exchange rate fixing (money supply endogenous). Let us now characterize the ERM as a regime that constrains inflation by limiting exchange rate movement within some set of margins except in bad times. We will implement this constraint by adding that under ERM $I \leq I^*$ ("no devaluation") except in bad times.

It should be noted that $I = I^*$ is not exactly the same as no exchange rate change, which only ensures that traded goods prices move by the change in their anchor currency value. In fact

$$I=(1-L)p=(1-t)(1-L)e+I_T+t(1-L)S$$

where L is the lag operator and $I_T=(1-L)p_T$, so that there is a complex dependence of I on the change in the state given any constraint on the exchange rate alone. Furthermore, the government does have two sorts of flexibility according to our interpretation of the ERM: it can move the exchange rate within the margins and it may, if absolutely necessary, revalue. The discipline is designed to hold inflation down by preventing devaluation except when $u=u_-$.

Let us first for simplicity assume that the economy starts out from $e=0=S$ (it enters the ERM from equilibrium). The government would then choose I^* and its ERM margins so that when u is not equal to u_- it can achieve $I=I^*$ by varying p_T (i.e., the exchange rate), that is

$$I_T=I^*-[(1-t)e+tS]$$

Using (A12) for e this yields

$$I_T=I^*-(th_0+a_0+b)^{-1}[(1-t)\{t(h_1+h_2)-a_1\}(I^e-I^*)$$

$$+\{(a_0+th_0)(1-t)+t\}S+(1-t)u]$$

The expression in square brackets (z) has all its terms positive. When $u=u_0=0$, $S>0$ and $u=0$; when $u=u_+$, $S=0$ and $u>0$. It depends in general on the parameters whether z is greater when $u=u_0$ (z_0) or for $u=u_+$ (z_+). But to minimize the margins that will just allow both to be accommodated, I^* will be set midway between z_0 and z_+, and the ERM margins set equal to $|I^*-z_{+\ or\ 0}|$.

Clearly, this calculation only works precisely for initial conditions of full equilibrium as assumed in the stylized treatment here. A realistic setting with repeated periods would require proper stochastic analysis of both shocks and initial conditions.

Note

This chapter is drawn from material first published in *Open Economies Review*, 5, 1994, 235–47, Permission of Kluwer Academic Publishers, Boston, to republish here is gratefully acknowledged.

I am grateful, for helpful suggestions, to Jürgen von Hagen and Michele Fratianni, and, for their comments, I thank other participants in a seminar at the University of Mannheim and in the 1993 Konstanz Seminar on Monetary Theory and Monetary Policy. This work was supported by the Esmee Fairbairn Foundation.

Postscript

Since this work was published in *Open Economies Review* I have benefited from further comments at this conference, for which I am grateful. Some discussion, especially by Alex Cukierman, Harald Uhlig and my discussant Jacques Sijben, focused on regime optimality: I have argued elsewhere ("Time-Inconsistency, Democracy, and Optimal Contingent Rules," *Oxford Economic Papers*, 1995, 47, 195–210) that the optimal regime – well known to be one where the domestic authorities have flexibility to respond to shocks and yet are precommitted to follow through on an inflation target otherwise – can be delivered by the electorate's monitoring of the government under floating exchange rates with domestic nominal targets. This could be efficiently specialized by the government delegating its monetary function to a central bank accountable to it and so to the electorate. The ERM regime set out in this chapter clearly does not have these optimal properties – nor could it be adapted to have them.

References

Giavazzi, Francesco and Pagano Marco, (1985), "The Advantage of Tying One's Hands: EMS Discipline and Central Bank Credibility," *European Economic Review*, 32, 1055–88.

von Hagen, Jürgen (1992), "Policy-Delegation and Fixed Exchange Rates," *International Economic Review*, 33, 849–70.

Lucas, R.E. Jr. (1972), "Expectations and the Neutrality of Money," *Journal of Economic Theory*, 4, 103–24.

Minford, Patrick (1992), *Rational Expectations Macroeconomics – An Introductory Handbook*, Oxford: Basil Blackwell.

Phelps, E.S. and Taylor, J.B. (1977), "The Stabilizing Powers of Monetary Policy under Rational Expectations," *Journal of Political Economy*, 85, 163–90.

Swan, T.W. (1963), "Longer-Run Problems of the Balance of Payments," in H.W. Arndt and W.M. Corden (eds.), *The Australian Economy: A Volume of Readings*, Melbourne: Cheshire Press, 384–95; Reprinted in R.E. Caves and H.G. Johnson (eds.), *Readings in International Economics*, Homewood, Ill: Irwin, 1968, 455–64.

Comment

JACQUES SIJBEN

Professor Minford's interesting and impressive theoretical chapter deals with the consequences of an anti-inflation commitment of the ERM-countries by tying their currencies to the Deutschmark as an anchor currency. In this way these countries are accepting the Deutschmark-external discipline with the associated credibility effects, preventing a time-inconsistent monetary policy behavior.

I agree with what Minford states in his chapter and I will just focus on some key issues, and try to elaborate a little more on some of these key points. He states that a prevailing overvaluation of the currency and the need for subsidies among countries pegging to the Deutschmark, are caused by the fact that those countries are faced with a lack of credibility or have not completely "tied their hands." This credibility is imperfect because there always exists the possibility that a country can change the exchange rate. Specifically, this may occur when the rate of inflation rises above the inflation in the anchor-country and the high-inflation country is not prepared to accept the negative real effects of the associated rise in the real exchange rate. According to the stylized model, this implies that the government is not willing to accept the resulting downward deviation of the actual rate of traded goods output from its natural level.

Therefore a devaluation possibility may be the reaction of policy makers in the high-inflation country to shift the needed internal adjustments with regard to income and fiscal policy to the sound, and lower-inflation countries.

Let us take France as an example. There was a long period when France frequently resorted to devaluation, because the authorities thought that it was a means of boosting growth, and business found it a convenient way to offset its lack of competitiveness. However, this discretionary exchange rate policy was not successful in the long run and the inflation rate in France was higher than that of its partners. All of the economic agents adjusted to devaluation and factored further depreciations of the currency and renewed inflation into their expectations. So in this way there exists a trade-off between surprise inflation and the associated negative real effects in the traded goods sector, on the one hand, and exchange rate stability, on the other hand. This implies that in an uncertain economic environment a risk of future devaluation, an exchange risk, arises at all times.

Minford presents subsidy protection as a strategy to generate the desired offsetting real effects for the domestic manufacturing sector. The subsidy rate is proportional to any reduction in traded output below its natural rate. He emphasizes the meaning of an asymmetry of policy makers in such a way that the pressure for a devaluation strategy will be intense during "bad times." Bad times are characterized as situations in which the natural rate of traded goods output is higher than the actual rate, and vice versa in good times.

This asymmetry of policy reaction creates a strictly positive expected devaluation at all times and then the reasoning goes as follows. The trade unions in their wage negotiations for the coming contract period count on a higher expected rate of inflation because of an expected large devaluation. This behavior generates a rise in the real exchange rate, reducing the competetiveness of the traded-goods sector, even in normal times. Policy makers are not prepared to accept the negative real effects for the traded goods sector and to offset this damage will award subsidies to the sector paid for by a general taxation. However this tax financed policy will not be beneficial for the total economy because of the resulting distortion to relative prices. So, in short, the expectation by trade unions of a devaluation will trigger a mechanism by which ultimately the total economy may be damaged.

In this stylized model, the expected rate of inflation is an average of inflation in bad times and in good times and is higher than the government's target for inflation. This target corresponds to no devaluation of the parity in normal and good times. In this way, the well-known "peso-problem" results. However, the expected rate of inflation is based on the crucial assumption of a symmetric distribution of good and bad times.

The objective function of the authorities aims at the protection of the traded goods sector from injury (thereby minimizing the difference between the actual and the natural rate in this sector), at reducing inflation, and at minimizing the distortion by the subsidy-cum-tax policy to the overall economy.

Now, a question comes to mind about how the policy makers can prevent the expectations of a devaluation and avoid the associated pressure for the tax-subsidy strategy. I hold the view that it is very important to gain or further strengthen policy credibility by rule-based and stability-oriented policies. This can be achieved by sticking to the "hard currency strategy" introduced within the EMS in 1983, that avoids compensating fully for past losses in competetiveness and takes a dynamic, future-oriented approach with emphasis on internal adjustment. At that time, Belgium had to accept a lower devaluation than it had initially sought and seemed justified by the commonly used indicators of external competitiveness. The devaluation also marked for Belgium the beginning of more decisive internal adjustment policies, initially in the area of prices and wages and later also in the budgetary field. Also, France adopted a stabilization program, making the commitment to stay in the EMS and to aim at a stable exchange rate credible by introducing a series of domestic adjustment measures. Pegging the franc to a strong currency helped reduce the costs of disinflation by curbing inflationary expectations and was also accompanied by credible economic policy commitments. After 1986, this policy helped reduce the real exchange rate of the franc *vis-à-vis* most of the other currencies in the system. This also gave rise to a lasting competitive advantage that helped change expectations concerning the French currency.

Since the mid-eighties, the EMS has gradually transformed itself into a commitment technology, a device that ensures the authorities' commitment to an announced plan, in this case a reduction of the inflation rate by the promise not to change the exchange rate. Anchoring exchange rates to the most stable currency in the system has in recent years provided many European countries with a new and enhanced basis of price stability, improving the prospects for economic growth in the medium term.

Gaining policy credibility and tying a policy maker's hands more completely are crucial issues in Minford's chapter. Eliminating the expectation of future devaluations can be achieved by a central bank, which has a clear mandate to maintain price stability and is largely independent of government instructions. However, to be successful and to avoid an overburdening of monetary policy, the exchange rate commitment also needs adequate support of credible fiscal and income policies. In my view, central bank autonomy offers no escape from the consequences of mismanagement of fiscal and income policies. In a repeated game, such a credible exchange rate policy may influence the distribution of bad times and good times in Minford's model, and thus the inflation distribution, so that the devaluation risk may be reduced, narrowing the difference between the expected rate of inflation and the government target of inflation (eliminating the "peso-problem").

Such a strong guideline can have benefits precisely because it restricts future discretionary exchange rate policies, and will give market participants a predictable framework, providing data for the wage and price policy of trade unions and firms. I think there are two lessons that can be learned from the EMS history. The first one is that a central bank's credibility is its most important asset and the second one is that this credibility can be maintained by sticking to a nominal anchor, i.e., a long-term nominal benchmark (a nominal quantity or a nominal price).

Finally, I will make the following remark. Exchange rate fluctuations, especially in the short run, have a rather weak link with movements in the relative price of domestic and foreign goods. According to the asset market approach, they originate primarily in financial markets, and as any other asset price are then determined by portfolio considerations. This implies that the maintenance of nominal parities is not so much challenged directly by the shocks affecting the real side of the economy, but by any market perception that policies or policy intentions will change. To my mind, what matters most are the market expectations of future policy actions. Policy makers should befriend the markets and enlist their help rather than make enemies of them. Policy is not an exercise in fooling markets. In the context of Minford's chapter, this means that the possibility of a future devaluation will be determined by whether markets perceive present and future policies to be compatible with a given constellation of exchange rates. Therefore policy stances of the different countries must not only be credible and time-consistent at the national level, but must also be perceived as mutually consistent by the players on the financial markets. This implies that a credible exchange rate system also needs a policy-coordination mechanism an institutional framework, to avoid competitive devaluations and reduce the chances of "bad times" in Minford's model. Otherwise, I think the exchange rate system is likely to function satisfactorily only for a short period of good times in the absence of asymmetric shocks and policy conflicts.

10 Unemployment benefits and redistributive taxation in the presence of labor quality externalities

1 Introduction

Unemployment benefit schemes have been explained by Bailey (1978) and Fleming (1978) as insurance against the risk of job loss. Boadway and Oswald (1983) and Wright (1986) have considered the political economy aspects of such insurance. Zeckhauser (1971) and Cooter and Helpman (1974), among others, alternatively rationalize transfer payments to the non-working poor as acts of altruism. This contribution offers a third rationale for unemployment benefits stemming from the fact that exits by relatively unproductive workers from the work force may in fact increase the productivity of remaining workers. This is the case if there are peer group effects in the work place in the sense that a worker's productivity depends on the quality of his co-workers as well as on his own quality. Henderson, Mieszkowski, and Sauvageau (1978) and Arnott and Rowse (1987) argue that such peer groups are important in the classroom setting, and they suggest that peer group effects may equally be important in the work place. Along similar lines, Sala-i-Martin (1992) introduces labor productivity externalities to explain mandatory retirement of older workers in a growth context.

Huizinga (1994) considers tax and transfer policy in a model of labor quality externalities for the case where the tax authorities have two fiscal instruments: (i) lump sum unemployment benefits, and (ii) proportional labor income taxes. This chapter extends Huizinga (1994) by introducing a third fiscal instrument: a lump sum tax (or transfer) to all workers regardless of their employment status. With this wider instrument set, the tax authorities can influence workers' employment status as well as their individual labor effort when employed. The chapter analyzes and contrasts the three variants of the model where only two of the three policy instruments are available. The sub-cases where only two instruments exist are analyzed for their own sake and to make the analysis comparable with earlier contributions on unemployment benefits and redistributive taxation. Finally, the case where all three policy instruments exist is also considered. Throughout, tax and transfer policy is examined from the perspective of a utilitarian social planner and of an electorate consisting of the universe of employed and unemployed workers.

If the policy set consists of universal lump sum transfers financed by proportional income taxation, then the model is very similar to Meltzer and Richards (1981). Lump sum transfers financed by labor income taxes will be favored by the median voter, if this voter has a lower than average labor income. Secondly, we consider the case where the instrument set consists of lump sum transfers to the unemployed financed by universal lump sum taxes. In this scenario, unemployment compensation generally benefits unemployed workers, who are direct beneficiaries, and the most qualified employed workers, who stand to gain the most on account of the peer group effect. As a result, a coalition of the unemployed and the highly qualified employed may support higher unemployment benefits than those preferred by the median quality worker.

As a third case, the instrument set consists of unemployment benefits financed by proportional labor income taxes. In this instance, the benefits and costs of higher unemployment benefits to employed workers are both shown to be proportional to individual labor quality (and income). As a result, all employed workers have equal preferences over different combinations of unemployment compensation and labor income taxes. The unemployed, of course, are simply interested in obtaining the maximum net-of-tax unemployment benefits. The unemployed as a group thus also have identical preferences over feasible pairs of unemployment compensation and labor income taxation. The employed and the unemployed thus will vote as separate blocs if tax and transfer policy is determined by elections. In this setting, equilibrium policy is determined by the median quality worker, after he has chosen whether he is better off as an employed worker or as an unemployed worker.

Finally, the policy set is assumed to consist of all three instruments: universal taxes or transfers, transfers to only the unemployed, and proportional income taxation. It is shown that there is a unique voting equilibrium, if the median quality worker can achieve highest utility as an unemployed individual. Unemployment benefits and labor income taxes are further demonstrated to be complementary in the sense that, starting from a political equilibrium where unemployment benefits exist, more people favor positive labor income taxation than in the absence of unemployment benefits.

The remainder of this chapter is organized as follows. Section 2 outlines the basic model. Section 3 considers the three cases where the policy instrument set consists of two of the three instruments examined in the chapter. Section 4 in contrast considers the case where all three instruments are at the authorities' disposal. Finally, section 5 concludes by drawing attention to the fact that the model is highly stylized. Several extensions are proposed that potentially affect the model's basic implications.

2 The model

There is a fixed population of workers that are heterogeneous in their quality. Worker quality, denoted a, can be in part innate and in part the result of education.[1] The variable a is distributed on the interval $[\underline{a}, \bar{a}]$ with density function $f(a)$ and distribution function $F(a)$. The size of the population is unity so that $F(\bar{a})=1$. The population mean value of a is denoted $\bar{\mu}$. Workers can choose to be employed or to be unemployed. Let S be the share of the population that is employed, which implies that $1-S$ is the unemployment rate. The mean quality of employed workers is denoted μ. All workers have one unit of time available. Individuals who are employed have to decide how much to work and how much leisure to consume. Let individual labor supply be denoted x so that leisure equals $1-x$. On account of peer group effects, the productivity of any worker depends positively on the mean quality of all employed workers, μ. Peer group effects may exist because workers can learn from and copy relatively highly qualified workers, or they may be purely psychological. Individual output, denoted y, is related to individual worker quality, a, the mean worker quality, μ, as well as to individual labor supply, x. Formally, individual output, y, is given as follows

$$y=xa\mu^{\alpha} \qquad \alpha>0 \tag{1}$$

Aggregate output, Y, is the sum of the output of all workers as follows

$$Y=\int_{\hat{a}}^{\bar{a}} xa\mu^{\alpha}f(a)da$$
$$=x\mu^{1+\alpha}S \tag{2}$$

where $\hat{a}$ is the borderline quality of a worker, if any, who is indifferent between working and not working.

Equation (2) displays what can be called increasing returns to average quality, as national output, Y, increases more than linearly with mean worker quality, μ, while there are only constant returns to scale, S.[2]

Individuals derive utility from consumption and from leisure. Let C be the level of consumption, and let $aV(1-x)$ be the subutility derived from leisure, with $V'>0$, $V''<0$. This specification reflects the assumption that a worker's enjoyment of leisure increases with his quality, a. The overall utility measure, denoted U, is assumed to be separable in consumption and leisure as follows

$$U=C+aV(1-x) \tag{3}$$

Let us now consider the policy instruments at the disposal of the fiscal authorities. As is usual, the government cannot observe or tax worker quality directly. A worker's employment status, however, is observable, and thus the government can implement a lump sum transfer, b, to only unemployed workers. Also, the government can tax labor income at a flat rate τ. For purposes of taxation, unemployment benefits are considered labor income. To balance the budget, the government finally provides a lump sum transfer, t, to all citizens regardless of their employment status. If negative, t represents a lump sum tax.

Employed workers have to decide how much they will work. The optimality condition regarding individual labor supply, x, if positive is as follows

$$V'(1-x)=(1-\tau)\mu^\alpha \tag{4}$$

Equation (4) reflects that individual labor supply, x, is independent of worker quality, a. A worker obtains utilities, U_e and U_u, if employed and unemployed, respectively. These two utility levels are given as follows

$$U_e=(1-\tau)y+aV(1-x)+t \tag{5}$$

$$U_u=(1-\tau)b+aV(1)+t \tag{6}$$

where in (5) individual labor supply x is chosen optimally.

Equations (5) and (6) reflect that employed and unemployed workers receive net labor incomes equal to $(1-\tau)y$ and $(1-\tau)b$, respectively.

An individual worker of quality a chooses to work if U_e in (5) exceeds U_u in (6), and vice versa. Setting $U_e=U_u$ from (5) and (6) implies that this borderline quality level, $\hat{a}$, is given implicitly as follows

$$(1-\tau)b+\hat{a}V(1)=(1-\tau)x\hat{a}\mu^\alpha+V(1-x) \tag{7}$$

All workers of quality higher (lower) than $\hat{a}$ clearly choose (not) to work. The labor participation rate, S, is now given by $1-F(\hat{a})$, while the unemployment rate equals $F(\hat{a})$.

From equations (6) and (7), we can derive how the unemployment benefit level, b, and the income tax rate, τ, affect individual labor supply, x, and the threshold worker quality level, $\hat{a}$, given that some workers are unemployed.

Qualitatively, the relationships between the fiscal variables, b and τ, and the labor market variables, $\hat{a}$ and x, are as follows

$$\frac{d\hat{a}}{db}>0, \quad \frac{dx}{db}>0, \quad \frac{d\hat{a}}{d\tau}>0, \quad \frac{dx}{d\tau}<0, \tag{8}$$

Exact expressions for the derivatives in (8) are provided in the appendix. Equation (8) first indicates that a higher benefit, b, increases the threshold quality level, $\hat{a}$, as a higher value of b induces the lowest qualified employed workers to exit from the work force. The resulting increase in the mean quality of remaining workers, μ, increases the productivity of remaining workers and, as seen in (8), their labor supply, x. Turning to the income tax rate, we see in (8) that a higher tax rate, τ, also increases the threshold quality level, $\hat{a}$. To understand this, note that employed workers receive relatively much labor income, and enjoy relatively little leisure. The labor income tax, τ, thus is borne relatively heavily by employed workers, and as a result it discourages the labor participation of marginal workers. Finally, we see in (8) that a higher labor income tax rate, τ, reduces individual labor supply, x.

It is interesting to consider how the unemployment benefit, b, and the tax rate, τ, affect aggregate output, Y. From (2), we can find that

$$\frac{dY}{db}=\mu^{1+\alpha}\,S\frac{dx}{db}+x\mu^{\alpha}[\alpha\mu-(1+\alpha)\hat{a}]\,f(\hat{a})\frac{d\hat{a}}{db} \tag{9}$$

$$\frac{dY}{d\tau}=\mu^{1+\alpha}\,S\frac{dx}{d\tau}+x\mu^{\alpha}[\alpha\mu-(1+\alpha)\hat{a}]\,f(\hat{a})\frac{d\hat{a}}{d\tau} \tag{10}$$

Using the qualitative expressions in (8), we see that higher unemployment benefits, b, unambiguously lead to higher aggregate output, Y, if $\hat{a}<\alpha\mu/(1+\alpha)$. This condition is more easily satisfied, the larger is the parameter α that reflects the strength of the relationship between individual output, y, and mean worker quality, μ, in (1). Equation (10) indicates that a higher labor income tax rate, τ, can also lead to a higher aggregate output, Y. In the limiting case where labor supply, x, is completely inelastic, for instance, we see that $\hat{a}<\alpha\mu/(1+\alpha)$ is a necessary and a sufficient condition for a higher income tax, τ, to lead to higher aggregate output, Y. These results are summarized as follows:

Proposition 1: A sufficient condition for $dY/db>0$ is $\hat{a}<\alpha\mu/(1+\alpha)$. The latter condition is a necessary and sufficient condition for $dY/d\tau>0$, if individual labor supply, x, is inelastic.

Next, let us consider the government budget. Let B be the government budget surplus. Formally, B is given as follows

$$B = \tau Y - (1-\tau)b(1-S) - t \qquad (11)$$

It is interesting to consider tax and redistributive policy, as determined by a social planner, as a benchmark. The social planner is assumed to have a utilitarian social welfare function, U_s, which is the sum of individual workers' utilities. Formally, social welfare, denoted U_s, is given as follows

$$U_s = \int_{\underline{a}}^{\hat{a}} U_u f(a)da + \int_{\hat{a}}^{\bar{a}} U_e f(a)da \qquad (12)$$

Alternatively, we will assume that fiscal policy is determined by popular vote. In a voting equilibrium, policy reflects the preferences of a decisive voter who, as we will see, may not be the worker of median quality. In all cases, however, the decisive voter is either employed or unemployed. A decisive voter thus wishes to maximize either U_e in (5) or U_u in (6). Whatever policy instruments are availabe, any equilibrium policy is thus always set so as to maximize U_s, U_e, or U_u, subject to the government budget constraint that $B \geq 0$. To facilitate the later analysis, the remainder of this section states the optimality conditions for a social planner, an employed worker, and an unemployed worker who maximize U_s, U_e, and U_u, respectively, subject to $B \geq 0$. Sections 3 and 4 then deduce the implications of these optimality conditions for equilibrium tax and transfer policy in various variants of the general model.

The social planner is interested in maximizing the Lagrangian expression $L_s = U_s + \lambda B$, where λ is the Lagrange multiplier associated with the government budget constraint. Note that if $\underline{a} > 0$, then unemployment benefits, b, also have to be positive to induce any individuals to leave the labor force. Let $\underline{b}$ be the unemployment benefit level such that workers of quality $\underline{a}$ are indifferent between working and not working. For any workers to exit from the labor force, we need $b \geq \underline{b}$. The optimality conditions of a social planner's maximization problem with respect to τ, b, and t are now as follows

$$\frac{dL_s}{d\tau} = -Y - b(1-S) + \alpha(1-\tau)Y\frac{\mu-\hat{a}}{\mu S}f(\hat{a})\frac{d\hat{a}}{d\tau} + \lambda\frac{dB}{d\tau} = 0 \wedge \tau \geq 0 \text{ or } \tau = 0 \qquad (13)$$

$$\frac{dL_s}{db} = (1-\tau)(1-S) + \alpha(1-\tau)Y\frac{\mu-\hat{a}}{\mu S}f(\hat{a})\frac{d\hat{a}}{db} + \lambda\frac{dB}{db} = 0 \wedge b \geq \underline{b} \text{ or } b < \underline{b} \qquad (13')$$

$$\frac{dL_s}{dt} = 1 - \lambda = 0 \qquad (13'')$$

where

$$\frac{dB}{d\tau}=Y+b(1-S)-(1-\tau)bf(\hat{a})\frac{d\hat{a}}{d\tau}+\tau\frac{dY}{d\tau}$$

$$\frac{dB}{db}=-(1-\tau)(1-S)-(1-\tau)bf(\hat{a})\frac{d\hat{a}}{db}+\tau\frac{dY}{db}$$

$$\underline{b}=\underline{a}[x\bar{\mu}^\alpha+\frac{V(1-x)-V(1)}{1-\tau}]\geq 0$$

and where use is made of the fact that $dB/dt=-1$.

An employed worker instead is interested in maximizing the Lagrangian expression $L_e=U_e+\lambda B$. The optimality conditions associated with this maximization problem with respect to τ, b, and t are as follows

$$\frac{dL_e}{d\tau}=-y+\alpha(1-\tau)y\frac{\mu-\hat{a}}{\mu S}f(\hat{a})\frac{d\hat{a}}{d\tau}+\lambda\frac{dB}{d\tau}=0\wedge\tau\geq 0 \tag{14}$$

or $\tau=0$

$$\frac{dL_e}{db}=\alpha(1-\tau)y\frac{\mu-\hat{a}}{\mu S}f(\hat{a})\frac{d\hat{a}}{db}+\lambda\frac{dB}{db}=0\wedge b\geq\underline{b}\text{ or }b<\underline{b} \tag{14'}$$

$$\frac{dL_e}{dt}=1-\lambda=0 \tag{14''}$$

Finally, an unemployed individual is interested in maximizing the Lagrangian expression $L_u=U_u+\lambda B$. The resulting optimality conditions with respect to τ, b, and t are as follows

$$\frac{dL_u}{d\tau}=-b+\lambda\frac{dB}{d\tau}=0\wedge\tau\geq 0\text{ or }\tau=0 \tag{15}$$

$$\frac{dL_u}{db}=(1-\tau)+\lambda\frac{dB}{db}=0\wedge b\geq\underline{b}\text{ or }b<\underline{b} \tag{15'}$$

$$\frac{dL_u}{dt}=1-\lambda=0 \tag{15''}$$

In the remainder of this chapter, we examine the implications for the setting of tax and redistributive policy of the sets of optimality conditions (13), (14), and (15).

3 The determination of policy with a limited set of policy instruments

This section considers the three cases where the policy instrument set consists of only two instruments in turn. The three cases are considered in three sub-sections.

3.1 Only income taxation and lump sum transfers available

In this sub-section, we consider that the proportional income tax at a rate τ and lump sum transfers, t, are the only policy instruments in existence. In the absence of unemployment benefits, all workers are employed. First, we can consider that the policy instruments, τ and t, are set by a social planner, as guided by optimality conditions (13) and (13″). From (13″), we see that $dL_s/dt=0$ implies $\lambda=1$. Noting $\lambda=1$, we see from (13) that optimally $\tau=0$.[3] This implies that a social planner optimally will not use income taxation to redistribute income. This is because income taxes only distort the labor supply decision without any offsetting benefits in terms of higher social welfare.[4] Next, let us consider what is the optimal policy from the perspective of an employed agent. For an employed person of quality a, the optimality conditions are (14) and (14″). Again (14″) implies that $\lambda=1$. Noting this, we can solve from the optimal income tax rate, $\tau^*(a)$, for an agent of quality a from (14a) as follows

$$\tau^*(a)=\frac{\bar{\mu}-a}{\bar{\mu}} \cdot \frac{1}{\epsilon_\ell} \text{ if } a \leq \bar{\mu} \tag{16}$$

where $\epsilon_\ell = -\dfrac{dx}{d\tau} \cdot \dfrac{1}{x} > 0$

If second-order conditions hold, there is a unique value of τ as in (16) that maximizes individual welfare and each agent's preferences over values of τ are single-peaked. From (16), we can infer that the optimal value of τ from an individual worker's perspective declines with his quality, a. In this instance, the median voter is the worker of median quality, denoted a_m. This result can be stated as follows:

Proposition 2: If lump sum transfers, t, are financed by income taxation at a rate, τ, then the voting equilibrium reflects the preferences of the median voter who is the median quality worker. This voter favors positive values of the income tax, τ, and the transfer, t, if his quality, a_m, is less than the mean quality, $\bar{\mu}$.

3.2 Only unemployment benefits and lump sum taxes available

In this sub-section, we consider the case where unemployment benefits, b, and lump sum transfers, t, are the available policy instruments. To start, we will consider the welfare implications of unemployment benefits just high enough to induce the lowest quality workers to exit from the labor force. Again, we will consider such unemployment benefits from the perspectives of a social planner, an employed individual, and an unemployed individual. For the social planner, the relevant first-order conditions are (13′) and (13″). The social planner favors the introduction of unemployment benefits if $dL_u/db > 0$ with $b = \underline{b}$ in (13a), where $\lambda = 1$ from (13″). This is the case if

$$\alpha Y \frac{\bar{\mu} - \underline{a}}{\bar{\mu}} > 0 \tag{17}$$

According to (17), the social planner favors unemployment benefits, if the social productivity externality resulting from the exit of a worker of quality $\underline{a}$ exceeds the unemployment benefit $\underline{b}$. It can be shown that (17) is satisfied if $\bar{\mu}/\underline{a} > (1 + \alpha)/\alpha$.[5] Next, we consider the determination of unemployment benefits from the perspective of an employed individual, guided by first-order conditions (14′) and (14″). An employed person of quality a is in favor of non-trivial unemployment benefits with $b > \underline{b}$ if

$$\alpha y \frac{\bar{\mu} - \underline{a}}{\bar{\mu}} > \underline{b} \tag{18}$$

A worker of quality a favors the introduction of unemployment benefits, if the effect on his own productivity (as indicated by the left-hand side of (18)) exceeds the unemployment benefit level, $\underline{b}$. As individual output, y, is proportional to labor quality, a, it follows from (18) that workers of a quality higher than a certain minimum level (if any) will support non-trivial unemployment benefits. Equation (18) implies, however, that the introduction of unemployment benefits financed by a lump sum tax may harm the lowest qualified employed workers.[6] The interests of poorly and highly qualified employed workers thus generally diverge, if unemployment benefits, b, are financed by a lump sum tax, t.

Finally, we can consider whether the introduction of non-trivial employment benefits actually helps the people rendered unemployed. To check this, note that an unemployed person's relevant optimality conditions are (15′) and (15″). The lowest qualified individuals, of quality $\underline{a}$, benefit from the introduction of non-trivial unemployment benefits if

$$1 - \underline{b}f(\underline{a})\frac{d\hat{a}}{db} > 0 \tag{19}$$

Equation (19) essentially indicates that the lowest quality unemployed benefit from higher unemployment benefits if the increase in the unemployment benefits outbalances the increase in the lump sum tax necessary to finance the higher unemployment benefits. A sufficient condition for (19) to be satisfied is $(\underline{a})\underline{a} < 1$.[7] The above results on the desirability of unemployment benefits are summarized as follows

Proposition 3: The introduction of low unemployment benefits, financed by lump sum taxation on all: (i) may or may not benefit those rendered unemployed and poorly qualifed employed workers, and (ii) it benefits employed workers of quality higher than a certain threshold level (if any).

Next, we consider in turn the optimal level of unemployment benefits from the perspectives of a social planner, an employed worker, and an unemployed worker. Starting with the social planner, we can solve from equation (13′) and (13″) for the socially optimal unemployment benefit level financed by lump sum taxation, $b^*_{t,s}$, as follows

$$b^*_{t,s} = \alpha Y \frac{\mu - \hat{a}}{\mu S} \tag{20}$$

Similarly, the optimal unemployment benefit from the perspective of an employed worker of quality a, $b^*_{t,e}(a)$, can be found from (14′) and (14″) as follows

$$b^*_{t,e}(a) = \alpha y \frac{\mu - \hat{a}}{\mu S} - \frac{1}{\epsilon_u} \tag{21}$$

where $\epsilon_u = \dfrac{d(1-S)}{db} \dfrac{1}{1-S} = \dfrac{d\hat{a}}{db} \dfrac{f(\hat{a})}{F(\hat{a})} > 0$.

The first term on the right of (21) is similar to expression (20). Expression (21), however, reflects that each worker is interested in how unemployment benefits affect his own output, y, rather than aggregate output, Y. Also expression (21) has a negative final term which reflects that an employed person, unlike the social planner, does not value increases in the benefit income of the unemployed per se.

Finally, we can solve for the optimal unemployment benefit from the perspective of all unemployed workers, $b^*_{t,u}$, from equations (15′) and (15″) as follows

$$b^*_{t,u} = \frac{S}{1-S} \cdot \frac{1}{\epsilon_u} \tag{22}$$

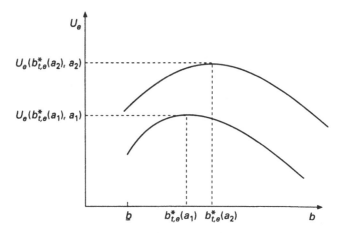

Figure 10.1 An employed worker's preference over benefits financed by lump sum taxes

The optimal unemployment benefit increases with the employed share of the population, S, that can help finance the unemployment benefits without being at the same time beneficiaries.

Before we consider voting on unemployment benefits, we have to examine agents' preferences over values of the unemployment benefits, as either employed or unemployed workers. To this end, let $U_e(b_t,a)$ be the welfare reached by agents of quality a as employed workers given that unemployment benefits, b, are financed by a lump sum tax, t. The utility index, $U_e(b_t,a)$, presupposes that the agent of quality a chooses individual labor supply optimally, while all other agents choose their employment status and labor supply optimally. We see immediately from (5) that $dU_e(b_t,a)/da>0$. At the same time, we know from (21) that the optimal value of b, $b^*_{t,e}(a)$ increases with a, provided $b^*_{t,e}(a)$ exceeds $\underline{b}$. The index $U_e(b_t,a)$ is presented in figure 10.1 for two worker quality levels a_1 and a_2, with $a_2>a_1$. The figure reflects the assumption that an agent's preferences as an employed worker over different levels of unemployment benefits, b, are single-peaked.

Next, we can define $U_u(b_t,a)$ to be the welfare obtained by agents of quality a as unemployed workers given that benefits, b, are financed by a lump sum tax, t. Again all other workers are assumed to have chosen their employment status and their individual labor supply, x, optimally. Using (6), we see that $dU_u(b_t,a)/da=V(1)$, which is independent of quality a. This confirms the result from (22) that the optimal unemployment benefit, $b^*_{t,u}$, from an unemployed worker's perspective, is independent of the transfer b. Figure 10.2 represents the index $U_u(b_t,a)$ for two worker quality levels a_1

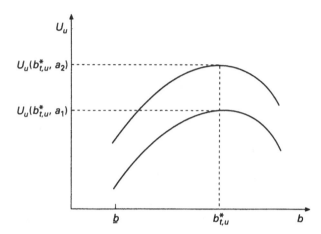

Figure 10.2 An unemployed worker's preferences over benefits financed by lump sum taxes

and a_2, with $a_2>a_1$. We assume that an agent's preferences as an unemployed worker over different levels of unemployment benefits, b, are single-peaked.

A worker of quality a chooses to be employed if $U_e(b_t,a)>U_u(b_t,a)$ and vice versa. In fact, for any benefit level, b, there is a borderline quality level $\hat{a}$, above (below) which agents choose to be (un)employed according to (7). Note that a worker's ability to change his employment status implies that preferences over different levels of employment benefits, b, are generally double peaked, even if preferences as either an employed or an unemployed worker are single peaked. In fact, an agent's preferences are double peaked, if (i) $b^*_{t,e}(a)<b^*_{t,u}$, and (ii) the worker decides to become unemployed at a benefit level below $b^*_{t,u}$.[8]

In this case of generally double-peaked preferences, there may still be a unique voting outcome. To see whether this is the case, we proceed as follows. We first consider what would be the outcome preferred by the median quality voter. Then we consider whether this solution can be beaten by a direct comparison with another outcome, and if so how. We now have to consider three cases: (i) $U_e(b^*_{t,e}(a_m),a_m)>U_u(b^*_{t,u},a_m)$ and $b^*_{t,e}(a_m)\geq b^*_{t,u}$, (ii) $U_e(b^*_{t,e}(a_m),a_m)>U_u(b^*_{t,u},a_m)$ and $b^*_{t,e}(a_m)<b^*_{t,u}$, and (iii) $U_e(b^*_{t,e}(a_m),a_m)\leq U_u(b^*_{t,u},a_m)$. In case (i), the median quality worker prefers to be employed at a benefit level exceeding b^*_u. Now all (employed) workers with $a>a_m$ wish to have higher benefits, while all workers with $a<a_m$, whether employed or unemployed, wish to have lower benefits. In this instance, the median quality worker's wishes are implemented. Case (ii) is somewhat more complicated. Now workers with $a>a_m$, who are employed, as before, wish to increase the benefit level beyond $b_{t,e}^*(a_m)$. This is also the case for unemployed workers, as $b_{t,e}^*(a_m)<b_{t,u}^*$. It follows that more than half the electorate is in favor of a small increase in b beyond $b_{t,e}^*(a_m)$. Thus the outcome preferred by the median quality worker cannot be a voting equilibrium. A complicating matter to determine possible voting outcomes in this case is that the coalition in favor of marginal increases in b may either decline or increase as b increases beyond $b_{t,e}^*(a_m)$, as the previously employed join the ranks of the unemployed who are in favor of higher values of b. As a result the existence of multiple voting equilibria cannot be excluded. Any equilibrium, however, will be larger than $b_{t,e}^*(a_m)$ and less than or equal to $b_{t,u}^*$. Finally, in case (iii) the median quality worker attains highest welfare at a benefit level $b_{t,u}^*$. This will be strictly the case for all agents with $a<a_m$. In this case, the benefit level $b_{t,u}^*$ is the unique voting outcome.

The most interesting result is, perhaps, that in case (ii) the median quality worker can be outvoted by a coalition of highly qualified employed workers and unemployed workers in order to increase the benefit level. This result is summarized as follows:

Proposition 4: If the median quality worker reaches highest utility as an employed person for a benefit level below $b_{t,u}^*$, then a coalition of the unemployed and of highly qualified employed workers will be able to implement a benefit level higher than the one preferred by the median quality worker.

This result indicates a potential conflict of interest between the poorly qualified employed and the highly qualified employed over the desired level of benefits. Underlying this conflict is the fact that higher benefits, in terms of higher individual productivity, accrue in proportion to an employed person's quality, while the tax burden, in the form of a lump sum tax, is equal for all employed workers. In the next sub-section, we instead consider unemployment benefits that are financed through a proportional tax on labor income. Labor income for employed workers, in turn, is proportional to labor quality. In this case, the benefits and costs of higher unemployment benefits for all employed workers are proportional to labor quality. As a result, there no longer is a potential conflict of interest among employed workers.

3.3 Only unemployment benefits and income taxes available

In this sub-section, unemployment benefits, b, are financed only by a proportional tax, τ, on labor income. The discussion in this sub-section closely follows Huizinga (1994). Let $U_e(b_\tau,a)$ now be the welfare of an individual of quality a as an employed worker if benefits, b, are financed by a labor income tax, τ. As before, we assume that all agents of quality other than a have chosen their employment status and their individual labor supply, x, optimally. It is immediate that $U_e(b_\tau,a)$ is proportional to labor quality a, which implies that $U_e(b_\tau,a)$ reaches a maximum for a value of b that is independent of a. Analogously, let $U_e(b_\tau,a)$ be the utility of an agent of quality a as an unemployed worker. Using the expression for U_u in (6), we see that $U_u(b_\tau,a)$ also reaches a maximum for value of b and τ that are independent of a. Let $b^*_{\tau,u}$ ($b^*_{\tau,e}$) now be the value of b and τ^*_u (τ^*_e) the tax rate that maximizes $U_u(b_\tau,a)$ ($U_e(b_\tau,a)$) for all workers. We can obtain the following result:[9]

Proposition 5: All agents prefer a higher benefit and tax rate as an unemployed worker than as an employed worker, i.e., $b^*_{\tau,u} > b^*_{\tau,e}$ and $\tau^*_u > \tau^*_e$.

Again, the welfare indices $U_e(b_\tau,a)$ and $U_u(b_\tau,a)$ are assumed to be single peaked in b. Agents can change their employment status, however, and, therefore, overall preferences over values of b generally are double peaked. Individual preferences, specifically, are double peaked for those agents that change their employment status for a value of b between $b^*_{\tau,e}$ and $b^*_{\tau,u}$.

In this model, the voting outcome will always reflect the preferences of the median voter. To see this, let us assume that the median quality worker prefers to be unemployed at a benefit level $b^*_{\tau,e}$. It is straightforward that all workers with $a < a_m$ also prefer to be unemployed at the same benefit level. Alternatively, the median quality worker can prefer to work at a benefit level $b^*_{\tau,e}$. In this instance, all workers with $a > a_m$ also prefer to work at the same benefit level. These results are summarized as follows:

Proposition 6: If the unemployment income, b, is financed by a proportional income tax, τ, then if the median quality worker prefers to be (un)employed at a benefit level $b^*_{\tau,e}$ ($b^*_{\tau,u}$) so will all workers of higher (lower) quality. As a result, the voting outcome reflects the preferences of the median quality worker.

Interestingly, the median voter can be indifferent between working and not working if $U_u(b^*_{\tau,u},a) = U_e(b^*_{\tau,e},a)$. In this instance, the outcome of the vote is not unique. More specifically, $b^*_{\tau,e}$ and $b^*_{\tau,u}$ are possible voting outcomes regarding the unemployment benefit level. While the median quality worker may be indifferent between the two possible voting outcomes, this is not the case for other workers. Workers of higher (lower) quality than the median quality worker, in particular, prefer the lower (higher) level of unemployment benefits. Note that the indifference between the two voting outcomes on the part of the median quality worker is fragile in the sense that a small change in the composition of the population can change the indifference by the median quality worker between the two outcomes. Small changes in the population, for instance resulting from migration, thus can bring about a large change in the unemployment benefit system with discrete changes in welfare for all but the median ability worker.[10]

4 All three instruments available

In this section, all three fiscal instruments, b, τ, and t, are available. As in section 3.1, the social planner will never use the income tax instrument, τ. Employed and unemployed persons, however, generally wish to employ all three instruments, if decisions are left to the individual. This section addresses two issues. First, starting from a voting equilibrium where only unemployment benefits, b, and lump sum taxes, t, exist, we address whether voters will favor the introduction of proportional income taxes. Second, we consider the issue of the voting equilibrium where all three fiscal instruments are available. At least in specific cases, we can say what the voting equilibrium entails.

Starting with the first issue, let us assume that there exists a voting equilibrium in the unemployment benefit level, b, and the lump sum tax, t. Which voters will be in favor of a positive level of the income tax rate, τ? Proposition 2 states that in the absence of unemployment benefits all voters of lower than the mean quality favor positive income taxes. Here we show that a broader segment of the population favors such an introduction if unemployment benefits are already in place. Specifically, we can state the following results:

Proposition 7 (i): If b and t are chosen optimally from the perspective of an unemployed worker, such that b, $t>0$, then this unemployed person favors a positive income tax rate, τ. (ii): Let b and t instead be chosen optimally from the perspective of an employed person of quality a such that b, $t>0$. This employed person can then benefit from a positive income tax level, if $a<(1-S)\hat{a}+S\mu$. The median quality worker, of quality a_m, specifically benefits from such an introduction if $a_m<(1-S)\hat{a}+S\mu$.

Comparing propositions 2 and 7, we see that the median voter is in favor of introducing positive labor income taxes under broader conditions if b, $\tau>0$ than if $b=\tau=0$, as $(1-S)\hat{a}+S\mu>\bar{\mu}$. In this sense, unemployment benefits and proportional income taxation are shown to be complementary.

To conclude this section, we consider how preferences of employed and unemployed workers over policy choices generally diverge, and the implication for voting in the case where all three instruments are available. We can state the following results:

Proposition 8 (i): If the three instruments are set so as to maximize the welfare of any unemployed agent, then all employed workers wish to implement lower values of b and of τ. **(ii):** If the three instruments are instead set so as to maximize the welfare of an employed agent of quality a', then (first) all employed agents of quality $a>a'$ wish to increase b and to reduce τ, and (second) all employed agents of quality $a<a'$ wish to reduce b and to increase τ, and (third) all unemployed agents wish to increase b and τ.

Regarding the voting equilibrium with all three instruments, the following can be said. If the median quality worker obtains highest welfare by being unemployed, then this is also the case for all workers of lower quality. In this instance, the median quality worker is the median voter and there is a unique voting equilibrium. Alternatively, the median quality worker can obtain highest welfare as an employed worker. As in section 3.2, there now is generally a majority coalition of unemployed and of highly qualified employed workers that wishes to increase the value of the benefit, b, for a given value of τ. The policy configuration preferred by the median quality worker thus cannot be a voting equilibrium. Voting for this case is not further pursued here.

5 Conclusion

This chapter starts from the premise that a worker's productivity depends on his own quality as well as on the quality of other employed workers. As a result, the model displays what can be called increasing returns to average quality: the output of a group of workers increases more than linearly with the average worker quality. A main feature of the model is that a system of unemployment benefits to low quality workers so as to remove them from the labor market can increase total output. In this setting, unemployment compensation has the dual role of bringing about efficient exits from the labor market and of redistributing income. The political process takes both aspects of the transfer system into account. The chapter considers policy as determined by a social planner and by majority voting.[11] A main result of the chapter is that it may be in the interest of employed workers to support unemployment benefits. This result is consistent with the reality that many countries have unemployment schemes, while the majority of voting age individuals do not receive unemployment benefits.

While the present model potentially rationalizes unemployment compensation, it cannot be taken to imply that any large-scale unemployment is in fact socially desirable. This reflects that the model is highly stylized in at least two respects: (i) the model is entirely static and (ii) workers can only be employed in a sector characterized by labor market external-ities or be unemployed. This negates that in practice workers may tem-porarily engage in training before entering or reentering the work place.

At the same time, real economies consist of many sectors that are characterized by labor quality externalities to different extents. To reflect this, the model could include an additional sector without any labor quality externalities at all. In this second sector, a worker's product could simply equal his own individual quality, or it could be a constant for all employed workers. In the second instance, employment in this second sector is immediately analogous to unemployment in the present model. In this amended model, there remains scope for tax policy to affect the allocation of workers between the two sectors, even if all workers are employed. More generally, there is scope for tax and transfer policy to affect employment in all the economy's sectors as well as unemployment.

Appendix

The derivatives in equation (8) are as follows

$$\frac{d\hat{a}}{db}=\frac{1}{\beta}>0 \tag{A1}$$

$$\frac{dx}{db}=-\frac{(1-\tau)\alpha\mu^\alpha\dfrac{\mu-\hat{a}}{\mu S}f(\hat{a})}{V''(1-x)\beta}>0 \tag{A2}$$

$$\frac{d\hat{a}}{d\tau}=\frac{\hat{a}(V(1)-V(1-x))}{(1-\tau)^2\beta}>0 \tag{A3}$$

$$\frac{dx}{d\tau}=\frac{\left[V'(1-x)-\dfrac{V(1)-V(1-x)}{x}\right]\beta+\left[\dfrac{V(1)-V(1-x)}{x}\right]\dfrac{b}{\hat{a}}}{V''(1-x)(1-\tau)\beta}<0 \tag{A4}$$

where

$$\beta=\frac{b}{\hat{a}}+x\hat{a}\alpha\mu^\alpha\frac{\mu-\hat{a}}{\mu S}f(\hat{a})>0$$

Proof of proposition 7

Part (i)

We wish to show that all unemployed workers can benefit from a positive value of τ. This is the case if $dL_u/d\tau>0$ in (15) for $\tau=0$ given that $dL_u/db=0$ in (15'). Thus we need to show that

$$-b+Y+b(1-S)-S\frac{d\hat{a}/d\tau}{d\hat{a}/db}>0$$

where $\dfrac{S}{d\hat{a}/db}$ has been substituted for $bf(\hat{a})$ from (15′) into (15). After substituting for $d\hat{a}/d\tau$ and $d\hat{a}/db$ from (A3) and (A1), we get

$$-b+Y+b(1-S)+S\hat{a}(V(1-x)-V(1))>0$$

$$Y-S[b-\hat{a}(V(1-x)-V(1))]>0 \qquad \text{(using (7))}$$

$$Y-S[x\hat{a}\mu^{\alpha}]>0 \qquad \text{(using (2))}$$

$$Sx\mu^{\alpha}(\mu-\hat{a})>0.$$

Part (ii)

We wish to show that agents of quality a lower than $(1-S)\hat{a}+S\mu$ can benefit from a positive value of τ, if b is set so as to maximize the welfare of an employed worker. Thus, we need to show that $dL_e/d\tau>0$ for $\tau=0$ in (14) given that dL_e/db and $\lambda=1$ in (14′).

This is the case if

$$-y+Y+b(1-S)+(1-S)\frac{d\hat{a}/d\tau}{d\hat{a}/db}>0$$

where $\dfrac{1-S}{d\hat{a}/db}$ is substituted for $\left(\alpha y\dfrac{\mu-\hat{a}}{\mu S}-b\right)f(\hat{a})$ from (14′) into (14).

Substituting from (A1) and (A3), we get

$$-y+Y+b(1-S)+(1-S)\hat{a}(V(1)-V(1-x))>0 \qquad \text{(using (7))}$$

$$-y+Y+b(1-S)-(1-S)[b-x\hat{a}\mu^{\alpha}]>0 \qquad \text{(using (2))}$$

$$x\mu^{\alpha}[-a+(1-S)\hat{a}+S\mu]>0$$

This shows that an individual of quality a can benefit from a positive income tax, τ, if $a<(1-S)\hat{a}+S\mu$.

Proof of proposition 8

Part (i)

Proposition 5 states that an employed person wishes lower values of b as well as of τ for the case of $t=0$. With $t=0$, the λ's in equations (14), (14′) and (15), (15′) are generally different from 1. However, the proof remains valid if $t\neq0$, which implies λ is equal to 1 in (14), (14′) and (15), (15′).

Part (ii)

To show the first and second statements note that

$$\frac{d^2L_e}{d\tau/da}=\frac{dy}{da}\left[-1+\alpha(1-\tau)\frac{\mu-\hat{a}}{\mu S}f(\hat{a})\frac{d\hat{a}}{d\tau}\right]$$

Noting that $dy/da=x\mu^\alpha$ and substituting for $d\hat{a}/d\tau$ from (A3) we see after rearranging

$$\frac{d^2L_e}{d\tau/da}=x\mu^\alpha.\frac{\alpha\frac{\mu-\hat{a}}{\mu S}[\hat{a}[V(1)-V(1-x)]-(1-\tau)x\hat{a}\mu^\alpha]f(\hat{a})-(1-\tau)\frac{b}{\hat{a}}}{(1-\tau)\left[b/\hat{a}+\alpha x\hat{a}\mu^\alpha\frac{\mu-\hat{a}}{\mu S}f(\hat{a})\right]}<0$$

Noting that $\hat{a}[V(1)-V(1-x)]-(1-\tau)x\hat{a}\mu^\alpha=-b(1-\tau)$ from (7) we see that the above expression is negative.

Also note that

$$\frac{d^2L_e}{db/da}=x\mu^\alpha\alpha(1-\tau)\frac{\mu-\hat{a}}{\mu S}f(\hat{a})\frac{d\hat{a}}{db}>0$$

These two derivatives imply the first and second statements. The third statement is the mirror image of part (i) of this proposition. The proof is therefore analogous.

Notes

I thank Petra Geraats for useful comments on an earlier draft.

1 The description of the basic model draws heavily on Huizinga (1994).
2 Kremer (1993) analyzes an alternative production function characterized by labor quality externalities. Production, in particular, is assumed to consist of a number of tasks that all have to be completed successfully for the produced output to have any value.
3 Note that in the absence of unemployment benefits we have

$$\frac{dL_s}{d\tau}=\tau\frac{dY}{dx}\frac{dx}{d\tau}=\tau\mu^{1+\alpha}\frac{\mu^\alpha}{V''(1-x)}<0$$

4 Income redistribution per se does not yield higher social welfare, as consumption, C, enters the utility specification in (3) linearly.
5 Using (2) and the expression for $\underline{b}$, we see that (17) is equivalent to

$$[\alpha\bar{\mu}-(1+\alpha)\underline{a}]x\bar{\mu}^\alpha+\underline{a}[V(1)-V(1-x)]>0$$

6 To see this, note that we can substitute for y from (1) and for $\underline{b}$ into (18) to reach,

$$\frac{\alpha a(\bar{\mu}-\underline{a})-\underline{a}\bar{\mu}}{\bar{\mu}}x\bar{\mu}^{\alpha}+\underline{a}[V(1)-V(1-x)]>0$$

The above inequality is not satisfied if, for instance, $a=\underline{a}$ with $\alpha<1$ and $V(1)=V(1-x)=0$.

7   To check this, note that (19) is equivalent to

$$[x\bar{\mu}^{\alpha}+V(1-x)-V(1)][1-f(\underline{a})\underline{a}]+x\bar{\mu}^{\alpha}[f(\underline{a})\underline{a}]\alpha\frac{\bar{\mu}-\underline{a}}{\bar{\mu}}>0$$

8   A sufficient condition for double-peakedness is that an employed agent loses from unemployment benefits that are increased from the minimum level $\underline{b}$.

9   For a proof, see Huizinga (1994).

10   Huizinga (1994) analyses how an influx of quality workers of mimimum quality affects the tax and transfer system if there are unemployment benefits financed by a proportional labor income tax. At some point a discrete drop in both the unemployment benefit and the tax rate occurs as the decisive voter is better off being employed than being unemployed.

11   Alternatively, it may be interesting to consider policy as affected by pressure groups in the present model. See Kirstov, Lindert, and McClelland (1992) for a recent analysis of pressure groups as they affect redistribution.

References

Arnott, Richard and Rowse, John (1987), "Peer Group Effects and Educational Attainment," *Journal of Public Economics*, 32, 287–305.

Bailey, Martin Neil (1978), "Some Aspects of Optimal Unemployment Insurance," *Journal of Public Economics*, 10, 379–401.

Boadway, Robin W. and Oswald, Andrew J. (1983), "Unemployment Insurance and Redistributive Taxation," *Journal of Public Economics*, 20, 193–210.

Cooter, R. and Helpman, E. (1974), "Optimal Income Taxation for Transfer Payments," *Quarterly Journal of Economics*, 88, 656–70.

Fleming, J.S. (1978), "Aspects of Optimal Unemployment Insurance: Search, Leisure, Savings and Capital Market Imperfections," *Journal of Public Economics*, 10, 302–425.

Henderson, Vernon, Mieszkowski, Peter, and Sauvageau, Yvon (1978), "Peer Group Effects and Educational Attainment," *Journal of Public Economics*, 10, 97–106.

Huizinga, Harry (1994), "The Political Economy of Unemployment Benefits in the Presence of Labor Quality Externalities," mimeo, Tilburg University.

Kremer, Michael (1993), "The O-ring theory of economic development," *Quarterly Journal of Economics*, 108, 551–75.

Kristov, Lorenzo, Lindert, Peter, and McClelland, Robert (1992), "Pressure Groups and Redistribution," *Journal of Public Economics*, 48, 135–63.

Meltzer, Allan H. and Richards, Scott F. (1981), "A rational theory of the size of government," *Journal of Political Economy*, 89, 914–27.

Mirrlees, J.A. (1971), "An Exploration in the Theory of Optimum Income Taxation," *Review of Economic Studies*, 38, 175–208.

Sala-i-Martin, Xavier (1992), "Transfers," NBER Working Paper No. 4186.

Wright, Randall (1986), "The Redistributive Roles of Unemployment Insurance and the Dynamics of Voting," *Journal of Public Economics*, 31, 377–99.

Zeckhauser, R. (1971), "Optimal Mechanisms for Income Transfer," *American Economic Review*, 61, 324–34.

Comment

CASPER VAN EWIJK

This chapter is concerned with the political economy of social security and unemployment. The central question is: Can we explain a political equilibrium with positive unemployment? More specifically, can unemployment be motivated as a deliberate choice of society to keep some (low quality) people out of the labour process? This is a very interesting and relevant issue, particularly in view of the European situation where many people are permanently outside the labor force, being unemployed or disabled.

The basic novelty of the chapter is that the author emphasizes labor quality externalities. Through "peer" effects the quality of one worker depends on the average quality of other workers. Incorporation of this effect has interesting political consequences since it may explain why employed workers support a social security system with positive benefits and unemployment, even without invoking altruism or insurance considerations. Keeping some "low quality" people out of the labor process may enhance overall efficiency, and therefore raise the income of all employed workers.

The chapter has a straightforward set-up. People live in a static world without uncertainty; every agent maximizes her own utility, there is no altruism. The political solution is obtained by applying the median voter theorem. The chapter derives the solution for different combinations of three instruments, a wage tax τ, a lump-sum tax t, and the unemployment benefit b. Yet, despite its clear set-up it is often difficult to grasp what really drives the results. Therefore, it is useful to unravel the mechanisms that underlie these solutions. We can distinguish three basic elements:

1 The first element is the well-known theorem that inequality can lead to a political equilibrium with distortionary taxation (see Persson and Tabellini, 1990). The basic idea is that people with less than average income benefit from a redistributive tax on income. Then, if the median voter has less than average income, this may lead to positive taxation, even if this reduces overall efficiency through the distortion it causes. In terms of Huizinga's model (neglecting the human capital externality) income can be written as $y=(1-\tau)ax-t$, where a is the (unobservable) quality of labor, and x is labor time. Upon substitution of the government budget constraint $t=\tau\bar{a}x$, where $\bar{a}$ is the average quality, it is clear that for any person with $a<\bar{a}$ the income tax is favorable, even if it distorts the labor–leisure choice (which causes a second-order loss).

2 Huizinga extends this idea to the case of unemployment. If people can freely choose to be unemployed or not, as Huizinga assumes, the median voter may choose a system with positive unemployment benefits if he is better off being unemployed and receiving $y_u=b-t$, than being employed and receiving $y_e=ax-t$.

It is obvious that this situation with positive unemployment benefits can only occur if the median voter is unemployed himself, which would require that at least half of the population is unemployed. Therefore, the theory so far cannot be regarded as a satisfactory explanation of real-world unemployment.

How to proceed? How could we explain that societies rationally choose for positive unemployment benefits? I can see three directions to solve this problem, two conventional ones, and the one taken by Huizinga. One conventional theory is to explain unemployment from an insurance point of view: if people do not know *ex ante* whether they will belong to the high quality workers or the low quality workers, they may choose for a social security system that insures them against bad luck. The other way to provide a rationale for unemployment benefits is to allow for equity considerations: if people are altruistic they may choose a social security system (with $b>0$) to prevent people from falling below some social minimum income. In a second-best world, unemployment benefits may be the most efficient – or better, least inefficient – way to do so. In both explanations, unemployment is clearly inefficient: it is better to have people at work rather than to have them idle at home; everybody can be useful at some place in the economy. Neither of these two conventional routes is taken by Huizinga; he chooses a third direction:

3   Huizinga argues that it may in fact be efficient to have certain workers unemployed. This is due to labor quality externalities, the "peer" effect. This is the core of his contribution. Together with the redistributive effects it may explain that also employed workers may favor a system with positive unemployment. In particular, the high quality workers are assumed to suffer from the negative labor externality when low quality workers enter the labor force. For their own sake, the very rich therefore join the unemployed in voting for positive unemployment benefits.

This is an interesting and striking result, at least from a theoretical point of view. However, does it also contribute to our understanding of unemployment in reality? Here I have some doubts. An obvious criticism would be that the author neglects any negative social costs of persistent unemployment through loss of skills, higher crime rates, social deprivation, etc. But even taking these costs for granted, one could doubt whether negative "peer effects" really matter for the unemployment; this depends crucially on the magnitude of these effects. Note in the first place that a negative externality is no reason per se for unemployment; the externality has to be so strong that entry of low quality workers leads to an absolute decrease in total production. That is, if production is given by $Y = S\mu^{1+\alpha}$ the negative effect of entry on average productivity μ should be so strong that Y is reduced!

This should at least be true for the unemployed with the lowest quality, $\underline{a}$. Take the extreme example: let $\underline{a} = 0$, then the relevant question is: Is society better off by letting this person work for free (note that his wage is zero too), or is it better to give him the prevailing benefit b (>0)? Note that the individual quality, a, is unobservable to the government, so that he would receive considerable rents. If we fill in this exercise with real world numbers, it is clear that the externalities must be quite large to be relevant, even for the lowest quality workers. If the externalities do not exceed the threshold of the "real world" b this explanation contributes little to our understanding of unemployment.

The next point concerns the microeconomic underpinnings of the peer effect. What happens when low quality workers are employed? According to the peer effect the productivity of all other workers decreases. In the way specified by Huizinga, high quality workers suffer most; this follows from his function $y = ax\mu^\alpha$ where the peer effect is proportional to quality a. This is the basis of his result that high quality workers may favor a system with positive benefits and unemployment. There is little evidence, however, that this is the proper way of specifying the peer effect. One could also imagine that the heterogeneity in quality leads to a segregation in the production process, with high quality workers in one firm (or one place) and low quality workers in another firm (place). Then the peer effect would in the first place influence the nearby workers, i.e., the medium and low quality workers. So, in that case the spillover would vary negatively with the distance in quality between workers, rather than positively as is assumed by Huizinga.

A related point is that, if the peer effect affects nearby workers, it is not clear why the peer effect is not internalized by the firm. If the peer effect is (mainly) a local effect, which occurs within a firm, it will simply be passed on to the individual worker causing it to reduce his wage. Consequently, there is no need for unemployment benefits to keep people out of the labor force: they will simply get no income from labor.

The upshot of these remarks on the microeconomic aspects is that there are still some important issues open for further theoretical and empirical research. It is not sufficient to simply transplant the idea of the peer effect, which is derived in the context of education theory, into a macroeconomic framework.

With regard to the policy level Huizinga assumes that unemployment benefits act as a simple and perfect screening device to filter out the people with lowest quality (and therefore largest negative spillovers). Then there is a one to one correspondence between low quality and being unemployed. However, this correspondence is lost when people are heterogeneous in other respects as well. For example, if people have different marginal utilities of leisure, it is well possible also that high quality people choose to be unemployed if they have a strong preference for leisure. It would therefore be interesting to allow for a second unobservable variable. This would also avoid the problem in Huizinga's model that quality is not truly unobservable as asserted by the author: if there is only one unobservable variable (a) the government can in fact simply infer a person's quality from his production y and the labor time x.

My final comment concerns the political equilibrium. The author distinguishes several different regimes according to the combinations of policy instruments that are available. It would be interesting to know more about the implications for welfare of the alternative regimes. In general, it is not always welfare improving when an instrument is added to the set of instruments. In a voting equilibrium, it may well lead to a decrease in welfare, as is also evident from our simple inequality–efficiency example given above. Therefore, it is crucial who decides on the instrument set, or, in a more dynamic context, who decides on the agenda for the successive steps in the voting process. By splitting up the problem in different regimes the author is able to solve each separate equilibrium. However, the next step should be that also the choice of the regime is explained from the political process. This may be a highly relevant exercise which could provide insight on the emergence and dynamics of social security systems from a political economy point of view.

Reference

Persson, T. and Tabellini, G. (1990), "Is Inequality Harmful for Growth? Theory and Evidence," mimeo, University of California at Berkeley.

Index

.

Printed in the United States
By Bookmasters